Institutions and Incentives in Public Policy

Economy, Polity, and Society

The foundations of political economy—from Adam Smith to the Austrian school of economics, to contemporary research in public choice and institutional analysis—are sturdy and well established, but far from calcified. On the contrary, the boundaries of the research built on this foundation are ever expanding. One approach to political economy that has gained considerable traction in recent years combines the insights and methods of three distinct but related subfields within economics and political science: the Austrian, Virginia, and Bloomington schools of political economy. The vision of this book series is to capitalize on the intellectual gains from the interactions between these approaches in order to both feed the growing interest in this approach and advance social scientists' understanding of economy, polity, and society. This series seeks to publish works that combine the Austrian school's insights on knowledge, the Virginia school's insights into incentives in non-market contexts, and the Bloomington school's multiple methods, real-world approach to institutional design as a powerful tool for understanding social behavior in a diversity of contexts.

Series Editors:

Virgil H. Storr, Associate Professor of Economics, George Mason University and Senior Fellow, F.A. Hayek Program for Advanced Study in Philosophy, Politics & Economics, Mercatus Center at George Mason University
Jayme S. Lemke, Senior Research Fellow, Mercatus Center at George Mason University

Institutions and Incentives in Public Policy

An Analytical Assessment of Non-Market Decision-Making

Edited by
Rosolino A. Candela,
Rosemarie Fike, and Roberta Herzberg

ROWMAN & LITTLEFIELD
Lanham • Boulder • New York • London

Published by Rowman & Littlefield
An imprint of The Rowman & Littlefield Publishing Group, Inc.
4501 Forbes Boulevard, Suite 200, Lanham, Maryland 20706
www.rowman.com

86-90 Paul Street, London EC2A 4NE

Copyright © 2022 by Rosolino A. Candela, Rosemarie Fike, and Roberta Herzberg

British Library Cataloguing in Publication Information Available

Library of Congress Cataloging-in-Publication Data

Names: Candela, Rosolino, 1984- editor. | Fike, Rosemarie, editor. | Herzberg, Roberta Q., editor.
Title: Institutions and incentives in public policy : an analytical assessment of non-market decision-making / edited by Rosolino Candela, Rosemarie Fike and Roberta Herzberg.
Description: Lanham : Rowman & Littlefield, [2022] | Series: Economy, polity, and society | Includes bibliographical references and index. | Summary: "Institutions and Incentives in Public Policy: An Analytical Assessment of Non-Market Decision-Making explores, both in theory and in practice, the consequences of using public policy as a tool to achieve specific individual and social goals, as well as its impact on private solutions to address such goals"—Provided by publisher.
Identifiers: LCCN 2022015702 (print) | LCCN 2022015703 (ebook) | ISBN 9781538160930 (cloth) | ISBN 9781538196168 (pbk.) | ISBN 9781538160947 (epub)
Subjects: LCSH: Policy sciences. | Public administration—Decision making.
Classification: LCC H97 .I44 2022 (print) | LCC H97 (ebook) | DDC 320.6—dc23/ eng/20220627
LC record available at https://lccn.loc.gov/2022015702
LC ebook record available at https://lccn.loc.gov/2022015703

Contents

List of Figures and Tables

FIGURES

TABLES

Introduction

Rosolino A. Candela, Rosemarie
Fike, and Roberta Herzberg

Since at least the days of Adam Smith, political economists have analyzed the role that alternative institutional arrangements play as a *means* for the fulfill- ment of particular public policy *ends*. The purpose of this volume, and its constituent chapters, is to address the following question: What role does in- stitutional analysis play in resolving public policy dilemmas? Addressing this question is by no means easy, since the positive analysis of institutions and its public policy implications, which are normative in nature, can never be easily disentangled. Therefore, we should begin, first, by defining what dilemmas are inherent to public policy choices and then developing an understanding of the role that institutions play in strategizing over policy alternatives.

Economic analysis, according to Lionel Robbins, "enables us to conceive alternative possibilities of policy. It does not, and it cannot, enable us to evade the necessity of choosing between alternatives" ([1932] 1952, 156). Central to this notion of "dilemma" is that public policy choices imply trade-offs, not solutions (see Sowell 2002, 17–19). There is only ever a solution to a problem in a world which does not face scarcity in choice. For example, at the time in which this introduction is being written, governments around the world have been implementing the distribution of vaccines to combat COVID-19. In a society that values life, rather than death, more vaccines are preferred, rather than less. Stated this way, it seems plausible to claim that "society" ought to devote more resources to providing greater vaccines as a "solution" to this problem. This claim neglects two important points for public policy analysis. First, "society" does not choose or act; only individuals choose and act. In order to make sense of public policy choices, we have to begin with the individual policymaker as the fundamental unit of analysis as well as the incentives *and* information motivating their policy choices. Second, the fact that individuals choose, not organizations or societies, implies that individuals make trade-offs, weighing opportunities against one another. And they make these trade-offs "at the margin" in the sense that they compare additional benefits of any activity with additional costs—including the additional opportunity cost of forgoing another activity. For example, given the goal of preventing death, there are trade-offs to the choice of releasing a COVID-19 vaccine "too early" or "too late": releasing the vaccine without proper testing against side effects may unintentionally contribute to fatalities against the wishes of a public policymaker. At the same time, however, delaying the release of an otherwise safe vaccine unintentionally contributes to fatalities by denying individuals a vaccination that could have saved their lives. The point here is that there is no solution, only dilemmas in choosing among public policy ends. The inevitable dilemma of public policymaking, particularly in achieving its desired ends, is not only adjudicating trade-offs in terms of the alternative uses resources have, but more importantly, adjudicating the competing demands that individuals have over such resources.

From this perspective, the purpose of public policy can never be to implement a pre-defined solution to a particular problem in accordance with the desires of "society." Rather, if we are beginning with the individual as the methodological basis of choices over public policy, then questions regarding public policy are redirected to understanding the following: (1) What incentives and knowledge are available to policymakers as the means to achieve the desired ends of public policy? (2) To what extent are policymakers incentivized to *learn* the desired ends of their constituency? (3) How will such ends be communicated? (see Aligica, Boettke, and Tarko 2019). Institutional analysis provides a theoretical framework for answering these questions.

Institutions, broadly speaking, are the "rules of the game," both formal and informal, that structure individual choice and social interaction. They provide not only the incentives that motivate individuals in their decision-making but also generate context-specific knowledge from which individuals learn. As Elinor Ostrom points out, "all institutional arrangements can be thought of as games in extensive form. As such, the particular options available, the sequencing of those options, the information provided, and the relative rewards and punishments assigned to different sequences of moves can all change the pattern of outcomes achieved" (1990, 23).

Policy outcomes can only be understood through a dual-level analysis. First, there is a "higher level" of analysis of the institutional context that generates incentives and information motivating policymaking. Only by acknowledging that policymaking does not take place in an institutional vacuum can we distinguish from a "lower level" of analysis regarding the selecting of different public policies. Once we realize that the selection of public policy decisions does not emerge from an institutional vacuum, the relevant choice for addressing unintended and undesirable consequences of public policy is neither to directly change the individuals implementing the policy nor to directly change the policy being implemented, per se. Rather, the emphasis becomes more subtle and indirect. That is, the relevant choice becomes one of changing the rules governing policymaking and, as a by-product, the incentives and information from which public policy outcomes are filtered, put on the table, and selected. Thus, the same players, under alternative institutional incentives, learn different games and implement different strategies. Simply changing the players without changing the rules governing public policymaking will not change the outcome.

The task for the political economist is, primarily, to assess the most effective means to implement a public policy end, not to impose a value judgment on the desired end of public policy. Institutional analysis is the theoretical tool to assess the coherence between a desired policy end and the means by which to achieve it. Returning to our example regarding COVID-19 vaccine testing, there are two sets of means by which to deliver safe and effective vaccines: the market and the government. To be clear, these are not mutually exclusive, since markets also, though not always, operate under government enforcement of private property rights and contracts. However, the fundamental distinction between markets and government lies in the nature of decision-making in a market setting and decision-making in a non-market setting, respectively. Here, again, the policy choice over whether to leave vaccine testing to the market or the government is a trade-off, neither of which provides a solution. Testing of a vaccine, left to profit-seeking firms in the market process, may allegedly be incentivized to undertest against undesired side effects, since the opportunity cost of additional testing is earning profits from selling a vaccine. Thus, the fear of under-provision of vaccine testing may justify government intervention to assure adequate testing before a drug is released. That being said, the issue is not whether we should, or should not, desire vaccine testing as a policy end, but rather the most effective way to implement vaccine testing that is consistent with its stated end, namely, to minimize death from the vaccine that may result passively by withholding it for excessive testing or actively from undertesting. Again, the issue at hand is not to implement a solution, but rather to adjudicate a trade-off.

In the market process, individuals are guided in their decision-making by profit *and* loss signals, the latter being the source of error correction and learning from error. Such learning in the form of profit and loss does not exist outside the context of private property, the institutional arrangement that distinguishes a market setting from a non-market setting. Though it may be the case that a pharmaceutical firm may sell a drug with unintended and lethal side effects, under the proper institutional setting of private property and freedom of contract under the rule of law, firms are residual claimants to their decision-making and must be held liable for such a mistake, either in the form of loss of future profits, civil lawsuit, loss of reputation, or a combination of all three. Private property implies a social liability to take account of one's decisions, not a social privilege to be excluded from responsibility of the consequences of one's decisions. With such ex-post error correction mechanisms in place, we could expect that pharmaceutical firms will learn to minimize such errors ex ante.

What incentives and knowledge are available to an individual decision-maker assessing the safety of vaccine in a nonprofit setting, such as the Food and Drug Administration (FDA)? Assuming no malevolent intent, what will more likely be identified as a "mistake"? Given the presumption that market processes will undertest relative to political processes, for reasons stated above, how will the cost of testing be assessed for a bureaucrat in a nonprofit setting? The logic of political processes is to concentrate benefits on well-organized and well-informed interest groups and disperse the costs on the ill-organized and ill-informed masses. In terms of motivation, FDA officials are no different from firms in a profit-seeking setting: they both seek income and job security. More importantly, like any nonprofit organization, the FDA is also a concentrated interest group, seeking to prevent job loss among its members. Given that illness or death from unintended side effects of a vaccine will be immediately visible and seen, this represents a concentrated cost on the FDA official accountable for early release of an otherwise unsafe drug. The benefits of over-testing, however, relative to the information costs of tracing the cause of deaths from withholding an otherwise safe drug implies that FDA officials will learn to identify undertesting as a "mistake" relative to the losses of life attributed to over-testing. The dilemma here, in terms of public policy outcomes, is not whether to choose the market process or the political process on the basis of the benevolence or malevolence of individual motivations but on the incentives and knowledge made available to individuals operating under these alternative institutional settings.

Thus, the relevant institutional question for public policy analysis, for our purposes here, is not whether individuals will make mistakes in their decision-making in either setting. Mistakes will always occur in both settings, which is why institutions are relevant in the first place! Institutions serve as an error correction mechanism for imperfect decision-making. Thus, taking the fact that human decision-making will always be prone to error, the question becomes not only whether individuals learn from their mistakes but also what will be identified as a "mistake" as the basis for correction under alternative institutional arrangements.

OVERVIEW OF THE BOOK

Each chapter in this volume applies institutional analysis to understand how incentives and context-specific knowledge motivate non-market decision-making, with a particular focus on the policy implications of the specific issues being addressed. The remainder of the book consists of eleven chapters, each of which frame public policy analysis within the broader literature on market process theory and public choice theory. It highlights, through a variety of case studies, the unintended consequences that are often neglected in the discussion and implementation of public policies that attempt to address pressing social, political, and economic issues.

This volume is subdivided into six sections, each of which focuses on particular aspects of public policy. These policy focuses are education policy, federal policy, international policy, public governance, environmental policy, and technology policy.

PART I: EDUCATION POLICY

In chapter 1, Martha Bradley-Dorsey provides a rich discussion of the history of the U.S. public education system and how that system evolved over the years. Through the lens of public choice, this chapter explores the effects of the Elementary and Secondary Education Act of 1965 and the No Child Left Behind Act of 2002 on the U.S. public education system. In particular, Bradley-Dorsey focuses on the incentives that bureaucrats face and how, as a result of these policy changes, the public school system has seen increased growth in the number of school district full-time staff with virtually no improvement in the performance of the schools.

Chapter 2, by Nathaniel Burke, explores some of the potential unintended consequences of forced desegregation policies that are often overlooked. Burke develops a model that highlights the important role informal institutions, such as cultural group identity, can play in determining the success of minority students attending schools outside of their own community. Burke's model forces us to consider a potential trade-off that policymakers often overlook because group identity factors have not been seriously considered. Specifically, he argues that under some circumstances, minority students who are bused to predominantly white schools may intentionally underperform in an attempt to signal their group identity. He then uses his framework to examine the case of Central High School in Little Rock, arguing that forced desegregation policies at the school district level do not address the problem of de facto segregation that occurs within the school because of pressures related to group identity. This chapter raises an important policy question regarding whether an integration strategy that grants families control over their possible schooling options would outperform ones that force students to attend schools outside of their own community.

PART II: FEDERAL POLICY

Can officials responsible for a wrongful conviction be held accountable for their errors in a way that does not violate individual rights? In chapter 3, Dora Duru examines the incentives created by alternative methods of compensating victims of wrongful conviction in order to answer whether wrongful conviction compensation schemes result in fewer wrongful convictions and whether they are consistent with a Hayekian view of liberty. Duru uses insights from both Austrian and public choice scholars to explore these questions. The analysis in this chapter helps explain why government officials are likely to oppose criminal justice reforms that raise the cost of decisions and actions that lead to wrongful convictions.

In chapter 4, Neil McCray examines the move in Medicaid programs across the states to public/private partnerships using a managed care platform. In particular, he considers the degree to which this move has impacted costs in Medicaid programs and suggests that the results have fallen short of those hoped for by policy reformers. He argues that these savings shortfalls may be attributed to two complementary explanations. First, Medicaid managed care has failed to introduce meaningful market competition that would incentivize real cost savings. The heavily bureaucratic process to award managed care contracts does not really provide the information and consumer and producer incentives to permit prices to adjust as expected in a competitive market. Second, McCray suggests that the form of managed care in Medicaid may actually disincentivize potential cost saving from competition or market forces because of rent-seeking behavior on the part of managed care organizations. As companies seek managed care contracts, they may find it more valuable to invest in politicians and policymakers through lobbying than to actually cut costs within the Medicaid delivery system. McCray notes that without real competition, the market impact of this strategy may be difficult to observe empirically. But he suggests the extent to which such rent-seeking behaviors are present in the Medicaid contracting and oversight process.

In chapter 5, Thomas B. Storrs presents a case study of evasive entrepreneurship in commercial banking. In the U.S. during the late nineteenth century, legal impediments marginalized borrowers from access to credit. Usury laws constrained lenders by mandating the maximum interest rate they could charge. As a result, extralegal markets existed to serve the borrowing needs of salaried employees. Or, borrowing was restricted primarily to, for example, pawnshops or financing from friends and relatives. Therefore, consumer lending from commercial banks catered primarily to wealthy customers who also carried large business accounts with the banks. Arthur J. Morris, a lawyer practicing in Norfolk, Virginia, managed, through some obfuscation, to charge an effective interest rate sufficiently high to turn a profit and provide loans to classes of borrowers underserved by the legally sanctioned financial system. This innovation heralded and hastened the massive rise in consumer debt that modernized America.

PART III: INTERNATIONAL POLICY

Chapter 6, by Anthony J. DeMattee, examines the social impact of laws and regulations governing the behavior of civil society organizations (CSOs). Specifically, this analysis explores the empirical relationship between three different types of legal restrictions on receiving foreign funding (prohibitive laws, red-tape laws, and notification laws) and three key measures of civil society robustness (CSO vitality, level of democracy, and foreign funding received). Through his empirical analysis, DeMattee challenges the dominant practice in this body of literature of treating all CSO laws as equal and making no distinctions across types. His findings suggest that the type of CSO restriction does in fact make a difference in terms of the effect it has on the robustness of civil society. Even slight differences in the institutional context matter.

PART IV: PUBLIC GOVERNANCE

In chapter 7, Vera Kichanova examines the dynamic development of urban areas, using the lens of Coasian transaction costs theory, to suggest that the imperfections in cities that impose costs offer an opportunity for market innovation that is often missed when all decisions for change are publicly directed through government. Private innovators who can respond more quickly to changing information and resident preferences are crowded out by public planners' intent on serving more fixed goals. As a result, some urban problems remain unsolved for too long. Instead of trying to change the legal environment in existing cities, Kichanova suggests that an alternative jurisdiction, such as entirely private cities, might provide a better avenue for reform. She argues that the private city can be a profitable enterprise and a legitimate alternative to conventional publicly governed cities, but only if the regulatory environment becomes more friendly toward such start-ups. To investigate this contention, she examines the case of Lavasa, a private city in India built over the last two decades, using the lens of Coasian transaction costs theory. From this case, she derives certain lessons for future private cities and suggests what might be required to facilitate such development in the future.

Building on the Bloomington school's work on polycentricity in service delivery, chapter 8 by Ifeoluwa M. Olawole examines the impacts of polycentric service delivery on political participation, with a specific application to the political context of Nigeria. Olawole analyzes the willingness of citizens to participate actively in systems where many different producers of goods and services operate in a polycentric form. Using contact with policymakers as a measure of political involvement in these multiproducer systems, she argues that political attitudes differ depending on *who* provides the basic goods and services. In Nigeria, with its context as a young democracy, she finds that non-state provision of goods reduces political participation with the state and argues that this reduced involvement can ultimately lead to the weakening of the state. As a result, she suggests that when the state provides services, citizens are more likely to participate in politics more broadly. Of course, it is difficult to sort out the extent to which political involvement, measured simply as citizen outreach to government, goes beyond simple customer service issues to more meaningful political accountability among citizens and political officials. But, at the very least, this work conveys the potential costs of involvement with multiple service providers that are borne by citizens. These costs must be considered as we think through the viability of polycentric forms. As such, it suggests some of the limitations of polycentric forms in developing countries.

PART V: ENVIRONMENTAL POLICY

In chapter 9, Emil Panzaru argues that the problem of social justice is exacerbated by a Hayekian knowledge problem during crises, which is an underexplored issue in the environmental justice (EJ) literature. Those seeking EJ argue that environmental resources should be allocated to those from disadvantaged social backgrounds based on race, gender, health, and occupation, as these groups have faced the greatest costs of disproportionate impact from past environmental degradation. Panzaru asks why champions of EJ fail to design institutions consistent with meeting these justice goals when it comes to natural disaster policy. Government agents are widely trusted with ensuring that the most vulnerable socioeconomic groups receive essential services after a natural disaster, yet they often fail to achieve this practice, especially under the conditions of crisis. He uses insights from public choice to better understand the source of these problematic patterns. Bureaucratic incentives are such that success is defined in terms of budget maximization and measurable output instead of improved environmental distribution. The solutions EJ advocates propose a focus on gathering information about the struggles of the least well-off rather than the context-specific knowledge needed to create real improvements. To accomplish these goals, policymakers need better knowledge about the preferences and needs of the individuals they hope to serve, but the usual sociological schemas are unable to capture the particularities of each person's diverse needs, no matter how well-designed or how well-intentioned the policymaker using them may be.

In chapter 10, Alison Grant explores the impacts of the meat industry using a mainline economics lens. Specifically, she examines the extent to which the production and consumption of meat pose a social externality in terms of health costs, environmental impacts, and respect for animal rights. She suggests that while there may be certain externalities associated with meat consumption and production, imposing a meat tax is not likely to improve overall social benefit. Both political and equity factors should be considered in evaluating the overall viability of a meat tax approach to reducing meat consumption, as depending on the way in which it is applied, it could simply shift use within meat products without reducing overall environmental or health impacts. Moreover, the problems of public choice may result in the implementation of such a tax favoring certain producers or social groups, creating greater inequity and market failures.

The way in which data is collected, processed, stored, and made available to researchers can have important consequences for the discovery of new ideas and the production of knowledge. In chapter 11, Alexis Garretson examines the various data stewardship practices of different herbaria across the United States. She explores the empirical relationship between the organizational type of the herbaria (cultural sector, public university, private university, or public land use) and the data collection practices employed at that organization. A richer data collection is seen as desirable and more consistent with the profession's established best practices. In this comparative analysis, particular attention is paid to the variation in incentives faced by actors across each type of organization due to differences in their unique organizational goals, the formal restrictions they face, the sources of their funding, and the availability of resources at their disposal.

PART VI: TECHNOLOGY POLICY

Using insights from new institutional economics, the final chapter (chapter 12) examines the incentives that hackers face and how those incentives shape their decision of whether to engage in illegal activities and what type of illegal services to provide. Karl Grindal argues that the size of the transaction costs involved in different types of data transfers will determine what type of illegal market will emerge to trade that information. In addition, public policies aimed at reducing the amount of data that is traded in these illegal markets face severe practical challenges. Such policies often directly increase transaction costs involved in making exchanges in illegal markets in an attempt to deter those exchanges. However, the potential gains from engaging in these illegal exchanges encourage individuals to create new institutional arrangements to reduce transaction costs once again. New technologies and new forms of contracts emerge in response to policies that increase transaction costs in these markets.

REFERENCES

Aligica, Paul Dragos, Peter J. Boettke, and Vlad Tarko. 2019. *Public Governance and the Classical-Liberal Perspective: Political Economy Foundations*. New York: Oxford University Press.

Ostrom, Elinor. 1990. *Governing the Commons: The Evolution of Institutions for Collective Action*. New York: Cambridge University Press.

Robbins, Lionel. [1932] 1952. *An Essay on the Nature and Significance of Economic Science*. 2nd ed. London: Macmillan.

Sowell, Thomas. 2002. *A Conflict of Visions: Ideological Origins of Political Struggles*. New York: Basic Books.

Part I

EDUCATION POLICY

Chapter 1

Rise of a Centropoly

Good Intentions, Distorted Incentives, and the Cloaked Costs of Top-Down Reform in U.S. Public Education

Martha Bradley-Dorsey

America's pragmatically idealistic beginning contrasts sharply with the formation of the U.S. public school system. While the two began in tandem, public education deviated and devolved into a set of monopolies, centralized first by states and later by the federal government into a massive bureaucratic structure. I call this monopolistic, layered bureaucratic creation the "centropoly."[1]

The American founders provided fertile ground for Adam Smith's notion of the "invisible hand" to flourish through a constitution designed to limit government and allow individual liberty. The founders' design gave the free market—of both goods and ideas—an optimal setting. Alexis de Tocqueville praised the resulting American civic society, stating that Americans maintain a correct understanding of self-interest, which tempers individualism by recognizing the need for social involvement *via* small, "free" organizations. Americans, he opined, operate under the assumption that sacrificing oneself for one's fellows is *useful* in maintaining one's own interests through maintenance of the government form. Herein, said Tocqueville, lies the nexus of individual liberty and social responsibility (Tocqueville [1835; 1840] 2010, 891, 920–23). While no human governance system is perfect, Tocqueville concluded that the combination of the invisible but efficient *informal* information systems and the conscious development of communities populated by responsibly acting individuals served both individuals and communities well in their quest for betterment.[2]

Schooling in America began in precisely this way: a *nonsystem* consisting of individual, community-organized schools. Historical twists, however, led public schooling to an alternate universe. Instead of remaining community-based, public schooling evolved into a centropoly—my term for the multi-level, monopolized government bureaucracy that controls American public schools. Extending from early reformers' actions, this change unfolded in pieces over time to eventually form the complex structure we have now. Through external reforms that have attempted to "repair" schools, social policy interventions have caused increasing centralization through larger and deeper formal institutions. This result has decreased information accuracy (a process explained by Tullock [2005, 148]), strengthened bureaucratic inflexibility (Downs 1967, 144–66), and left numerous students vastly underserved.

I explain the system's evolution in two parts. First, I trace the larger early movements that shifted public schooling to a system both centralized and monopolized, thereby launching the centropoly. Second, I specifically examine twentieth-century reforms adopted under the most significant federal education act, the Elementary and Secondary Education Act of 1965, which was intended to improve the educational outcomes of disadvantaged youth. I provide evidence that the attempts to improve the education of low-income and minority students have failed largely because of the reforms' effect on public school system bureaucratization.

I base my analysis on public choice theory, which is an essential part of broader mainline economics theory. As Boettke, Haeffele, and Storr (2016, 3) state, mainline economics is "a set of positive propositions about social order." These propositions include three on "the nature of human action and the role of institutions" (ibid., 4). First, there are "limits to the benevolence" on which humans can rely, resulting in knowledge limits in navigating the social world. Second, as a result of these limits, both formal and informal institutions influence activity. Third, and key to mainline economics, "social cooperation is possible without central direction." The authors conclude, "Stated another way, by relying on the emergent and human-devised rules of conduct, agents possessing both the capacities and the failings of the typical human being can nonetheless work together to achieve their individual and collective goals" (ibid., 4).

Public choice theory, which operates under this overarching mainline theory, contemplates choices inside *formal* (e.g., public) institutions. The theory can be explained using three relatively simple concepts: individual incentives are similar inside and outside institutions, information accuracy decreases as organizations grow, and organizational individuals seek increased resources as the natural outcome (Boettke, Haeffele-Balch, and Storr 2016; Buchanan and Tullock 1999; Tullock 2005; Downs 1967; Niskanen [1971] 2017). Mises ([1949] 1998, 13) aptly connected public choice theory to mainline economic theory when he wrote, "Action is a real thing. What counts is a man's total behavior, and not his talk about planned but not realized acts."

While I discuss the entire system using this theoretical lens, in the second part of this chapter I show evidence of specific consequences. After summarizing the formative history of the public school system, I specifically analyze the influence of the Elementary and Secondary Education Act of 1965 (ESEA), an umbrella act containing far-reaching federal education policy interventions intended specifically to improve the education of targeted disadvantaged students. In doing so, I provide evidence that these federal interventions, though well-intentioned, have further centralized and thereby thickened public educational bureaucracy beyond what early state actions had already done. I argue that these federal policies have contributed to increased bureaucratization at all three levels of government: federal, state, and local. Bureaucratic thickening has resulted in further reducing of the information available to decision-makers, rendering their decisions increasingly less effective. This, in turn, has led decision-makers to do what they know best: work to increase resources. I show evidence of policy consequences in several ways, including a description of spending over time. I provide related evidence regarding the number of education staff at each of the three levels of government over time along with empirical evidence of the associations between various ESEA amendments and staff growth. Finally, I review research evidence that these efforts, though intended to reverse the effects of disadvantage, appear instead to have distorted and largely defeated the ultimate goal of improving the lot of disadvantaged students by producing little to no educational gain. On the contrary, centropolization has exacerbated achievement gaps, and it has hardened and formalized income, racial, and ethnic segregation based on zip codes. Increased funding has become a proxy for the educational improvement of disadvantaged students despite the fact that it has done relatively little to improve outcomes.

In the next two sections of this chapter, I show how reforms turned individual schools into district monopolies and, further, how reformers superimposed state and federal government controls onto the emerging monopolized system, at first only loosely, yet over time, stubbornly connected layers, hence giving birth to the hybridized educational centropoly. As monopolies, the purpose of the institution is simply to maintain the institution. With very limited or no external incentives to serve school constituencies (since many constituencies are essentially prevented from seeking alternative schooling), the only real incentives are those held by the individuals employed in public school monopolies.

Public choice theorist Anthony Downs (1967) explains that the same becomes true of any organization that becomes a bureaucracy, regardless of monopoly status. Downs (1967) identifies bureaus as a subset of organizations, which must exhibit all of four characteristics: (1) they are *large*—a term that could expand, at least in relation to the public school system, to include the effect of layering government levels;[3] (2) most of a bureau's members are full-time employees who *depend on their employment* in the organization for most of their income; (3) hiring, promotion, and retention are at least partly based on achievement-related characteristics that can be judged by performance assessment, as opposed to ascribed characteristics (religion, race, class, connections) or election to office; and (4) their *output is not subject to external market evaluation* (ibid., 25; emphasis added). Downs then describes how increasing bureaucracy defends and expands itself, and then rigidifies (ibid., 144–66).

A central tenet of public choice theory is that information suffers as distance increases between decision-makers and those who provide input. Tullock (2005, 148–52) describes this phenomenon by analogy to an American army experiment used as a teaching device, wherein trainees stood in a large circle outside hearing distance of each other. An officer would pass a message orally to one soldier, who then ran to the next soldier in the circle to deliver the same message orally, and so on until all soldiers had received the message. When the last soldier repeated the message, it normally no longer resembled the original. Tullock (ibid.) ascribed this not to a defect inherent in using oral over written transmission, but instead to distortions arising "in the brains of each man" (ibid., 148). Tullock elaborates regarding bureaucracies, explaining bureaucrats are not "mere postmen" but are interpreters as well (ibid., 150). As bureaucracies have multiple hierarchical levels, so the possibility of multiple (mis)interpretations increases.

Niskanen ([1971] 2017) furthered public choice theory by explaining that public bureaucracy employees maximize utility through rational decisions regarding survival and personal growth. Alternatively stated, officials, acting rationally, seek strategies to maximize their budgets. Regarding incentives, Downs (1967, 82) states, "Utility maximization [. . .] means the rational pursuit of one's goals [. . .] In order to predict what officials will do, we must know their goals." Downs juxtaposes *social functions*—the overt, publicly stated goals of an organization—against individual officials' private motives (ibid., 82). Private motives include increased power among organizational leaders, job retention, and pay increases for employees and others. Here, we come full circle to the first concept: humans operating with the same motives inside and outside institutions.

According to Blais and Dion (1990, 657), "The Niskanen model predicts that the bureaucrat's personal utility is a function of the budget and that bureaucrats attempt to maximize their budgets." Specific considerations include salary, benefits and other perquisites, power, and reputation, all of which Niskanen theorizes constitute "a positive monotonic function of the total budget" (ibid., 656). Public bureaucracy officials, according to Niskanen, also maximize their budgets for survival purposes (ibid., 656).

Because humans populate institutions, organizational behavior is fundamentally human behavior. However, the layering of institutional control over humans produces layered responses with the deepest layers—and their motives—cloaked to some extent. Assuming, as with the public choice model, that "every official acts at least partly in his own self-interest" (Downs 1967, 83), one must take private motives into account when examining the actions of a bureau, particularly a layered one. Downs (ibid., 5) cites Calhoun (1953): "Each [individual] [. . .] has greater regard for his own safety or happiness than for the safety or happiness of others, and, where these come in opposition, is ready to sacrifice the interests of others to his own." Hearkening again to the words of Mises ([1949] 1998, 13), it is a person's actions that ultimately count.

Importantly, it was not bureaucratization, centralization, or monopolization alone that created the U.S. public school system. The three combined to generate the layered and hyper-inflexible centropoly we have today. I add to the literature in two ways: first, historically, by explaining the myriad changes reformers wove together to centralize what was once decentralized, and second, by closer examination of the top layer *via* federal policy example. I use a public choice lens to explain public education as the hybridized, layered system it has become, and I provide evidence of this assertion.

"EXIGENCIES OF AN EARLIER ERA": FORMATION OF THE U.S. SCHOOL SYSTEM AND THE DAWN OF THE CENTROPOLY

Considerable support exists for state educational oversight. Early philosophers such as Plato and Locke defended education as fundamental to the well-being of a society. The issue in the United States, however, is not *that* American states took control of their schools, but rather *how* they did so. Importantly, American reforms led to centralized, bureaucratic, and monopolistic control.

Contrary to what public education has become, informal organizations drove early American school efforts. Public schools began with both public and private roots as individual, voluntary efforts in small communities before the nation's establishment.[4] In some areas, private schools were permitted to operate in community schoolhouses. In other areas, parents and others volunteered to form and operate schools. Legislators permitted and funded still other schools *via* a "rate bill," for which only the users of the school would pay (Cubberley 1916, 4). In fact, education in America did not begin as a *system* at all, let alone a centralized one. Cubberley (1916, 3) notes that since the U.S. Constitution does not mention "any form of education for the people" and education was not mentioned during the debates of the Constitutional Convention, "education became one of the many unmentioned powers 'reserved to the States'" under the Tenth Amendment to the U.S. Constitution.

A country as large and diverse as America, however, is bound to be affected by many forces. Among them for schools, concerns developed around diversity itself. Reformers uneasy about the country's growth and diversification in many aspects, including religion, culture and race, industry, and population density, began to exert more control over the relatively unconnected schools in individual communities.

These reforms were not carefully planned; instead, they occurred in piecemeal fashion over time and through various social and cultural changes. As Hess (2010, 40) explains, defenders of the current public school system frequently "impute [. . .] [a] high-mindedness to what are in fact makeshift responses to the exigencies of an earlier era." In this chapter, I employ instead a perspective of historical mindfulness to what these exigency-based reforms have actually produced in the aggregate.

THE EARLY INFLUENCES: RELIGIONS, WARS, AND THE BEGINNING OF A CENTRALIZED STRUCTURE

Before the Revolutionary War, schools were community-centered and largely religion-focused, a logical arrangement when religious congregations were the dominant forms of social organization. Early school organizational efforts were interwoven with religion.

For example, in 1647, Massachusetts adopted what became known as the Old Deluder Satan Act. Known as the first compulsory education law in America,[5] the Act clearly identified its purpose as maintaining true "knowledge of the Scriptures" instead of being "clowded by false glosses of Saintseeming deceivers" (Old Deluder Satan Act 1647). Despite its stated religious purpose, the Act only required towns of 100 or more to provide a Latin grammar school.[6] "Old Deluder" is arguably a precursor of laws that, while requiring towns to provide education for all children, could have allowed towns to direct education as each saw fit.[7]

Ultimately, the anti-Deluder model did not prevail. Cubberley (1922, 356) observes that the half-century after the Revolutionary War could be seen as a transitional period from church to state control of education.[8] Common School leaders concerned about post-war educational decline began to focus not only on providing similar content, but on providing that content _via_ a similar structure to all children, including those who otherwise could not afford an education.[9]

Beginning around 1825, new cities arose, and older cities began to grow, hence transforming the nation's previously rural, agricultural, and pioneer character. Educational and social conditions changed first for people in the Central and Northern states (ibid., 363–64). Southern states held their agrarian, slavery-based economic system until long after the civil war ended (ibid.). With city growth also came large-scale manufacturing, leading to the demise of small industries and the apprenticeship system. The 1810s also initiated the suffrage movement by extending voting rights to non-property-owning males. With the extension of voting rights, general knowledge and civic virtue grew in importance, lending support for educational purposes beyond religion (ibid., 366).

The new focus on education's importance brought changes in school structure and lesson content. National growth, fueled in large part by immigrants different from each other and from those who had settled earlier, helped spark Common Schoolers to work toward civic unification through education. Religious diversity accompanied immigration, resulting in religious tension that surfaced in the schools and school reform movements. With increased Catholic immigration, anti-Catholic Protestants, including politicians and Common Schoolers, mobilized to suppress the spread of Catholicism in the schools (van Raemdonck and Maranto 2018, 549; Hess 2010, 87–88).

Common Schoolers focused on much more than just religious instruction. The movement's efforts to unify the delivery of American education led, by extension, to a perceived need for a formal structure by which to do so. Importantly, a visit to Prussia in the 1840s influenced Common School movement leader Horace Mann to advocate for schools to be organized by age-based grade levels. Prussia, notes Hess (2010, 81–82), had adopted such a system to help rebuild national pride when the country faced defeat at the hands of Napoleon in the early nineteenth century. Mann approved of the orderly structure, regardless of why Prussia had implemented it in the first place, and he recommended it be adopted in the United States. This rigid, Prussian War–inspired organizational structure remains dominant today.

CENTRIPETAL FORCES APPEAR: UNIFORMITY AND THE POWER OF PROGRESSIVE IDEAS

American public schools became a unified system through various means. Among the more important are the formation of the district system, the establishment of state constitutional clauses, and the creation of a mass-production teacher preparation model.

School Districts

Near the time states began forming state public school systems, the growing number of individual community schools began forming into districts. Some experts saw school districts as the "natural" organizational unit, since schools whose areas adjoined did not follow extant city or township boundaries and instead became smaller and irregularly shaped school districts. Cubberley (1916, 5) states, "As a unit of organization, the district was well suited to the needs of the time [. . .] Districts could be formed anywhere, of any size and shape, and only those families or communities desiring schools need be included in the district organization." Cubberley (and others) therefore embraced the district system, describing it as a creation of the state (ibid., 14).

District formation created American public school monopolies, which continue today. School district geographic boundaries provided demarcation lines, inside which resident students attended school. As districts grew, district officials further subdivided districts into school attendance or "catchment" areas (Cubberley 1916, 6–8; National Center for Education Statistics n.d., The Boundary Collection), wherein a student attended the school located in the catchment area that includes the student's residence. State constitutional provisions and resulting state laws then codified the monopolistic district system, making it difficult to eradicate.

State Constitutional Clauses

Due perhaps in part to a renewed religious conflict, more states began to include education in their constitutions. Six of the fourteen state constitutions framed by 1800 did not mention education, and several others did so only briefly (Cubberley 1916, 3). As of 1834, almost half of the states had adopted education clauses (Tractenberg n.d.). Between 1835 and 1912, the number of states with constitutional education provisions doubled, and most of these were explicit regarding the establishment and funding of free common school systems (ibid.).[10]

Given the country's constitutional guarantee of religious freedom, one could argue that the goal of religious preference is a private function as opposed to the more general social functions of literacy and citizenship. Yet, religious tension helped to solidify state constitutional education provisions. A new wave of immigrants brought religion back into focus, thereby contributing to permanent structural changes to public education. With millions of additional Catholics immigrating to the United States in the mid-1840s (Byrne 2000), Catholic political power increased, and Catholics began using their power to combat Protestant efforts to de-Catholicize their children *via* the common schools (DeForrest, II.C.). Education became more diversified in various locales, but this result was short-lived (Maranto and van Raemdonck 2015). Ultimately, this religious battle spawned several unsuccessful attempts at U.S. constitutional amendments to prohibit federal resources from being given to religious groups or schools. Maine Congressional Representative and presidential hopeful James Blaine proposed one such amendment in 1875 as a springboard to the office of president. Upon failure at the federal level, Blaine amendments began surfacing in states' constitutions. At this writing, thirty-seven states have Blaine amendments in their constitutional education clauses (Parker 2016; Institute for Justice n.d.; DeForrest, II.C.).[11]

Overall, state constitutions served to solidify the fifty partially centralized and largely monopolized educational systems into their layered, state-centralized form, thus setting the stage for a future layer—the federal government—to complete the centropoly. State constitutions generally call for the state to not only fund but also *govern* the public schools in a manner that, structurally speaking, originates at the state level. This more or less universal constitutional system generally sets forth a state-elected individual (chief state school officer, governor) or body (state board of education) to oversee the state system (Railey 2017). As pointed out by Friedman (1955, [1962] 1982), a state government could instead fund but not manage or control individual schools. This important observation is predicated upon the public choice notion that, as an organization thickens, two results materialize. First, the information distance lengthens (and accuracy suffers) between an organization's leaders and those it serves (Tullock 2005). Second, this increased distance further exacerbates the natural tendency for leaders' private incentives to override concern for those being served (Downs 1967).

Teacher Preparation

Reformers unified teacher preparation as well, lowering its quality as a result. The Common School movement spurred efforts to establish a formal teacher preparation system, and the state normal school became the Common Schoolers' major teacher preparation effort. As Labaree (2018, 293) notes, given limited resources to establish normal schools, "normal school leaders ended up choosing relevance [reaching more prospective teachers by 'skimping on professional preparation'] over rigor [providing 'a few model teachers' with rigorous professional training]." The development of teachers' colleges in the late nineteenth and early twentieth centuries to prepare new teachers hence brought considerable uniformity while also deemphasizing content knowledge of teachers and leaders (Maranto and Wai 2020, 6).

The Progressives and Scientific Management

The Progressives not only further solidified a central public education vision but also created a centralized delivery system. Continued rapid socioeconomic change, including increased immigration and urbanization in the mid- to late 1800s, brought wholesale transformation not only in specific areas of U.S. social policy but also in the way policy was implemented. Having viewed the American "freedom experiment" a failure, Progressives set to work to design a system that would rein in and thus significantly reduce the influence of the *invisible hand* approaches to society and government, exchanging them for a top-down system of control through bureaucratic governmental agencies. Centralizers thus pushed for their arguably *private* view of government—private because it is in direct contradiction to the social functions of American government explicated in the country's founding documents.

Woodrow Wilson, the twenty-sixth U.S. president and academic who advocated Progressivism, wrote prolifically on the Progressive role of government administration, arguing that "a professional class of experts" constitutes a better, more efficient way to implement policy (Pestritto 2007). He dismissed the founders' limited-government social function by stating that "administrative principles and constitutional principles [are] distinct" so constitutional principles (e.g., checks and balances) "interfered with efficiency and should not be applied to the exercise of administrative power" (ibid.). In response to the Progressives, policymakers began developing programs to serve particular groups of Americans or accomplish particular policy missions, with agencies employing *professional* bureaucrats. For the Progressives, the professionals, guided within rule-bound bureaucracies, knew what was best for the public.

The Progressives transformed public education. Thought leaders like Ellwood Cubberley worked to bureaucratize schools specifically to control them. While the first state systems originated in the early 1800s (e.g., New York State in 1812 [Cubberley 1916, 9]), states' educational administrators gradually began adopting the Progressives' ideas.

As mentioned previously, the school district/catchment area system resulted in a state-sanctioned arrangement of monopolies motivated to maintain their status—one that, when coupled with the Progressive-led move toward centralization and bureaucratization, tended to insulate the public school system from those it was intended to serve. Rather than considering a return to local schools, reformers doubled down on centralization, pushing harder for uniformity under growing numbers of professional "experts" who would impose the supposedly "best" business practices.

In the early 1900s, Frederick Taylor's Scientific Management Theory spread into public education, first in magazines and education journals that attacked schools as inefficient and unprofessional (Callahan 1962, 51).

In 1918, the Commission on the Reorganization of Secondary Education presented the Cardinal Principles of Secondary Education, which recommended curricular content that was less academic and more uniform across schools while at the same time tracked students within schools (Commission on the Reorganization of Secondary Education, Appointed by the National Education Association 1918). Often termed the "factory model" of education, school leaders began assigning students based on age (elementary and secondary grades) or subject matter (secondary grades), largely for the convenience of school personnel. This single, "one size fits all" reform has resulted in additional problems for students, such as impersonalization and social promotion—policies gravely affecting disadvantaged students who are tracked and passed through bureaucratic systems whether they learn or not (Doherty 2004).

The question of how much control states should exert over their public school systems evolved erratically across states. As a thought leader, Cubberley (1916, 24–25) discussed the consideration of elements that could balance a state system between too little and too much state control. Ultimately, he did not equivocate on *whether* and, to a great extent, *how* the state should control the public education system by controlling the schools.

> The authority and power to develop [public schools] have come from the State and *not, except secondarily*, from the community [. . .] The school district [. . .] [was] erected for the purpose of better local administration. The State creates these subdivisions of itself and then endows them with their powers [. . .] as the best interests of the State may seem to require. It has been the people as a whole, represented in the legislature of the State, and not portions of the people here and there, who have been supreme in the matter of educational legislation. (ibid., 14; emphasis added)

The Progressives thus pushed for centralizing separate community schools under state—instead of community—control. They advocated placing that control in the hands of professionals who were removed from the schools. Under public choice theory, every such move increases the distance between the decision-makers and their constituencies. Mises ([1949] 1998, 7) states, "There is no such thing as perfection in human knowledge, nor for that matter in any other human achievement. Omniscience is denied to man." Building upon this fact, Tullock (2005, 76–77) expounds upon bureaucratic actors' incentives:

> While it is probable that the subordinate will know more about any given situation than his superior, it is also true that the ambitious and intelligent bureaucrat will tend to cut himself off from external reality, unless he is a conscious

hypocrite. The official who is not hypocritical about his task soon learns than an active curiosity leads [. . .] to quarrels with superiors [. . .]; hence he suppresses his curiosity.

Thus, as organizations become more centralized, organizational actors become even more separated from complete or accurate information. This fact helps to explain how and why centralization is the antithesis of optimal community action. In the case of public education, every step toward greater centralization has further distanced the decision-makers from the consumers of education (Downs 1967; Payne 2008).

CENTROPOLY, SEGREGATION, AND SYSTEMATIC INEQUITY

Apart from other educational considerations, the district monopoly system has given schools captive consumers whom bureaucrats can now frequently ignore (Bradley-Dorsey and Maranto 2021). More egregious, however, the school monopoly apparatus has trapped large numbers of U.S. schoolchildren whose families cannot afford to move to a different district or school. This includes, systematically, disadvantaged students and many students of color.[12]

A pointed example of the school monopoly effect can be traced through the systematic segregation of African Americans. Early anti-Black public policy actions are perhaps more widely known than those occurring in the twentieth century; however, the Black-white gaps observed by civil rights leaders in the early 1900s widened further with the advent of the Great Depression and the subsequent New Deal policies (National Advisory Commission on Civil Disorders 1968, 223). Central among these policies that further disadvantaged Black citizens was public housing. For example, New Deal housing, initially administered by the Public Works Administration in 1933, was rigidly segregated and indeed created new segregated neighborhoods, as did later government housing-related programs (Rothstein 2017, 20–24).

Because districts maintained geographic boundaries atop a system of racially and economically segregated communities, the "common" school system envisioned by Mann, Cubberley, and others served educational communities whose needs were anything but uniform. Given racial and economic segregation, the children enrolled in these "uniform" schools differed markedly across districts—and within districts' schools—hence rendering education and its delivery unequal. Beginning in the mid-twentieth century, awareness of this inequality grew and fueled a massive reform movement at the federal level. I turn now to the largest federal reform initiative and argue that these external efforts were ultimately attempts to reform the extant, flawed system of vastly unequal schools serving markedly different student populations. Instead, though, the resulting educational system grew in the United States and its bureaucracy strengthened, increased in complexity, and hardened into a hybridized centropoly, ill-equipped to deal with the problems it attempted to address regarding the needs of the vastly diverse American student population in a rapidly changing world.

One of the most grievous overarching repercussions of American educational reforms can be explained by examining this formalized school segregation in terms of public choice—specifically, with what Downs (1967, 144–66) referred to as control processes and the rigidity cycle. As bureaucracies grow, control increases through processes such as monitoring and the creation of monitoring agencies (ibid., 144–54). Operating bureaus respond by assigning personnel to provide information to the monitors—information that sheds the best light possible on the operating bureau. "In potentially controversial matters," notes Downs, "they often devote extra resources to 'beefing up the record' to provide ample justification for their behavior" (ibid., 152). Downs describes the rigidity cycle as what happens to some bureaus as they grow larger—effects I ascribe to the hybridized super-bureau, or centropoly. Layering additional government levels automatically increases an organization's size. Leaders' resulting "leakage of authority [. . .] leads to [. . .] a growing rigidity of behavior and structure within the bureau [. . .]" (or, in this case, within the hybridized super-bureau; ibid., 152). Control by monitors results in "ever more complex and ever more restrictive regulations upon the operating [super-] bureau [. . .] [T]he bureau also tends to devote ever more resources to figuring out ways of evading or counteracting the monitors' additional regulations" (ibid., 159). The author also notes that specialization increases, and operating authority escalates (ibid., 159), resulting in the "incapability for fast or novel action" (ibid., 160).

I demonstrate these effects to some extent in the remainder of this chapter, which proceeds as follows. In the next section, I summarize the Elementary and Secondary Education Act of 1965 (ESEA) and its reauthorizations and other amendments. Contained within this section is an examination of several consequences of the many policies adopted. I then conclude by summarizing evidence of the consequences in both theoretical and student-outcome terms.

DYSFUNCTIONAL REFORM FOR THE DISADVANTAGED: THE ELEMENTARY AND SECONDARY EDUCATION ACT OF 1965 (ESEA)

School segregation, propagated by educational, housing, and economic public policies, set the course for the famous 1954 *Brown v. Board of Education*

U.S. Supreme Court decision that "the 'separate but equal' doctrine adopted in Plessy v. Ferguson [. . .] has no place in [. . .] public education."[13] President Eisenhower's 1957 decision to send troops to Little Rock evidenced the slow response to the 1954 *Brown* decision (Clark 2020). Dr. Martin Luther King Jr.'s famous "I Have a Dream" speech preceded the Civil Rights Act of 1964 by approximately one year and the ESEA by less than two years. The mid-1960s brought President Lyndon B. Johnson's Great Society and War on Poverty. The Civil Rights Act expressly prohibited school segregation, deeming invalid state and local laws permitting such segregation. Yet, public school leaders had already established and continued to maintain government monopolies *via* district and school catchment area boundaries. The ESEA, intended to improve the educational outcome of students disadvantaged by virtue of being in low-income families, this goal was considered a major part of the War on Poverty. Its spotlight intervention was funding targeted to district public schools with large low-income student enrollments.

Many expressed concerns regarding federal intervention into education prior to the ESEA. As an early example, even before calls came to focus federal attention on America's disadvantaged, the most significant education legislation had been the National Defense Education Act of 1958 (NDEA). A direct response to Russia's launching of Sputnik, the NDEA authorized funding for teaching specific secondary school subjects such as math and science. Although dwarfed in size by the ESEA, Senator Barry Goldwater warned, "If adopted, [the NDEA] will mark the inception of aid, supervision, and ultimately control of education in this country by federal authorities" (Collins 2014, 9; internal references omitted).

Reformers pursued funding focused on education for America's poor soon after the NDEA's passage. But these federal reforms faced obstacles, such as the role of the federal government in education, inclusion of religious schools, and mistrust of local school district officials. President John F. Kennedy's Aid to Education bill failed in 1961, in large part because it excluded aid to private schools (Sorensen 1965, 360).

During the debate preceding the ESEA, civil rights activists argued that public school administrators had placed low priority on education for disadvantaged students and that the schools had been unresponsive to these students' needs (McLaughlin 1974, 1).[14] An anonymous civil rights activist stated forthrightly, "Title I will be money down a rathole unless it includes some measure to protect the interests of poor children" (ibid., 1). Democratic Senator Robert F. Kennedy expressed similar concerns during the 1965 Congressional hearings on the ESEA. Kennedy noted that "[. . .] the school itself has created an educationally deprived system" (ibid., 4). Kennedy made a last-minute demand for an amendment to the legislation mandating reports of educational achievement. "What I want to make sure of is not just that the money is not wasted, because you can find more money, [. . .] but the fact that the lives of these children are not wasted," he stated (Thernstrom and Thernstrom 2003, 215). The senator's demand for achievement evidence, however, resulted only in a requirement that districts or state education departments receiving federal funds file an annual report (ibid., 215). Innocuous though well-intentioned, this language would lay the groundwork for the use of statewide achievement testing to evaluate schools instead of focusing on individual student success (Koretz 2008).

THE ORIGINAL ACT AND ITS AMENDMENTS

Enacted in 1965, the ESEA marked the onset of rapidly growing federal involvement in education—which, in turn, further centralized public education, thickened educational bureaucracy, and solidified into the centropoly. The chain of amendments and reauthorizations itself illustrates the rapid increase of this hybridized government organizational structure.[15] Together with its eight reauthorizations and several other weighty amendments, the ESEA has been the single most significant federal education legislation in the United States. According to Klein (2015, n.p.), "[. . .] [F]or the most part, each new iteration has sought to expand the federal role in education." The only federal education legislation to surpass the original 1965 act in scope has been some of its reauthorizations, most notably the No Child Left Behind Act (NCLB), which will be discussed in detail later.

The original 1965 act consisted of five titles, of which Title I was the Act's main focus (Collins 2014, 14).[16] Title I, "Financial Assistance to Local Education Agencies for the Education of Children of Low-Income Families," originally funded at $1.06 billion, authorized the provision of assistance to schools with large proportions of low-income, "educationally deprived" students *via* formula-driven grants to compensate for this educational deprivation by providing additional funding specifically for these students. Titles II through V created several additional programs, hence adding to federal educational intervention (ibid., 14–20; McGuinn and Hess 2005, 295–96). Ironically, the original Act expressly prohibited federal control of education (Collins 2014, 16). However, with successive reauthorizations came additional programs and requirements. Congress has amended the ESEA many times to contain provisions and government bodies relating to education for disabled students, bilingual education, and other programs and entities. It is certain, however, that these programs contributed to government growth at all three levels of government: federal, state, and local. Each successive law added funding, government bodies, staffing, or a combination thereof. Not all the amendments addressed the needs of the originally targeted student groups, but they contributed to federal centralization of education through funding, requirements tied to receipt of the funds, and other, perhaps unanticipated, incentives resulting from law changes.

Congress reauthorized ESEA every three years during the first fifteen years, focusing increasingly on "resource accountability" (e.g., ensuring the funds were spent on schools enrolling low-income students and students with lowest achievement levels) (Puma and Drury 2000, 3). Schools frequently used "pull-out" programs for eligible students wherein remedial teaching staff removed students from the regular classroom to instruct them. Criticism of pull-out programs led to a 1978 amendment that allowed for schools whose enrollment was at least 75 percent low-income to focus on school, instead of individual student, improvement (ibid.). The local matching fund requirements, still in place, kept most schools from implementing schoolwide programs (ibid.), but this would change in 1988 when Congress discarded the local match requirement.

The 1981 reauthorization under Reagan constituted an attempt to reduce federal intrusion into public education. Under Reagan, federal regulations were reduced from seventy-five to fourteen pages, and Title I—the largest ESEA-funded program—was renamed Chapter 1 (though this changed back in later legislation). The 1988 reauthorization began to focus on "program improvement" efforts where Chapter 1 students showed inadequate gains in achievement (ibid.).

The law changed again with the 1994 reauthorization. Two important revisions were a mandate that all states adopt standards-aligned assessment systems by 2000–2001 and a reduction in the poverty-rate threshold for operating a schoolwide Title 1 program, from 75 to 50 percent poverty (ibid., 4–5).

In summary, the ESEA's evolution so far had led to promotion of external, school-based accountability while reducing focus on student-targeted improvement provisions. But reauthorizations to this point were minor steps when compared to the changes coming through the NCLB under George W. Bush.

NO CHILD LEFT BEHIND ACT: ESEA CHANGE IN FEDERAL INTERVENTION

Other than the original Act, the ESEA reauthorization with the greatest impact was the NCLB. Enacted in 2002, the NCLB "[. . .] effectively scaled up the federal role in holding schools accountable for student outcomes" (Klein 2015, n.p.).

Arguably, the NCLB's most important element is made obvious from the Act's title: *No child* was to be ignored, translated in the Act as focusing on disadvantaged students. Kymes (2004, n.p.) notes that research conducted by Bush's administration "concluded that many present-day educational systems were still attempting to serve a population that has not existed since the 1950s [. . .]." The country's disadvantaged had long since become not simply those who were not interested in academics, but students who, more pointedly, were tied to factors anchored in the histories of minorities and the poor.

Ironically, then, the NCLB represented a recognition that the same problems existed which the original Act was purposed to address nearly four decades earlier. Even though the goal of the original ESEA was to improve educational outcomes of this student group, the NCLB made specific demands that attempted to ensure districts and schools would not ignore disadvantaged students. These demands included mandatory reporting at student subgroup levels (e.g., income, race, or ethnicity) so that districts and schools could not hide achievement gaps by averaging overall student performance.

Second, the NCLB was the first-ever federal attempt at an outcome-based educational accountability system. Previous iterations of the ESEA contained provisions that focused on aspects of accountability, such as testing and reporting, but the NCLB contained a federal mandate that states meet specific outcome measures. Prior to this, several states had adopted standards- or outcome-based accountability programs beginning in the 1980s and continuing into the 1990s. The state-level programs grew out of concerns arising from *A Nation at Risk*, a 1983 report describing America's educational system in dire terms (National Commission on Excellence in Education 1983).[17] Many found themselves still aware that America ranked in the middle among other nations regarding educational performance (Hanushek and Luque 2003, 485). Some concluded action was needed at the national level—again, doubling down on top-down reform.

The cornerstone of the NCLB accountability provisions was the requirement that all students, with rare exceptions, reach the "proficient" level on state math and reading tests by the 2013–2014 school year. Under the law, each state was required to (1) define the test score levels that met the state's "proficiency" designation and (2) set and meet its annual targeted "Adequate Yearly Progress" (AYP), or percentage of students achieving at the state's self-prescribed "proficiency" level for each year.

Consequently, state testing became an integral part of the newly mandated high-stakes accountability system created through the NCLB.[18] States had to create tests to measure students' proficiency status in math and literacy in specified grades while also reporting on student subgroups such as those from low-income families, those with limited English proficiency, and students with disabilities.

This testing itself changed administrator and teacher behavior toward their students as well as student learning behaviors and outcomes. According to Koretz (2008, 47), in the United States, the "primary [function] of large-scale achievement" testing changed from helping individual *students* (*via* diagnosis) to group-based accountability (holding schools, districts, and teachers accountable)—the latter being precisely the purpose of the NCLB-based testing.

The ESEA (and particularly, the NCLB reauthorization), therefore, helped create the *institutional* accountability movement.[19] The concern about disadvantaged students, which resulted in the Act's passage, evolved into measurement of disadvantaged student progress, which then drove the group-based testing accountability movement (ibid., 54). This progression represented a step in the incremental march toward a more centralized and illogically based institution, as the focus became even more centered on the success of the school instead of the success of the student.

This well-intentioned testing mandate is a prime example of centralization gone awry. The mandate took attention away from the constituents—students—as public school system employees focused on ways to make their institutions look better, or at least deflect punishment. All such behaviors reflect the "circling of wagons" around the institution itself—precisely the behavior that public choice theorists had described.

During the latter years of the NCLB, raising AYP (the percent-proficient measure) became increasingly difficult for states. Supporters and critics alike began to question this provision. Because of this and other factors, the federal Education Secretary implemented a directive allowing for a waiver from the continued mandated increases. Using the ESEA Flexibility Waiver, the U.S. Department of Education (USDOE) waived states meeting certain requirements from the mandate to increase their proficiency levels. Forty-two states received flexibility waivers under the NCLB (Balingit 2015).

However, many of the NCLB's institutional effects survived. By holding districts and schools accountable—perhaps a natural inclination, given their prior performance regarding disadvantaged students—the Act served to focus on the institution and not on the students themselves. In other words, students became the instruments to reflect school and district success rather than the constituency to be served.

ESEA: CONNECTIONS TO GOVERNMENT GROWTH AND CENTRALIZATION

Being the primary driver of public school education involvement at the federal level, the ESEA has had a dramatic impact on government growth and centralization. Several indicators of growth and centralization at all levels of government can be attributed, at least in part, to the adoption of the ESEA and its subsequent reauthorizations.

Federal Funding

Though not the sole driver of federal education funding increases, the ESEA figured prominently. Federal funding rose from $652 million in fiscal year (FY) 1960 to $3.22 billion in FY 1970 (second reauthorization). By approximately FY 1975, spending had increased to about $25 billion, after which it fluctuated, rising to a $29.7 billion high in FY 1980. That year was followed by a sizeable and sustained spending decrease that lasted until after the fifth reauthorization in FY 1988. Revenues climbed for approximately the next eight years, with fluctuations and an abrupt decline due to the Great Recession.

In recent fiscal years, the amount of federal ESEA funding has stabilized at around $14 to $16 billion. In FY 2017, ESEA Title I funding was just over $14 billion, and total federal funding for public school education was over $57 billion. Total federal revenues per pupil, based on the $57 billion amount, was more than $2,000 (National Center for Education Statistics 2020, 7).

Staffing: Federal, State, and Local Levels

As with federal funding, the number of federal full-time equivalent (FTE) education staff for public school education functions has increased markedly since the passage of the ESEA. As of 1965, the Office of Education within the Department of Health, Education, and Welfare employed more than 2,100 people. Forty-five years later, in 2010, the USDOE employed almost 4,300 people. The federal public school-related workforce increased dramatically upon the upgrade of the federal education function to a cabinet-level agency in 1979. Before the change, the Office of Education had approximately 3,000 employees (USDOE 2010).

The staffing increases were not confined to the federal government. School district FTE staff grew from fewer than 1.5 million FTE in 1957 to about 3.9 million in 1997. Total state and local staff grew from about 2 million FTE in 1957 to more than 7 million in 1997. Subtracting, this means that state-level public education FTE grew over the same period from 0.5 million to about 3.1 million.

The student-to-staff ratio provides another illustration of public education employment increases over time. In FY 1950, the number of students per staff member was 19.3 (Maranto and McShane 2012, 28). By FY 1993, the ratio had dropped to 10.1. From FY 2000 to FY 2018, the ratio hovered between

8.0 and 8.9, with the exception of FY 2015, when the ratio jumped to 9.4. The ratio for FY 2018 was 8.5.

Empirical Evidence: The ESEA Is Associated with State and Local Staff Growth

Although the descriptive evidence appears to show general growth in staff numbers, not all states grew in staff over the more recent years, and staffing levels differed markedly among states. The following longitudinal, fixed-effects regression analyses provide a clearer picture of the relationship between the ESEA over the years and public education staffing levels. To conduct this regression model, I obtained panel data covering multiple years for each of the fifty states from two sources: (1) 1965–1992 data from the U.S. Census of Governments (COG) conducted every five years, wherein I calculated the average change for the years in between the five-year intervals; and (2) the NCES Common Core of Data (CCD) for 1993–2009. The lack of a single, continuous data set presents a limitation. The CCD data might be preferable since annual data are available, but they do not cover the earlier ESEA years. Although the COG data were gathered only every five years, it is possible that earlier, smaller school organizations paid more careful attention to data reporting. Either way, because there is a clear change between the two data sets, as shown in figure 1.1, I could not combine them. Therefore, I conducted two separate longitudinal panel data, fixed-effects regression analyses, both of which follow the same model:

$$logFTE_{it} = \beta_0 + \beta_1 Act_{1,it} + \beta_2 Act_{2,it} + \ldots + \beta_r Act_{r,it} + \partial_1 logPov_{it} + \partial_2 logPop_{it}$$

My dependent variable, $logFTE_{it}$, is the natural log of state and local public education FTE staff for each year beginning two years after the relevant amendment group. This measurement is to account for the time lag between a law's adoption and the changes implemented as a result.

My independent variables of interest are categorical variables representing all sets of law changes beginning just after the adoption of the original ESEA. The variable value is "1" if the amendments were in effect for a particular year. For example, the variable for the 1981 reauthorization would contain a value of "1" in the years 1981 and all years thereafter. I compare the resulting associations relative to the original 1965 enactment. Hence, law change coefficients are additive.

In this relatively simple model, I employ fixed-effects panel regression to account for nonrandom, unmeasured differences within individual states,

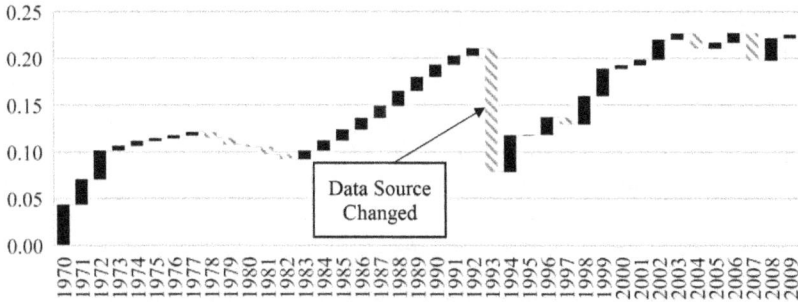

Figure 1.1   Percent Change in Mean State-Local School FTE per 100 Population from Previous Year. *Note*: Black rectangles show growth over previous year. *Source*: *Population*: U.S. Census: 1970–1980—Population Distribution Branch, Intercensal Estimates of the Resident Population of States, 1970–1980; 1981–1990—Population Distribution Branch, 1981–1989 Intercensal Estimates of the Resident Population of States, and Year-to-Year Components of Change (all data consistent with the intercensal estimates shown in Table 2 of CURRENT POPULATION REPORTS Series, P25-1106); 1990–2000—ST-99-7 State Population Estimates and Demographic Components of Population Change: Annual Time Series, April 1, 1990, to July 1, 1999, Population Estimates Program, Population Division; 2000–2010—Table 1. Intercensal Estimates of the Resident Population for the United States, Regions, States, and Puerto Rico: April 1, 2000, to July 1, 2010; 2010–2019—Population Division, Table 1. Annual Estimates of the Resident Population for the United States, Regions, States, and Puerto Rico: April 1, 2010, to July 1, 2019 (NST-EST2019-01). *Staff:*1972 Census of Governments, Vol. 3 Public Employment, No. 2 Compendium of Public Employment, Table 13 Full-Time Equivalent Employment of State and Local Governments. 1982 COG, Vol. 3, No. 2; 1992 COG, Vol. 3, No. 2; U.S. Department of Education, National Center for Education Statistics, Common Core of Data (CCD), "Local Education Agency (School District) Universe Survey," 1992–1993 v.1a, 1993–1994 v.1a, 1994–1995 v.1a, 1995–1996 v.1a, 1996–1997 v.1a, 1997–1998 v.1a, 1998–1999 v.1c, 1999–2000 v.1b, 2000–2001 v.1a, 2001–2002 v.1a, 2002–2003 v.1a, 2003–2004 v.1b, 2004–2005 v.1c, 2005–2006 v.1a, 2006–2007 v.1c, 2007–2008 v.1b, 2008–2009 v.1a; "State Nonfiscal Public Elementary/Secondary Education Survey," 2008–09 v.1c, 2018–19 v.1a.

such as economic conditions. I add controls for the natural log of the state's population in poverty and of the state's total population each year as reported by the U.S. Census.

As discussed previously, figure 1.1 shows a clear pattern of increase in the mean proportional state and local education FTE in most ESEA amendment years, with the exception of FYs 1978–1982. Only three of this group of 17 years experienced a mean proportional FTE decrease over the previous year. Considering all fiscal years shown in both data sets, there is an overall growth pattern over the years, and proportional FTE growth occurs in most, but not all, years. It is possible that most of the absolute growth in the overall mean state and local public education FTE occurred in the first set (i.e., FYs 1965–1992—using the first data set). During this period, the number of FTE grew from less than 1.5 in 1965 to almost 2.1 in FY 1992 for every 100 people. During the second period (using the second data set), the mean FTE dipped to 1.8 per 100 people in FY 1993 and rose again to 2.1 in FY 2009. (Note, however, the sizeable interruption in values between the two data sets, as shown in figure 1.1.)

Table 1.1   Associations between State and Local Education Full-Time Equivalent (FTE) Staff (Log) and ESEA Amendments by Year Adopted

Earlier ESEA Amendments[1]		*Later ESEA Amendments*	
1966	0.061***	1994	0.074***
	(0.008)		(0.018)
1968	0.071***	2002	0.055***
	(0.009)		(0.012)
1970	0.074***	Number in Poverty (log)	0.096
	(0.008)		(0.078)
1972	0.045***	Population (log)	0.900***
	(0.008)		(0.122)
1974	0.012	Constant	−3.758***
	(0.008)		(1.311)
1977	0.007	Observations	840
	(0.010)	Number of States	50
1978	−0.013	R-squared	0.438
	(0.010)	Standard errors in parentheses	
1981	−0.012	*** $p < 0.01$, ** $p < 0.05$, * $p < 0.1$	
	(0.008)		
1983	0.011		
	(0.010)		
1984	0.034***		
	(0.009)		
1988	0.080***		
	(0.005)		
Number in poverty (log)	−0.194***		
	(0.013)		
Population (log)	1.035***		
	(0.018)		
Constant	−2.284***		
	(0.184)		
Observations	2,395		
Number of states	50		
R-squared	0.944		

[1]Because the two datasets could not be combined, I ran separate regressions.
Source: Author created.
Standard errors in parentheses

Table 1.1 reveals the results of the regression analyses. The first column, reflecting the first and largest set of the ESEA laws, shows that of the eleven law changes in the regression, six (those enacted in 1966, 1968, 1970, 1972, 1984, and 1988) reveal highly statistically significant (p = 0.01) FTE staff growth. Of the remaining five laws (those enacted in 1974, 1977, 1978, 1981, and 1983), two are associated with FTE staff decreases, but none are statistically significant. Of the two laws associated with FTE staff decreases, the 1981 law might be expected to show a negative association since the 1981 reauthorization was President Reagan's attempt to reduce federal education influence.

To interpret the model, it is important to remember that all laws are in operation from their enactment year forward. Additionally, because the law variables are binary, all are relative to the original 1965 act's passage. Finally, the model assumes staffing changes two years following the adoption of the law. Therefore, to interpret the regression results, one must consider that the 1965 act's staffing influence continues in all years since and including 1967 (two years after passage, the assumed staff change delay), the 1966 reauthorization's staffing influence continues in all years since and including 1968, and so on. This means, for example, that the 1966 law change, for which the assumed staffing change is in effect from 1968 forward, is associated with a 6.1 percent FTE increase. The 1968 law, in effect from 1970 forward, is associated with a 7.1 percent FTE increase, and so on. The population coefficient is expected to be large and highly statistically significant, since states' populations have grown sizably over the past decades. Controlling for population eliminates this variable's impact from the law change associations.

Importantly, however, the log of the number in poverty is highly statistically significant (p=0.01) associated with a 0.194 percentage point FTE *decrease*. In other words, poverty is associated with a decrease in FTE separate and apart from the law changes and the population control. This could have additional, and concerning, implications for the nation's poorest students. More research is necessary to further examine this coefficient.

The second column in table 1.1 shows a similar analysis for the 1994 and 2002 laws. As shown, these laws are associated with highly significant (p = 0.01) total FTE staff increases of 7.4 and 5.5 percent, respectively. The poverty coefficient in this model is not statistically significant.

In summary, over the two analyses (using two data sets), there are positive associations between FTE increases and eight of thirteen ESEA law changes. None of the five remaining law changes analyzed were associated with a statistically significant FTE change, and only two of those five (nonsignificant) associations were negative. The negative association between poverty and FTE in the first analysis needs further examination, as it might be concerning in its own right.

THE EDUCATIONAL CONDITION OF
DISADVANTAGED STUDENTS

The obvious question becomes whether the sizeable resource increases, due at least in part to the passage of the ESEA and its subsequent iterations, have resulted in educational improvements for the disadvantaged students they were intended to help. Clearly, the ESEA was adopted to reduce or even close achievement gaps between low-income students and others. Also, clearly, research evidence reveals it has not done so—especially when considering the multiple billions of dollars spent over time.

Addressing only the ESEA's Title 1, Sousa and Armor (2016) review prior research evaluating the program's effectiveness in closing achievement gaps between disadvantaged and non-disadvantaged students using a research synthesis approach to summarize studies conducted between 1966 and 2011. After reviewing five peer-reviewed evaluation studies and conducting their own standardized national assessment score trend analysis, the authors conclude that there is "very little evidence that the Title I compensatory education program has significantly improved the academic achievement of disadvantaged students nationwide" (ibid., 309).

In summary, none of the studies used randomized control trials (RCT), considered the only true experimental design, because RCT has never been used to evaluate the overall Title I program across the nation. This is likely due to the "near universal implementation of Title I," which negates the pos-sibility of a control group.

Nevertheless, Sousa and Armor (2016) examine five peer-reviewed studies: two meta-analyses, two National Assessments (conducted by the USDOE), and one panel data analysis of state-level results of the standard-ized national assessment (National Assessment of Educational Progress, or NAEP).[20] They also conduct their own summary analysis of NAEP data span-ning from 1990 to 2013.

Three peer-reviewed studies evaluated Title I's effectiveness at closing gaps during school years prior to 2000 (i.e., before the NCLB was imple-mented). These studies showed "[no] meaningful gap reductions" and, in fact, widening achievement gaps in one of the studies (ibid., 309). The two later peer-reviewed studies provide evidence suggesting the NCLB "had modest effects on fourth grade test scores, especially in math, and these gains were somewhat stronger for disadvantages [*sic*] students" (ibid., 309). One of these studies conducted a quasi-experimental examination in which the study authors compared states that had implemented NCLB-like accountability reforms prior to the NCLB with states that had no such reforms. The authors found that, by 2003, states with pre-NCLB accountability reforms reduced the gap between Black and white students by 7 points compared to 5 points for states without the pre-NCLB reforms (ibid., 310). Note that this study focused on a different gap—Black-white—than did the other studies (which focused on poverty), likely due to the fact that NAEP changed its reporting focus to racial groups (ibid.).

Finally, Sousa and Armor (2016) conduct an overall analysis of 1990–2013 NAEP data. The authors conclude, "The overall progress is disappointing, particularly for the poverty gap. The achievement gaps between [low-income] students [. . .] and those not [low-income] have remained virtually constant for reading and math at both grade levels [i.e., fourth and eighth grade]" (ibid., 310). Black-white and Hispanic-white gaps showed better results. The authors then comment on the distinction between results before and after the NCLB, noting that "after 2000 [the national approach] was to adopt accountability practices which had proven effective in some states during the late 1990s" (ibid.). However, as previously noted, others have expressed concerns with the institutional accountability approach adopted through the NCLB. Additionally, concerns have been raised that, post-NCLB, achievement scores might have dropped. Since the Sousa and Armor study ends at 2013 and the NCLB waivers were generally granted in 2014 and 2015, additional study is necessary to determine what happened later because of the NCLB as well as what happened after the NCLB was no longer in effect.

WHY THE ESEA REFORMS FAILED: A PUBLIC CHOICE EXPLANATION

Given the layered structure of the school system, it is not difficult to explain why hundreds of billions of federal reform dollars amounted to little, if any, progress for disadvantaged students. The district monopolies provide personnel with negligible incentive to improve student outcomes. The layering that had begun *via* early state control has only increased in the ensuing years as federal and state controls have expanded, thereby thickening educational bureaucracy. The centropoly has thus formed and strengthened. Relatedly, a key disincentive to change, quite simply, is that most educational administrators and school boards prefer schools to remain as they are, not as some (e.g., some policymakers and much of the public) would like them to be (Maranto and Wai 2020; Downs 1967).

The entire infrastructure of laws, agencies, and staffing resulting from the ESEA and its iterations was superimposed, in waves, upon an already centralized and monopolized public education system, hence bringing to life the hybridized U.S. educational centropoly with its layers of government operating above each student. The effects of this large-scale evolution *should* be emphasized. Layering has contributed to what Tullock (2005) discussed regarding communication distortions and to what Downs (1967) refers to as the rigidity cycle. Government layering has produced additional bureaucracy that, in turn, has led to reduced information as well as increased monitoring, regulation, and defensive moves, of and by the centropoly.

Additionally, as Mises (1944, 57–63) explains, a public bureaucratic manager has only his/her set of rules to govern behavior. This happens because public enterprises, such as public schools, lack the simple information device of the profit motive. Absent the profit motive, public managers have no way of determining the *public's* needs or demands or how these compete among different groups of people, but they do understand that (1) "[. . .] the appearance of a deficit is not considered a proof of failure [. . .]"; and (2) "every service can be improved by increasing expenditures" (ibid., 61–62). Since the primary interest of each such manager is "improving the satisfaction of needs only in their special branches of activity" (ibid., 62), the focus becomes budget maximization.

Finally, the centropoly has decreased focus on schools' constituencies. Stated alternatively, increased defensiveness and information distance further emphasize private motives (Tullock 2005). Disadvantaged students and their parents were captive in school districts in 1965, and they remain captive today because they cannot afford to move to a different district or school or to enroll their children in a private school. Educational captivity places these students and their parents under the control of officials—at three levels of government—working in settings offering job security in numerous ways, *via* the school system's now-centropolized status. Professional educators frequently tell complaining or questioning parents to leave their children's education to the professionals. Yet, these professionals not only have limited information relative to that of the parents, but they also prioritize their own private interests ahead of those of the students.

As shown, in U.S. public education centropoly, the purpose of the institution is to maintain the institution. The public school system fits Downs's (1967) description of bureaus—actually, of an organization (more precisely, a *bureau*) made up of several bureaus. A state educational system is composed of the state education bureau and its many school district organizations or bureaus. The imposition of federal control—tied to the "golden handcuffs" offered by the additional federal funding—has further centralized and bureaucratized the public education system: now, the states as well as their monopolistic school districts are required to follow *federal bureau* mandates in addition to their respective *state bureau* requirements.

The public school system frequently defends itself against perceived threats, such as funding cuts or school choice legislation, by publicly stating that its goal is to serve the children. Public choice theory, however, helps to explain how the public education system primarily serves itself. The schools and states exhibit collective willingness (of multiple organizational participants) to take the strings attached to higher-level (e.g., federal) money, thereby becoming more bureaucratic. This, in combination with the fact that the bureaucracy is separated, often by several levels, from its constituency, means that self-interested bureaucrats decide, with woefully inadequate information, what is best for the students under their control.

Given these circumstances, what is the education centropoly's incentive to focus on improving, for example, achievement gaps evidenced in the NAEP scores? The students will remain regardless of personal or institutional achievement. Given widespread public sector job protection and teacher tenure in particular, neither low-performing teachers nor poorly performing school leaders are incentivized to prioritize student achievement. Finally, their monopoly status coupled with their political clout means that public schools will remain unchanged regardless of their performance or lack thereof. Widespread measurable success—indeed, much success at all—under such a system could be viewed as the exception, not the rule.

NOTES

1. My deepest thanks go to my adviser, Dr. Robert A. Maranto, for his steadfast guidance and support. Thanks also to my team of quantitative advisers, Dr. Jon Mills, Nathaniel Burke, and Dr. Aaron Novotny, for helping me so much. Thank you always, David and Patrick.

2. Indeed, later the work of Elinor and Vincent Ostrom regarding successful efforts by communities to overcome community ("commons") challenges absent centralized control would reinforce Tocqueville's impression (see Cole and McGinnis 2015). Although public education could have benefited from the Ostrom model, reformers took it in a different, and more centralized, direction.

3. Of course, not all U.S. school districts are large; indeed, many are small organizations. However, as will be explained further, the layered bureaucracy resulting from state and federal involvement changes the structure to some extent, effectively making even small districts operate as larger entities. State and federal involvement result in decreased information flow and flexibility of even the small districts.

4. The nation's response to the 2019 pandemic has included a return to small-group schooling (often referred to as "pods," micro-schools, or hybrid homeschooling). See Watson (2020); Burke (2020); and Manning, Kennedy, and Kerr (2020).

5. Although the law was indeed compulsory, Hazlett (2011, abstract) notes that it and other similar compulsory education laws were not "strictly enforced until Horace Mann advocated schooling for all, with his Common School Movement leading to free, public, and locally controlled elementary schools, beginning with Massachusetts in 1852."

6. Latin grammar schools, having originated in Europe, were essentially college preparatory schools. The first one in America was the Boston Latin School, established in 1635, also known as the first public school in what would become the United States (National Geographic, n.d.). Hess (2010, 41) notes that "historian Gerald Gutek has observed, 'The colonists believed in a two-track system of schools—one for the poor and another for the wealthy.'" Latin schools, he says, were for upper class (male) children. Hazlett (2011, abstract) notes that "[the] law's title was derived from its purpose, as teaching youth to read allowed access to the [Protestant] Christian *Bible*, with their presumably subsequent faith and doctrinal adherence producing virtuous citizens."

7. In fact, Vermont and Maine established the first school voucher programs in the United States. Implemented in 1869 and 1873, respectively, the states' town-tuitioning programs provide for towns without a public school to provide tuition to send their students to a public or private, non-religious school in another location (EdChoice 2019). Additionally, early American schools were more likely to be religiously diverse (at least in terms of Christian denominations), given the fact that immigrants to America frequently had escaped religious persecution (van Raemdonck and Maranto 2018, 550).

8. Ellwood P. Cubberley was both an academic scholar and a (progressive) thought leader in the field of education. Here, I use his historical writings. Some have questioned Cubberley's historiography because of his particular point of view regarding the formation of the U.S. school system. See Cartwright (1996).

9. The Common School movement had roots in philanthropic group efforts. Philanthropic groups began founding schools through the Sunday School movement, providing both religious and minimal secular learning: the City School Societies, fashioned after the English charity schools to provide a rudimentary education to the poor; the Lancastrian (or monitorial school) movement, a system under which the more advanced students taught less advanced students; and the Infant-School Societies, establishing schools for children between the ages of four and eight (Cubberley 1922, 357–63). According to Cubberley, "These four important educational movements [. . .] all arising in philanthropy, came as successive educational ideas to America during the first half of the nineteenth century, supplemented one another, and together accustomed a new generation to the idea of a common school for all" (ibid., 363).

10. The Anti-Catholic state Blaine amendments—indicative of private motives as opposed to social functions—would become highly instrumental in the late twentieth and early twenty-first centuries in preventing attempts to move away from this centralized public education system to one involving parental choice. Equally important, however, the amendments represent evidence that centralized state educational systems became the consequence of reformers' attempts to balance the desires for limited government, individual liberties, and natural markets against a social concern for national unity in the face of diversity. But national unity can easily evade a nation's grasp if what constitutes a "unified" view is contentious. As Hayek ([1973; 1976; 1979] 1982, 170) explains, "The common welfare or the public good has [. . .]

remained a concept most recalcitrant to any precise definition and therefore capable of being given almost any content suggested by the interests of the ruling group."

11. The state Blaine amendments only recently lost their power to separate religion and public education: in June 2020, the U.S. Supreme Court (in *Espinoza v. Montana Department of Revenue*, 18-1195, June 30, 2020) ruled that states cannot exclude religious families and schools from school choice programs (Institute for Justice n.d.).

12. Indeed, despite widespread acceptance of the Tiebout Effect theory (i.e., that the public can "vote with their feet" to pursue public goods such as schooling by moving to different neighborhoods), the Tiebout Effect is also widely disputed even for those with the financial means to move. See Fedako (2018).

13. See *Brown v. Board of Education* (1954).

14. For example, ten years after the momentous *Brown v. Board of Education* (1954) U.S. Supreme Court decision ordering school desegregation—and one year before passage of the ESEA—the vast majority of African American students in the South still attended segregated schools (Sunstein 2004).

15. School district consolidation is arguably another policy designed to correct underlying systemic problems while creating or exacerbating extant problems. Driven largely by policymakers' desire to improve efficiency, the number of school districts nationally has dropped from more than 127,500 in 1932 to fewer than 20,000 in the early 1970s and fewer than 15,000 in the 2001–2002 school year (Coulson 2007). As researchers find diminishing returns to the efficiency of larger districts, it is also noteworthy that larger organizations frequently result in further centralization, hence greater separation from information.

16. The act also included a title for "general provisions."

17. Considered hyperbole by some, the report claimed: "If an unfriendly foreign power had attempted to impose on America the mediocre educational performance that exists today, we might well have viewed it as an act of war." See *A Nation at Risk* (National Commission on Excellence in Education 1983, paragraph 2). By 2000, forty-eight states were involved in standards-based accountability systems. The state plans varied in content, implementation, and success levels.

18. As mentioned previously, however, not all aspects of the NCLB accountability system were mandatory. The act permitted states to set their own proficiency (and other achievement) levels.

19. One could analyze the transformation from student to institutional focus, resulting from just the NCLB, in great detail. Another such example is that the federal government revised its AYP target requirements to allow for states to meet AYP in a particular year by improving subgroup performance while not meeting its stated targeted goals. See, *EducationWeek* (2008).

20. NAEP, mandated by Congress, is "the only assessment that measures what US students know and can do in various subjects across the nation [and] states [. . .]" (National Center for Education Statistics n.d., About NAEP). Although limited (i.e., it samples each state's fourth- and eighth-grade student bodies), NAEP measures include public school reading and math scores.

REFERENCES

Balingit, Moriah. 2015. "Virginia, Four Other States to Remain Exempt from No Child Left Behind." *The Washington Post*: March 31. https://www.washingtonpost.com/local/education/virginia-four-other-states-to-remain-exempt-from-no-child-left-behind/2015/03/31/6ed61d48-d710-11e4-ba28-f2a685dc7f89_story.html.

Blais, André and Stéphane Dion. 1990. "Are Bureaucrats Budget Maximizers? The Niskanen Model and Its Critics." *Polity* 22 (4): 655–74.

Boettke, Peter J., Stefanie Haeffele-Balch, and Virgil Henry Storr, eds. 2016. *Mainline Economics: Six Nobel Lectures in the Tradition of Adam Smith.* Arlington, VA: Mercatus Center, George Mason University.

Bradley-Dorsey, Martha and Robert Maranto. 2021. "Bureaucracy Has Conquered Schools. Joe Biden Won't Fix It." *National Review*, March 21. https://www.nationalreview.com/2021/03/bureaucracy-has-conquered-schools-joe-biden-wont-fix-it/.

Brown v. Board of Education 347 US 483. 1954. Transcript. https://www.ourdocuments.gov/doc.php?flash=false&doc=87&page=transcript.

Buchanan, James M. and Gordon Tullock. 1999. *The Collected Works of James M. Buchanan, Volume 3. The Calculus of Consent: Logical Foundations of Constitutional Democracy.* Indianapolis, IN: Liberty Fund.

Burke, Lindsey M. 2020. "'Pandemic Pods' Are Fundamentally Reshaping K-12 Education." *The Heritage Institute*, July 1. https://www.heritage.org/education/commentary/pandemic-pods-are-fundamentally-reshaping-k-12-education.

Byrne, Julie. 2000. "Roman Catholics and Immigration in Nineteenth-Century America." *National Humanities Center*. http://nationalhumanitiescenter.org/tserve/nineteen/nkeyinfo/nromcath.htm.

Calhoun, John C. 1953. *A Disquisition on Government.* New York: Bobbs-Merrill Company, Inc.

Callahan, Raymond E. 1962. *Education and the Cult of Efficiency.* Chicago, IL: The University of Chicago Press.

Cartwright, William H. 1966. "Review of *The Wonderful World of Ellwood Patterson Cubberley: An Essay on the Historiography of American Education*, by Lawrence A. Cremin." *The American Historical Review* 71 (2): 725–26.

Clark, Alexis. 2020. "Why Eisenhower Sent the 101st Airborne to Little Rock after *Brown v. Board.*" *History.com*, April 8. https://www.history.com/news/little-rock-nine-brown-v-board-eisenhower-101-airborne.

Cole, Daniel H. and Michael D. McGinnis, eds. 2015. *Elinor Ostrom and the Bloomington School of Political Economy: Volume 1, Polycentricity in Public Administration and Political Science.* London: Lexington Books.

Collins, Courtney A. 2014. "Reading, Writing, and Regulations: A Survey of the Expanding Federal Role in Elementary and Secondary Education Policy." Working Paper, Mercatus Center at George Mason University.

Commission on the Reorganization of Secondary Education, Appointed by the National Education Association. 1918. "Bulletin, 1918, No. 35: Cardinal Principles of Secondary Education." Washington, DC: Department of the Interior, Bureau of Education.

Coulson, Andrew J. 2007. "School District Consolidation: A Brief History and Research Review." *Mackinac Center for Public Policy*, May 22. https://www.mackinac.org/8663.

Cubberley, Ellwood P. 1916. *Public School Administration: A Statement of the Fundamental Principles Underlying the Organization and Administration of Public Education.* Boston, MA: Houghton Mifflin Company.

———. 1922. *A Brief History of Education: A History of the Practice and Progress and Organization of Education.* Boston, MA: Houghton Mifflin Company.

DeForrest, Mark Edward. 2003. "An Overview and Evaluation of State Blaine Amendments: Origins, Scope, and First Amendment Concerns." *Harvard Journal of Law & Public Policy* 26 (2): 551–626.

Doherty, Kathryn M. 2004. "Social Promotion." *EdWeek*, September 21. https://www.edweek.org/ew/issues/social-promotion/index.html.

Downs, Anthony. 1967. *Inside Bureaucracy.* Boston, MA: Little, Brown, and Company.

EdChoice. 2019. "America's School Choice Programs by Dates Enacted and Launched." *EdChoice.org*, Last Modified August 19, 2019. https://www.edchoice.org/school-choice/enacted-and-launched-table.

EducationWeek. 2008. "Schools Seek 'Safe Harbor' from 100 Percent Proficiency." *EdWeek.org*, June 5. http://blogs.edweek.org/edweek/NCLB-ActII/2008/06/charlie_barones_reacts_to_the.html.

Fedako, Jim. 2018. "Voting with Our Feet? Local Government 'Services' and the Supposed Tiebout Effect." *Mises Institute*, May 29. https://mises.org/library/voting-our-feet-local-government-services-and-supposed-tiebout-effect.

Friedman, Milton. 1955. "The Role of Government in Education." In *Economics and the Public Interest*, edited by Robert A. Solo. New Brunswick, NJ: Rutgers University Press.

———. [1962] 1982. *Capitalism and Freedom.* Chicago, IL: The University of Chicago Press.

Hanushek, Eric A. and Javier A. Luque. 2003. "Efficiency and Equity in Schools around the World." *Economics and Education Review* 22: 481–502.

Hayek, F. A. [1973; 1976; 1979] 1982. *Law, Legislation and Liberty: A New Statement of the Liberal Principles of Justice and the Political Economy.* Padstow, UK: T. J. International Ltd.

Hazlett, Lisa A. 2011. "American Education's Beginnings." Forum on *Public Policy Online* 1–13.

Hess, Frederick M. 2010. *The Same Thing over and Over: How School Reformers Get Stuck in Yesterday's Ideas.* Cambridge, MA: Harvard University Press.

Institute for Justice. n.d. "Blaine Amendments." https://ij.org/issues/school-choice/blaine-amendments/.

Klein, Alyson. 2015. "The No Child Left Behind Act: An Overview." *EdWeek*, April 10. https://www.edweek.org/ew/section/multimedia/no-child-left-behind-overview-definition-summary.html.

Koretz, Daniel. 2008. *Measuring Up: What Educational Testing Really Tells Us.* Cambridge, MA: Harvard University Press.

Kymes, Nancy. 2004. "The No Child Left Behind Act: A Look at Provisions, Philosophies, and Compromises." *Journal of Industrial Teacher Education* 41 (2): article 6.

Labaree, David F. 2018. "An Uneasy Relationship: The History of Teacher Education in the University." In *Who Decides Who Becomes a Teacher?* edited by Julie Gorlewski and Eve Tuck. New York: Routledge.

Manning Kennedy, Kate and Liam Kerr. 2020. "We Can't Stop Pandemic Pods. But We Can Fight for All Kids to Be Included." *WBUR (NPR Boston)*, August 10. https://www.wbur.org/cognoscenti/2020/08/10/pandemic-pods-for-all-kate-manning-kennedy-liam-kerr.

Maranto, Robert A. and Michael Q. McShane. 2012. *President Obama and Education Reform: The Personal and the Political.* New York: Palgrave Macmillan.

Maranto, Robert A. and Dirk C. van Raemdonck. 2015. "Letting Education and Religion Overlap: Why Expanding Vouchers to Include Parochial Schools Is a Good Idea." *The Wall Street Journal*, January 8. https://online.wsj.com/articles/robert-maranto-and-dirk-c-van-raemdonck-letting-education-and-religion-overlap-1420761949?reflink=desktopwebshare_permalink.

Maranto, Robert A. and Jonathan Wai. 2020. "Why Intelligence Is Missing from American Education Policy and Practice, and What Can Be Done about It." *Journal of Intelligence* 8 (1): 2.

McGuinn, Patrick and Frederick Hess. 2005. "Freedom from Ignorance? The Great Society and the Evolution of the Elementary and Secondary Education Act." In *The Great Society and the High Tide of Liberalism*, edited by Sidney M. Milkis and Jerome M. Mileur, 289–319. Amherst, MA: University of Massachusetts Press.

McLaughlin, Milbrey W. 1974. "Evaluation and Reform: The Elementary and Secondary Education Act of 1965, Title I." *The Rand Corporation.* https://www.rand.org/pubs/reports/R1292.html.

Mises, Ludwig von. 1944. *Bureaucracy.* New Haven, CT: Yale University Press.

———. [1949] 1998. *Human Action: A Treatise on Economics.* The Scholar's Edition. Auburn, AL: Ludwig von Mises Institute.

National Advisory Commission on Civil Disorders. 1968. *The Kerner Report.* Princeton, NJ: Princeton University Press.

National Center for Education Statistics. n.d. "About NAEP: A Common Measure of Student Achievement." https://nces.ed.gov/nationsreportcard/about/.

———. n.d. "The Boundary Collection, School Attendance Boundary Survey." https://nces.ed.gov/programs/edge/SABS.

National Center for Education Statistics. 2020. "Revenues and Expenditures for Public Elementary and Secondary Education: FY 17." Washington, DC: US Department of Education. https://nces.ed.gov/pubs2020/2020301.pdf.

National Commission on Excellence in Education. 1983. *A National At Risk.* https://www2.ed.gov/pubs/NatAtRisk/risk.html.

National Geographic. n.d. "Apr 23, 1635 CE: America's First Public School." *NationalGeographic.com.* https://www.nationalgeographic.org/thisday/apr23/first-public-school-america/.

Niskanen, Jr., William A. [1971] 2017. *Bureaucracy & Representative Government.* New York: Routledge.

Old Deluder Satan Act. 1647. https://www.mass.gov/files/documents/2016/08/ob/deludersatan.pdf.

Parker, Emily. 2016. "50-State Review: Constitutional Obligations for Public Education." *Education Commission of the States.* https://www.ecs.org/wp-content/uploads/2016-Constitutional-obligations-for-public-education-1.pdf.

Payne, Charles M. 2008. *So Much Reform, So Little Change: The Persistence of Failure in Urban Schools.* Cambridge, MA: Harvard Education Press.

Pestritto, Ronald. 2007. "The Birth of the Administrative State: Where It Came from and What It Means for Limited Government." *The Heritage Foundation,* November 20. https://www.heritage.org/political-process/report/the-birth-the-administrative-state-where-it-came-and-what-it-means-limited.

Puma, Michael J. and Darrel W. Drury. 2000. *Exploring New Directions: Title I in the Year 2000.* Alexandria, VA: National School Boards Association.

Railey, Hunter. 2017. "State Education Governance Structures: 2017 Update." *Education Commission of the States.* https://www.ecs.org/wp-content/uploads/State_Education_Governance_Structures_-_2017_update.pdf.

Rothstein, Richard. 2017. *The Color of Law: A Forgotten History of How Our Government Segregated America.* New York: Liveright Publishing Corporation.

Sorensen, Ted C. 1965. *Kennedy: The Classic Biography.* New York: Harper Perennial Modern Classics.

Sousa, Sonia and David Armor. 2016. "The Effectiveness of Title I: Synthesis of National-Level Evidence from 1966 to 2013." *Universal Journal of Educational Research* 4 (1): 205–311.

Sunstein, Cass R. 2004. "Did Brown Matter?" *The New Yorker,* May 3. https://www.newyorker.com/magazine/2004/05/03/did-brown-matter.

Thernstrom, Abigail and Stephan Thernstrom. 2003. *No Excuses: Closing the Racial Gap in Learning.* New York: Simon & Schuster.

Tocqueville, Alexis de. [1835; 1840] 2010. *Democracy in America, Volumes I and II.* Edited by Eduardo Nolla. English ed. Indianapolis, IN: Liberty Fund.

Tractenberg, Paul L. n.d. *Education Provisions in State Constitutions: A Summary of a Chapter for the State Constitutions for the Twenty-first Century Project.* https://statecon.camden.rutgers.edu/sites/statecon/files/subpapers/tractenberg.pdf.

Tullock, Gordon. 2005. *The Selected Works of Gordon Tullock, Volume 6: Bureaucracy.* Edited by Charles K. Rowley. Indianapolis, IN: Liberty Fund.

US Department of Education. 2010. "An Overview of the U.S. Department of Education." Washington, DC: US Department of Education.

van Raemdonck, Dirk C. and Robert A. Maranto. 2018. "Prisoners of History: Explaining Why Statist Belgium Has School Vouchers While Liberal America Does Not." *Journal of School Choice* 12 (4): 546–66.

Watson, Angela. 2020. "Parent-Created 'Schools' in the U.S." *Journal of School Choice* 14 (4): 595–603.

Chapter 2

Group Identity and Unintended Consequences of School Desegregation

Nathaniel Burke

Much has been written to evaluate the range of policies intended to deseg-regate primary and secondary institutions in the decades following the U.S. Supreme Court's historic decision in *Brown v. Board of Education.* Some metropolitan areas used a more relaxed approach in which limitations of admission based on race were simply removed and students were enrolled into schools where they resided, and some were more aggressive and set racial proportions to be achieved, requiring some students to cross district lines to balance out the demographics of neighboring districts.

Initial actions to integration were met with considerable hostility and pushback as is expected when there is a significant change in the status quo. A famous example of this was when the Little Rock Nine had to be escorted into Little Rock Central High School as the first Black students allowed in the school after "separate but equal" was ended as a policy. While we have come a long way from these early experiences, we struggle to explain why Blacks underperform relative to their white counterparts. This performance gap is observable across the curriculum but is particularly apparent in core subjects such as math, science, and reading.[1] For example, Black students in their fall semester of kindergarten test at .638 standard deviations lower than white students in math and .401 standard deviations lower in reading. This gap is reduced to .102 and .093 standard deviations, respectively, when controlling for other non-race factors; however, many non-race factors have some predictability of race such as Special Supplemental Nutrition Program for Women, Infants and Children (WIC) participation, number of children's books at home, and socioeconomic status (Fryer and Levitt 2004). The test score gap has been shown to persist in later grades, with a difference of .738 standard deviations in third grade math and .814 by eighth grade (Clotfelter, Ladd, and Vigdor 2009). Many recognize the continued problem of differential results, but few suggest what can be done to change this trajectory of underperformance. The gains that have occurred still leave behind significant potential that might be achieved. This could be likened to the deadweight loss that occurs in an inefficient market with a monopoly operating. There are additional benefits that formerly excluded students might gain, but they are prevented by the government refusing to allow alternate models. Specifically, minority students may do better in integrated environments, but not necessarily all minority students do better in these environments. A broader set of policies might move forward those who continue to lag under the existing approach.

This chapter examines how desegregation education policies failed to fully evaluate the benefits of identity and why policies that seek to force integration may end up marginalizing some within the previously segregated communities. In some school districts, current desegregation policies have taken the decision-making ability away from individual students and their households concerning participation in busing programs. This has caused a failure to optimize educational access and outcomes for minority students because the desegregation program does not consider their group identity when assigning them to schools to meet a racial quota. Some students perform better when sent to schools farther from their communities while many do worse because they have a different sensitivity to their group identity being maintained. The practice of forced desegregation also removes human capital from lower-performing neighborhoods earlier by moving potentially higher-performing students to other neighborhoods for schooling. These higher-performing students will then base a major portion of their social capital out of their communities' post-graduation.

I examine the existing literature on the positive impacts of desegregation through this broader lens to consider the overall effects on the previously segregated communities, specifically Black communities. During this exploration, I also look at the educational achievement gaps in testing and graduation rates between schools local to the previously segregated communities and the target schools of desegregation. Recognizing that the advancement of a community through education is a complex, multifactor problem, I also consider how teachers' labor decisions were impacted by desegregation and the continuing concerns of Black communities relating to segregation. Building on this educational literature, I survey the related literature on group identity and the economics of education to understand how including identity can enhance the traditional framework used to consider educational policies. This analysis incorporates the social components from the group identity literature to suggest that there is lost potential in the current policies that are almost exclusively experienced by Black students and communities. Further, I examine the case of Little Rock Central High School from 2016 to 2018 to consider how desegregation policies can end up creating segregation within a school (Smith 2009). Also, I discuss how giving the student and community more choice in desegregation participation can improve outcomes for high-achieving minority students without harming other minority students. I conclude with some key questions that need further exploration. The arguments in this chapter suggest that despite the good intentions of policymakers, there are unintended consequences of the existing policies that have limited their effectiveness.

LITERATURE REVIEW

When analyzing how desegregation policies impact the group that those policies aim to assist, we must first consider the original intention. Often, a perceived policy failure is not an actual policy failure but an unintended consequence. When the landmark *Brown* case was taken up, the focus was on the concept of "separate but equal," with the primary argument being that there was no way to be equal as long as there was enforced separation. Since then, desegregation has reversed somewhat toward "desegregated and equal," but that may be too far in the other direction. Desegregation policy intends to improve the opportunities available and the educational outcomes in the Black communities, which it has done to some degree. Two concerns remain as an extension of the desegregation results that should be considered. The first is the original skepticism that was expressed by many Black communities in the 1960s, 1970s, and 1980s, which is the consequence of not investing in minority communities but instead just busing minorities into other communities to get their education. The second issue is whether a greater level of student potential can be achieved.

The general goals of desegregation policies are simply to create an environment of equally accessible quality education, improve the academic performance of low-income minorities, improve their post-secondary opportunities, and improve racial relations and diversity. Desegregation policies tend to target the demographic makeup of a school. Higher levels of racial, cultural, and socioeconomic diversity in schools often result in non-white students doing better in school while also increasing the likelihood that those students live and engage in a multicultural setting later in life (Joondeph 1998).

There is a lot of work looking into how desegregation has impacted the performance and outcomes of students (Cook 1984; Diette et al. 2021; Irvine and Irvine 1983; Wortman and Bryant 1985). This work starts in the late 1960s when researchers started looking at models of how different proportions and distributions of racial groups could account for segregated patterns

without explicit segregation policy and what it would take to get distributional convergence (Schelling 1969).

In general, the research agrees that there is a strong and positive effect on
the academic performance of Black students when there are strong desegregation initiatives in place (Guryan 2001). However much of this gain is due
to an increase in resources available and does not consider the counterfactual
of improving existing schools in predominantly Black communities. This
has been used by researchers to understand how previous segregation policies have had disproportionately, and likely exclusively by design, negative
intergenerational impacts on Black communities that were previously denied
access to equal resources contributing to human capital. The earliest report on
the unequal availability of educational resources was compiled in a 737-page
report to Congress by James Coleman (1966) to inform the *Civil Rights Act*.
This report found that in the segregated South, there were lower achievement
levels measured by standardized testing and academic attainment in low-
income minority areas. However, it was not due to funding differences, but
rather a difference in home life and family educational background. Coleman
concluded that students, particularly those from working-class families,
would benefit from more background diversity. The diversity he discussed
was not only affluence but also family education levels and emphasis. It is
important to note that one of the major downsides previously stated in the
Coleman Report was that desegregation would lead to "white flight" from
desegregated areas. However, later research has found that this phenomenon,
while it does occur, is not causally related to the desegregation of schools
(Pettigrew and Green 1976; Rossell 1975) and instead is caused by neighborhood ethnic composition, not the school district composition, which is often
a conglomeration of multiple neighborhoods and may have an irregular shape
(Van Hook and Snyder 2007; Wilson and Taub 2007). In more recent times,
there has been a greater aversion to foreign-born neighbors than domestic
minorities.

Some previous studies have expanded on the question of Black short-term
educational returns by looking at long-run improvements in adult socioeconomic indicators of "success" or welfare (Johnson 2015; Wells and Crain
1994). In particular, the study done by Wells and Crain looks at a selection of
twenty-one other studies that took place from the 1960s to the 1990s to better
understand how desegregation impacted the opportunities available to Black
students beyond the immediate impacts of educational achievement and
dropout rates decreasing (Guryan 2001). The underlying mechanism besides
disproportionate availability of resources that made graduates from predominately Black schools so much worse off in value is based on the National
Association for the Advancement of Colored People (NAACP)'s core argument from *Brown v. Board of Education*. This argument was centered around

the theory that degrees from prestigious universities would always hold more weight and act as a key to access higher-status employment opportunities, institutions, and the support of more powerful social networks. This means that any graduate, regardless of racial background or identity, would be better off by pursuing an academic pedigree from a more well-known predominately white institution since these were the academic institutions that provided such prestige and access. While this does not negatively impact the potential quality of the educational value, it limits the employment and postgraduate prospects. This leads to an inherent "separate and unequal" expected outcome for Black students resulting from being allowed into these institutions, regardless of ability or education level. Of course, this picture looks a little bit different at the primary and secondary levels of education, but it is still closely connected.

Some research has found a "frog-pond" effect, where a student from a high-ranking high school will have a harder time getting into an elite university due to being a small frog in a big pond (Espenshade, Hale, and Chung 2005). This result should not be taken as evidence that students at higher-ranked high schools have it harder because there is more to the story of any given college applicant. The idea breaks down to when you have two students with similar profiles, intelligence, and scholastic achievement, the student from the lower-performing school will be seen as relatively stronger due to how much better performing they are compared to the other students in their academic environment. In other words, they are a big frog in a small pond, whereas the student at the higher-performing school will be relatively more average since they are surrounded by more high performers in their respective academic environments. The naive conclusion would be that a student is better off targeting a lower-ranked high school so that they can have a better chance of admission into an elite college, but this would exclude the prospect that a student from an inferior academic environment would be less likely to have a similar or better profile than a student from a superior academic environment. The investment into human capital starts with the available resources for a student before the respective student has any optimizing decision to make concerning how they invest in their human capital. One of the major results that illustrates this is that a student passing an AP test increases their odds of being admitted into an elite school. Specifically, Espenshade, Hale, and Chung (2005) find this gain to be a 31 percent increase with just one successfully passed AP exam in a student's portfolio, with more AP exams being cumulative. The problem with this finding is that multiple studies have shown there is a limited number of AP courses available for students in low-income and urban minority schools in the United States (Horn and Kojaku 2001; Klopfenstein 2004; Zarate and Pachon 2006). The natural thought would be that an aggressive desegregation process would alleviate these concerns of access and prestige rankings but the education system is a three-sided problem, where all three sides interact and are a circular function of each other: (1) the students, (2) the teachers, and (3) the community.

In any given jurisdiction, teachers in the public schools are all paid according to a common base income. This does not typically change if you teach at a high-performing public high school or a low-performing public high school, even if they are just 1 mile down the street from each other. Given this, it is reasonable that teachers would target school districts for other utility-generating factors rather than income if they are geographically specific about what area they want to work in (Jackson 2009). Typically, teacher pay is based on horizontal salary rules that are based on tenure standards within a school district. This incentivizes teachers to take the job at the best performing school within each given school district to make their ratings higher, which are often based on student achievement on standardized testing. Thus, educational institutions directly impact the outcomes of public policies that work to improve community outcomes due to uniformity of pay within school districts, despite heterogeneity in the work environment and effort requirement for teachers. Jackson's (2009) work looks at the teacher side of the equation in the Charlotte-Mecklenberg School District in North Carolina when they stopped their busing model of desegregating that involved busing minority students to predominately white neighborhoods to increase school diversity. This natural experiment allowed the author to observe how the labor market reacted to a demographic change in student population when the area switched to a neighborhood school choice model that resulted in an outflow of Black students from suburban schools and inflow of those same students back to the schools closer to their neighborhoods, which were predominately Black. The results found that schools that experienced an overall increase in Black student enrollment ended up losing in their proportion of experienced teachers and teachers with higher scores on their licensure exams. This point is also in line with the institutional issue of teacher pay and the way the teachers are incentivized when it comes to choosing the schools at which they want to teach. The quality of both Black and white teachers decreases in schools that gain more Black students. There was also a decrease in measured teacher value-added in these schools.[2] Related to this, however, and like results found from desegregation literature on the student side, white teachers were found to be no more likely to leave schools that had an increase in Black students than to leave schools that did not. Jackson (2009) conversely finds that Black teachers tended to stay to receive Black students when there was an exogenous shock, meaning that they were more likely to stay in a location that experienced a net inflow of Black students. This is one of the first studies that takes an experimental approach to find suggestions of teacher quality and race to be more than a function of co-location but also a question of racial identity–impacted preferences. Jackson (2009) is explicit when pointing out that Black teachers are more likely to experience discrimination in schools with higher shares of white enrollment. However, the decrease in teacher quality in increasingly Black schools is robust to the race of the teachers leaving. This also speaks to the heterogeneous nature of teacher preferences after salary considerations when there is a reshuffling of students. When there is a change in the student composition, the social capital of the student body also changes, and there is a requirement for teachers to adjust to the changing cultural backgrounds and expectations of the student population. At the most surface level, we can observe that there are differences in preference weighting when it comes to school quality, location, and student characteristics.

Most of the constructive skepticism surrounding desegregation comes from the inner city and minority communities which, at least empirically, seem to have the most to gain. The downside viewed by some in minority neighborhoods is that these policies are more focused on making schools balanced on paper rather than investing in the minority neighborhoods. A strictly empirical view of the results would make a nuance like this seem unnecessary to distinguish when considering that the students are Pareto improved. However, when we consider the behavioral implication of institutional action and the secondary effects on others involved in that action (e.g., students, teachers, and the community), then it becomes important to consider our policy end goal regarding student performance and educational quality and whether that end goal is as encompassing as it should be.

Identity is a relatively new concept in economics and has only been seriously considered in behavioral models for the last twenty years, starting with Akerlof and Kranton's (2000) seminal work. They explained how a person's identity does not just guide their decision-making out of compulsion but can actually feed back into their utility function (Akerlof and Kranton 2000). Their later work directly applies this model to the economics of education to help explain why a student's time discounting of future outcomes make more rational sense, considering the social identities that exist within schools and just how salient a respective student's self-image is to their utility function (Akerlof and Kranton 2002). This work was taken into a more applied context by considering the differing interactions Black and Latino students face in the way they must signal group identity from their white counterparts, specifically when avoiding being ousted by their groups due to concerns of "acting white" (Austen-Smith and Fryer 2005), which manifests in linguistic behavior code-switching (Durkee and Williams 2015). The analysis of "acting white" takes into consideration that, because education had been a white exclusive activity for so long, to differentiate and try to maintain cultural identity over looked-down-upon acts of assimilation, Black and Latino students began associating most academically focused activities with being white. Simply put, the forced desegregation puts students in a situation where they are afraid of visibly "acting white" in a mixed-identity environment. Some students are more susceptible to this than others at the individual level and have some degree of capability in self-sorting. The fear of "acting white" for those more susceptible to identity pressure would be less salient in an environment where everyone is a member of the identity group. Some are higher performing in this environment, but there is no need to code-switch or engage in any other out-of-group behaviors to fit into higher-performing social circles.

Ideas of group signaling can be harmful when social and policy goals push for greater levels of academic achievement, but this is both an internal and external identity pressure. A nice example of this can be seen on the campuses of historically Black colleges and universities (HBCUs), such as Howard University in Washington, DC. Howard is one of the top-ranked minority-serving institutions in the United States and is home to many historic actors in the Black community as well as the birthplace of many highly desired Black social groups (Poyer 2008). Even though academic campuses highly prioritize academic success, Austen-Smith and Fryer (2005) have found that Black students are pressured away from high-achieving academic pursuits to send appropriate identity signals. There is an obvious explanatory factor in self-selection, where high-achieving or goal-oriented students will self-select into Howard. There is also the overriding identity that Howard brings that can offset the negative pressure from the baseline identity. A factor that has not been heavily considered is that in the absence of external pressure to conform, the within-group members can expand what their sense of group identity signaling is. HBCUs also provide greater gains in social mobility, despite not typically being highly ranked in college and university rankings (Hardy, Kagandra, and Arguete 2019).

As a more tangible example, Fryer and Torelli (2010) extend Austen-Smith and Fryer's earlier economic analysis and identify specific activities that were empirically viewed as white activities. This list included activities such as being good at math, increased effort in school, cheerleading, and having high grades in general. When matched with other people of their own identity, people are more likely to act selflessly and be less envious, which would impact the strength of a negative signal such as "acting white" (Chen and Li 2009). However, if the "acting white" concern existed absolutely, then we would expect a low rate of occurrence of strong academics in a place that is predominately Black or Hispanic. This goes back to the idea that there may be two sides to group identity pressure. Pressure by members of their present identity group has an impact on a given individual's decision-making just like pressure by members outside of the group. We know from the applied identity literature in economics that there are varying levels of salience for group identity. This is based on the identity, but it is also idiosyncratic to the weighting of the identity group in the individual's utility function. This leads to the major gap in the current literature to be considered. While, on average, desegregation policies have been Pareto efficient, they are not guaranteed to be the best possible implementation.

MODELING THE POLICY

To illustrate the potential missing productivity by making desegregation mandatory rather than allowing self-selection, I propose a simplified identity model, similar to what has been used by Akerlof and Kranton (2000) in their seminal identity paper and their education and identity work (Akerlof and Kranton 2002) and utilized and adapted by Austen-Smith and Fryer (2005). This simplified model looks at an individual's success as a function of not only their innate ability but also their group identity, adjusted by the presence of external and internal pressure. It also includes the personal cost of busing, which is often not discussed in the literature but seen in examples such as Little Rock, AR, and St. Louis, MO, where students must be bussed from their home neighborhoods to whichever school they are assigned. This is a tax-funded service, so the individual family does not have to directly pay for the service, but the student can incur a high utility cost of time since some of these bus rides can be up to an hour long in each direction and can prove to be a limiting factor when the student tries to engage in activities that are positively associated with achievement, labor market outcomes, and higher education outcomes. Consider that a community's utility from an education policy is roughly the student's gains from education additive with the returns to the community such that

$$U_j\left(\theta\right)=\sum_{i=1}^{n}u_{ij}\left(\theta\right)+V_j\left(\theta\right) \tag{1}$$

where θ is the policy, $U_j(\theta)$ is the total utility experienced by community j as a function of that policy, $u_{ij}(\theta)$ is the individual utility experienced from that policy by the students within the community, and $V_j(\theta)$ represents the returns to the community from students who are part of the educational policy. $V_j(\theta)$ could be expressed as $V_j(\theta) = V_j(u_{ij}(\theta))$. Simply put, the benefits to a community from any given policy are going to be the sum of how much the students directly benefit and how much the community gets back from the students who benefited. There can be a range of impacts, such as more productive human capital living in the community, increased investment, or decreased crime rates.

The identity aspect of how policy interacts with the community can be found in both parts of the simplified model: student and community returns. The student side is drawn directly from the literature on identity and education. This model follows a canonical Spence signaling model with a key social component variation that would be influenced by the education policy:

$$u_j\left(\theta,\ w,\ \alpha,\ s,\ \tau\right) = \left(1 + \alpha\,\gamma_{i,j}\right)\left(1 - s\right) + w(s) - c\left(s,\ \varphi_j\right) \qquad (2)$$

where α is a dummy variable representing whether a student is accepted into their group or not,

$(1+\gamma)(1-s)$ is the amount of leisure for an individual with education s that is accepted by their group versus $(1-s)$ for an individual not accepted. w is the payoff of choosing education s in future wages with a cost of $c(s, \varphi_j)$, based on the socioeconomic background of community j and also the distance that students have to be bussed from their home community to their school each day to account for the opportunity cost of time. An individual student gains some direct utility from leisure and some future payoff from education in terms of wages. The leisure component of an individual's utility is magnified by whether they are accepted as part of the in-group. The specific part of this that has not been fully questioned is the behavior of γ, which is the effect from the group and how it is weighted. Consider that $\gamma = \gamma_i\,(p)$, where p is the proportion of students that are of the same-group identity within an academic environment. This would mean that the impact of the group on the student's signaling behavior is going to change based on this proportion. Considering the HBCU example, at some point when the proportion is very large, students would be expected to place less emphasis on the group identity signaling due to a decreased potency of the identity as it becomes more of the normal. Also consider the other extreme where there are only a few students of a particular identity, such as only having two or three Black students in a class with twenty or more white students. The Black students would not face criticism while actively participating in the class because the rest of the class would expect participation to be the norm (Fryer and Torelli 2010). The issue is that in many desegregation policies, there is a very specific balance that is trying to be achieved regardless of how the individual student weights the importance of that diversity balance. In younger years, the group identity phenomenon is not as strong, but by the time a student reaches tenth grade, it seems to be at its peak. When students can self-select into programs, such as in St. Louis's desegregation program that ended a few years ago, we see a much stronger relative impact. This means that students and their parents are likely more sophisticated than the school district in determining how they would fare in a "desegregated school" as opposed to staying in their neighborhood where there may be more racial homogeneity. This suggests that the ideal *p* is going to be best determined by the student and community weighting of the identity. Some will naturally want more diversity, some less, which should be considered by policymakers.

The other side of the impact to consider is the community returns from the policy, which was presented as $V_j(\theta)$. On the one hand, higher-achieving students traveling to a desegregated school in another community will bring back higher returns to their community in terms of human capital. The counterfactual concerns Blacks' hesitancy about having to send their students away to be educated outside of their communities as opposed to investing in their local schools. Students who attend more diverse schools outside of their neighborhoods are more likely to be comfortable leaving their neighborhoods, which improves the student's long-run opportunities but detracts from the suggested long-term benefit to the community (Jackson 2009). There would be a higher rate of return for the community when there is an investment, or at least the option of investment, into the local community's ability to provide an education. This raises the question of whether the busing programs that are implemented are reinforcing the current socioeconomic status of these lower-income communities. This relates to the teacher's labor decisions as well, since the more experienced and higher-skilled teachers are more likely to work at and move to communities with higher-performing schools. This is an area where educational institutions at the school district and state level have a direct effect on public policy's effort to improve the outcomes for community development. When students have the opportunity to maximize their utility as a function of their identity while still achieving academically, then policy efforts do not need to contradict institutional actions in the education sector. As it stands, there is a loss of utility that is modeled that policy is continuously trying to make up for in terms of reinvestment into communities. When students are allowed to decide for themselves, they will naturally improve the return to the community at a higher rate after they graduate if they self-select appropriately to maximize utility from identity and educational achievement according to their utility functions and district standards.

LITTLE ROCK CENTRAL HIGH SCHOOL

Little Rock Central High School, or "Central" as it is known in Arkansas, is famously known for being the site of forced desegregation in 1957 after the U.S. Supreme Court ruled segregated schools to be unconstitutional. In the present day, Central is a national historic landmark, and its relevant school district is under state control. While Central is technically desegregated in the sense that students are no longer prohibited from attending based on race, they have a different problem. Within Central, there are two different sides of the school. One side is the general population and the other is referred to as the "AP Wing." The AP Wing is so named due to the majority of AP classes being concentrated in this one wing of the building, thus AP track students primarily have their classes in this wing. This academic segregation may seem to make sense on the surface, but it has deeper implications.

Central High School is considered one of the better schools in the Little Rock area based on AP enrollment, with a participation rate of 54 percent taking at least one AP test (*U.S. News & World Report* 2020). The issue with this ranking is that it only looks at the AP test-taking rate, not persistent AP enrollment. It also fails to consider the general academic performance of the student body. This is where we must consider some of the underlying mechanisms that could lead an individual student at Central toward or away from the AP track. Currently, the overwhelming majority of AP students at Central are white. Even though the school is majority Black—55 percent Black, 31 percent white, 7 percent Asian, 5 percent Hispanic—the AP enrollment weighs heavily toward the white students (Dunn 2011; US News & World Report 2020). AP enrollment in the Little Rock School District is also heavily biased toward white students. The heavy skew toward white students dominating AP classes would normally go relatively unnoticed in the day-to-day functioning of the school unless someone specifically surveyed AP courses or was sitting in on a class. But the setup at Central means that the AP Wing itself becomes very homogenous. If we consider that one of the primary goals of desegregation was to help encourage the interaction of minority students with other students to form different academic and cultural backgrounds, having an AP wing is directly counter to this goal. Central has two worlds that exist within it: the mostly white, upper-middle-class "AP world" and the Central that everyone else attends. If students attend Central as members of the AP world, then they may not even notice that anything is wrong with the school; they attend the high-ranked public high school that has plenty of opportunities, resources, and academic encouragement (Dunn 2011; Renaud and Renaud 2007).

Considering the physical separation that this system has created, there are bound to be strong impacts on the group identity interaction with enrollment and AP track courses. Typically, we would think the decision to take an AP course is primarily based on the student's performance in the course before it, which is true for the initial entry into the AP track (CollegeBoard 2020). However, when students enroll in an AP course at Central, they are not only enrolling in the class but are also committing themselves to be in a class that is on the "white" side of the building, and the decision is readily observable. Due to the internal segregation of the school that flows from the status and location of their classes, that class decision becomes part of the identity signaling in a public way. The student's decision is more heavily influenced if they value their identity group. In the context of the proposed model, γ_i would represent the proportion of Black students and it would be at a more extreme value, not only because of the skew in the proportion of same-group students in the school but also because of the high visibility of this decision as a very "white" activity (Akerlof and Kranton 2002; Fryer and Torelli 2010). Black students at Central often have to deal with being rejected by members of their identity group, as well as out-group members, when they do decide to follow the AP track, enduring taunts like "Oreo" that directly attack their sense of identity (Dunn 2011; Renaud and Renaud 2007). The resulting atmosphere encourages Black students to stay in the general wing to avoid strong identity repercussions. The way the AP track is set up, avoiding AP classes early on makes it harder to take them later.

Segregation does not mean opportunities inherently disappear. While the AP enrollment at Central is primarily from white students, there are still Black students who are in the AP Wing who are involved in student leadership and who excel despite the environment in which they have to make their decisions. Therefore, the impact from identity, as a function of racial proportions, γ_i, has been modeled as an individual-level factor. While all members of any group experience some level of group weight on their decision-making, some members of a group are less likely to be hindered by negative group pressure than others. The ideal proportion of students, p, to optimize the decision-making environment is potentially quadratic since it seems that students in very low-density and very high-density environments excel—comparing the two or three Black students per AP class to the students at Howard University, for example. Letting students and their families decide for themselves which environment they want to be educated in spreads the burden of balancing optimal school composition between policymakers and families. The points where this function rises or falls would be based on how well the individual student can adjust to the identity proportions and excel despite not having the support of their in-group, such as high-achieving Black students at Central. It would then follow, as a policy consideration, that students should have the option to opt in or opt out of a proposed busing program that aims to spread out the number of minorities. The current policy that is in place in the Little Rock School District results in the closure of more minority-neighborhood high schools and the busing of those students to Central and a few other primary and secondary schools in more suburban, whiter neighborhoods (Dunn 2011; Sealy 2016).

CONCLUSION

Desegregation has been seen and empirically shown to be a net positive policy result. There are different ways of implementing it, ranging from relaxed to explicit busing protocols to ensure demographic balances across schools in different communities. This chapter is not in contention with any of the previous literature's findings that Blacks end up better off under these controlled desegregation policies. Rather, the analysis of the policy here establishes that there may be an overlooked consequence that could be improved upon by rethinking the way policy for desegregation is implemented. Black students, on average, find gains in educational outcomes in the short run, lower dropout rates in the short run, higher college admission rates, and long-run gains in socioeconomic indicators as adults.

One of the bigger areas that leaves room for improvement is in the analysis of what is left on the table for students in potential gains to education and utility from that education. When individual students are forced into a busing program, they do not get to provide input on their preferences concerning education value versus social/cultural value or whether they are highly susceptible to group peer pressure. Students with higher weighting on their payouts from education and lower weighting on their group identity multiplier for leisure would rationally choose to be in a desegregation busing program such as the previous program in St. Louis, given that the opportunity cost of this was not too high in terms of time, specifically. This means that the students leaving their community to go to school, on average, have a lower susceptibility to negative identity peer pressure and are less likely to detract from other students of the same identity background at the school they attend. This increases the potential educational returns within the individual's utility function at the new school because they lower their risk of being rejected by their identity group if they engage in actions that are "acting white." This self-selection through school choice concept may be the key to understanding why places with high proportions of self-selected Black students, like Howard University, are still both identity cultural centers and strong educational communities. This means that those with a preference to stay within the community can stay, and with the appropriate investment into local schooling options, you would still see an increase in community human capital.

A policy consideration here is that community investment could focus on structuring teacher salaries so that there is a greater benefit for talented teachers who accept positions at underperforming schools where the marginal impact of their teaching efforts would arguably have a higher return. This would mean giving teachers an incentive to be at the schools where they are most needed, rather than seeking out schools with the easiest workload for the same rate. We saw with the Charlotte-Mecklenburg school district that teachers are making their decisions based on student characteristics. We know that white students do not gain much when these higher-experienced teachers move around. This has been suggested to be due to the academic environment that already exists where most of the white students live and go to school. However, there is a significant change for Black students living in lower-income communities, likely again due to the academic environment from which they are primarily coming. This means that, without being detrimental to student learning, teachers can be incentivized through a more market-based structure to work in areas that are not typically desired but have high needs.

Future work is still needed to fully understand the potential impacts of lower-level policies. Specifically, work needs to be done to experiment with group identity signaling thresholds. This will be especially important to suggest the point at which group identity becomes a factor within a respective environment. Another area that should be explored is the returns to communities in the short–medium run based on different types of desegregation policies—specifically, how neighborhoods are impacted when students are bussed away for school, whether those neighborhoods lose human capital in the long run, and case studies to help identify a policy where investments are instead made to improve the community's educational environment.

NOTES

1. The achievement gap is empirically observable using standardized testing during multiple preset points, particularly in fourth, eighth, and twelfth grades. These tests evaluate reading, science, math, history, and writing with special emphasis usually placed on reading, writing, and math evaluations. There is a consistent achievement gap found between Black and white students where Black students underperform in all categories, getting worse as the students age, particularly for boys (Hanushek and Rivkin 2006).

2. Value Added Models (VAM) attempt to measure how much value a teacher adds to a school through student performance outcomes measured in longitudinal student data linked to the respective teachers (McCaffery et al. 2004).

REFERENCES

Akerlof, George A. and Rachel E. Kranton. 2000. "Economics and Identity." *The Quarterly Journal of Economics* 115 (3): 715–53.
———. 2002. "Identity and Schooling: Some Lessons for the Economics of Education." *Journal of Economic Literature* 40 (4): 1167–201.
Austen-Smith, David and Roland G. Fryer, Jr. 2005. "An Economic Analysis of 'Acting White'." *The Quarterly Journal of Economics* 120 (2): 551–83.
Chen, Yan and Sherry Xin Li. 2009. "Group Identity and Social Preferences." *The American Economic Review* 99 (1): 431–57.
Clotfelter, Charles T., Helen F. Ladd, and Jacob L. Vigdor. 2009. "The Academic Achievement Gap in Grades 3 to 8." *The Review of Economics and Statistics* 91 (2): 398–419.

Coleman, James S. 1966. *Equality of Educational Opportunity, Summary Report* (Vol. 1). US Department of Health, Education, and Welfare, Office of Education.

CollegeBoard. 2020. *AP Program Particpation and Performance Data 2020.* https://research.collegeboard.org/programs/ap/data/participation/ap-2020.

Cook, Thomas. 1985. *School Desegregation and Black Achievement.* Washington, DC: The National Institute of Education.

Diette, Timothy M., Darrick Hamilton, Arthur H. Goldsmith, and William A. Darity. 2021. "Does the Negro Need Separate Schools? A Retrospective Analysis of the Racial Composition of Schools and Black Adult Academic and Economic Success." *RSF: The Russell Sage Foundation Journal of the Social Sciences* 7 (1): 166–86.

Dunn, Mimi M. 2011. "Segregation by Any Other Name: Central High School and Integration in American Memory." *Rhodes Institute for Regional Studies.*

Durkee, Myles I. and Joanna L. Williams. 2015. "Accusations of Acting White: Links to Black Students' Racial Identity and Mental Health." *Journal of Black Psychology* 41 (1): 26–48.

Espenshade, Thomas J., Lauren E. Hale, and Chang Y. Chung. 2005. "The Frog Pond Revisited: High School Academic Context, Class Rank, and Elite College Admission." *Sociology of Education* 78: 269–93.

Fryer, Roland G., Jr. and Steven D. Levitt. 2004. "Understanding the Black-White Test Score Gap in the First Two Years of School." *Review of Economics and Statistics* 86 (2): 447–64.

Fryer, Roland G., Jr. and Paul Torelli. 2010. "An Empirical Analysis of 'Acting White'." *Journal of Public Economics* 94 (5–6): 380–96.

Guryan, J. 2001. "Desegregation and Black Dropout Rates." Working Paper, National Bureau of Economic Research.

Hanushek, Eric A. and Steven G. Rivkin. 2006. "School Quality and the Black-White Achievement Gap." Working Paper, National Bureau of Economic Research.

Hardy, Precious M., Elizabeth J. Kaganda, and Mara S. Aruguete. 2019. "Below the Surface: HBCU Performance, Social Mobility, and College Ranking." *Journal of Black Studies* 50 (5): 468–83.

Horn, Laura J. and Lawrence K. Kojaku. 2001. "High School Academic Curriculum and the Persistence Path through College Persistence and Transfer Behavior of Undergraduates 3 Years after Entering 4-Year Institutions." *National Center of Education Statistics.* https://nces.ed.gov/das/epubs/pdf/2001163_es.pdf.

Irvine, Russell W. and Jacqueline Jordan Irvine. 1983. "The Impact of the Desegregation Process on the Education of Black Students: Key Variables." *The Journal of Negro Education* 52 (4): 410–22.

Jackson, C. Kirabo 2009. "Student Demographics, Teacher Sorting, and Teacher Quality: Evidence from the End of School Desegregation." *Journal of Labor Economics* 27 (2): 213–56.

Johnson, Rucker C. 2015. "Long-Run Impacts of School Desegregation & School Quality on Adult Attainments." Working Paper, National Bureau of Economic Research.

Joondeph, Bradley W. 1998. "Skepticism and School Desegregation." *Washington University Law Quarterly* 76 (1): 161–70.

Klopfenstein, Kristen. 2004. "Advanced Placement: Do Minorities Have Equal Opportunity?" *Economics of Education Review* 23: 115–31.

McCaffrey, Daniel F., J. R. Lockwood, Daniel Koretz, Thomas A. Louis, and Laura Hamilton. 2004. "Models for Value-Added Modeling of Teacher Effects." *Journal of Educational and Behavioral Statistics* 29 (1): 67–101.

Pettigrew, Thomas F. and Robert L. Green. 1976. "School Desegregation in Large Cities: A Critique of Coleman 'White Flight' Thesis." *Harvard Educational Review* 46 (1): 1–53.

Poyer, David A. 2008. "The Black Enterprise Magazine Ranking of Colleges for African Americans: A Structural Analysis." *The Review of Black Political Economy* 35 (1): 19–29.

Renaud, Brent and Craig Renaud, directors. 2007. *Little Rock Central: 50 Years Later*. HBO, 1 hr., 10 min.

Rossell, Christine H. 1975. "School Desegregation and White Flight." *Political Science Quarterly* 90 (4): 675–95.

Schelling, Thomas. 1969. "Models of Segregation." *The American Economic Review* 59 (2): 488–93.

Sealy, Neil. 2016. "School Closings in Little Rock: Whose Schools? Whose Neighborhoods?: Residents Speak about the Potential Impact of Closings in Neighborhoods South of I-630." *Arkansas Community Institute.* http://arkansas-comm.org/wp-content/uploads/2018/08/LRSD-Closures-6.22.16.pdf.

Smith, Justin D. 2009. "Hostile Takeover: The State of Missouri, the St. Louis School District, and the Struggle for Quality Education in the Inner-City." *Missouri Law Review* 74 (4): 1143–69.

US News & World Report. 2020. "Central High School in Little Rock, AR." *US News Best High Schools.* Accessed September 30, 2020. https://www.usnews.com/education/best-high-schools/arkansas/districts/little-rock-school-district/central-high-school-1373#students_teachers_section.

Van Hook, Jennifer and Jason Snyder. 2007. "Immigration, Ethnicity, and the Loss of White Students from California Public Schools, 1990–2000." *Population Research and Policy Review* 26 (3): 259–77.

Wells, Amy Stuart and Robert L. Crain. 1994. "Perpetuation Theory and the Long-Term Effects of School Desegregation." *Review of Educational Research* 64 (4): 531–55.

Wilson, William Julius and Richard P. Taub. 2007. *There Goes the Neighborhood: Racial, Ethnic, and Class Tensions in Four Chicago Neighborhoods and Their Meaning for America*. New York: Vintage Books.

Wortman, Paul M. and Fred B. Bryant. 1985. "School Desegregation and Black Achievement: An Integrative Review." *Sociological Methods & Research* 13 (3): 289–324.

Zarate, Maria Estela and Harry P. Pachon. 2006. *Equity in Offering Advanced Placement Courses in California High Schools*. Los Angeles, CA: The Thomas Rivera Policy Institute.

Part II

FEDERAL POLICY

Chapter 3

Compensating the Innocent

Hayekian Considerations for Wrongful Conviction Compensation Statutes

Dora Duru

WRONGFUL CONVICTIONS AND HAYEK

Much has been written on the topic of compensation laws for wrongful convictions in the United States. Much of the literature on wrongful convictions focuses on what should or ought to be done (i.e., how much should be given) to undo the injustice done to the wrongfully convicted[1] (Mostaghel 2011, 524). However, beyond addressing injustice through compensating the wrongfully convicted, there are broader goals that compensation statutes can seek to accomplish—ways to pair short-term relief with long-term criminal justice reform.

This chapter's analysis is based on the Austrian school of economics, specifically the work of F. A. Hayek. Hayek argued that some forms of government intervention are consistent with a free market and that government actions that assist the spontaneous forces of the free market are acceptable (Hayek 1960, 331). Hayek argued that individual responsibility is an important component of liberty and that individuals should be held accountable even for negligent actions that cause harm to others because it will cause people to bear the consequences of their actions in mind and influence them to act in ways that are more desirable for society (ibid., 133, 138). He wrote, "Liberty not only means that the individual has both the opportunity and the burden of choice; it also means that he must bear the consequences of his actions and will receive praise or blame for them" (ibid., 133). The premise of this chapter is that compensation laws can be constructed to promote the Hayekian conception of liberty in a free market by holding individual actors, such as prosecutors, individually responsible for any role they play in wrongful convictions.[2] This connection between compensation laws for the wrongfully convicted and the Hayekian conception of liberty is an idea currently unexplored in the existing literature.

The remainder of this chapter is organized as follows: Section II will provide a review of the literature describing reasons for and against compensation statutes for the wrongfully convicted. Section III will discuss some current mechanisms for compensation. Section IV will discuss Hayek's idea on how individual responsibility is connected with liberty, the Hayekian knowledge problem, and the collective versus general interest problem. Finally, Section V will provide some public choice and Austrian insights into the interplay between knowledge, incentives, and outcomes, and Section VI will conclude.

ARGUMENTS FOR AND AGAINST WRONGFUL CONVICTION COMPENSATION STATUTES

Compensation statutes for the wrongfully convicted come in many shapes. For example, Texas has the *Tim Cole Act*. Under this act, an individual can receive compensation if he served at least part of a prison sentence and received a full pardon for innocence or received relief based on actual innocence (Shaw 2011, 610). There is also a provision for families of a deceased innocent person to receive compensation (ibid., 611).

There are a number of policy goals that legislators may seek to accomplish through compensation statutes for the wrongfully convicted, but these purposes are not necessarily stated in the statute itself. For example, a South Carolina bill states, "The purpose of this act is to ensure that those persons who were wrongfully convicted and imprisoned by the State receive, under appropriate circumstances, compensation" (South Carolina General Assembly 2019, sec. 1). On the face of the law, nothing is stated about reducing prosecutorial misconduct or preventing potential crimes of persons released from prison (ibid., secs. 1–3).

There are arguments for and against states adopting compensation statutes for wrongfully convicted persons. Professor Mostaghel of Golden Gate University of Law discusses that state compensation statutes for the wrongfully convicted are economically feasible (Mostaghel 2011, 529). Through an analysis where each state averaged only two to three exonerees per year from 1989 to 2003, Mostaghel argues that compensation statutes will not destroy state budgets. Mostaghel's argument that state budgets can afford compensation for wrongful convictions may rest on the assumption that the number of exonerations where compensation is provided by the state will not increase significantly (ibid., 529). Drawing from the work of Adele Bernhard, Mostaghel argues that it is becoming less common for wrongfully convicted persons to rely on DNA evidence to free them because it is more common to do DNA testing at the investigatory stage. Many cases that once lacked DNA evidence now have it, and many of the prisoners whose cases lacked DNA evidence are dying (ibid., 529–530).

Some states fear not only the cost of administering state compensation regimes, but that a regime may compensate those who do not merit compensation; Mostaghel argues that this fear is unfounded because state statutes place strict standards on persons claiming wrongful conviction, requiring them to prove actual innocence and not merely restate trial evidence (ibid., 530). Also, with the introduction of DNA evidence, it is easier to prove actual innocence in cases involving DNA (Smith 2007, 7).

Mostaghel argues that state compensation statutes for the wrongfully convicted should be drawn from prosecutor and police budgets. Because prosecutors and police have access to information that others do not have access to and "their actions directly create or prevent" wrongful convictions, they are uniquely positioned to avoid wrongful convictions (Mostaghel 2011, 534).

Mostaghel's view that prosecutor and police officers should be held accountable for wrongful convictions seems consistent with Hayek's view that individuals should be held accountable for their actions (Hayek 1960, 139). Hayek wrote that general and equal laws offer "the most effective protection against infringement of individual liberty," which is "due mainly to the habit of tacitly exempting the state and its agents from them and of assuming that the government has the power to grant exemptions to individuals" (ibid., 318). If prosecutors' and police officers' contributions to wrongful convictions are not excusable under the law, this can serve as a type of shield to protect individuals from wrongful convictions (Mostaghel 2011, 534).

Mostaghel discusses that it is important to focus on the prosecutor office as a whole rather than individual prosecutors because "taking some portion of the compensation money from the budget of prosecutors would exact 'a sufficient political price' because any prosecutor could expect to lose funding whenever damages are awarded" (ibid., 535).

According to public choice theory, people in public office (such as prosecutors) act primarily in their own self-interest just as other individuals outside of the political sphere (Shugart n.d., para. 3). "Electing better people will not, by itself, lead to much better government" (ibid., para. 16). With that said, shaping public policy is not about finding better people, but rather it is about changing the incentives that individuals can respond to, which can lead to more socially desirable outcomes, such as fewer wrongful convictions. Holding prosecutor offices financially responsible (at least to some degree) when there are wrongful convictions can help to shift power dynamics and cause prosecutors to change their behavior.

Public choice economics often infers intentions from outcomes (Ikeda 2003, 67). This line of reasoning implies that when prosecutors obtain wrongful convictions, they intended to obtain them. More realistically, though, the public choice implications for a prosecutor who obtains a wrongful conviction may be that the prosecutor intended to take actions that were more focused on securing a conviction rather than proving the actual guilt of an individual.

"Public Choice treats deception, the divergence between announced and intended intentions, as an instrument that promotes narrow private interests over broader public ones" (ibid., 66). Relating this idea to prosecutorial misconduct in wrongful convictions, prosecutors may announce intentions that are different from their intentions. For example, prosecutors may work hard to increase the number of convictions they gain in a given year (even if this means doing sloppy work) and claim it is to make their city safer, when truly the greater incentive is to advance their careers. This is not to say that prosecutors cannot have mixed motives, but this use of the tool of deception can help them to achieve their private interests at the expense of the broader public goal of a fair criminal justice system (ibid., 66).

Under Austrian economic theory, "man engages in purposeful action, and his purpose, his ends, are what drive him" (Leeson and Boettke 2003, 2). Austrian economic theory suggests that prosecutors are motivated by incentives, particularly the end results of their actions. The threat of civil liability and the fear of that "end" may thus motivate prosecutors to change their behavior and make more careful and prudent choices about what cases to pursue. Prosecutors may value freedom from liability over the benefits to their career of securing convictions.

One of the purposes of compensating people is the fact that "remedies represent a vehicle for achieving corrective justice" (Encarnacion 2017, 251). One goal of providing damages is the attempt to make victims whole (ibid., 251). However, an alternate way of justifying compensation for the wrongfully convicted is through the principle of "restitutionary justice, which forces parties to relinquish unjust gains"—this concept can help justify the existence of compensation statutes (Encarnacion 2016, 141). Encarnacion further explains:

> The unjust gains at issue are fair wages withheld from those performing crime-deterrence services. That is, this paper claims that prisoners, like law enforcement officials, perform crime-deterrence services simply by virtue of their incarceration. The state might fairly withhold compensation from the guilty for their crime-deterrence role, on the grounds that we should avoid rewarding individuals for their wrongdoings. But this rationale for withholding payment does not apply to innocent prisoners; innocent prisoners are in effect pressed into service as instruments of criminal deterrence without being compensated

for this task. Fair compensation cannot be justly withheld from the innocent, any more than the state may justly withhold compensation from conscripts unwillingly pressed into military service. (ibid., 141)

Even if wrongfully convicted persons do not actually help deter crime, Encarnacion argues that there is still justification for compensating them for that purpose because, for example, even when police officers do not actually deter crime, they are still paid (Encarnacion 2016, 151–52). While Encarnacion argues that the restitutionary justice approach offers a better justification for state compensation statutes for the wrongfully convicted than the corrective justice approach, he also acknowledges that there is benefit in reparative relief, and he agrees with states providing for medical and educational expenses (ibid., 146).

Encarnacion's rationale that compensation statutes can be justified by granting just wages to individuals who may potentially deter crime indirectly through their wrongful imprisonment is consistent with Hayek's view that true freedom cannot exist when there is coercion (Encarnacion 2016, 141; Hayek 1960, 58). According to Hayek, coercion is "such control of the environment or circumstances of a person by another that, in order to avoid greater evil, he is forced to act not according to a coherent plan of his own but to serve the ends of another" (Hayek 1960, 71). When persons are wrongfully convicted, they are subject to the coercion of the state agents who imprison them, but true freedom exists where an individual "is not subject to coercion by the arbitrary will of another or others" (ibid., 58). In a society with wrongful convictions, individuals have often been subject to the arbitrary will of prosecutors or police officers and their livelihoods largely depend on how competent these officials are at doing their job. A person could become wrongfully convicted merely because a prosecutor decided to bring a case due to public outcry and pressure to convict someone, despite the existence of insufficient evidence. Hayek writes that the "task of a policy of freedom must therefore be to minimize coercion or its harmful effects, even if it cannot eliminate it completely" (ibid., 59). Criminal justice reforms that aim to reduce wrongful convictions and promote this Hayekian view of freedom will likely focus on trying to reduce the coercive power of officials, such as prosecutors, who can play crucial roles in the outcomes of cases (ibid., 59).

Fon and Schäfer (2007) discuss how holding states[3] liable for wrongful convictions can deter crime, thus lowering the crime rate (270). They also discuss how compensating persons who have been wrongfully convicted may negatively affect a judge's utility, depending on which state agency is responsible for the compensation and the judge whose wrongful conviction judgment has led to the compensation. If the compensation comes out of the court's budget, then the judge may suffer adverse career prospects;

the judge may be affected less if the compensation comes from the budget of the municipality. Additionally, if compensation comes out of the court's budget or is otherwise too closely connected to the judge, judges might strive to avoid this by making it even harder to prove guilt, thus increasing the number of guilty who are acquitted (ibid., 281). Fon and Schäfer discuss that this pitfall can be avoided by ensuring compensation comes from a branch of government that is more removed from judges and the courts so as not to influence court behavior (ibid., 283). Influencing court behavior may help achieve certain policy goals. However, there may exist a balance that policymakers strive to strike between not increasing the number of acquittals for guilty persons while increasing the number of acquittals for innocent persons. It is not always clear if motivating judges through incentives, such as a threat to reduce their budgets if there are wrongful convictions, will simultaneously achieve both of these goals.[4]

According to public choice theory, judges, just like other individuals, are motivated to fulfill their narrow personal interests. The Chicago public choice theorists believe that judges act with perfect information, whereas the Virginia public choice theorists believe that judges act with partial ignorance. But both schools agree that judges are acting to serve their own interests. While this self-seeking behavior is not unique to judges, it can help to explain why certain judges might be resistant to the idea of wrongful conviction compensation funds if the money will be taken out of their court budgets (Ikeda 2003, 68). For example, if a judge's salary were to depend on the court budget, then a wrongful conviction fund that took from the court's budget could directly impact the financial interests of a judge, thus providing that judge with a perverse incentive to resist wrongful conviction funds. Furthermore, the embarrassment of having a budget reduced due to wrongful convictions could also jeopardize a judge's reputation and career prospects, providing judges with another reason to not support wrongful conviction funds.

Lawrence Rosenthal (2009) describes the work of Daryl Levinson, who takes issue with the idea of a governmental liability regime. Since government's main goal is not maximizing profits, but rather reacting to political costs and benefits, government cannot be trusted to achieve an efficient outcome. Rosenthal seems to agree with Levinson that government actors do not have the incentive to keep costs at their lowest and maximize profits, like the private sector does (Rosenthal 2009, 129). Reflecting on the work of Gordon Tullock, Stefanie Haeffele and Anne Hobson write:

> While private and government bureaucracies may have similar hierarchical structures and incentivize similar behavior, there is a key difference—private products and services, whether produced in a small or large business, have to pass the market test. The external market pressure of the profit and loss

mechanism allows private organizations to tend toward efficiency, by signaling what products and services consumers desire and which processes are most effective. (Haeffele and Hobson 2019, para. 8)

They further discuss: "Without prices, profit, and loss, nonprofits and governmental organizations operate in a more amorphous atmosphere, where signals cannot clarify what processes, products, and services are of value to the public and are the most effective means for achieving their goals" (ibid., para. 9). This analysis from Haeffele and Hobson underscores Rosenthal's idea that government cannot be trusted to bring about efficient outcomes (Rosenthal 2009, 129).

Rosenthal discusses Levinson's idea that imposing strict liability on public officials for wrongful convictions could create the problem of overdeterrence, such that public officials internalize the costs but not the rewards of their work to bring offenders to justice (ibid., 129). Rosenthal also discusses Levinson's idea about the likelihood that public officials would rely on indemnification from public entities, such as state or local governments, so they do not have to take responsibility for their actions. If indemnification is *not* present, wrongfully accused persons may be less likely to sue, as a public official would not likely have enough assets to compensate them with a substantial amount for damages (ibid., 130). For example, in *Wright v. State*, the New Jersey Supreme Court considered whether the actions of county prosecutors and their subordinates fell under the umbrella of state functions in deciding that the state could be required to indemnify them: "We hold that the State of New Jersey may be required to indemnify and defend SCPO's [Somerset County Prosecutor's Office] prosecutors and their subordinates for tortious conduct committed during the investigation, arrest, and prosecution of Isaac Wright, under the relevant provisions of the TCA [New Jersey Tort Claims Act]" (*Wright v. State* 2001, 454, 456). Furthermore, according to Connecticut law Section 7-465, cities, towns, and boroughs assume legal liability for their employees acting within the scope of their employment (State of Connecticut n.d., sec. 7-465). These entities are responsible for

damages awarded for infringement of any person's civil rights or for physical damages to person or property, except as set forth in this section, if the employee, at the time of the occurrence, accident, physical injury or damages complained of, was acting in the performance of his duties and within the scope of his employment, and if such occurrence, accident, physical injury or damage was not the result of any wilful or wanton act of such employee in the discharge of such duty. (ibid., sec. 7-465)[5]

Rosenthal is skeptical of some of Levinson's views and appears to be more convinced than Levinson that creating a liability regime will affect the

behavior of government actors. According to Rosenthal, a regime of governmental liability will create incentives for the government to avoid liability;
however, there are limits. If spending resources in reducing wrongful convictions also makes it more difficult to convict the truly guilty, then the benefits
of reducing wrongful convictions may not outweigh the costs, particularly for
government actors such as prosecutors whom voters elect. Therefore, government officials who are politically accountable may feel more constrained
in their efforts to combat wrongful convictions[6] (Rosenthal 2009, 131).
However, regardless of how constrained these government officials may feel,
under Hayek's conception of liberty, individuals will nonetheless receive
praise or blame for their actions—prosecutors will receive praise for convicting actual perpetrators of crimes and blame for convicting innocent persons.
Hayek believed that when individuals possess the knowledge that they will
be held responsible for their actions, their conduct will be more likely to take
a desirable direction (Hayek 1960, 133). Therefore, to reduce wrongful convictions, impressing the consequences of negligent or intentionally wrongful
conduct upon key state actors is paramount.

Rosenthal draws a distinction between a compensation regime based on
strict liability versus fault liability (Rosenthal 2009, 132). Basically, a fault
liability regime requires a person contesting their conviction to prove fault,
whereas in a strict liability regime, the person does not have to prove fault
(Encarnacion 2016, 153). No-fault statutes or strict liability statutes "do not
require the plaintiff or claimant to demonstrate their wrongful conviction
was the result of government misconduct" (Gutman and Sun 2019, 707).
Rosenthal (2009) describes strict liability as a system that puts the burden
of internalizing the costs of wrongful convictions on the government (128).
Encarnacion (2016, 153) discusses that exonerees do not need to prove that
official misconduct led to their wrongful imprisonment because "incarcerating the innocent can be construed as a form of strict liability wrong." If exonerees do not have to prove that there was a particular actor who did something
wrong, this would likely make it easier for exonerees to receive compensation
since there is less to prove. Also, if compensation were subtracted from police
and prosecutor budgets, then this reality could motivate prosecutors and
police officers to be more careful with conducting accurate investigations, as
even if no fault were attributed to them, their offices could still be liable for
damages to wrongfully convicted persons.

Mandery (2005, 1) questions the usefulness of a strict liability compensation regime centered on prosecutors, meaning that when it is discovered that
persons have been wrongfully convicted, prosecutors would bear the cost,
regardless of whether it was their fault. Mandery also mentions that strict
liability does not necessarily function the same way when the government
is a potential defendant (ibid., 6). Governments may not react to a risk of

liability the same way that individuals or corporations do, and it is not certain that citizens would opt into an insurance plan against wrongful convictions in a private sector (ibid., 6). Furthermore, due to the existence of governmental tort immunity doctrines, many governmental actions, even wrongful ones, leave no room for compensation, including "wrongful death caused by tortuous governmental conduct" (Rosenthal 2009, 134).

Hayek's understanding of liberty is probably more consistent with a fault liability regime over a strict liability regime due to his emphasis on individual responsibility. In fact, under Hayek's conception of liberty, individuals should not be held responsible for the actions of others, so prosecutors who have not contributed to wrongful convictions should not necessarily see a reduction in their office budgets. Hayek wrote:

> Freedom demands that the responsibility of the individual extend only to what he can be presumed to judge, that his actions take into account effects which are within his range of foresight, and particularly, that he be responsible only for his own actions (or those of persons under his care)—not for those of others who are equally free. (Hayek 1960, 146)

This quote suggests that prosecutors should not be liable for wrongful convictions that they do not cause. Hayek does state that collective responsibility is valid in situations where individuals are individually and severally responsible: "Responsibility, to be effective, must be individual responsibility. In a free society there cannot be any collective responsibility of members of a group as such, unless they have, by concerted action, all made themselves individually and severally responsible" (Hayek 1960, 146). Based on this quote, Hayek might argue that prosecutor offices can be held liable if the individual prosecutors are jointly and severally liable.

Not only may there be reluctance to pay for wrongful conviction compensation schemes that have the potential to be very expensive, but these schemes may also lead to wealth transfers from impoverished individuals with minimal political power to the wrongfully convicted (Rosenthal 2009, 132). It is important to note, however, that there is a relationship between the rate of wrongful conviction and the race of the wrongfully convicted person; race often has implications about the political power and income level of individuals. While only 13 percent of the population, African Americans comprise 47 percent of wrongful convictions in the United States, based on exonerations listed in the National Registry of Exonerations (Gross, Possley, and Stephens 2017, ii). In addition, incompetent lawyering is a key cause of wrongful convictions, and low-income individuals are more likely to receive incompetent lawyering, as they cannot afford more expensive and potentially better quality attorneys (Rutberg 2011, 303).

Rosenthal might still argue that, given that a budget is limited, a wrongful conviction fund means resources are being diverted from other important uses. "Programs that benefit thousands in disadvantaged communities would be replaced by jackpot-type awards to a relative handful. The ethical argument in favor of such a wealth transfer is contestable, to say the least" (Rosenthal 2009, 135). In spite of this argument that Rosenthal raises, the fact is that many wrongfully convicted persons are disadvantaged individuals—racial minorities or people with incompetent legal counsel. Therefore, this reality casts doubt on Rosenthal's argument about compensation for wrongfully convicted persons leading to wealth transfers from disadvantaged groups to people potentially not as disadvantaged (Gross, Possley, and Stephens 2017, ii; Rutberg 2011, 303). Furthermore, while Hayek did argue that collective interests are only general interests when their "benefit outweighs the cost imposed on the other members of society not part of the collective," given that everyone has the potential to be wrongfully convicted, having a general fund to address this possibility is arguably beneficial to all (Hayek 1978, 18).[7]

Also (assuming that there is an ethical duty to fix a problem if someone causes the problem), if a governmental actor causes an individual harm, perhaps this creates an ethical duty to act. This duty is distinguished from what may be expected of governmental actors when factors outside of the governmental actors' control cause an individual harm. Perhaps Rosenthal assumes it will not be possible to take away funds from other programs that are not specifically intended for disadvantaged groups. Rosenthal (2009, 136) counteracts this point by stating that even if broad-based program funding is reduced rather than programs specifically for the disadvantaged, a fund for wrongfully convicted persons still might not lead to a net gain in social welfare.

With that said, compensating the wrongfully convicted may lead to an increase in social welfare if it leads to improvements in the criminal justice system. For example, if prosecutors internalize the costs of wrongful convictions and end up making fewer mistakes as a result of this pressure, this can lead to more accuracy in convictions in general, which may benefit the public overall. Assuming wrongfully convicted persons were productive members of society before their wrongful convictions, these convictions rob persons of their opportunities to make productive contributions to society, and the wealth that is lost from their wrongful convictions cannot be redeemed. Besides the foregone wealth of wrongfully convicted persons, taxpayers also end up paying for the costs of incarcerating people.

Rosenthal (2009, 136) states that compensation will improve the lives of the exonerated but questions its ability to reduce errors in the criminal justice system. Moreover, due to prosecutorial immunity in most cases, if compensation for the wrongfully convicted depends on proving a prosecutor was at fault, there may not be a robust compensation scheme (ibid., 149). It is not clear that a fault-based liability regime against prosecutors and police officers will reduce misconduct (ibid., 153). Thus, abolishing prosecutorial immunity or weakening it would probably be one potential avenue for reducing prosecutorial conduct. This would also be consistent with Hayek's idea of individual responsibility: "If I have caused harm to somebody by negligence or forgetfulness, 'which I could not help' in the circumstances, this does not exempt me from responsibility but should impress upon me more strongly than before the necessity of keeping the possibility of such consequences in mind" (Hayek 1960, 138). Holding prosecutors responsible for wrongful convictions when they have contributed to the wrongful convictions may motivate them to consider the potential consequences of handling cases in a sloppy or imprudent way. Even if prosecutors cannot pay for wrongful convictions out of their own pockets, other costs could be imposed on them, such as losing their job or being demoted.

There is evidence suggesting that the amount of compensation given to wrongfully convicted persons released from prison has an effect on their behavior. Exonerees who received more than $500,000 for compensation are less likely to commit offenses after being released from prison than those who receive less than this amount. This is not to say that exonerees had already committed prior offenses, but evidence suggests that time in prison is related to offending later in one's life. Exonerees who were compensated more than $500,000 committed offenses post-prison at the same rate as those with no prior criminal histories (Mandery et al. 2013, 556). There are different theories on why the amount matters: (1) a certain base amount of funding is necessary to successfully reintegrate an exoneree back into the world and (2) exonerees who believe they are more fairly treated by the criminal justice system may be less likely to commit a crime after prison (ibid., 576). On this second point, research exists indicating that "perceptions of systemic procedural fairness affect criminal conduct" (ibid., 556). A greater amount of compensation is linked to a lower rate of criminal activity, perhaps because those who can afford rent, feed their families, and fulfill their basic needs are less likely to commit crimes (ibid., 579).

Encarnacion (2016), on the other hand, notes that there may exist perverse incentives if there are no caps on compensation and if the amount of compensation is high. For example, if compensation is about $100,000 per year, this might lead some officials to withhold admitting mistakes or misconduct and to resist efforts to release truly innocent persons from prison (ibid., 151).

One potential goal of compensation for the wrongfully convicted is to reduce prosecutorial misconduct, but there are many reasons why a compensation regime for the wrongfully convicted may not cause prosecutors to change their behavior. Rosenthal argues:

Given the political potency of aggressive prosecutions that produce convictions—and their career-enhancing advantages for the prosecutors themselves—
and the limited political accountability that prosecutors have for taxing and
spending, we can have no real confidence that whatever political incentive the
threat of civil liability might create to avoid the riskiest prosecutorial tactics
would not be offset by the powerful political and professional incentives for
prosecutors to put what they regard as their strongest case before a jury, and to
prosecute all suspects that they believe a jury is likely to convict. (Rosenthal
2009, 159)

If prosecutors do not pursue what seem to be winnable cases out of fear of
future liability, they may suffer the political cost at the next election. But
these trade-offs are not unique to prosecutors, and this may actually be in the
general interest (ibid., 159).

It is perhaps difficult to determine if the incentive to avoid civil liability
would be sufficient to overcome the political pressures and incentives for producing convictions. However, this does not mean that attempts to shape prosecutorial conduct are valueless. Hayek grappled with the question of whether
"the person upon whom we place responsibility for a particular action or its
consequences is the kind of person who is accessible to normal motives" and:

whether in the given circumstances such a person can be expected to be influenced by the considerations and beliefs we want to impress upon him. As in
most such problems, our ignorance of the particular circumstances will regularly be such that we will merely know that the expectation that they will be
held responsible is likely, on the whole, to influence men in certain positions
in a desirable direction. Our problem is generally not whether certain mental
factors were operative on the occasion of a particular action but how certain
considerations might be made as effective as possible in guiding action. This
requires that the individual be praised or blamed, whether or not the expectation
of this would in fact have made any difference to the action. Of the effect in the
particular instance we may never be sure, but we believe that, in general, the
knowledge that he will be held responsible will influence a person's conduct in
a desirable direction. (Hayek 1960, 138)

Hayek's work suggests that, at least sometimes, prosecutors will be motivated
to change their conduct if they possess knowledge of potential civil liability.

On a related note, Hayek also discusses the "knowledge problem," which is
the idea that no one can acquire perfect knowledge (Hayek 1945). Therefore,
while prosecutors might have some idea of their potential for civil liability,
they will not necessarily know how probable civil liability will be. Thus, if
they are not convinced that an undesirable outcome is likely from maintaining
the status quo, they may not actually be motivated to change. Hayek's work

suggests that it is imperative to try to provide people, especially those whose decisions carry great weight, with as much accurate information as possible. Assuming there will be liability for prosecutorial misconduct, the less imperfect the knowledge of prosecutors is, the more it seems that knowledge can motivate them to pursue their cases more carefully.

TYPES OF COMPENSATION SCHEMES FOR THE WRONGFULLY CONVICTED

There exist two main ways for wrongfully convicted persons to be compensated. One method is by state statute, which does not require the plaintiff or claimant to prove that their wrongful conviction was caused by government misconduct; these are known as no-fault statutes. Under these statutes, plaintiffs generally must prove factual innocence. After post-conviction relief, some states require that a civil suit commence in state trial court. The second method for obtaining compensation is by filing federal civil rights cases under 42 U.S.C. § 1983 against counties, municipalities, or state actors, including prosecutors, police officers, state experts, or others who may have taken unconstitutional actions that led to the wrongful conviction (Gutman and Sun 2019, 707).

There is a great disparity in compensation schemes for the wrongfully convicted who have experienced incarceration. Just to provide an idea of the amounts provided, eighteen states, the federal government, and the District of Columbia provide at least $50,000 of compensation per year for wrongful incarceration, but several states do not have any laws to compensate the wrongfully convicted (Innocence Project 2019). It is important to note that the states' laws only apply to wrongfully convicted innocent persons and thus do not extend to other populations who may have also been wrongfully convicted due to reasons such as police corruption or prosecutorial misconduct (Cardozo 2016, 13). States' laws reflect differences in the amount provided, the circumstances under which someone is eligible for compensation, and whether the award is available as per statute, litigation, and/or special legislative authorization (Innocence Project 2019).[8]

Only thirty-five states, the District of Columbia, and the federal government have legislation that permits compensation for innocent persons who have experienced both a wrongful conviction and incarceration (ibid.). In the other states, exonerees have to engage in litigation or seek relief through special legislative bills if they want compensation (Cardozo 2016, 13). Also, there are many prerequisites and disqualifying factors that could prevent someone from receiving compensation, such as if the person contributed to his wrongful conviction (University of Michigan Law School 2018, 1–16).

Under some state compensation regimes, exonerees are not eligible for compensation if they in any way contributed to their convictions (i.e., pleaded guilty to the crime or gave a false confession to police). In some states, only exonerees with official government pardons are eligible for compensation. In other states, only DNA-exonerated persons can receive state compensation. Some state statutes include provisions stating that there is a statute of limitations for an exoneree to bring a claim, and these periods can be quite short, such as California's statute that has a period of two years (Mandery et al. 2013, 559).

The exoneree also bears the burden to prove (could be by a preponderance of the evidence depending on the state) the following:

> The claimant did not commit the crime or crimes for which the claimant was convicted and was not an accessory or accomplice to the acts that were the basis of the conviction and resulted in a reversal or vacation of the judgment of conviction, dismissal of the charges or finding of not guilty on retrial. (Innocence Project 2019, 1)

Oftentimes, states use the court system to adjudicate compensation claims. Furthermore, sometimes exonerees seek state compensation in addition to filing a federal civil rights lawsuit. Some states do not allow exonerees to receive both state compensation and compensation from a federal claim, so if an exoneree who received state compensation later wins a federal claim, he is obligated to reimburse the state. Contrarily, if an exoneree wins a federal claim first, any state compensation gained would first subtract out the federal amount received (Innocence Project 2019).

Different theories have been advanced for how the state can or should compensate individuals who have been wrongfully convicted and later released from prison. Shawn Ambrost supports a holistic compensation model that involves providing not only financial support but also job training support and health care. Cathleen Burnett suggests using an individualized approach based on the restorative justice model to reintegrate wrongfully convicted persons back into the world (Mandery et al. 2013, 563).

One possible solution entails providing jobs to the wrongfully convicted in addition to compensation for years of wrongful imprisonment. Providing jobs and waiving educational and/or vocational fees would help wrongfully convicted persons to become productive members of society. According to Mandery's study sample, 56.8 percent of wrongfully convicted persons had at least one prior criminal conviction, 42.4 percent had no prior record, and 38.1 percent were convicted of at least one crime after they were released (ibid., 568, 570). Post-release offending is an issue for some persons released after a wrongful conviction, and compensation of at least $500,000 decreases the likelihood of post-release offending (at least based on Mandery's sample) (ibid., 572).

HAYEK DISCUSSION: INDIVIDUAL RESPONSIBILITY, THE "KNOWLEDGE" PROBLEM, AND COLLECTIVE VERSUS GENERAL INTERESTS

Individual Responsibility

"Liberty and responsibility are inseparable" (Hayek 1960, 133). According to Hayek's philosophy on individual responsibility, each individual must bear the consequences of his actions, including government actors who are prosecuting innocent victims. Therefore, if individual liberty is the institutional foundation of a free market, then it follows that wrongfully convicting individuals is inconsistent with a free market, since wrongfully convicting individuals implies a system in which government actors (e.g., judges, prosecutors) are (1) not being held accountable for the full consequences of their actions and (2) there is no error correction mechanism to rectify such wrongful prosecution. Even a comprehensive compensation scheme will not fully undo the "wrongs" that wrongfully convicted persons have endured.

Knowledge Problem

Hayek writes that it is "the character rather than the volume of government activity that is important" (ibid., 331). Hayek would not likely argue that providing compensation to the wrongfully convicted goes against the foundation of a free market, especially if this can lead to more productive individuals (wrongfully convicted persons). But as Hayek points out, no one can acquire 100 percent perfect knowledge (Hayek 1945). Hayek wrote that the economic problem of society is "a problem of the utilization of knowledge which is not given to anyone in its totality" (ibid.).

Due to the knowledge problem, state and local government officials will find it difficult to choose an optimal amount of compensation for a wrongfully convicted person. If the correct amount is not chosen, this may complicate potential policy goals of compensation schemes, such as reducing prosecutorial misconduct and re-integrating the prison population back into society to become more productive members.

Given that officials are unable to know how to distribute compensation to victims of wrongful convictions in a welfare-enhancing manner, there may be a general increase in compensation for the wrongfully convicted, even without empirical evidence that this is more socially desirable. Rather than wrongful conviction compensation being a means to an end for policymakers, the Hayekian knowledge problem suggests that a by-product of this problem is that it may become an end in itself. It may also lead bureaucrats to resist correcting such mistakes if they think that correcting mistakes will lead to large settlements as well.

The problem about how much compensation to choose is not unique to the wrongful conviction context. However, state officials can use recommendations from organizations such as the Innocence Project as a starting point for discussions about compensation amounts.[9] The Innocence Project recommends that states "provide a minimum of $50,000, untaxed, per year of wrongful imprisonment and $100,000, untaxed, per year on death row. This amount is based on the federal government's standard created through the Innocence Protection Act of 2004" (Cardozo 2016, 5). The Innocence Project designed these recommendations after consultation with exonerees and their families, lawmakers, social workers, and psychologists, so they may have some expertise in the field that state officials can draw from (ibid., 5). Hayek also speaks about

> the knowledge of the particular circumstances of time and place. It is with respect to this that practically every individual has some advantage over all others because he possesses unique information of which beneficial use might be made, but of which use can be made only if the decisions depending on it are left to him or are made with his active cooperation. (Hayek 1945, 521–22)

This knowledge seems to mirror that of what a prosecutor may have. Because the prosecutor is in a unique position to have "knowledge of the particular circumstances" of a case that others may not possess, the prosecutor is best suited to avoid wrongful convictions. Prosecutors may have access to knowledge that others do not have and in some situations, they are required to disclose that knowledge. In *Brady v. Maryland* (373 US 83 (1963)), the U.S. Supreme Court held that "the suppression by the prosecution of evidence favorable to an accused upon request violates due process where the evidence is material either to guilt or to punishment, irrespective of the good faith or bad faith of the prosecution" (*Brady v. Maryland* 1963, 87). There is a clear link between *Brady* violations and wrongful convictions, so any effort to reduce the rate of wrongful convictions should also address *Brady*.[10] In one particular case, "John Thompson spent 18 years in prison for a robbery and murder he did not commit. 14 of them on death row in solitary confinement in the infamous Angola prison in Louisiana. He was exonerated after evidence covered up by New Orleans prosecutors surfaced after his seventh and final execution date was issued on May 20, 1999" (Witness to Innocence n.d., para. 1). Thompson's case is just one of many that reveal how dire the consequences of *Brady* violations and prosecutorial misconduct can be. The *Brady* violation is an illustration of knowledge problem. But if prosecutors' budgets are impacted by compensation for wrongful convictions, then perhaps the number of *Brady* violations could decrease.

If higher compensation is linked to a lower probability of future criminal conduct, this is an argument in favor of higher compensation schemes. However, because of the imperfect knowledge problem, it is unclear how bureaucrats would be able to determine an ideal amount of compensation to reduce likelihood of future criminal conduct. For example, $500,000 may seem like a high number for some people, but for someone who spent twenty years in prison, this amount may seem low, especially compared with income potentially unearned during that time frame. Determining a range for optimal compensation is an area for future research.

Directly related to the knowledge problem is the fact that Hayek viewed competition "systematically as a procedure for discovering facts" (Hayek 1968, 9). Given that a legal trial and litigation can be regarded as a competitive process between defendants and plaintiffs, the outcome of which is the discovery of the truth of the matter (this is what the word "verdict" implies), then how the competition is run will likely have a bearing on whether "truth" is actually discovered. If the playing field is not even and prosecutors (for example) illegally withhold information from defense counsel, this affects the integrity of the discovery process and may impede the truth from actually being uncovered. Also, the pursuit of truth may not necessarily be the goal of a prosecutor or defense attorney. Without the goal of discovering truth, prosecutors may employ tactics that are inconsistent with truth discovery.

This line of reasoning suggests that, besides ex-post compensation, ex ante, the rules governing prosecution must be restructured to concentrate greater liability on the part of prosecutors for wrongful prosecution so that the "learning process" of court litigation would yield greater fairness as a by-product of the legal proceeding. The result would be less wrongful prosecution and, as a by-product, less need for compensation schemes in the first place.

Collective versus General Interests

Hayek writes that "it is often erroneously suggested that all collective interests are general interests of the society; but in many instances the satisfaction of collective interests of certain groups may be decidedly contrary to the general interest of society" (Hayek 1978, 18). Hayek argues that collective interests are only general interests when their benefit outweighs the cost imposed on the other members of society who are not part of the collective[11] (ibid., 18). If there are state compensation laws for the wrongfully convicted, does that serve a collective interest or a general interest? How can compensation laws be constructed to satisfy not only the collective interest but also the general interest? The answer lies in crafting them in such a way that leads to criminal justice reform.

PUBLIC CHOICE AND AUSTRIAN ECONOMICS: KNOWLEDGE AND THE RELATIONSHIP BETWEEN INCENTIVES AND OUTCOMES

Besides the desire to pursue self-interest, pure public choice theorists also believe that political agents possess perfect knowledge, which cuts against Hayek's theory that such agents cannot acquire perfect knowledge (Boettke and Lopez 2002, 112; Hayek 1945, 521–22). Public choice is one of the varieties of neoclassical political economy that discusses the idea of perfect knowledge (Ikeda 2003, 72):

> One of the central ideas that define neoclassical economics is that of perfect knowledge, which refers to that state of affairs in which actors possess information relating to their future plans sufficient to avoid ex post regret. Where there is perfect knowledge, it follows that the future outcomes of present actions will never generate disappointment, i.e., what we expect to happen, and only what we expect to happen, will indeed happen. This identity of intended and actual outcomes means that there is no real possibility of error on the part of the actor. Faced with all relevant costs, benefits, and probabilities he will always make the right choice. But if actors always get what they want, in a world of perfect information it would seem to follow that they must have wanted what they have gotten. That is, the assumption of perfect information would also clear the way for the political economist to infer the actual intentions of public choosers from the outcomes of public policy. (ibid., 66)

This idea of inferring intentions from outcomes probably makes more sense for the Chicago public choice theorists who believe in perfect information because if actors have imperfect information, as they do for the Virginia public choice theorists, then it seems that results may not necessarily mirror intentions (ibid., 68).

Public choice theory lays out the following relationship between intentions and outcomes:

> Inferring intentions from outcomes under the assumption of perfect information (or perfect probabilistic information) implies that public choosers always get what they want, and what comes to pass is what they wanted to come to pass even if others suffer net harm by it as a result. *In a neoclassical framework,*

*government failure does not mean that public choosers fail to produce the
intended outcome with their policies, but that the intervention produces deadweight losses*, which those public choosers are prepared to live with and no one
else has an incentive to remove. (ibid., 66)[12]

The fact that results may cause harm to others or even be classified as a government failure does not mean the results were not intended, but this argument also implies that sometimes public choosers will deliberately choose
to pursue inefficient outcomes that result in net losses to society (ibid., 66).
Considering that public officials have many incentives and interests that
motivate them, it becomes clearer why some may be willing to accept wrongful convictions if it helps them to secure their own interests.

Hayek favored a hybrid approach between public choice theory and
Austrian economics (Boettke and Lopez 2002, 112). As it relates to wrongful convictions, the public choice theory may attribute perfect knowledge to
prosecutors. In that scenario, prosecutors would have no defense in claiming
that they did not know that someone was innocent because perhaps their
thorough investigation should have revealed that innocence. Thus, constructive knowledge is imputed to them. It seems that, at least as it concerns the
knowledge issue, pure public choice theorists would hold prosecutors who
contribute to wrongful convictions to a higher standard than Hayek, since
persons with perfect knowledge cannot use lack of knowledge as an excuse
for making poor choices (Boettke and Lopez 2002, 112; Hayek 1945, 521–
22). On the other hand, the Austrian economic theorists believe more in the
"structural uncertainty of the future and the diffuseness and subjectivity of
knowledge" (Boettke and Lopez 2002, 112). An Austrian outlook on wrongful convictions suggests that prosecutors do not have perfect knowledge;
while they have subjective knowledge, their "knowledge" is not infallible
(ibid., 112).

"The Austrian concept of government failure is thus very different from
that of Public Choice insofar as the latter views government failure in
terms of deviations from an ideal optimal state. Government failure from
the Austrian perspective refers therefore to the failure of an intervention
to produce the outcome sought by its proponents" (Ikeda 2003, 67). Under
the public choice model, perhaps the ideal optimal state would be a society
where there were no wrongful convictions; if so, then any government effort
that did not completely eradicate wrongful convictions could be considered
a government failure. However, under the Austrian model, if a governmental
action sought to reduce the number of wrongfully convicted persons by 15
percent over the next three years and that goal was achieved, there would
not be a government failure even though some wrongful convictions would
still exist.

CONCLUDING REMARKS AND POTENTIAL
AREAS FOR FURTHER RESEARCH

Compensation statutes for the wrongfully convicted can lead to criminal justice reform that produces fewer wrongful convictions and thus less of a need for wrongful conviction compensation statutes. Changing the incentives of various actors in the criminal justice system by causing these actors to internalize some of the costs related to the wrongful convictions they contributed to may lead to fewer wrongful convictions.

Even if public officials may stand against wrongful convictions, in theory, they are motivated by various incentives, just as other individuals in society. Some of those interests may be directly opposed to wrongful conviction compensation schemes, particularly if they have to pay personal costs when these schemes are enacted (Ikeda 2003, 68). By creating a system where individuals are held accountable for their own mistakes, lapses of judgments, or misconduct in relation to wrongful convictions, compensation statutes for the wrongfully convicted can be consistent with a Hayekian idea of liberty (Hayek 1960, 133). Hayek argued that even negligent actions that cause harm should be punished, and individual responsibility cannot be separated from liberty (ibid., 133, 138). Wrongful convictions are inconsistent with the Hayekian view of liberty because they coerce individuals to endure punishment without cause; these convictions do even more harm when there is not an effective method for correcting mistakes (ibid., 71). While people cannot regain the years they have lost after being wrongfully imprisoned, compensation statutes can provide a way for those responsible to be held accountable for their actions.

Areas for further research include further exploration of the various incentives that prosecutors face in determining how to prosecute a case, the various incentives police officers face in determining how to conduct their investigations, and the various incentives that judges face in determining how to handle cases in their courtrooms. By analyzing incentives, perhaps the journey to changing those incentives can begin. It all starts with knowledge. Hayek argued that, when faced with the knowledge of certain adverse consequences, individuals will generally be led to engage in more socially desirable conduct (ibid., 138). Another area of research could also look into the feasibility of holding public officials responsible for wrongful convictions and the implications this would have for government immunity doctrines.

NOTES

1. "But if the state should make amends to those it fails to protect from crime, it should equally make amends to those it fails to protect from its own processes when they go awry" (Mostaghel 2011, 524).

2. This would likely require abolishing prosecutorial immunity or at least weakening it. This paper focuses more on the role of prosecutors than, say, police officers, but this does not mean that they do not also contribute to wrongful convictions.

3. By "state," they are likely referring to state actors.

4. Nevertheless, Professor Cassell from Utah Law discusses that it is possible to formulate a regime where the innocent can be protected and the guilty convicted for crimes they commit through a criminal justice system that focuses more on substance than procedure (Cassell 2017, 1). Cassell discusses that, with the exception of a homicide, a single wrongful conviction may cost society more than one violent crime when comparing (for example) jury verdicts or civil settlements in wrongful conviction versus criminal assault cases. However, Professor Cassell also acknowledges that if a prisoner is released from prison, there is a possibility that multiple violent crimes will be committed. Particularly for those who have committed crimes in the past, there are high rates of recidivism (ibid., 6). Cassell argues that one way for defense counsel to focus more on actual claims of innocence while also prioritizing convicting the guilty is if the exclusionary rule were to be abolished, as this rule can be viewed as more of a procedural rather than a substantive rule (ibid., 14–15). The exclusionary rule prevents the government from using (in a criminal case) most evidence collected that violates constitutional rights; it does not apply to civil cases (Cornell Law School Legal Information Institute n.d., para. 1). Cassell's argument about abolishing the exclusionary rule seems to rest on an unsubstantiated assumption that there is not a significant number of innocent people who will be found guilty without the protection of the exclusionary rule. The exclusionary rule could theoretically prevent a prosecutor from using evidence obtained through a warrantless search of someone's apartment when evidence was planted in the person's home (ibid., para. 1). It is not at all clear that the exclusionary rule is mainly helping guilty persons as Cassell suggests (Cassell 2017, 15).

5. There seems to be an error in the law. It should read "willful."

6. The public is divided in terms of whether it values ensuring the innocent are free versus the guilty being imprisoned (Ekins Institute 2016). According to a survey conducted by the Cato Institute, 60 percent of Americans believe it is worse to have 20,000 innocent people imprisoned versus 20,000 guilty people free and 40 percent believe the opposite (ibid.). If these percentages reflect reality accurately, it would seem that avoiding wrongful convictions would be a greater priority for prosecutors than imprisoning the guilty if they are greatly concerned about satisfying public opinion (for reelection purposes). In fact, some prosecutor offices have taken programmatic steps to combat wrongful convictions through the creation of conviction integrity units. "A Conviction Integrity Unit (CIU) is a division of a prosecutorial office that works to prevent, identify, and remedy false convictions." In 2018, for example, CIUs assisted in fifty-eight exonerations (The National Registry of Exonerations 2019, 12).

7. "A collective interest will become a general interest only in so far as all find that the satisfaction of collective interests of particular groups on the basis of some principle of reciprocity will mean for them a gain in excess of the burden they will have to bear" (Hayek 1978, 18).

8. To find a comparison of wrongful conviction statutes across states, please consider this link on the University of Michigan website: www.law.umich.edu/special/

exoneration/Documents/CompensationByState_InnocenceProject.pdf. Also at this website, you can find an interactive map with a list of exonerations by state: www.law .umich.edu/special/exoneration/Pages/Exonerations-in-the-United-States-Map.aspx.

9. "The Innocence Project, founded in 1992 by Peter Neufeld and Barry Scheck at Cardozo School of Law, exonerates the wrongly convicted through DNA testing and reforms the criminal justice system to prevent future injustice" (Innocence Project n.d.).

10. To learn more about *Brady* violations, you can visit this link: https://theappeal .org/the-epidemic-of-brady-violations-explained-94a38ad3c800/.

11. "A collective interest will become a general interest only in so far as all find that the satisfaction of collective interests of particular groups on the basis of some principle of reciprocity will mean for them a gain in excess of the burden they will have to bear" (Hayek 1978, 18).

12. "Deadweight loss refers to the loss of economic efficiency when the equilibrium outcome is not achievable or not achieved. In other words, it is the cost born by society due to market inefficiency" (CFI n.d.).

REFERENCES

Boettke, Peter J. and Edward Lopez. 2002. "Austrian Economics and Public Choice." *The Review of Austrian Economics* 15 (2–3): 111–19.

Brady v. Maryland, 373 US 83. 1963.

Cardozo, Benjamin N. 2016. "Making Up for Lost Time: What the Wrongfully Convicted Endure and How to Provide Fair Compensation." *Innocence Project.* https://www.innocenceproject.org/wp-content/uploads/2016/06/innocence_project _compensation_report-6.pdf.

Cassell, Paul. 2017. "Can We Protect the Innocent without Freeing the Guilty? Thoughts on Innocence Reforms That Avoid Harmful Tradeoffs." In *Wrongful Convictions and the DNA Revolution: Twenty-Five Years of Freeing the Innocent,* edited by Daniel S. Medwed, 264–90. Cambridge, UK: Cambridge University Press.

Corporate Finance Institute. n.d. "Deadweight Loss." Accessed April 15, 2021. https://corporatefinanceinstitute.com/resources/knowledge/economics/deadweight -loss/.

Cornell Law School Legal Information Institute. n.d. "Exclusionary Rule." Accessed April 15, 2021. https://www.law.cornell.edu/wex/exclusionary_rule.

Encarnacion, Erik. 2016. "Why and How to Compensate Exonerees." *Michigan Law Review First Impressions* 114: 139–54.

———. 2017. "Backpay for Exonerees." *Yale Journal of Law & the Humanities* 29 (2): 245–71.

Ekins, Emily. 2016. "Blackstone's Ratio: Is It More Important to Protect Innocence or Punish Guilt?" Cato Institute, December 07. https://www.cato.org/policing-in -america/chapter-4/blackstones-ratio.

Fon, Vincy and Hans-Bernd Schäfer. 2007. "State Liability for Wrongful Conviction: Incentive Effects on Crime Levels." *Journal of Institutional and Theoretical Economics* 163 (2): 269–84.

Gross, Samuel, Maurice Possley, and Klara Stephens. 2017. "Race and Wrongful Convictions in the U.S." *National Registry of Exonerations*, March 7. http://www .law.umich.edu/special/exoneration/Documents/Race_and_Wrongful_Convictions .pdf.

Gutman, Jeffrey and Lingxiao Sun. 2019. "Why Is Mississippi the Best State in Which to be Exonerated? An Empirical Evaluation of State Statutory and Civil Compensation for the Wrongfully Convicted." *Nebraska Law Review* 11 (2): 694–789.

Haeffele, Stefanie and Anne Hobson. 2019. "Inside Leviathan: Lessons from Gordon Tullock's *Bureaucracy*." *Econlib*, November 4. https://www.econlib.org/library/ Columns/y2019/HaeffeleHobsonbureaucracy.html.

Hayek, F. A. 1945. "The Use of Knowledge in Society." *The American Economic Review* 35: 519–30.

———. 1960. *The Constitution of Liberty*. Chicago, IL: University of Chicago Press.

———. 1968. "Competition as a Discovery Procedure." Translated by Marcellus S. Snow. *The Quarterly Journal of Austrian Economics* 5 (3): 9–23.

———. 1978. *Law, Legislation and Liberty, Volume 2: The Mirage of Social Justice*. Chicago, IL: University of Chicago Press.

Ikeda, Sanford. 2003. "How Compatible Are Public Choice and Austrian Political Economy?" *The Review of Austrian Economics* 16 (1): 63–75.

Innocence Project. n.d. "About." Accessed April 15, 2021. https://innocenceproject .org/about/.

———. 2019. "Key Provisions in Wrongful Conviction Compensation Laws." https://www.innocenceproject.org/wp-content/uploads/2019/09/Key-Provisions-in -Wrongful-Conviction-Compensation-Laws.docx.

Leeson, Peter T. and Peter J. Boettke. 2003. "An 'Austrian' Perspective on Public Choice." In *Encyclopedia of Public Choice*, edited by Charles K. Rowley and Friedrich Schneider, 351–56. Boston, MA: Kluwer Academic Publishers.

Mandery, Evan J. 2005. "Commentary: Efficiency Considerations of Compensating the Wrongfully Convicted." *Criminal Law Bulletin* 41 (3): 492–506.

Mandery, Evan J., Amy Schlosberg, Valerie West, and Bennett Callaghan. 2013. "Compensation Statutes and Post-Exoneration Offending." *The Journal of Criminal Law and Criminology (1973-)* 103 (2): 553–83.

Mostaghel, Deborah. 2011. "Wrongfully Incarcerated, Randomly Compensated–How to Fund Wrongful-Conviction Compensation Statutes." *Indiana Law Review* 44 (2): 503–44.

Rosenthal, Lawrence. 2009. "Second Thoughts on Damages for Wrongful Convictions." *Chicago Kent Law Review* 85 (1): 127–61.

Rutberg, Susan. 2011. "Wrongfully Convicted: The Overrepresentation of the Poor." In *Vulnerable Populations and Transformative Law Teaching*, edited by Society of American Law Teachers and Golden Gate University School of Law, 299–312. Durham, NC: Carolina Academic Press.

Shaw, John. 2011. "Exoneration and the Road to Compensation: The Tim Cole Act and Comprehensive Compensation for Persons Wrongfully Imprisoned." *Texas Wesleyan Law Review* 17 (4): 593–618.

Shugart, William F., II. n.d. "Public Choice." Accessed April 15, 2021. https://www.econlib.org/library/Enc/PublicChoice.html.

Smith, Meggan. 2007. "Have We Abandoned the Innocent? Society's Debt to the Wrongly Convicted." *American University Criminal Law Brief* 2 (2): 3–15.

South Carolina General Assembly. 2019. "Wrongful Conviction Bill." Last Modified February 13, 2019. https://www.scstatehouse.gov/sess123_2019-2020/bills/3303.htm.

State of Connecticut. n.d. "Sec. 7-465. Assumption of Liability for Damage Caused by Employee of Municipality or Member of Local Emergency Planning District. Joint Liability of Municipalities in District Department of Health or Regional Council of Governments." Accessed April 15, 2021. https://www.cga.ct.gov/current/pub/chap_113.htm#sec_7-465.

The National Registry of Exonerations. 2019. "Exonerations in 2018." April 09. https://www.law.umich.edu/special/exoneration/Documents/Exonerations%20in%202018.pdf.

University of Michigan Law School. 2018. "Compensation Statutes: A National Overview." Last updated May 21, 2018. https://www.law.umich.edu/special/exoneration/Documents/CompensationByState_InnocenceProject.pdf.

Witness to Innocence. n.d. "John Thompson (1962-2017)." Accessed April 15, 2021. https://www.witnesstoinnocence.org/single-post/john-thompson#:~:text=John%20Thompson%20spent%2018%20years,infamous%20Angola%20prison%20in%20Louisiana.&text=Thus%2C%20the%20robbery%20conviction%20was,35%20minutes%20to%20acquit%20John.

Wright v. State, 169 NJ 422. 2001.

Chapter 4

Rent-Seeking in Medicaid Managed Care

Neil McCray

A perspective advanced by privatization advocates in public policy discussions in the United States, especially since the 1980s, is that the private sector will tend to be more efficient than the public sector at accomplishing a range of objectives. That perspective is exemplified in arguments in favor of Medicaid managed care: "Advocates of contracting out Medicaid to managed care plans often cite instilling market discipline and bringing competitive market forces to bear on lowering program spending, familiar arguments for outsourcing any government function" (Goldsmith, Mosley, and Jacobs 2018b, para. 17). Private companies have a profit motive and thus a different set of incentives than do public institutions and bureaucrats, which might yield such market discipline; a competitive market environment should also tend to lower prices and improve quality. Despite the theoretical arguments for managed care in Medicaid, there is little peer-reviewed empirical evidence suggesting managed care in Medicaid leads to reductions in cost relative to a publicly administered system (Sparer 2012; Congressional Budget Office 2018; Goldsmith, Mosley, and Jacobs 2018b). The paucity of peer-reviewed evidence for managed care's success with regard to budget impacts has not affected its spread in Medicaid: as of July 2019, forty states had risk-based managed care contracts for at least a portion of their Medicaid recipients (Hinton et al. 2019). By 2017, "over two-thirds (69 percent) of all Medicaid beneficiaries received their care through comprehensive risk-based MCOs" (Hinton et al. 2019, para. 4).

A reasonable person might be curious why most Medicaid beneficiaries are enrolled in managed care plans despite a lack of evidence indicating such plans yield savings. Referring to a quote from a state Medicaid director, one Robert Wood Johnson Foundation report termed the phenomenon of transitioning populations for which evidence may not be available into managed care the "managed care 'leap of faith'" (Sparer 2012, 14). While this chapter cannot answer that question definitively, it will address several reasons why states have transitioned toward managed care in Medicaid, present a perspective of Medicaid managed care as a system that incentivizes rent-seeking behavior on the part of managed care organizations, and discuss reasons why managed care might realize fewer savings than would be theoretically expected.

Section II will present background information on Medicaid, including its history and purpose, and the history of managed care and Medicaid managed care specifically. Section III will review available literature on Medicaid managed care savings. Section IV will discuss competition and implications for the knowledge problem in state Medicaid program administration, and section V will offer arguments relating to Medicaid budgeting and perspectives from public choice. The chapter will offer concluding observations in Section VI.

BACKGROUND

Medicaid is a means-tested program that provides government-funded health insurance "to millions of Americans, including eligible low-income adults, children, pregnant women, elderly adults, and people with disabilities" (Centers for Medicare & Medicaid Services n.d., para. 1). The program, which is jointly funded by the federal and state governments, cost over $592 billion in federal fiscal year 2018 (Kaiser Family Foundation 2019) and as of November 2019 covered over 71 million people (Kaiser Family Foundation 2020)—over a fifth of the population of the United States.

Medicaid was established in 1965 by Title XIX of the Social Security Act. While the program has expanded from its initial form, its design intent was similar in nature to its present form: to provide health insurance for people with low incomes, with the goal of helping people access needed healthcare services. States were tasked with designing and administering their own Medicaid programs, and the federal government would pay for a portion—at least half—of each state's Medicaid costs. There were requirements set for certain essential services that states had to cover in their programs and states also had to cover specific populations. However, states had the discretion to cover services beyond those that were federally mandated and to include populations, such as the medically needy, which were not federally mandated to get coverage via Medicaid. Since the program's inception, Medicaid has undergone substantial changes in eligibility criteria, the structure and generosity of benefits, and its payment systems. "The cumulative effect of these changes—combined with state decisions regarding the scope of their programs—has been to expand Medicaid well beyond its original focus on furnishing principally acute care services to public assistance recipients" (Smith et al. 2005, 19).

While Medicaid has evolved in many ways since its inception, the primary change of interest in this chapter is the shift in its payment models. The traditional payment model in Medicaid is known as "fee for service" (FFS). Under a FFS system, providers bill and are paid for each service they perform. In traditional FFS Medicaid, providers that see Medicaid patients would directly bill the state Medicaid program for services rendered. However, FFS systems have long been observed to have questionable incentive structures. If providers want to earn higher incomes in a FFS system, they merely need to increase the quantity of services they are providing. Because healthcare consumption is driven at least in part by providers—they indicate to patients what tests or services are necessary for patient care—there is a clear incentive for physicians, in order to maximize incomes, to provide a higher volume of services and more expensive types of care than may be strictly necessary (Ikegami 2015). An alternative version of the problem might be that providers are incentivized to provide whatever combination of services maximizes their incomes; this is more complicated than simply providing more services generally, as different services have different associated fees. However, a general criticism of FFS is that it may lead to increased utilization of services and spending without, at least necessarily, any improvements in quality—or potentially, with reductions in quality associated with the mix of services provided. In general, in a system where providers are paid by volume of services provided, the incentives are perverse: providers are pushed to provide more services, not fewer. An additional cause for increased utilization, specifically in the Medicaid space, relates to low reimbursement levels. Medicaid reimburses providers at a level typically far below that of private insurers, and this may push providers to increase services rendered in order to maintain income levels.

That objection is one primary reason that states have transitioned away from FFS as a payment model. At its core, FFS will tend to incentivize physicians and other providers to offer higher volumes of care and more care than is necessary. This argument is borne out empirically as well: one study on Medicare fees found that changes to the fee schedule led to statistically significant changes to the types of procedures doctors chose to perform on patients (Gong, Jun, and Tsai 2017); (i.e., doctors responded to payment incentives by changing the types of care they provided).

That Medicaid reimbursements are typically lower than Medicare or private payers leads to another problem managed care might address: limited provider networks. Low reimbursement rates and the speed with which providers are reimbursed lead some providers to not accept Medicaid patients.

Given the incentive-based arguments against FFS as a payment system as well as Medicaid's growing cost and its growing share of states' budgets, states have looked for ways to reduce spending, make spending more predictable, and provide stronger provider networks. One option to which states have appealed, especially since the 1990s, is Medicaid managed care, a system in which states contract with private health insurance companies to provide services to Medicaid recipients. These private companies, or managed care organizations (MCOs), accept a per-member per-month (PMPM) capitated payment from the state government, and the companies are responsible for managing the care of Medicaid recipients.

Risk-based capitated managed care is an answer to the above objections to FFS systems. Capitation means payment on a per-person basis. The contracted private companies are paid a capitation by the state Medicaid agency to manage the care of Medicaid recipients. The risk associated with the contract comes in the form of expenses for the MCO: if they keep their per-person expenses for the Medicaid recipients whose care they manage below the capitation payment paid by the state, then they can keep those savings—or, depending on the level of savings, a portion of them. If their per-person costs rise above the level of the capitation payment from the state, then they lose money. This is the risk associated with capitated managed care. That risk is the source of the critical incentive structure that undergirds the theory of risk-based capitated managed care. MCOs are incentivized to find methods to reduce costs; if they succeed in getting costs below the capitation payment, they make money.

The benefits to the state from risk-based capitated managed care are numerous. In addition to having the potential to reduce costs in the Medicaid program, which for many states is the largest single line item in state budgets, capitated managed care also reduces volatility in program spending and makes it more feasible for states to project and appropriately budget for future Medicaid spending. Managed care has the potential to allow states, via their MCOs, to more carefully monitor and manage the care provided to and utilized by Medicaid recipients. In theory, MCOs are incentivized to carefully monitor care and promote cheaper preventive care in the place of more expensive retroactive treatment for certain conditions. An additional critical benefit of managed care is that, while states may have limited provider networks due to low reimbursement rates, MCOs may be able to provide more robust provider networks. So, theoretical benefits of managed care in Medicaid include improvements in access to care, improvements in quality of care or increases in preventive care, reductions in Medicaid spending relative to FFS systems, and improvements in state capacity to project and budget appropriately.

Those theoretical benefits to managed care in Medicaid represent critical reasons that states have transitioned administration from the state toward private companies. The result of that transition is that "[F]or almost all [. . .] states the Medicaid program has been effectively privatized at the operational level [. . .] While there are a few states where state bureaucracies administer Medicaid, the trend is toward private management" (Pauly 2019, 12).

An alternative perspective to that theoretical approach considers other effects that incentives might have on the private companies. They may be subject to pressure to generate profits, but that would not necessarily lead only to the conclusion that they must improve healthcare quality and reduce costs by cutting unnecessary care or increasing access to preventive care. Several objections are noted by the Medicaid and CHIP Payment and Access Commission (n.d.): capitated managed care will also incentivize undertreating patients to keep costs down, and it will incentivize companies to find ways to exclude or discourage expensive or high-cost beneficiaries from participating in those plans. The effect, then, may be that capitated managed care in Medicaid establishes an opposite perverse incentive from that of FFS: companies will face pressure to find ways to cut costs, and two ways to cut costs are to reduce utilization of care, even potentially much-needed care, and to discourage participation of more expensive members. It should be noted that there is little peer-reviewed research examining this issue (ibid.), and many states use risk-adjustment approaches and include quality metrics in contracting in an attempt to prevent just this sort of outcome from occurring. And, if MCOs expected members to be covered under the same plan for the long term, this might present an incentive for MCOs to prioritize preventive care to avoid higher costs down the road. However, Medicaid experiences high degrees of churn, with members moving from eligibility to ineligibility over time and switching plans.

An additional objection, which will be introduced here but more fully fleshed out in Section V, is that managed care in Medicaid may incentivize rent-seeking behavior. Rent-seeking, as explicated by Tullock (1967) and Krueger (1974), can be understood as "the fact or practice of manipulating public policy or economic conditions as a strategy for increasing profits" (Lexico n.d., n.p.). In the context of Medicaid managed care, rent-seeking might take multiple forms. MCOs might use resources to get state governments to expand the scope of managed care in Medicaid, including new populations or groups not previously covered in managed care. Companies might lobby the government to ensure that they are given managed care contracts. Once they have business, companies could proactively lobby the government to get higher capitated rates before signing contracts, or, in the case of losses, they could retroactively seek higher rates to recoup some of the loss. It is not clear that profit motives would push private companies only to cut costs and improve quality, as seems to be the traditional narrative. Rather, profit motives operate in complex ways. They might push companies to cut costs, but they might also push companies to simply try to get more money from the government. These forms of rent-seeking are distinct from those that exist in a FFS system. Providers have a clear incentive to lobby for higher reimbursements from Medicaid, for example, but in a FFS system, there is no clear reason for health insurance companies to lobby Medicaid. In a managed care system, there may still be such provider lobbying for higher reimbursements—as many states still set fee schedules used by MCOs to pay providers—and there is then additional incentive for health insurance companies to lobby Medicaid, as in the above examples.

There is little or no research on any of the objections to managed care in Medicaid mentioned above (Medicaid and CHIP Payment and Access Commission n.d.; Sparer 2012; Congressional Budget Office 2018; Goldsmith, Mosley, and Jacobs 2018b). The next section will review available literature on savings in Medicaid managed care.

LITERATURE REVIEW

Despite the optimistic theoretical expectations of savings for risk-based capitated managed care in Medicaid, results are generally far from positive. Most of the research into whether Medicaid managed care programs lead to savings for states has been done by consulting firms paid by MCOs or health plan advocacy groups like America's Health Insurance Plans (Sparer 2012). One report by Sparer (2012) reviewed available literature, including both academic and non-academic research, on Medicaid managed care savings and quality impacts. That literature review found mixed results and concluded that Medicaid managed care does not yield savings except in very specific circumstances for certain states, largely as a result of their own generous benefits prior to the transition to managed care. In general, Sparer found that Medicaid managed care is either cost neutral or may actually be more expensive than FFS.

Two noteworthy peer-reviewed studies use national-level data, not specific state programs, to consider the impact of managed care on Medicaid spending. Duggan and Hayford (2013) found "that shifting Medicaid recipients from fee-for-service into MMC [Medicaid Managed Care] did not on average reduce Medicaid spending. If anything, our results suggest that the shift to MMC increased Medicaid spending and that this effect was especially present for risk-based HMOs" (ibid., 505). Perez (2018) found, contrary to other findings of limited or no savings in national estimates of Medicaid managed care savings, that "a 10% increase of managed care enrollment reduces state Medicaid spending by 2.94%" (Ibid., 1).

Duggan and Hayford (2013) base their analysis on Medicaid enrollment, managed care enrollment, and spending data for all states from 1991 to 2009.

One concern with this span of data is that substantial changes to Medicaid have been made since the end of that time period: states have expanded the scope of managed care in Medicaid, and many states have expanded Medicaid eligibility via the *Affordable Care Act*. Using an ordinary least squares regression (OLS) with fixed state and year effects and state-specific time trends, they examine the relationship between the fraction of state Medicaid recipients in managed care and state spending on Medicaid. Selection into managed care is probably not random—states, counties, and individual recipients presumably made their decisions relating to managed care plans for specific reasons. As such, there may be systematic differences between states with more or less managed care, and thus simple OLS approaches might be less appropriate. To that end, they also use an instrumental variable approach that allows them to instrument enrollment in managed care using state or county managed care mandates. Standard OLS results indicate managed care costs more than FFS; instrumental variable methods found no statistically significant result. In either case, no findings suggested savings.

Perez (2018, 4) uses "a novel dataset of Medicaid enrollment, spending, and fiscal stress in forty-eight states gathered from multiple CMS publications and other sources from 1998 to 2008." One primary contribution by Perez, other than findings that differ significantly from other peer-reviewed academic literature, is the method by which Perez estimates savings from managed care and the nature of the populations being compared. Perez assesses the impact of managed care across all populations and in all states except for Hawaii and Alaska. The study uses a dynamic panel framework, which is a novel treatment of Medicaid managed care. Perez finds savings in Medicaid in several different and increasingly robust specifications of the model.

Other than the recent paper from Perez, the consensus in the literature seems to be that there is little peer-reviewed evidence indicating savings in Medicaid managed care. There are a variety of reasons that capitated managed care might not be saving states money compared to their FFS systems. Some of those reasons are programmatic in nature and might be due to details in the managed care systems. These reasons will be discussed next. Other reasons relate to the incentive issues with which this chapter will engage; those reasons will be addressed in sections IV and V.

Goldsmith, Mosley, and Jacobs (2018b) discuss a variety of unanswered questions with regard to Medicaid managed care, including several issues that could impact managed care savings. First, administrative savings may be limited if states have to maintain state-level administration for areas of the state or populations that are not covered by MCOs. That is, even if managed care is more administratively efficient than a state-run system, unless MCOs cover the entire population of Medicaid beneficiaries in the state, states must maintain IT infrastructure and networks to cover the remainder of beneficiaries, which limits capacity for administrative savings.

Second, savings in many states will be limited by the degree to which states build savings assumptions into their capitation rates. In some states, MCOs do not bid in a competitive process on capitation rates themselves—that is, the state sets capitation rates, and there is no MCO competition to lower rates. States typically have actuaries that help them set rates based on standards of actuarial soundness; the rates are based on data from prior years in the Medicaid program, with different types of adjustments applied that might vary by state. Adjustments might include risk adjustment, adjustment to account for anticipated future medical cost trends, adjustment for completion of data (incurred but not reported analysis, or IBNR), fee schedule adjustments, and managed care savings, to name a few. Once preliminary rates are set, there might be an opportunity for MCO, state, and federal government feedback; then, rates are finalized. In most states, finalized rates are set for all MCOs that want to participate. Thus, there is no price competition on the part of MCOs to win contracts. Because there is no competition to offer lower prices to the state to win business, the primary force working to lower capitation rates is the state's selection of the managed care savings assumption—the percentage decrease in rates they assume will occur due to private care management. If states set an aggressive savings assumption in the rates, they may stand to have higher savings; if savings assumptions are less aggressive, savings will be lower.

An additional issue that may limit the ability of managed care to yield savings relates to the type of contracting used by MCOs themselves when working with providers. Despite the incentive-based ideas behind risk-based capitated managed care, many MCOs have historically used a standard FFS approach to pay providers. That is, MCOs will establish their own care management and gatekeeping practices to restrict access of patients to specialists or broader networks or to encourage patients to utilize preventive care services prior to requiring more expensive treatments. However, when it comes to patients actually visiting providers, MCOs commonly pay providers just as the state does in a FFS system: based on a pre-established set of fees. Despite the incentives present in risk-based managed care for MCOs to manage care in a way that reduces costs, having what are ultimately decentralized FFS payments means providers themselves do not necessarily have any incentive to change the types of services they offer or to focus more on preventive services than on more expensive reactive treatments later. Embedding a sort of decentralized FFS system within risk-based capitated managed care may limit the effectiveness of such managed care programs. Note that there are examples of innovative payment structures used by MCOs to avoid this problem; this is just an issue that will occur for MCOs that use standard FFS payment with their providers. This is not to say that MCOs have no innovative payment solutions; there are subcapitation arrangements and other approaches used to avoid the problems inherent to FFS systems. However, in at least some cases, MCOs do seem to use simple decentralized FFS payment systems to pay providers.

Layton, Ndikumana, and Shepard (2018) offer an excellent discussion of the structure of competition in Medicaid managed care markets. While MCOs may not typically compete to offer lower rates to the state, as noted in Goldsmith, Mosley, and Jacobs (2018a), the Layton paper notes two additional approaches that are used to induce price competition in Medicaid managed care.

First, during the procurement process, states can select MCOs based on price or quality metrics. While states may tend to set their own capitation rates, they can look to the historical experience of an MCO to get information about that MCO's performance and the price at which they can operate in the state; that information can both inform decisions about which MCOs to choose and at what level to set rates/aggressiveness of savings assumptions.

Second, in managed care systems, Medicaid recipients can often select their plans. When recipients do not choose a plan, states may assign them automatically. The auto-assignment process by which recipients are assigned to plans can itself be used as a negotiation tool with MCOs to encourage lower prices or higher quality. Such an approach would be preferable to that currently taken by the twenty-three states that auto-assign passive recipients to plans with the lowest share of active enrollments to balance enrollment across all plans.

"This method has the odd (and likely perverse) effect of favoring plans that actively choosing enrollees have signaled to be less desirable. Given the high rates of auto-assignment in many states (45% in the median state), a state's decision of how to allocate these enrollees is likely to have a significant effect on MMC plan behavior" (Layton, Ndikumana, and Shepard 2018, 552).

This discussion of potential sources of price competition constitutes a useful segue into Section IV, which will discuss competition and price in Medicaid managed care and offer a perspective from literature on the knowledge problem.

COMPETITION, PRICES, AND THE
KNOWLEDGE PROBLEM

While Layton, Ndikumana, and Shepard (2018) outline a few ways price competition might be induced by states, it is worth observing that the examples are not currently common practice—note that twenty-three states use the perverse incentive auto-assignment system mentioned above instead of one that might be more aptly used for contracting incentives. And insofar as states are setting capitation rates in a uniform way for all participating MCOs, competition is less efficiently affecting prices than it otherwise might, if it is doing so at all.

Managed care might save states money for a host of reasons: more efficient care management might lead to more preventive, cheaper care and healthier members; MCOs might contract more efficiently with healthcare providers than would the state; and MCOs might find innovative approaches to cut costs and improve quality. While any of these might be possible, these are just programmatic changes. That is to say, states could create care management systems and administer those systems themselves (and some have). States could create innovative payment structures with providers that avoid FFS arrangements, even absent capitated managed care plans. States could improve their contracting and get better rates with providers just as private companies could. The primary difference between MCOs and states is not that MCOs have those capacities and states do not; rather, the primary difference relates to the nature of MCOs as (typically) for-profit enterprises with different types of incentives compared to state Medicaid agencies. MCOs, as private, for-profit companies, seek profits; their CEOs may answer to shareholders and investors. State agency employees answer to the state legislature, maybe to a governor, and ultimately to the state's taxpayers. One factor that is critical to distinguishing between the expected performance of a private MCO versus the state is the degree to which competition features in the market. If private companies participate in a market, but the market lacks substantive competition, then the primary incentives to behave more efficiently, and specifically to behave differently than would the government, cease to function.

Setting aside the potential sources of price competition noted above and excepting states that allow MCOs to compete to offer lower rates (most do not), in general, managed care organizations do not compete on prices in state Medicaid markets. They might compete to offer better quality services to the state to win a contract or offer better services to recipients to encourage recipients to enroll in their plans, but that competition does not generally affect the pricing of capitation rates. Because many states set their capitation rates—their prices—the rates/prices do not ultimately reflect competitive market forces. This leads to one of several knowledge problems endemic to Medicaid programs with which this chapter will engage.

Kiesling (2015) outlines two formulations of Hayek's knowledge problem: First, the "Complexity knowledge problem. The difficulty of coordinating individual plans and choices in the ubiquitous and unavoidable presence of dispersed, private, subjective knowledge" (para. 8). Second, the "Contextual knowledge problem. The epistemic fact that some knowledge relevant to such coordination does not exist outside of the market context" (para. 9). Because knowledge is dispersed among many different people, Hayek observed, "'the man on the spot' cannot decide solely on the basis of his limited but intimate knowledge of the facts of his immediate surroundings. There still remains the problem of communicating to him such further information as he needs to fit his decisions into the whole pattern of changes of the larger economic system" (Hayek 1945, 524–525). The primary thrust of this criticism is aimed toward central planning. Hayek argued that (1) no central planner could ever successfully aggregate all the dispersed knowledge of society in order to plan economic activity for the society as effectively as the decentralized society itself would otherwise do, and (2) even if a central planner could aggregate all the explicit knowledge, some knowledge only exists in market contexts, and absent market transactions such knowledge ceases to exist, so a central planner could not access it. The solution to the problem of coordinating between all the dispersed bits of knowledge, Hayek instead proposed, was the price system. Price is a surrogate for all the dispersed knowledge that contributes to it (Kiesling 2015). Price confers information about scarcity and value, and it accounts for supply and demand dynamically.

One implication of this perspective is that, while prices are a solution to the problem of coordinating dispersed knowledge, the solution functions only insofar as prices are free to fluctuate based on the dispersed knowledge (i.e., as prices grow more rigid or fixed, they function less well as a knowledge surrogate and are less useful for coordination).

In a managed care system with capitation rates set by the state, prices are not free to fluctuate. Further, prices may have very little relation to market forces at all. Rather than being a function of the supply of managed care services and the demand for those services, prices are typically set based on Medicaid claims and enrollment experience from previous years, with a variety of adjustments included. States may have good reason for this: if MCOs could bid competitively on rates, rates might be set at a level so low that MCO costs would be higher than their revenue, and MCOs would be forced to leave the market, potentially causing instability for many Medicaid recipients in the state. (This has happened in rate-setting states without price competitive systems as well.) Avoiding instability might be an important goal for states; if such were the case, then price competition might be inappropriate. An analogous example of such behavior might be private insurance companies offering plans on the ACA's state exchanges. Policy instability, competition, and other factors led plans to set insufficient rates, which led to considerable rate hikes and/or plans exiting markets.

State Medicaid programs are subject to the knowledge problem in several other ways. One relates to prices faced by consumers of health care financed by Medicaid: recipients typically are not subject to either premiums or cost sharing in Medicaid plans, which means they do not face exposure to the cost of their care. This leaves individual Medicaid recipients largely incapable of assessing market prices for goods or services rendered (and might also lead to moral hazard concerns if care is not managed effectively, but that is a separate topic). While this is a knowledge problem for Medicaid, this is notably a feature, and not a bug, of the program. The intent of Medicaid is to provide health insurance coverage, and to thus pay for healthcare services, for people with low incomes or certain disabilities. If recipients are considered unable to pay for care, then insulating them from market prices for that care is purposeful. Even so, it is worth acknowledging here that this very protection from cost sharing and market prices also has strong implications for how Medicaid addresses and manages cost. In a private insurance plan, one powerful tool insurance companies can use is cost sharing via copays, deductibles, and coinsurance. By forcing members to pay a portion of their incurred costs, MCOs can check growth in demand for healthcare services. In Medicaid, MCOs often cannot use cost sharing arrangements; the result is that MCOs must appeal to care management or other tools considered above to manage costs instead.

Another major manifestation of the knowledge problem for Medicaid programs stems from the nature of Medicaid agencies as public bureaucracies: individuals in state agencies bear neither the costs nor the benefits of their decision-making. While the agency may be responsible for purchasing managed care services from MCOs, the agency is hardly the consumer in the transaction. Instead, the consumer is the Medicaid recipient whose care is being managed by the MCO. And while the agency disburses funds to MCOs, the agency is not itself the source of those funds. Those funds come from the state's taxpayers and taxpayers from across the United States. One implication of this problem is that agencies have limited ability to learn how well MCOs provide services to Medicaid recipients. Further, agencies may have difficulty learning how well the state's Medicaid program as a whole functions for its "consumers"—the state's Medicaid recipients. Forms of this objection might also apply to FFS Medicaid, given similar, though not identical, knowledge problems would exist in that system as well. The primary factor of difference in this case is that instead of the Medicaid agency lacking knowledge of how it provides services to recipients, the problem in a managed care setting is assessing how well a hired contractor does the same work. In addition to being a knowledge problem, this could also be a principal-agent problem. The Medicaid agency is in this case the principal making decisions for consumers, the agents.

Understanding whether state Medicaid programs are "successful" can itself be a difficult question. While not the primary goal of this chapter, a brief discussion will illustrate the complications involved. Ought Medicaid directors look to increasing Medicaid rolls as a sign of success? Medicaid is a counter-cyclical entitlement program, which means that in general, enrollment increases are tied to economic downturns, with the exception of recent Medicaid expansions. Ought directors look to cutting spending as a sign of success? Because the program is jointly financed by states and the federal government, that means any dollar saved in Medicaid saves the state at most 50 cents (and in many cases much less when the federal government's proportion of the bill is higher, as is the case with Medicaid expansion populations). Cutting spending might improve the state's budget outlook, but at least half of the savings are passed on.

One additional knowledge problem faced by Medicaid agencies relates back to the problem of the lack of price competition in managed care. Because prices are set, knowledge is unavailable to the agency when determining which firms receive managed care contracts. While Medicaid agencies can act based on available information relating to a firm's previous prices in other markets, or based on the firm's quality, lacking market-based pricing information leaves critical knowledge on the table. Given observations from the public choice literature discussed in Section V, it is also worth noting that politics can be considered an exchange process. If bidding is not competitive, favor trading or some other form of lobbying might influence contract allocation decisions.

BUDGETING, PUBLIC CHOICE, AND RENT-SEEKING BEHAVIOR

For a variety of reasons, some relating to features specific to Medicaid and some caused by the knowledge problems outlined previously, there are good reasons to expect general upward pressure on state Medicaid budgets. Because Medicaid is counter-cyclical, cutting budgets when times are good can lead to complications in an economic downturn if enrollment rises past the level supported by the budget. So, when times are bad, the tendency would be to push for higher budgets in case times get worse. When times are good, the tendency would be to maintain or push for higher budgets to prepare for a downturn and corresponding enrollment jumps.

When states look for line items to cut or reduce in order to improve their budget outlook, Medicaid is also not the easiest option. Remember that for every dollar saved in Medicaid, a state typically only sees up to 50 cents because the federal government also benefits from the savings. So, if a state wanted to save $50 million in their budget, they would have to cut at least $100 million (or potentially much more) to get those savings from Medicaid. For another program that was fully state-funded, cutting $50 million would actually yield $50 million in savings. While states may consider Medicaid when faced with budget cuts, other programs tend to yield savings more easily from a state budget perspective (regardless of the actual ease of finding savings in a specific program).

Public choice economics also informs the issue of Medicaid budgets. Because Medicaid agency employees cannot "learn" how to succeed at providing services in the way that firms do in a competitive marketplace (as noted in Section IV) where the survival mechanism is meeting consumer demand, they might instead tend toward a nonprofit survival mechanism: expanding their agency budget. This is a Niskanenian argument: bureaucrats will tend to be rational agents and thus maximize their agency budgets (Niskanen 1968). This can be difficult to measure empirically, but Kaiser Family Foundation surveyed Medicaid directors in fifty states on a variety of topics, and one critical finding in 2020 was that "[e]ven when state economic and budget conditions are more favorable, state Medicaid directors remain focused on the task of managing the Medicaid budget with a goal to constrain growth while preserving eligibility, covered services, and provider access" (Gifford et al. 2019, 79). When asked directly, Medicaid directors indicate that in times of favorable economic conditions they want to constrain budget growth, which might be some evidence against the Niskanenian perspective, though it is critical to note a distinction between Medicaid directors' stated goals and what actions they might take during such periods.

One additional complication, from a budget perspective, is that Medicaid presents a classic case of concentrated benefits and diffuse costs. Medicaid recipients and healthcare providers stand to benefit from additional spending in Medicaid, such as higher provider reimbursements. However, the costs of additional spending are diffused: all the taxpayers in a state bear the burden of the state's portion of Medicaid spending, and all the taxpayers in the nation and the nation's debt bear the burden of the federal share of each state's Medicaid spending.

The combination of issues raised here, including knowledge problems faced by state Medicaid agencies, public choice issues, and upward pressure on state budgets, all make the possibility of rent-seeking behavior on the part of MCOs stronger. While this chapter cannot conclusively demonstrate that rent-seeking behavior is going on, it will present a few arguments for the perspective. There are clear incentives for MCOs to engage in rent-seeking behavior, and some of those incentives flow directly from the structure of Medicaid and its knowledge problems. Rent-seeking might take two forms: (1) initial efforts to either create or oppose creation of a new rent and (2) attempts to partake of an already created rent.

Before proceeding to assess incentives for the second type of rent-seeking behavior, this chapter asks whether MCOs may have engaged in the first form of rent-seeking already. When Medicaid managed care was in its infancy and not yet as prevalent as it is today, there existed either no or almost no evidence, peer-reviewed or otherwise, about its effects on state budgets or outcomes. Most of the early research into Medicaid managed care was funded by MCOs or health insurance lobbying groups. Given that such evidence tended to find more positive outcomes than more recent peer-reviewed academic research have and that such research was used to justify massive expansions of Medicaid managed care, which has given private companies billions of dollars in profits (Goldsmith, Mosley, and Jacobs 2018b), it could be argued that funding for such research could itself be considered a form of rent-seeking behavior. There existed a massive untapped health insurance market, but before insurance companies could enter that market they first had to convince states to open their Medicaid programs to managed care. The health insurance industry funded research with findings that were pro-managed care and that were used to support further expansion of private managed care in Medicaid.

This is the most explicit example of potential rent-seeking behavior that might illustrate the more general point in this chapter, and it is worth noting that this may be tenuous. Rent-seeking ought properly also be socially costly because "resources could have been (but were not) used in pursuit of socially productive activities" (Laband and Sophocleus 2019, 51). It could certainly be argued that someone had to pay for the first research into Medicaid managed care, and of course companies were going to fund that research first. And the research was socially beneficial because it created knowledge regardless of the funding source. Here is only one response on that point: perhaps the source of the funding matters quite a bit in terms of the reliability of the research and for the types of research questions being asked. When surveyed by Pew, 58 percent of Americans indicated they trusted scientific results less when they found out those results were funded by industry (Johnson 2019), and one literature review in the *American Journal of Public Health* found that "corporate funding of research with commercial implications drives the research agenda away from public health priorities" (Fabbri et al. 2018, e15).

This is not to argue that all industry research is inherently rent-seeking. Rather, this perspective merely seeks to call into question the idea that there is a clear distinction between money spent on lobbying as nonproductive versus money spent on research and development as productive. In at least some cases, the lines between research and lobbying may be blurred, and in those cases, research itself might also be lobbying and a form of rent-seeking.

Outside of this question about the first type of rent-seeking, there are several other opportunities for companies to engage in rent-seeking behavior of the second type. Companies might lobby Medicaid agency employees, state legislators, or even governors to increase the probability that they win managed care contracts with the state. Once companies have contracts, they might lobby any or all of those parties or even involved parties at the federal level, such as employees with the Centers for Medicare and Medicaid Services (CMS) who oversee state Medicaid managed care rate-setting processes, to encourage the state to set higher capitation rates. Even in states with actuarial rate setting that do not have price competition or rate negotiation, MCOs might threaten to leave the market if rates are set lower than they prefer, leading to instability for members and administrative problems for the state. Once they are an incumbent MCO, they might encourage the state to limit the number of MCOs allowed in the state's Medicaid program or create other regulations that benefit them to the detriment of other companies. If MCOs lose money because their rates did not cover their costs, they might lobby to get retroactive rate increases to regain some or all of those losses, despite the very nature of capitation being risk-based. In some cases, states might grant those requests.

That there is opportunity for rent-seeking behavior does not demonstrate incentive. That there are incentives to engage in such behavior is clear once the stakes are made apparent and the knowledge problems are illustrated. Of the $592 billion spent on Medicaid in FY 2018, over $265 billion was spent on managed care plans. In California alone in 2014 and 2015, MCOs made $5.4 billion in profits—that is profit, not revenue—and "two prominent investor-owned firms generated 7.1 percent and 8.2 percent margins on their contracts" (Goldsmith, Mosley, and Jacobs 2018a, para. 3). Consider these figures compared to the health insurance industry average profit margin of 1.1 percent and 0.6 percent in those years, respectively, and an average 3 percent margin over the last ten years (National Association of Insurance Commissioners 2020).

In addition to opportunity and motive on the part of MCOs, knowledge problems faced by the state Medicaid agencies also make rent-seeking difficult to avoid. Because in many states capitation rates are set rather than negotiated, the rates are subject to the lobbying behaviors described above, and the state agency lacks critical information because prices are not allowed to develop as a result of market competition. One of the two methods mentioned above that states can use to generate price competition among MCOs is to select MCOs based on price and quality metrics during procurement. One critical feature of that approach is that it requires a credible threat of exclusion from the market, which would imply that one of the best methods states can use to boost price competition may actually require states to limit market entry, at least somewhat inhibiting competition once firms have entered the market.

CONCLUSION

States have transitioned from state-administered FFS Medicaid systems toward privately administered Medicaid managed care since the 1990s despite very little peer-reviewed evidence indicating that such an approach improves states' budget outlooks. This chapter assesses several reasons why managed care might not generate savings as expected and offers several perspectives. First, managed care in Medicaid may not introduce competition or market forces as theorized, which would limit its effectiveness in reducing costs. Second, some of the knowledge problems and other issues that limit competition in managed care may also incentivize rent-seeking behavior on the part of MCOs. Different types of rent-seeking behavior are presented, and the chapter questions whether industry-funded research might be considered a form of rent-seeking behavior alongside more traditional lobbying.

Future research should assess an important question raised by this chapter: What influence did industry-funded research have on the transition to managed care from the 1990s to the present? This could be assessed through qualitative document reviews and interviews and potentially via quantitative analysis of the effects of specific studies on state decisions. A qualitative research project could interview current and previous state Medicaid agency employees to learn about their perspectives on managed care. Interviewing authors of industry-funded research might also yield interesting findings relating to their perspective on the motives for research or other issues.

While measurement of rent-seeking behavior is difficult, future studies also ought to attempt to track more typical rent-seeking behavior in the form of industry lobbying of politicians. Such quantitative analysis might be able to show effects of rent-seeking on Medicaid regulations or policy decisions. Social network analysis might examine the relationships between state Medicaid agency employees, legislators, and the MCOs they regulate as well as potential revolving doors between the agency and the MCOs.

REFERENCES

Centers for Medicare & Medicaid Services. n.d. "Medicaid." Accessed March 18, 2020. https://www.medicaid.gov/medicaid/index.html.

Congressional Budget Office. 2018. "Exploring the Growth of Medicaid Managed Care." August 07. https://www.cbo.gov/system/files/2018-08/54235-MMC_chartbook.pdf.

Duggan, Mark and Tamara Hayford. 2013. "Has the Shift to Managed Care Reduced Medicaid Expenditures? Evidence from State and Local-Level Mandates." *Journal of Policy Analysis and Management* 32 (3): 505–35.

Fabbri, Alice, Alexandra Lai, Quinn Grundy, and Lisa Anne Bero. 2018. "The Influence of Industry Sponsorship on the Research Agenda: A Scoping Review." *American Journal of Public Health* 108 (11): e9–16.

Gifford, Kathleen, Eileen Ellis, Aimee Lashbrook, Mike Nardone, Elizabeth Hinton, Rudowitz, Robin, Maria Diaz, and Marina Tian. 2019. "A View from the States: Key Medicaid Policy Changes – Results from a 50-State Medicaid Budget Survey for State Fiscal Years 2019 and 2020." Kaiser Family Foundation. http://files.kff .org/attachment/Report-A-View-from-the-States-Key-Medicaid-Policy-Changes.

Goldsmith, Jeff C., David Mosley, and Anne Jacobs. 2018a. "Medicaid Managed Care: Lots of Unanswered Questions (Part 1)." *Health Affairs Blog*, May 3. https:// www.healthaffairs.org/do/10.1377/hblog20180430.387981/full/.

———. 2018b. "Medicaid Managed Care: Lots of Unanswered Questions (Part 2)." *Health Affairs Blog*, May 4. https://www.healthaffairs.org/do/10.1377/ hblog20180430.510086/full/.

Gong, Dan, Lin Jun, and James C. Tsai. 2017. "Trends in Medicare Service Volume for Cataract Surgery and the Impact of the Medicare Physician Fee Schedule." *Health Services Research* 52 (4): 1409–26.

Hayek, F. A. 1945. "The Use of Knowledge in Society." *American Economic Review* 35 (4): 519–30.

Hinton, Elizabeth, Robin Rudowitz, Maria Diaz, and Natalie Singer. 2019. "10 Things to Know about Medicaid Managed Care." Kaiser Family Foundation. http://files.kff.org/attachment/Issue-Brief-10-Things-to-Know-about-Medicaid -Managed-Care.

Ikegami, Naoki. 2015. "Fee-for-Service Payment – an Evil Practice That Must Be Stamped Out?" *International Journal of Health Policy and Management* 4 (2): 57–59.

Johnson, Courtney. 2019. "Most Americans Are Wary of Industry-Funded Research." Pew Research Center Blog. October 4. https://www.pewresearch.org/fact-tank /2019/10/04/most-americans-are-wary-of-industry-funded-research/.

Kaiser Family Foundation. 2019. "Total Medicaid Spending." Kaiser Family Foundation, September 12. https://www.kff.org/medicaid/state-indicator/total -medicaid-spending/.

———. 2020. "Total Monthly Medicaid and CHIP Enrollment." Kaiser Family Foundation, February 11. https://www.kff.org/health-reform/state-indicator/total -monthly-medicaid-and-chip-enrollment/.

Kiesling, Lynne. 2015. "The Knowledge Problem." In The Oxford Handbook of Austrian Economics, edited by Peter J. Boettke and Christopher J. Coyne, 45–64. http://www.oxfordhandbooks.com/view/10.1093/oxfordhb/9780199811762.001 .0001/oxfordhb-9780199811762-e-3.

Krueger, Anne O. 1974. "The Political Economy of the Rent-Seeking Society." *The American Economic Review* 64 (3): 291–303.

Laband, David N. and John P. Sophocleus. 2019. "Measuring Rent-Seeking." *Public Choice* 181 (1): 49–69.

Layton, Timothy J., Alice Ndikumana, and Mark Shepard. 2018. "Chapter 18 - Health Plan Payment in Medicaid Managed Care: A Hybrid Model of Regulated Competition." In *Risk Adjustment, Risk Sharing and Premium Regulation in Health Insurance Markets: Theory and Practice*, edited by Thomas G. McGuire and Richard C. van Kleef, 523–61. San Diego, CA: Elsevier Science & Technology.

Lexico. "Rent-Seeking." https://www.lexico.com/en/definition/rent-seeking

Medicaid and CHIP Payment and Access Commission. n.d. "Managed Care's Effect on Outcomes." Accessed October 29, 2018. https://www.macpac.gov/subtopic/managed-cares-effect-on-outcomes/.

National Association of Insurance Commissioners. 2020. "U.S. Health Insurance Industry | 2019 Annual Results." https://content.naic.org/sites/default/files/inline-files/2019%20Health%20Industry%20Commentary_0.pdf.

Niskanen, William A. 1968. "The Peculiar Economics of Bureaucracy." *The American Economic Review* 58 (2): 293–305.

Pauly, Mark V. 2019. "Will Health Care's Immediate Future Look a Lot Like the Recent Past?" American Enterprise Institute, June 7. https://www.aei.org/research-products/report/health-care-public-sector-funding/.

Perez, Victoria. 2018. "Effect of Privatized Managed Care on Public Insurance Spending and Generosity: Evidence from Medicaid." *Health Economics* 27 (3): 557–75.

Smith, Gary, Cille Kennedy, Sarah Knipper, and John O'Brien. 2005. "Chapter 2: Essential Features of the Medicaid Program." In *Using Medicaid to Support Working Age Adults with Serious Mental Illnesses in the Community: A Handbook,* 19–30. Washington, DC: Office of Disability, Aging, and Long-Term Care Policy; Office of the Assistant Secretary for Planning and Evaluation; and US Department of Health and Human Services.

Sparer, Michael. 2012. "Medicaid Managed Care: Costs, Access, and Quality of Care." Robert Wood Johnson Foundation, September 4. https://www.rwjf.org/content/dam/farm/reports/reports/2012/rwjf401106.

Tullock, Gordon. 1967. "The Welfare Costs of Tariffs, Monopolies, and Theft." *Economic Inquiry* 5 (3): 224–32.

Chapter 5

Banking on the Masses

Mainstreaming Marginal Legal Entrepreneurship along with the Trappings of Transitional Gains, 1910–1940

Thomas B. Storrs

Consumer borrowing in the United States began to emerge from the margins of the financial mainstream, such as regulated commercial banks and insurance companies, just over a century ago, largely as the result of one man's battles on the borderlands above the law. These interactions on the edge of legality emerged dynamically as markets and cultural change pushed against governments and entrenched interests. The legal entrepreneur Arthur J. Morris evaded Gordon Tullock's "transitional gains trap" for over two decades by creating a new business that served American borrowers of modest means as American modernity emerged. Tullock (1975, 671) stated that "the profit record of these protected industries does not seem to differ systematically from the nonprotected." Arthur J. Morris, along with one of his protégés Thomas Boushall, sustained this enviable record for two reasons. First, they had not been granted a government privilege like the businesses to which Tullock refers. Instead, they innovated a new means of lending money barely within the law and then continued to improve upon this method. Second, their position on the edge of the law protected one flank from competition that might reduce their profit margins. The diminishment of profit margins came in the 1930s when their other flank, commercial banks, dove into consumer lending.

This chapter will present a case study of how markets better serve consumers when they operate nominally within the law. In the late nineteenth century, extralegal markets arose to serve the borrowing needs of salaried employees, while pawnshops continued to serve the needs of a wide range of borrowers. Small business owners relied on financing from friends and relatives. These classes of borrowers almost never received personal loans from commercial banks, which restricted their consumer lending to wealthy customers who also carried large business accounts with the banks. Usury laws constrained lenders by mandating the maximum interest rate they could charge. Arthur J. Morris, a lawyer practicing in Norfolk, Virginia, managed, through some obfuscation, to charge an effective interest rate sufficiently high to turn a profit and provide loans to classes of borrowers underserved by the legally sanctioned financial system. This innovation heralded and has-tened the massive rise in consumer debt that modernized America.

In Gordon Tullock's 1975 article "The Transitional Gains Trap" he uses the example of blue laws, where businesses cannot operate on Sundays, and the mercantile community's support for them. The businesses can accomplish their weekly sales with six-sevenths of the operating costs as opposed to being open seven days a week. The initial implementation of blue laws led to a transitory excess of profits for the mercantile community due to the reduced costs, but this soon returned to normal profits. Society would be better off with shopping seven days a week, but the mercantile community resists this change because their operating costs would increase. Thus, the blue laws are a trap with a deadweight loss and no way out (Tullock 1975, 673–674).

The Morris Plan institutions achieved moderately persistent excess profits through transitional gains along with societal gains. I will explain Tullock's understanding of operating hours through an entirely figurative example. Traditional commercial banks are open from 9:00 a.m. to 5:00 p.m. These are the daylight hours in which banking was accomplished for the socially acceptable: businesses and high-net-worth individuals. Many forms of con-sumer lending, such as immigrant banks, loan sharks, and salary lenders, were attacked by Progressive reformers, and we can think of them as taking place, once again figuratively, in the overnight hours. Morris's innovation was to find some daylight at the beginning and end of each day, not in the dark and not in the established financial institutions' time, in which to con-duct a consumer lending business. He could rest assured that he would have no legal competition in the nighttime hours and that the existing bankers would keep to their regular schedules completely in the daylight. Morris persisted in this legal and commercial twilight for decades—the second two decades of the twentieth century—before the traditional financial institutions joined him and competed away the excess profits.

While Arthur J. Morris brought consumer lending out of the shadows, Thomas Boushall, founder and president of the Morris Plan Bank of Virginia, completed the next step in mainstreaming consumer lending (i.e., making it operate at the same hours as commercial banks, figuratively, by using a Morris Plan framework in an institution with a commercial banking charter beginning in 1922). Both of these incremental steps aided the rise of U.S.

consumer lending in the twentieth century, which fueled purchases of auto-
mobiles, appliances, and college educations. Alongside economic growth and
greater financial autonomy, though, often came greater debt for working-
class Americans.

In 1910, working-class consumer lending in the United States remained
culturally and legally suspect—expensive, hard-to-scale, and occupying a
shadowy fringe of society. Yet by 1940, most commercial banks across the
country made consumer loans. Credit fueled the indomitable American consumer's indispensable contribution to economic growth and higher standards
of living. Change in consumer lending in the first half of twentieth-century
America came about through the interaction of cultural, social, economic,
legal, and political forces alongside the actions of specific individuals. By
illuminating the interaction between these forces, a useful and broadly applicable history emerges. Arthur J. Morris received training as a lawyer at the
University of Virginia and launched the Morris Plan of consumer lending in
1910 in Norfolk, Virginia. Wealthy individuals that had business relationships with commercial banks could secure personal loans, and poorer individuals with acceptable collateral could borrow from pawnbrokers (Easterly
2008). Salaried workers that needed to borrow money could not tap banks
and might not have appropriate collateral. The failure of lending institutions
to serve this market did not result from a failure of markets, but rather a
failure of government (Candela and Geloso 2018, 79). The usury rate—the
maximum interest rate that could be legally charged—prevented lenders from
profitably serving the working class.

Arthur J. Morris overcame these constraints by devising a system of lending that resulted in an effective interest rate much higher than the legal rate
prescribed by usury laws—6 percent at that time in Virginia. The Morris
Plan worked by lending a borrower, for example, $100 for one year. Six
percent was immediately prepaid as interest along with a 2 percent investigation fee. Thus, the borrower received $92 and then made twelve equal
monthly payments over the course of the year to pay back the $100. The loan
was unsecured except for the borrower's promise to repay along with two
cosigners—or co-makers in Morris Plan parlance—who agreed to repay the
loan if the borrower did not. The lender, the Morris Plan institution, earned
an effective interest rate more than double the legally prescribed ceiling of
6 percent (Robinson 1931). This increased profitability of unsecured consumer lending, and greater economies of scale allowed the Morris Plan to
rapidly spread across the country.

Fortuitously for Morris, the Russel Sage Foundation and other Progressive
Reform activists were simultaneously attacking his extralegal competitors,
the loan sharks or salary lenders. Morris positioned his enterprises as socially
beneficial and took advantage of the changing mores that questioned the

wisdom of usury laws to evade condemnation for his evasion of those laws. The elimination, or in some cases relaxation, of a millennia old tradition of usury laws represents a supracyclical phenomenon that continues, in fits and starts, to this day. The Morris Plan facilitated this transition by more firmly establishing the property rights of lenders and borrowers in loans than previous lending facilities run by loan sharks and salary lenders had done, highlighting the importance of secure property rights in a felicitously functioning debt marketplace (Dixit 2007). The property rights of the lenders were established by requiring cosigners on the loans. Loan sharks and salary lenders relied on violence and other extralegal forms of persuasion to enforce their contracts. By bringing consumer lending into legality, the loans became a better and more secure deal for consumers and a more profitable and stable business for lenders.

While Arthur J. Morris brought consumer lending out of the shadows of extralegality, Thomas Boushall brought consumer lending into the mainstream by using the platform developed in the Morris Plan and molding it effectively into the world of commercial banking. Boushall founded the Morris Plan Bank of Virginia (MPBoV) in 1922 and secured a banking charter from the state of Virginia. Many commercial banks took up consumer lending following the passage of the National Housing Act and its Title I of the Federal Housing Authority (FHA) in 1934. Title I encouraged commercial banks and other financial institutions to make loans to individuals through a provision that covered the first 20 percent of lending institutions' losses on home improvement loans during the Great Depression (Coppock 1940).

Through innovative advertising and effective regulatory arbitrage, though, Boushall placed the MPBoV ahead of the curve. As other banks expanded into consumer lending, Boushall expanded outward from consumer lending as a primary focus. The MPBoV's relative strength during the Great Depression allowed it to move into more traditional banking activities while continuing to advertise itself as prioritizing individuals. The MPBoV, though, secured a banking charter upon opening in 1922. This meant, unlike most Morris Plan institutions, the MPBoV could accept demand deposits rather than selling investment certificates, thus expanding its sources of funds.

With the increasing prevalence of commercial banks in consumer lending, the late 1930s, through a combination of market opportunities and the incentives provided by FHA Title I to commercial banks, saw the decline of industrial banks (i.e., banks without a formal banking charter that operated under general incorporation laws or special industrial banking laws depending on the state, of which the Morris Plan institutions constituted the majority as standalone entities). The Morris Plan ushered consumer lending from the legal wilderness to the financial mainstream. Industrial banks operated under a cornucopia of legal arrangements in different states. While the MPBoV secured a banking charter at its inception in 1922 in part to pursue legitimacy, many other institutions operated under a state's general incorporation laws. In a 1940 study, Raymond Saulnier stated that "an industrial banking company is held to be an institution which extends consumer loans repayable on an instalment basis, and obtains at least part of its working funds from the acceptance of deposits or the sale of investment certificates" (Saulnier 1940, 12).

BACKGROUND

This study fills a lacuna between current and past scholarships while also centering the discussion on the ways in which public policy affects and is affected by the private and nonprofit sectors. Among this scholarship, first is Michael Easterly's UCLA dissertation, *Your Job is Your Credit*, about the rise of salary lenders in New York City and their eventual demise due to social movements and the Morris Plan (Easterly 2008). Second, Louis Hyman's *Debtor Nation* tracks the rise of consumer finance in the United States from the interwar period but entirely neglects the Morris Plan institutions as crucial innovators in this sector (Hyman 2011). Additionally, the borrowers in Easterly's account are the salaried "visible hands" in Alfred Chadler's *Visible Hands*, which tracks the rise of modern American business (Chandler 2002). Chandler and Oliver Zunz, in *Making America Corporate*, follow a rise in the systemization of American business that came late to the fragmented financial industry (Zunz 1992).

On the subject of financial innovation, many historians have focused on the 1960s as a key period at the beginning of financial deregulation in the United States (Storrs 2019; Rose 2019). While that period leads neatly to today, such a periodization focuses heavily on commercial banks. The legal historian John Coffee proposed a theoretical regulatory sine curve in which regulations tightened in the immediate aftermath of a crisis and then slowly loosened until the next crisis (Coffee 2012). Also, the FHA's Title I encouraged and subsidized greater consumer lending to stimulate the economy in the depths of the Great Depression. On net, this resulted in a deregulation and expansion of consumer lending in a crisis counter to some scholars' characterization of the paradigmatic government response to a crisis of increased regulation (Higgs 2012). While theoretically interesting, Morris Plan innovation does not follow these patterns. A more pertinent parallel can be found in the brewers of fifteenth-century Cologne, where profitable opportunities managed to overcome the transitional gains trap (Thomas 2009). Innovation came by way of moving within regulations, and crisis brought liberalization of consumer lending. The differences are attributable in part to the fact that consumer lending is generally not regarded as systemically important and, in fact, was not regarded as particularly important at all before the New Deal. The Morris Plan institutions did not have the political power to maintain their exclusive gains in consumer lending in the face of the federal government's desire to rapidly increase consumer lending by bringing in new lenders to the market, and the Morris Plan's profitable niche in consumer lending on the sidelines of the financial establishment became part of that establishment. This example illustrates how crises are an opportunity not just for more regulation but also to overcome the privileged positions of entrenched interests.

The historiography of the Progressive Era often neglects private businesses as actors. The Morris Plan, though, clearly represents an institution in line with the goals of many Progressives, who sought to eliminate extralegal lenders, such as immigrant banks, that they viewed as exploitative of working classes (Benton-Cohen 2018). This chapter will provide breadth to the historiography of the Progressive Era while also engaging the literature on the notion of origins for change. Michael Willrich's *City of Courts* examines Chicago's rationalization of its criminal justice and welfare systems and argues for the importance of local origins (Willrich 2003). The Morris Plan was developed in Norfolk, Virginia, and it relied on local control to administer its businesses even as it spread. At the other end of the spectrum is Daniel Rodgers's *Atlantic Crossings*. Rodgers delves into the extensive communications and innovations that were exchanged between Europe and North America (Rodgers 2001). While Arthur J. Morris claimed to have invented the Morris Plan, Michael Easterly effectively argues that credit is in fact due to a Russian immigrant named David Stein, who based the idea upon European precedents (Easterly 2008, 210). The issue of the morality of lending to the poor at relatively high interest rates persists in scholarly debates today, just as it did in the Progressive Era, with research showing that the poor can handle debt better than most experts expect (Allcott et al. 2021). Of course, Morris understood that borrowers shunned by traditional bank lenders were good credit risks.

The Morris Plan's reliance on the reputation of borrowers and their cosigners, rather than group characteristics, might have diminished racial disparities in access to credit. When lending against physical collateral, the race of the borrower proved less important to the lender, as argued by Martha Olney from data in the 1918–1919 BLS Consumer Purchases Survey. Olney (1998) argues that Black families had greater access to installment credit on durable goods that served as collateral than merchant credit that relied on the reputation of the borrower. Photos of MPBoV staff generally show exactly one African American member out of 20 to 40 staff members total, suggesting that serving Black borrowers represented a small but existent proportion of their lending business (Morris Plan Bank of Virginia n.d.). For working-class borrowers in general from the late 1910s to the Great Depression, the Morris

Plan represented the most significant new source of borrowing and fueled a boom in consumption that helped leverage America into modernity (Olegario 2016, 128–131).

Despite later claims, Arthur J. Morris did not invent the Morris Plan of industrial banking. Morris's contemporary fame and fortune also did not derive from especially brilliant financial acumen. Instead, he excelled at positioning his enterprise just inside the fence of legality and leveraging reputational capital to found a business model that suited his changing times. For a quarter-century, from 1910 to 1935, the Morris Plan revolutionized consumer finance in the United States and led directly to the world of consumer debt that Americans know today. This study will examine the point at which consumer and small business debt made a decisive jump into legality and social acceptability. This process of bringing extralegal activity into the legal realm offers a wide array of insights into public policy issues of both contemporary and historical concern. Though many persons may find a market process socially distasteful, societal welfare may potentially benefit from that process occurring in a legal manner. This study will also highlight the importance of legal regimes for understanding the constraints on economic innovation, financial or otherwise.

THE MORRIS PLAN IN ACTION

In order to appreciate the innovation that the Morris Plan represented, it is crucial to understand the way most Americans borrowed money prior to the plan. Pawnbroking existed since the fifth century in China and since the Middles Ages in Europe. Pawning goods served as the primary means to borrow money for the vast majority of nineteenth-century Americans. Historian Wendy Woloson thoroughly investigates the historical practices of pawnbrokers in the United States up until 1920. She recounts that what many historians view as a "fringe" activity constituted the mainstream of American life (Woloson 2009, 7). Arthur J. Morris changed small-scale lending by substituting intangible assets as collateral for tangible assets. A borrower's good name, along with those of her cosigners, thus replaced a timepiece, work tools, or a fine bonnet as the lender's protection against the failure to repay a loan.

The tenuous legality of the Morris Plan lending scheme rested on the benevolence of state authorities and a vigorous legal defense. Arthur J. Morris founded the first Morris Plan Company in 1910 in Norfolk, Virginia. Trained as a lawyer, he had already been making loans from his law office for the previous four years to those unable to obtain bank loans. His initial foray into lending proved remarkably successful, as every single bank loan he cosigned for borrowers was repaid. As his law partners became frustrated by his side projects, Morris opened a small lending office and cut the banks out of the lending process (Black 1961, 165).

While banks would not loan money to these borrowers, Morris found through his investigations that they "held steady jobs with fair earning power and were persons of good character" (Black 1961, 165). The loans in the Morris Plan relied on the character and earning power of the borrower plus the guarantees of at least two co-makers—what would be called cosigners today. The loans, though, differed from mutual aid societies in which there was a prior relationship between the lender and borrower. The Morris Plan investigated each borrower and was open to anyone with demonstrated earning power that could find co-makers of roughly equal or better financial status. In 1911, Morris copyrighted the Morris Plan name and sought to establish quasi-franchises in cities across the country. Most of the growth of the system occurred between 1911 and 1917, when seventy-one of the ninety-four units in existence in 1940 originated (Saulnier 1940, 15).

The efforts to expand the Morris Plan system began in a simple manner. Arthur J. Morris would go to a new city and convene a meeting with business and civic leaders. A group emerging from this meeting would set up a legal entity that conformed to the laws of that state and sell stock. The local leaders would subscribe to some of the stock and serve on the board of the local institution. This pattern was subject to wide variation. The parent company, the Industrial Finance Corporation (IFC), formed in 1914 and owned about 25 percent of the outstanding stock in local Morris Plan companies. By 1938, a large range of ownership levels arose as the IFC held controlling interests in eleven companies, minority shares in fifty companies, and no equity at all in twenty-nine others (Saulnier 1940, 17–18).

Historian Louis Hyman, in his book *Debtor Nation: The History of America in Red Ink*, argues that modern consumer credit did not take off until after World War I. The essential prerequisites were a relaxation in usury laws, the increase in consumer product availability (especially automobile financing), and the ability of lenders to buy and sell debt (Hyman 2011, 10–11). Without the ability to charge higher than legally allowable interest rates, lenders apparently considered lending to average workers to be unprofitable (Glaeser and Scheinkman 1998). The Morris Plan, in fact, found a way around the legal limits on usury almost a decade before that point.

Writing *in The American Economic Review* in 1931, Louis Robinson claimed that the Morris Plan charged an effective interest rate of approximately 19.2 percent. Robinson distilled the Morris Plan as "a scheme of lending money on endorsed notes at a high rate of interest with repayment in installments" (Robinson 1931, 222). Elsewhere, he called it "mainly a scheme to enable the lender to charge more than the ordinary legal or contract rates of interest in force in most states" (Robinson 1930, 241). Raymond Garver calculated an effective interest rate of 18.8 percent and a variety of figures in the high teens as arguably correct (Garver 1931, 694). While Robinson's curt style implies some distaste with the Morris Plan, he actually saw it as in line with the credit options for the class of borrowers served. He explained how the plan worked in this theoretical transaction:

> Let us suppose that a man wishes to borrow $100. If, after he has found two suitable endorsers or co-makers, his application is granted, the Morris Plan company or bank discounts his note for one year at the legal rate of interest plus a fee or commission usually of 2 or 3 per cent. The borrower will then be given, in case the legal rate is 6 per cent and the commission 2 per cent, $92. He purchases simultaneously from the company or bank on the installment plan two Class C certificates amounting in all to $100, agreeing to pay $1.00 a week on each of these. He gives these certificates to the company or bank as additional security for his note. When he has paid for these Class C certificates he is allowed the privilege of using them as a means of paying off his note. (Robinson 1931, 223)

The introduction of competition from commercial banks in consumer lending served both to legitimize Morris Plan companies and provide, in the longer term, a grave competitive threat. In the short term during the mid-1930s, the entry of commercial banks into the market, hastened by FHA Title I, took place alongside an increase in the business of Morris Plan companies. Although, it is difficult to disambiguate this trend from the concurrent economic recovery. Additionally, commercial banks appear to have catered to a slightly more affluent customer base (Harold 1938, 145).

Morris Plan companies operated under a wide variety of legal conditions owing to the constraints of the state laws where they operated. They managed, in some cases, to enjoy the approximate privileges of commercial banks, such as accepting quasi-deposits and making loans without the constraints of regulations (e.g., reserve requirements and strict adherence to usury laws). As commercial banks encroached on their territory in the mid-1930s, Morris Plan companies, in turn, expanded into the territory of commercial banks. In 1936, Morris Plan loans for all entities included about 13 percent in FHA Title I loans, which also served as a bridge for commercial banks into consumer lending. In 1936, the number of co-maker loans, the traditional vast majority of Morris Plan loans, dipped below half with the rest of the remainder coming from automobile, collateral (i.e., similar to pawns), and other forms (Harold 1938, 145–146). This convergence of business lines across distinct legal forms developed in a similar manner to the convergence of banks and non-banks in the field of interest-bearing deposits in the 1970s (Kane 1981).

Fidelity Saving and Trust opened in Norfolk, Virginia in 1910. This small institution served as the model for all Morris Plan institutions going forward. The minutes from the board meetings of this company remain extant and offer a window into the complexities of operating a novel type of lender. All loans went to the board for approval. The board also negotiated a complicated relationship between Fidelity and its legal counsel, the firm of Morris, Garnett, and Cotton, of which Arthur J. Morris was a partner ("Fidelity Savings and Trust Minute Book, 1911–1917," n.d., 19).

Early on, Fidelity did not adhere to a strict policy of only taking loans with co-makers. For example, on September 14, 1911, they approved a $1,000 loan to H. Sugarman with a deed of trust on two pieces of real property conditional on the loan not increasing beyond $1,200 and a guarantee from a third party to bid at least $14,000 on the properties in the event of foreclosure ("Fidelity Savings and Trust Minute Book, 1911–1917," n.d., 16). On November 16, 1911, M. H. Mills borrowed $75 with Arthur J. Morris as a cosigner and a diamond ring as additional collateral (ibid., 28). The former loan incorporated some elements of a building and loan association real estate loan, while the latter differed in some respects very little from the operations of a pawnbroker. Nonetheless, these types of early Fidelity loans comprised a minority of the transactions funded, and each incorporated a cosigner in some sense.

The loan to Miss Bessie Lasdan on November 23, 1911, was more typical of the types of loans that Fidelity made. She borrowed $200 with Marcus Cohen, S. A. Markel, and the Virginia Confectionary and Grocery Company serving as cosigners ("Fidelity Savings and Trust Minute Book, 1911–1917," n.d., 31). Also typical is the loan on December 28, 1911, to John Kyatt, a manager at the NY Cleaning Company. His two cosigners were two pilots, William Baulch and Cecil B. Guy (ibid., 38; Hill Directory Company 1911, 90, 251, 317).

In earlier years, these borrowers would have sought loans from loan sharks or pawn brokers. Michael Easterly (2008) explains the rise of the Morris Plan institutions as an inside-the-law response to the disreputable loan sharks. They also allowed borrowers without any acceptable collateral, or who desired not to risk such collateral if they had it, to secure loans. The awareness and zeal for reform against the loan sharks was developed in large part by the Russell Sage Foundation. Incorporated in 1907, the Sage Foundation raised awareness about the ills of workers caught in a mire of debt from salary lenders who often operated outside the law (ibid., 144). After a life of eleemosynary activities hamstrung by her husband's tightfistedness, the widow Margaret Olivia Sage gave $10 million to begin a foundation in her husband's memory. In line with the Progressive Era's emphasis on effective, data-based philanthropy, this new organization sought to systematically cure the ills of society.

At the beginning of the 1920s, Arthur J. Morris stood as a successful pioneer in consumer finance after a decade of phenomenal growth and innovation. Nonetheless, the investment certificates that he used to fund his loans could not attract sufficient funds to break into the mainstream of the financial community and continue the growth of Morris Plan institutions as industrial banks. The next step required further innovation and the translation of the profitable consumer lending formula to a commercial bank setting. This link, between Morris's successful negotiation of the limits of usury laws in the 1910s and the mainstreaming of consumer lending in the 1930s, was forged with his ambivalent support by Morris's protégé.

THE MORRIS PLAN GROWS UP IN VIRGINIA

In 1922, Thomas Boushall, a young veteran of both National City Bank and World War I, finagled a meeting in New York City with Arthur J. Morris. The young North Carolinian came out with a mission to try to buy up and consolidate Morris Plan franchises in North Carolina and Virginia. The new Morris Plan Bank of Richmond, as it was initially called, immediately ruffled feathers among the Morris Plan old guard. They began to pay interest on the loan payments by replacing the certificates in widespread use with a savings account. The new policy stated: "You assign your savings account as collateral to your loan, build it up to a sum equal to your loan and the savings account wipes out the loan at maturity. And we will pay you 3 percent interest per annum on your assigned savings deposits on a quarterly basis provided you make the required deposits regularly and on time" (Wessells 1973, 25–26). The new policy amounted to a shift toward amortization in consumer financing and a significant step on the road to adding respectability to the Morris Plan model.

When he arrived in Richmond in 1922, Boushall recalled seeing a large outdoor billboard that read: "Banking Centuries Old Today Stands Complete." Eighty percent of Americans did not have access to bank credit at that time, and that began to change, in large part through Boushall's actions. Commercial banks up until the Great Depression lent money almost exclusively to established businesses and wealthy individuals. Part of their preference stemmed from a bias against the creditworthiness of working-class borrowers. Another reason was the fixed costs of making a loan. As the loan got smaller, the fixed costs consumed a greater proportion of the loan, and the fixed costs of making a loan stood basically unchanged for millennia prior to that point.

Boushall took the initial Morris Plan concept, then active in thirty-seven states, and tweaked it into a form that was acceptable in a commercial bank. As banking came to embrace consumer lending in the 1930s, the MPBoV ventured into more traditional lines of business. In some ways, the Morris

Plan proved a victim of its own success as its services became less unique. Boushall understood the vast resources that were available with a commercial bank charter to serve the four-fifths of Americans who were cut off from traditional bank services. By the 1950s, virtually every commercial bank in the United States offered consumer credit along the lines that he pioneered. After Morris snuck consumer credit into legality, Boushall wriggled it into broad acceptance among established financial institutions. Referring back to the billboard from 1959, Boushall correctly stated that "These intervening 37 years seem to have refuted that concept" (Boushall 1959).

The Morris Plan made money by making small to medium-sized loans largely to individuals with no collateral beyond the borrower's and their cosigner's—co-maker in Morris Plan parlance—creditworthiness. After taking a discount of about $8 per $100 loaned (2 percent as investigation fee and 6 percent as interest), the borrower repaid the money in equal monthly installments. The MPBoV described this method by claiming: "Amortization banking is the adaption of an individual's necessities to his capacities" (Morris Plan Bank of Virginia n.d., "Confidential," 1). While such a scheme resulted in an effective interest rate far above the advertised rate of 6 percent, the Morris Plan made much of its heroic work in bringing reasonably priced borrowing to the masses. Before their arrival, "the business of helping the average man meet his obligations and keep his head above water was in the hands of fly-by-night salary buyers, usurious pawnbrokers, and loan sharks whose interest rates ranged from 240% to 1000% a year" (ibid., "Confidential," 1).

Throughout the 1920s, Boushall pushed for growth at the expense of profitability. The bank expanded throughout the state with branches from Roanoke in the Shenandoah Valley to Norfolk on the Atlantic Seaboard. The banking establishment in Virginia's reaction shifted from amused apathy toward the queer upstart to growing hostility as its assets approached the largest banks in the state and its footprint outpaced them all. However, the Norfolk and Roanoke branches required a backroom deal to come to fruition. In 1928, the banking establishment approached Boushall with a deal: they would allow the two new branches if he agreed with their legislation to limit interest in savings accounts to 4 percent. The newly named MPBoV had been paying 5 percent on deposits, greater than the 3 to 4 percent that all other banks in the state paid on savings accounts. In exchange for the two new branches, state legislation in 1928 capped interest rates on savings accounts at 4 percent. Boushall became a force to contend with in Virginia banking politics and fortuitously managed to lower the cost of funds just ahead of turbulent times (Morris Plan Bank of Virginia, n.d."Confidential," 39–43).

Marketing materials for Morris Plan loans suggested a myriad of ways to use the borrowed money. One pamphlet suggested dentist bills be paid for with a Morris Plan loan. "There is no red tape. You call at the bank or write for a simple application form which is immediately given together with a note to be signed by you and your co-makers, who may be relatives or friends having regular employment and salaries in keeping with the amount of the loan" (Morris Plan Bank of Virginia, n.d., "Paying Your Dentist on the Morris Plan").

While the MPBoV used the tagline "Bank for the Individual," it also cultivated business through a variety of marketing techniques. They stated up-front that their lending services should be treated as supplementary to traditional commercial banks because they did offer demand deposits or "commercial borrowing accounts." While their loans to individuals ranged from $50 to $10,000, corporations and firms could borrow between $500 and $50,000. The MPBoV marketing material gave examples of its success stories working with businesses. Dairy farms were particularly active borrowers. In one example, the MPBoV lent $3,000 to a farmer to buy more milk cows and accepted as security an endorsement from his wife and a lien on the new cows as well as an equal number of old cows. The farmer then deposited $250 per month from his increased milk sales for the next year to pay off the loan. The loan cost the farmer a 6 percent discount at the beginning, $180, and he received 3 percent interest on the $250 monthly principal payments once the loan was paid in full (ibid., "Building Business for Individuals, Firms and Corporations through the Morris Plan Bank").

The MPBoV also made marketing efforts explicitly targeting women. In a 1920s pamphlet with turquoise embellishments, the bank enumerated ways in which women used the Morris Plan because "in this modern age [. . .] [t]o take advantage of her new possibilities, woman must have the same financial backing that man enjoys, and the Morris Plan Bank, believing in the future of the American Woman, is always glad to help her accomplish her purpose" (ibid., "How Women Use the Morris Plan Bank," 6). The uses of a Morris Plan loan for a woman included home improvements, outstanding bills, household appliances, children's college tuition, and starting a business. In a 1930s brochure on heavy matte paper with elegant pastel pink wording entitled "She Holds the Key to Progress," the bank laid out its case with an illustrative example. They told the story of a woman who cannot understand why her family cannot save any money. Upon investigation, she discovers that many of their outlays go toward payments on small debts that her husband has accumulated. A Morris Plan loan allows her to consolidate the family's debt into a smaller monthly payment and put the difference into savings at the bank. The fictional housewife, of course, thought this plan was excellent: "Why that sounds wonderful. My husband said something not long ago about borrowing some money; but it seemed to me that it would make us just that much worse off. I never thought of it as really HELPING us to get ahead." As gendered and patriarchal as it may be, this brochure reveals that the bank sought new market opportunities in traditionally underserved communities, namely the half of the population that was not male. However, the 1929 Annual Report began with the salutation, "Gentlemen" (1929 Annual Report, 5).

One historian looks to 1928 as a banner year in consumer lending because Boushall's alma mater, National City Bank in New York, opened a consumer lending department (Hyman 2011). The MPBoV, though, had a head start in the daunting logistics of handling such a large quantity of loans. Consumer lending brought in customers who had never interacted with a bank before depositing or borrowing a small sum. The difference in costs, through interest and fees, between a small consumer loan and a large commercial loan reflected, for the most part, the increased personnel costs of servicing small loans rather than greater risk. In fact, the small consumer loans diversified risk by spreading it over a larger number of borrowers. As the MPBoV grew rapidly, it also had to hire many more staff per dollar lent than traditional commercial banks in order to process the large volume of loans with frequent payments.

The MPBoV also innovated with home improvement loans in 1926. This program served as a model for the Title I home loans under the FHA in 1934 during the depths of the Great Depression. The FHA actually brought Boushall to Washington, DC, to explain how to implement the program ((Wessells 1973, 72). These Title I loans served as the first experience with extensive consumer lending for most commercial banks in the United States. Under the program, the FHA insured lenders for the first 20 percent of their losses. These training wheels opened the doors to a profitable new stream of lending to consumers during the turbulent Great Depression years, and the MPBoV acted as a pioneer. The U.S. government rebuilt the financial system on the foundation laid over the previous two decades by Morris and Boushall. From a start barely within the bounds of the law, the crisis of the Great Depression provided the government with the means and opportunity to expand its reach by bolstering new lines of business for the country's stodgy commercial banks (Higgs 2012).

The 1929 report, coming on the heels of the October stock market crash, emphasized that the bank intended to stay true to the Morris Plan's three principles of operation: safety, service, and profits, listed in descending order of importance (1929 Annual Report, 5). A fourth principle, related to the three stated, underlay Thomas Boushall's modification into the mainstream of the Morris Plan: growth. In the previous fiscal year, MPBoV accounted for a quarter of the growth in resources among Virginia's 323 state-chartered banks. The bank also acquired locations in Wilmington, NC and Washington, DC. The eleven locations—four in North Carolina, one in DC, and six in Virginia—constituted an impressive interstate banking organization. In 1929, the bank also established a holding company controlled by the MPBoV to hold the assets outside of Virginia.

The MPBoV weathered the Great Depression by successfully competing for the savings of the community by offering a high rate of return and reassuring their depositors that their savings were safe. In a 1931 confidential pamphlet for employees, the bank laid out the other reasons "why the Morris Plan Bank cannot fail." The MPBoV counted first on the diversity of its lending, as between its founding and 1931, it lent $53 million to 182,000 people for an average loan per person of $291. The bank also carried high reserves that were nominally 5.1 percent of assets but 8.3 percent with the inclusion of non-withdrawable payments made on loans—the monthly principal payments. The required reserves were 3 percent against savings deposits.

The bank's roaring growth in the 1920s would have resulted in failure during the Great Depression had it been structured like a traditional bank. Most banks rely on demand deposits for most of their funding. Demand deposits, as the name implies, are available to the depositor whenever demanded. The MPBoV did not accept demand deposits and relied solely on savings deposits as well as borrowed money for some initiatives, such as its automobile lending program. These savings deposits carried with them a stipulation that, at the bank's discretion, withdrawals could be limited in a crisis. This funding structure made the bank more like a building and loan association—the largest home mortgage lenders in the country at the time—than a commercial bank (Morris Plan Bank of Virginia. n.d., "Confidential," 49). The annual report for 1932 showed a remarkable first decade. In 1932, the bank had $10.4 million in assets, 106 employees in five cities, and 29,400 savings accounts. Over the decade, the bank lent $66.8 million in 224,000 loans (1932 Annual Report, 61–62).

By 1938, the MPBoV began to fully shed its Morris Plan heritage. It was the sixth largest bank in Virginia and the 276th largest bank in the country. It began to accept demand deposits and joined the Federal Reserve. It used Title II of the FHA to make insured home mortgage loans with much longer maturities than traditional consumer loans that lasted a year or two at most (Wessells 1973, 83–89). In short, it started to look and act like other banks.

As other banks became more like the MPBoV by adding a consumer lending function, it became more like traditional banks. The extraordinary profits afforded by the Morris Plan's innovations faded away as other financial institutions absorbed and employed their knowledge.

As Gordon Tullock argued in his article "The Transitional Gains Trap," firms granted a special privilege by government privilege will not make extraordinary profits in the long term (Tullock 1975). Morris and Boushall innovated their way into special privileges around usury laws generally and then extended this into commercial banking, respectively. In the span of about a decade in each case, their firms achieved extraordinary growth. As their special knowledge became more widely dispersed, their special advantages faded away. In the long run, Morris and Boushall became irrelevant as their innovations dispersed. But to understand change over time in American financial history and how new long-term equilibria are established, the contributions of Morris and Boushall are essential.

REFERENCES

Allcott, Hunt, Joshua Kim, Dmitry Taubinsky, and Jonathan Zinman. 2021. "Are High-Interest Loans Predatory? Theory and Evidence from Payday Lending." w28799. Cambridge, MA: National Bureau of Economic Research. https://doi.org/10.3386/w28799.

Benton-Cohen, Katherine. 2018. *Inventing the Immigration Problem: The Dillingham Commission and Its Legacy*. Cambridge, MA: Harvard University Press.

Black, Hillel. 1961. *Buy Now, Pay Later*. New York: William Morrow and Company.

Boushall, Thomas C. 1959. *Banking for Main Street, U.S.A. (1922-1959): An Address at Richmond*. New York, San Francisco, and Montreal: The Newcomen Society in North America.

Candela, Rosolino A. and Vincent J. Geloso. 2018. "The Lightship in Economics." *Public Choice* 176 (3–4): 479–506. https://doi.org/10.1007/s11127-018-0573-x.

Chandler, Alfred Dupont. 2002. *The Visible Hand: The Managerial Revolution in American Business*. 16. print. Cambridge, MA: Belknap Press of Harvard University Press.

Coffee, John C. Jr. 2012. "Policitcal Economy of Dodd-Frank: Why Financial Reform Tends to Be Frustrated and Systemic Risk Perpetuated." *Cornell Law Review* 97: 1019.

Coppock, Joseph D. 1940. *Government Agencies of Consumer Instalment Credit*. National Bureau of Economic Research, Inc.

Dixit, Avinash K. 2007. *Lawlessness and Economics: Alternative Modes of Governance*. 2. print., and 1. paperback print. The Gorman Lectures in Economics. Princeton: Princeton University Press.

Easterly, Michael Edward. 2008. "Your Job Is Your Credit: Creating a Market for Loans to Salaried Employees in New York City, 1885-1920." Dissertation. UCLA.

"Fidelity Savings and Trust Minute Book, 1911-1917." n.d. Norfolk, VA. Virginia Museum of Culture & History, Richmond, VA.

Garver, Raymond. 1931. "The Mathematics of Small Loans." *The American Economic Review* 21 (4): 693–95.

Glaeser, Edward L. and Jose Scheinkman. 1998. "Neither a Borrower Nor a Lender Be: An Economic Analysis of Interest Restrictions and Usury Laws." *The Journal of Law and Economics* XLI (April): 36.

Harold, Gilbert. 1938. "Industrial Banks." *The Annals of the American Academy of Political and Social Science* 196: 142–48.

Higgs, Robert. 2012. *Crisis and Leviathan: Critical Episodes in the Growth of American Government*. Independent Institute.

Hyman, Louis. 2011. *Debtor Nation: The History of America in Red Ink. Politics and Society in Twentieth-Century America*. Princeton: Princeton University Press.

Kane, Edward J. 1981. "Accelerating Inflation, Technological Innovation, and the Decreasing Effectiveness of Banking Regulation." *The Journal of Finance* 36 (2): 355–67. https://doi.org/10.1111/j.1540-6261.1981.tb00449.x.

Morris Plan Bank of Virginia. n.d. "Morris Plan Bank of Virginia Collection." Virginia Museum of Culture & History, Richmond, VA.

Norfolk & Portsmouth, Virginia 1911 Directory. 1911. Hill Directory Co. https://cdm15987.contentdm.oclc.org/digital/collection/p15987coll2/id/47.

Olegario, Rowena. 2016. *The Engine of Enterprise: Credit in America*. Cambridge, MA: Harvard University Press.

Robinson, Louis N. 1930. "Review of Review of The Morris Plan of Industrial Banking, by Peter Herzog." *Journal of Political Economy* 38 (2): 241–43.

———. 1931. "The Morris Plan." *The American Economic Review* 21 (2): 222–35.

Rodgers, Daniel T. 2001. *Atlantic Crossings: Social Politics in a Progressive Age*. Cambridge, MA; London: Belknap.

Rose, Mark H. 2019. *Market Rules: Bankers, Presidents, and the Origins of the Great Recession*. 1st ed. American Business, Politics, and Society. Philadelphia: PENN/ University of Pennsylvania Press.

Saulnier, Raymond J. 1940. *Industrial Banking Companies and Their Credit Practices*. National Bureau of Economic Research, Inc.

Storrs, Thomas B. 2019. "'This Will Drive Them Wild. . .Wild': Comptroller James Saxon's Transformation of American Banking, 1961-1966." *Management & Organizational History* 14 (4): 408–22. https://doi.org/10.1080/17449359.2019 .1683035.

Thomas, Diana W. 2009. "Deregulation despite Transitional Gains: The Brewers Guild of Cologne 1461." *Public Choice* 140 (3–4): 329–40. https://doi.org/10.1007 /s11127-009-9420-4.

Tullock, Gordon. 1975. "The Transitional Gains Trap." *The Bell Journal of Economics* 6 (2): 671–78. https://doi.org/10.2307/3003249.

Wessells, John H. 1973. *The Bank of Virginia: A History*. Charlottesville: University Press of Virginia.

Willrich, Michael. 2003. *City of Courts: Socializing Justice in Progressive Era Chicago. Cambridge Historical Studies in American Law and Society*. Cambridge, UK; New York: Cambridge University Press.

Woloson, Wendy A. 2009. *In Hock: Pawning in America from Independence through the Great Depression*. Chicago; London: The University of Chicago Press.

Zunz, Olivier. 1992. *Making America Corporate: 1870–1920*. Paperback ed. Chicago: University of Chicago Press.

Part III

INTERNATIONAL POLICY

Chapter 6

Taking Time and Distinct Law Types Seriously

How the Effects of CSO Laws Vary by Type and Unfold over Time

Anthony J. DeMattee

What laws and policies, if any, help or hinder civil society? A growing number of human rights defenders have called attention to the laws that regulate civil society organizations (CSOs) and caution that these laws are part of a global crackdown on the freedom of voluntary association. This chapter asks two questions of this increasingly researched topic. First, do laws and restrictions that appear different in content also have different outcomes? I argue that CSO laws that are qualitatively different have varying effects on civil society, democratization, and foreign funding levels. The second question asks, how quickly and completely do such laws affect society? While some study CSO laws as having an immediate and complete effect on society, I maintain an important temporal dynamic is at play. This analysis uses a specialized time series model to understand how quickly and for how long changes in CSO laws affect societies. The data are a sample of 2,464 country-year observations from 135 low- and middle-income countries (1994–2013). My findings suggest that the CSO laws studied here—specifically, three distinct types of foreign funding restrictions—affect societies in minimal ways and distribute those effects over decades. These impacts are minimal for two reasons: First, it demonstrates that it is insufficient to study only a narrow type of legal provision without accounting for other rules within the larger regulatory regime. Second, these laws may have stronger impacts on more granular indicators such as the number of CSOs operating in a country and the amount of money they spend. Readers should not interpret these findings to mean that CSO laws are unimportant. Quite the contrary, CSO laws profoundly shape the degree to which citizens can enjoy the fundamental human right to freely and voluntarily associate. How and why governments use laws to shape the government-CSO relationship is a concerning matter that we cannot afford to misunderstand. This chapter argues that studying only one type of foreign funding restriction oversimplifies CSO laws to the point of distortion.

Drawing on the metaphor of a greenhouse helps us understand the conditions under which CSO laws shape the government-CSO relationship.[1] The metaphor is useful in four ways. First, greenhouses minimize pests and provide a conducive environment for growth. In this metaphor, greenhouses represent the legal institutions that shape the environment for the civil society garden to grow. The legal institutions prevent profiteers from abusing the legal form, provide CSOs with rights, and incentivize individuals to start and join voluntary associations. Second, merely having a greenhouse does not guarantee a healthy garden. Including the freedom of association in a constitution or making an international commitment to safeguard human rights does not guarantee such civil liberties. Third, like greenhouses, CSO laws do not erect themselves. Like gardeners, governments are responsible for enacting and maintaining the legal institutions in which civil society exists and grows. Fourth, not all greenhouses are identical, and a greenhouse ideal for one climate is not necessarily appropriate for another. Likewise, the legal institutions erected in liberal democracies may look quite different from those built under autocratic regimes. The former is likely to have all the qualities our mind's eye associates with the perfect greenhouse: optimal growing conditions, ample room to expand, no pests, and minimal disturbance from gardeners. An autocratic gardener, by contrast, builds greenhouses that fail to keep out pests, overheat certain plants, and deny the garden the elements it needs to flourish.

This chapter contributes to the "closing space" literature, a research program studying the global trend in which governments enact restrictive CSO laws to repress and weaken civil society. This pattern of legalized repression occurs when governments enact laws to monitor, repress, and control CSOs within their borders (Carothers 2006; Wiktorowicz 2000; Gershman and Allen 2006; Swiney 2019; Christensen and Weinstein 2013; DeMattee 2020). Discourse within the research suggests that democracies pass permissive laws that help CSOs and protect the freedom of association (World Bank 1997; Kiai 2012), while nondemocratic regimes enact restrictive laws that weaken civil society and undermine the bulwark (Wolff and Poppe 2015; Mendelson 2015; Gyimah-Boadi 1998; Tripp 2017). My primary contribution in this chapter is to assess the "effectiveness" of these CSO laws in 135 countries by replicating data from two studies. I accomplish this by evaluating CSO laws' predicted effects on three concepts comparable across societies: civil society vitality, level of democracy, and foreign funding received. To be precise, I analyze CSO laws as policy interventions and ask the following questions:

Do different legal restrictions have different effects? And how quickly do those legal restrictions affect society? I predict that restrictive legal provisions will dampen civil society vitality, reduce the level of democracy, and decrease foreign funding received. To preview my findings, my analysis finds that restrictive legal provisions have only a nominal impact on the societal indicators we expect them to affect. The implication is that attempts to weaken society with a CSO law—specifically, a foreign funding restriction—will not have a full and immediate impact. My findings also indicate that the effects of legal restrictions vary by type and that those effects unfold over several years and sometimes decades.

The next section of this chapter reviews civil society theory and discusses the "closing space" argument. I then discuss the research design, which uses a specialized time series model to evaluate the impact of these legal restrictions over 20 years in 135 low- and middle-income countries. After discussing the findings, I close the chapter with a challenge to analysts for better conceptualizations within this particular policy domain. Fundamental freedoms are at stake, and research should rise to meet this challenge.

THEORY

Many disciplines give civil society serious consideration when discussing important issues such as governance, democracy, interpersonal trust, and political behavior (Tocqueville [1835; 1840] 2010a; Putnam 1993; Fukuyama 1995; Aligica 2018; Skocpol and Fiorina 1999; Warren 2001; Grzymała-Busse 2015; E. Ostrom 1990; Mutunga 1999; Johnson and Koyama 2019; Linz and Stepan 1996). Civil society is a broad concept that includes interpersonal ties within society as well as between groups of men and women. Hegel ([1821] 1991) defined *civil society* as that which fulfills the system of needs that exists between the family and the state (ibid., xviii), and later that century Tocqueville described it as voluntary associations of free persons where "self-interest rightly understood" and "habits of the heart" produced the skills and norms necessary for democracy in America (Tocqueville [1835; 1840] 2010a). Inspired by Dewey (1927), Habermas ([1962] 1989), and Gramsci (1971), scholars have conceptualized civil society as a public forum in which citizens voluntarily interact, debate, build social capital, and pursue numerous forms of social and political behavior. For this chapter, I use Mark E. Warren's definition of *civil society* as "the domain of society organized through associative media, in contrast to organization through legally empowered administration (the core of state power and organization), or market transactions mediated by money (the core of economic power and organization)" (Warren 2001, 2011, 377).

Civil society is related to but distinct from CSOs. The distinction is similar to the distinction between an industry and the firms that comprise it.[2] CSOs are the non-market, nongovernmental entities that exist within the civil society domain. These organizations are often legally registered organizations, but some exist as informal groups. CSOs include churches, charitable organizations, private- and public-interest advocacy organizations, social clubs, professional associations, and affinity groups held together by shared interests or ideologies. Thus, I define *CSOs* broadly as self-governed, private organizations established on the principle of voluntary association for purposes other than political control and economic profit.

Like plants in a greenhouse, CSOs' ability to bear fruit and contribute to positive sociopolitical outcomes is profoundly shaped by the legal institutions that structure their activity. CSO laws have the potential to either bolster or upend democratic transitions and good governance because of the laws that give CSOs positive and negative rights. CSOs use those rights to establish themselves, engage and challenge government, and provide the organizations in which individuals associate freely. Removing these rights diminishes their ability to contribute to positive sociopolitical outcomes directly. As a secondary effect, a weakened civil society limits opportunities for citizens to understand the "science of association," learn how to overcome the weakness of individuals in democratic societies (Tocqueville [1840] 2010b, 902), and develop the political capacity necessary to engage society and make democracy a viable way of life (V. Ostrom 1973, 106–107; 1997, 272–273).

Scholars have offered many frameworks that describe the government-CSO relationship in detail (e.g., Bratton 1989; Brass 2016; Cammett and MacLean 2014; Edwards 2004). Emphasizing an economic rationale, Young (2000, 2006) categorizes CSOs' relationship with the government in three modes: complementary to improve service delivery; supplementary to provide services when the government is unresponsive; and adversarial, where CSOs advocate for better services or policy change. Young's categories are valuable for their ability to transcend contexts, study change over time, and analyze regulatory variation by sectors within a country. Still, these categories do not consider the political context in which the government-CSO relationships unfold. Bratton (1989) provides an alternative framework that focuses on politics to explain a government's posture toward CSOs. Bratton (1989) proposes that a government's confidence in its grip on power determines both the strategies it uses to regulate CSOs and the operating space given to CSOs. Two lower-conflict strategies are monitoring and coordination, while higher-conflict strategies are cooptation and dissolution (ibid., 577–79). Combining Young's economic-centric categories with Bratton's politics-based theory offers a more complete picture of when and how governments regulate CSOs.

There are two caveats worth mentioning. First, it is important not to conflate "low-conflict" with "democratic." Indeed, some nondemocratic regimes have engineered a low-conflict, symbiotic relationship wherein the government permits CSOs to provide public service goods if they limit democratic claims-making (Spires 2011). The second caveat is that no government-CSO relationship is unidirectional or permanent. As "new policies create new politics," governments will change the legal rules that regulate CSOs (Schattschneider 1935, 288). Ultimately, CSO laws comprise the legal institutions that develop over time and constrain CSO behavior and structure the incentives of the government-CSO relationship (DeMattee 2020).

THE "CLOSING SPACE" ARGUMENT

Researchers have studied CSO laws and regulations for over 35 years (Brass et al. 2018). Human rights defenders have recently drawn our attention to governments around the world that use laws to crack down on CSOs within their borders. Practitioners and scholars refer to this pattern as the "closing space" or "shrinking space" phenomenon. It occurs when nondemocratic regimes enact laws that contain restrictive rules that stifle CSOs. Civil society is the target of these legalized crackdowns because it is often a source of—or resource for—political challengers.

I define *restrictive rules* as those that erode society's trust in CSOs and decrease demand for such organizations. These rules may also empower government agencies to repress and intimidate CSOs and their members, thereby reducing the supply of voluntary associations (Swiney 2019; DeMattee and Swiney 2021; DeMattee 2020). Restrictive rules give the government the authority to choose whether CSOs can self-regulate and the types of CSOs that can emerge (Mayhew 2005; Poppe and Wolff 2015; Maru 2017; Rutzen 2015). Other examples endow regulators with broad discretion to suspend or cancel any organization's legal registration (Ndegwa 1996; Kameri-Mbote 2002; Tiwana and Belay 2010; Hodenfield and Pegus 2013; Gugerty 2017; Maru 2017; Cunningham 2018). Still others give the CSO regulator the ability to intervene in a CSO's internal operations or external activities (Salamon and Toepler 2000; Kameri-Mbote 2002; Mayhew 2005; Hodenfield and Pegus 2013; Poppe and Wolff 2015; Maru 2017; Cunningham 2018) and narrowly specify what CSOs are permitted and forbidden to do with their financial and non-financial resources (Kameri-Mbote 2002; Tiwana and Belay 2010; Hodenfield and Pegus 2013; Appe and Marchesini da Costa 2017; Christensen and Weinstein 2013; Poppe and Wolff 2015; Maru 2017; Sidel 2017). The restrictive rules studied here (i.e., restrictions on foreign funding to locally operating CSOs) are perhaps the most analyzed type of restrictive

legal provision (Dupuy and Prakash 2020; Dupuy, Ron, and Prakash 2015,
2016; Dupuy and Prakash 2017; Carothers 2006; Gershman and Allen 2006;
Christensen and Weinstein 2013; Rutzen 2015; Poppe and Wolff 2016;
Bromley, Schofer, and Longhofer 2020; Oelberger and Shachter 2021).

The "closing space" argument's working hypothesis is that restrictive rules
are part of new legal institutions meant to weaken civil society so that CSOs
are less "problematic" for the current regime. In simpler terms, nondemocratic regimes have an incentive to enact restrictive CSO laws so that they
can prolong their stay in power. However, governments encounter incentive
problems after they enact laws that restrict foreign funding to locally operating CSOs. The first is that restrictive CSO laws risk upsetting the symbiotic
relationship in which governments rely on CSOs to provide unmet public service goods. Low- and middle-income countries may be highly dependent on
welfare- and service-oriented CSOs because those domestic and international
organizations fulfill fundamental social needs unmet by the government
(Bratton 1989; Lorch and Bunk 2017; Spires 2011; Brass 2016; Toepler,
Pape, and Benevolenski 2020; Toepler et al. 2020). CSO laws intended to
hinder democracy-promotion activities may dampen service provision and
damage the regime's output legitimacy.

The second incentive problem is that disturbing the flow of foreign funding may decrease the regime's influence. A country's laws can direct foreign
funding to specific locations. And once at those locations (e.g., deposited at
particular banks, placed in escrow at government ministries, or channeled
to favored or coopted organizations) the regime has multiple opportunities
to use those funds to increase its influence and resource base (Dimitrovova
2010, 528–29; Lewis 2013, 329). Centrally planned, large-scale, top-down
government-supported aid packages may be especially susceptible to this
form of corruption and undermine their effectiveness (Williamson 2010;
Easterly and Williamson 2011; Moyo 2009; Coyne and Ryan 2009). The
incentive problem is that CSO laws intended to starve CSOs of financial
resources may also shrink the regime's resource base. In the end, a government faces multiple incentive problems concerning how CSO laws affect the
regime's immediate and long-term goals (Lorch and Bunk 2017). As I explain
later in this chapter, governments can navigate this incentive problem by
allowing partiality to guide enforcement and permitting rules-in-use to deviate from rules-in-form.

In this chapter, I argue that distinct legal restrictions have different effects.
There are three distinct restrictions to which I refer. *Prohibitive laws* contain
strong language regarding what organizations cannot do (DeMattee 2019a,
1234–35; 2020, 70–72). Such laws are prohibitive and highly restrictive
because they prohibit particular activity concerning receiving foreign funding.[3] *Red-tape laws* are moderately restrictive and communicate ex ante

conditions that CSOs must meet before receiving foreign funds (ibid.).[4] *Notification laws*, finally, are minimally restrictive and contain instructions for what organizations must do after receiving foreign funding (ibid.).[5] I maintain that presuming CSO laws are homogenous and studying them as conceptually equivalent distorts their true impacts.

Elsewhere, I have argued that it is best to study CSO laws as bundles of different rules and that various factors (e.g., international commitments to protect human rights, constitutions, preexisting laws, international influence) predict the enactment of distinct law types (DeMattee 2019a, 2019b, 2020). This chapter analyzes law types following coding outlined in Dupuy, Ron, and Prakash (2016), where all laws are treated as identical and DeMattee (2019a, 1237), where qualitatively different laws are recoded as distinct law types. Research has not yet considered whether these distinct restrictions have varying effects on society. In this chapter, I specifically argue that highly restrictive legal provisions have the strongest negative long-run effects, while minimally restrictive legal provisions have the weakest. Moreover, "pooling" all laws together and treating them as identical is misleading because it understates the harm done by highly restrictive laws and overstates the shock of minimally restrictive ones.

My other argument is that societies do not experience the effects of CSO laws immediately. It may be possible for some legal provisions to have a stepwise property whereby the effects are immediate, complete, and permanent. Implementation challenges (Pressman and Wildavsky 1973; Hill and Hupe 2002) and the social world's complexities make this an unlikely possibility. I argue that the effect of these laws unfolds over time. The following hypotheses make these arguments explicit and testable:

Hypothesis 1: Restrictive CSO laws have a negative effect on the dependent variables; however, the magnitude of the effect varies by law type. The effect is strongest for highly restrictive laws and wanes for moderately and minimally restrictive laws.

Hypothesis 2: The total effect of enacted laws takes multiple years to affect civil society.

Framed in terms of the analysis, the first hypothesis predicts that each response variable (i.e., civil society vitality, level of democracy, and foreign funding received) will decrease in countries that enact a legal provision restricting foreign funding. The estimated effect will be strongest for highly restrictive laws and smaller for less restrictive types. The second hypothesis predicts that countries do not experience the full effect of the CSO law immediately. Instead, the effect slowly accretes before each response variable regresses to its long-run mean.

RESEARCH DESIGN

This research design uses an autoregressive distributed lag (ADL) model to assess the dynamic relationship between enacting different CSO laws on three outcomes comparable across societies: civil society vitality, level of democracy, and foreign funding received. Tests show each outcome is nonrandom and correlates with itself over time. I use a general ADL model with no ad hoc restrictions to account for this serial correlation. De Boef and Keele (2008, 186) offer three methodological reasons to use the general model: it makes no assumptions on the lag-lengths at which X_t influences Y_t, it is consistently estimated by ordinary least squares, and it is a useful starting point to test the appropriateness of restrictions. And unlike other models that assume a static process whereby "all movement in X_t translates completely and instantaneously to Y_t" (ibid., 188), the general form ADL with one-year lags allows me to discuss each law type's long-run effect and the speed at which it affects different response variables.

The data analyzed are the observations from recent scholarship studying the adoption of different law types in 138 low- and middle-income countries from 1993 to 2012 (Dupuy, Ron, and Prakash 2016; DeMattee 2019a). Data are organized as a panel dataset with group controls that remove unobserved heterogeneity between different countries. Clustered standard errors account for within-country correlation. The sample includes 2,643 country-year observations from 135 countries from 1994 to 2013.[6] The average number of observations per country is 19.6 (min = 11, max = 20).

Response Variables

I repeat the analysis three times using the same sample and different response variables to test my findings for robustness. Three concepts serve as response variables: civil society vitality, level of democracy, and foreign funding received. *Civil Society Vitality* is the degree to which civil society and individuals enjoy autonomy from the state and are free to pursue political and civic aims. According to the stated hypotheses, a government's enactment of a restrictive CSO law should adversely affect CSOs and decrease civil society vitality. The negative effect should be strongest for highly restrictive foreign funding provisions and decrease for moderately and minimally restrictive ones. I measure the concept using the civil society robustness index formed by taking the point estimates from a Bayesian factor analysis model of indicators measuring CSO entry and exit, government repression of CSO, and CSO participatory environment (Coppedge et al. 2018, 237–38). The index is an interval (0 = low robustness, 1 = high robustness) produced by the Varieties of Democracy Project (V-Dem).

Level of Democracy is the second response variable. This concept represents the presence of both democratic and autocratic institutions. Democratic institutions constrain executive power, guarantee civil liberties, and allow citizens to express their preferences concerning policies and leaders. Autocratic institutions, by contrast, are those that suppress participation, restrict political competition, and nominally constrain the chief executive. Conceptualized this way, higher levels of democracy have more democratic institutions and fewer autocratic ones. Following the theory that suggests a positive relationship exists between civil society and democracy, the stated hypotheses predict that enacting restrictive CSO laws undermines the bulwark and decreases democracy in a society. I measure the concept using the Freedom House/ Imputed Polity variable produced by V-Dem (ibid., 290). The variable uses Freedom House Political Rights and Civil Liberties values and the original Polity2 variable to impute values for countries where Polity data are missing. The continuous measure ranges from least democratic to most democratic (*0* = autocracy, *10* = democracy) and has stronger validity and reliability than its component indicators (Hadenius and Teorell 2005).

Foreign Funding Received is the third response variable. Restrictive foreign funding legal provisions may affect foreign funding received in two ways. The first process is the direct effect of enacting a restrictive provision. Each type of CSO law increases the transaction costs CSOs face to obtain financial resources from foreign sources.[7] These sources may include international organizations, government agencies, and private funders. The second process unfolds when a foreign government withholds bilateral assistance because a regime enacted a restrictive CSO law. For example, the Cold War's geopolitics led many countries to overlook Kenyan president Daniel arap Moi's authoritarianism and human rights abuses. This arrangement persisted as long as both Kenya's president remained an ally to the West on the international stage (Branch 2011, 142, 151, 172) and the USSR remained a credible threat to Western interests. After the Cold War ended, however, Kenya's strategic location and anti-communist position lost considerable importance. In turn, the international community devalued President Moi's strategic importance and international assistance became conditional on political and economic reforms (Brass 2016, 67; Branch 2011, 185; Mutua 2008, 68; Haugerud 1995, 14, 202). It is beyond this chapter's scope to determine what causal process accounts for variation in foreign funding received. According to the stated hypotheses, a government's enactment of a foreign funding restriction should decrease foreign funding received. I measure foreign funding received using net official development assistance received (constant 2014 US$) normalized on a per capita basis. The World Development Indicators (World Bank 2018) provide country-year data for both population and net official development assistance. I add a one-year lag to these response variables to account for autocorrelation. The appendix contains a table summarizing the descriptive statistics for all variables.

Independent Variables

Testing the stated hypotheses requires analyzing the effects of different CSO law types. The four types I study here—pooled (laws are identical), prohibitive (highly restrictive), red-tape (moderately restrictive), and notification laws (minimally restrictive)—follow the coding outlined in prior research (Dupuy, Ron, and Prakash 2016; DeMattee 2019a). *Pooled* is the default coding for whether a country adopted any type of CSO law. This category is nondiscriminatory and analyzes all laws as if they are identical. *Prohibitive laws* are highly restrictive and contain strong language regarding what organizations cannot do. Laws are prohibitive/highly restrictive if they prohibit particular activity concerning receiving foreign funding. *Red-tape laws* are moderately restrictive and communicate ex ante conditions that civil society organizations must meet before receiving foreign funds. *Notification laws*, finally, are minimally restrictive and contain instructions for what organizations must do after receiving foreign funding. The coding protocol used terms such as "notification," "reporting," and "taxation" to code notification/minimally restrictive laws (DeMattee 2019a, 1237). Table 6.1 defines each law type and provides relevant examples. The binary variable for all categories switches from *0* to *1* in the year the country adopted the law and retains that value for the rest of its observations. I add one-year lags to model to estimate the speed at which laws affect the response variable.

Control Variables

My analysis uses four control variables. *International Commitment to Guard Civil and Political Rights* (*Commitment to Guard Human Rights* for short) provides information on a country's formal commitment to the international community to support human rights. Making such a commitment creates a preexisting institution that retards attempts to undermine civil and political rights (e.g., enacting restrictive CSO laws). I measure this concept as whether a country ratifies the International Covenant on Civil and Political Rights (ICCPR), which commits its parties to promote human rights and fundamental freedoms, such as voluntary association (Donnelly 2013; Henkin 2000). The binary variable switches from *0* to *1* in the year a country ratified the ICCPR according to the UN Office of Legal Affairs.

Constitutional Rules Strengthen International Commitments (*Constitution Bolsters Commitments* for short) represents constitutional systems that explicitly place international treaties such as the ICCPR above ordinary legislation.

Table 6.1   Continuum of Restrictive CSO Laws

	Notification Laws	Red-Tape Laws	Prohibitive Laws
Level of Restrictions	Minimal	Moderate	High
Definition	Impose ex-post instructions for what CSOs must do after receiving foreign funding.	Erect ex ante conditions that CSOs must meet before receiving funds.	Contain strong language forbidding certain CSO activities.
Examples	•Caps on funding •Must not exceed threshold of budget spent on overhead •Must pay taxes on unrelated business activities •Must provide an annual report of financial flows •CSOs must follow reporting requirements •Taxation of foreign funding	•CSO allows the government to monitor financing agreements and contracts •Must route money through government financial institution •CSOs must be approved to receive funds •One-time approval for all future transactions •Government approval is necessary for each transaction	•Foreign funding prohibited •Certain CSOs forbidden to receive foreign funds •CSOs cannot operate in a sector if they received foreign funds •Restrictions on the source of funds •Stigmatization of foreign funding •Restrictions on use of funds

Source: Adapted from (DeMattee 2019a, 1235; 2020, 72).

The measure comes from the Comparative Constitutions Project (Elkins, Ginsburg, and Melton 2009, 2014). The variable equals *1* for all constitutional systems that explicitly state international treaties are superior to ordinary legislation. The variable equals *0* if the constitution does not mention international treaties or gives them a status equal or inferior to ordinary legislation.

Rule of Law is an index that measures the degree to which laws are fairly enforced and to what extent the actions of a government comply with the law. V-Dem calculates the index as a latent variable using a Bayesian factor analysis of fifteen indicators (Coppedge et al. 2018, 235–236). Methodologists show the index is superior to using a single indicator or averaging several measures (Linzer and Staton 2015).

Finally, the World Development Indicators collection (World Bank 2018) provides country-year data for population and GDP (constant 2010 US$). I normalize GDP on a per capita basis to produce the control variable *Economic Development*. I include one-year lags for each of these control variables to account for serial correlation in the response variable.[8]

FINDINGS AND IMPLICATIONS

This section contains one subsection for each research question and hypothesis presented above. The data justifies using a specialized time series model to assess the dynamic relationship between the enactment of different law types on three response variables (see table 6.4 in the appendix). In each panel, the lagged response variable (LRV) is large and robust across model specifications. The coefficient represents the "temporal stickiness" of the response variable (i.e., the amount of variation in Y_t explained by Y_{t-1}) with higher values indicating a stronger temporal interdependency. In time series analysis parlance, this temporal interdependency is known as "autocorrelation" or "serial correlation" (Box-Steffensmeier et al. 2014). The LRVs for civil society vitality ($0.97, p < 0.001$) and level of democracy ($0.95, p < 0.001$) have similar levels of autocorrelation. And while the LRV for foreign funding received has less temporal interdependency ($0.79, p < 0.001$), the response variable is serially correlated and nonrandom.

Highly Restrictive CSO Laws Are Associated with a Weaker Civil Society over Time

My analysis provides straightforward estimates for the contemporaneous effects of each law type (i.e., pooled, prohibitive, red-tape, and notification) on three response variables: civil society vitality (table 6.4, first panel), level of democracy (table 6.4, second panel), and foreign funding received (table 6.4, third panel). The sample and model specifications are consistent across response variables. I begin with civil society vitality which has a sample mean of 0.67 (0 to 1 scale) and demonstrates significant autocorrelation. The immediate average enforcement effect across all law types (model 2, "pooled") is -0.002 ($p = 0.86$), which is negligible with respect to the sample mean. For prohibitive laws (model 3), the immediate enforcement effect is -0.016 ($p < 0.05$), which is relatively much larger than the pooled laws but still quite small compared to the response variable's sample mean. The immediate average enforcement effect is nearly zero for red-tape laws (model 4, $p = 0.99$) and notification laws (model 5, $p = 0.54$). Comparing the immediate average enforcement effects across law types shows prohibitive laws have the largest immediate impact on civil society robustness. This variation in effect sizes provides initial evidence supporting my first hypothesis that argues that the effect of CSO laws varies by law type.

Effect sizes also vary across law types in the other response variables. Level of democracy has a sample mean of 5.70 (0 to 10 scale) and shows signs of strong autocorrelation. As predicted by my first hypothesis, prohibitive laws have the strongest negative effect on level of democracy (-0.033, $p=0.64$). Although the effect is small compared to the response variable's sample mean, it is double the estimated effect size of pooled laws (-0.015, $p=0.81$) and notification laws (-0.016, $p=0.82$). Red-tape laws, meanwhile, have a slightly positive short-term effect on level of democracy (0.009, $p=0.90$). None of these immediate effects are statistically significant on level of democracy. These null results do not mean CSO laws are irrelevant and may reflect the slow speed at which political institutions change.

The foreign funding received variable, which has a sample mean of $54.58, shows indications of autocorrelation and a similar pattern as the other response variables. Prohibitive laws have the strongest negative impact (-7.639, $p=0.12$), followed closely by notification laws (-6.837, $p=0.08$). The estimated effects for pooled (-2.129, $p=0.46$) and red-tape laws (-1.804, $p=0.57$) are both weaker. Taken together, this variation in effect sizes within three different response variables provides evidence supporting my argument that the effect of CSO laws varies by law type. These short-run effects, however, represent only the contemporaneous effect of law type on the response variable. In the next section, I show that each law's long-run effect is much larger than the immediate effect and that these long-run effects take years and sometimes decades to play out fully.

Temporal Dynamics of Different Laws

Table 6.2 provides information concerning the degree to which different foreign funding restrictions in CSO laws affect society. The first column repeats the immediate effect across three response variables, and the second column shows the estimated long-run effect of each CSO law type. I display the long-run effect in table 6.2 as an aggregate value. Readers should interpret these effects with caution due to the lack of statistical significance of coefficients (see table 6.4 in the appendix). Furthermore, this long-run effect is distributed over multiple years rather than experienced in a single moment. The third column, mean lag length, represents the average amount of time it takes for the long-run effect to play out fully.[9]

Comparing immediate and long-run effects shows that the latter are much larger in all cases. Comparing these long-run effects across law type provides additional support for my first hypothesis that the effects of CSO laws vary by law type. For all response variables, prohibitive laws' long-run effects are generally two to three times larger than other law types. The aggregate long-run effect of a prohibitive foreign funding restriction decreases civil society

Table 6.2   Estimated Temporal Dynamic of CSO Law Types

	Immediate Effect	Long-Run Effect	Mean Lag Length (yrs.)
Civil Society Vitality (sample mean: 0.67)			
Pooled Law	<0.00	−0.21	29.4
Prohibitive Law	−0.02	−0.47	29.3
Red-Tape Law	<0.00	−0.16	30.6
Notification Law	−0.01	−0.23	30.4
Level of Democracy (sample mean: 5.70)			
Pooled Law	−0.02	−0.64	17.6
Prohibitive Law	−0.03	−1.21	17.7
Red-Tape Law	0.01	−0.44	17.8
Notification Law	−0.02	0.29	17.9
Foreign Funding Received (sample mean: 54.58)			
Pooled Law	−2.13	−11.65	3.8
Prohibitive Law	−7.64	−24.84	3.8
Red-Tape Law	−1.80	−2.58	3.8
Notification Law	−6.84	−24.04	3.8

Source: Author created.

vitality by a value equal to 70 percent of the sample mean (−0.47). This non-trivial effect is stronger than pooled laws (−0.21), red-tape laws (−0.16), and notification laws (−0.23). The long-run effect of a prohibitive restriction decreases level of democracy by a value equal to 21 percent of the sample mean (−1.21). This effect is stronger than pooled laws (−0.64), red-tape laws (−0.44), and notification laws (0.29). Finally, the long-run effect of enacting a prohibitive law decreases foreign funding received by a value equal to 46 percent of the sample mean (−24.84).

Regardless of law type, it takes approximately 30 years for any foreign funding restriction to fully affect civil society vitality (table 6.2, third column). This does not mean that the long-run effect is in place for 30 years. It means instead that society experiences portions of the total, long-run effect throughout the three-decade period. The same is true for other response variables. The long-run effect of any foreign funding restriction takes nearly eighteen years to play out fully with respect to level of democracy but only four years for foreign funding received. These findings support my second hypothesis that it takes multiple years for foreign funding restrictions to affect society. Moreover, the analysis suggests that the time it takes for the long-run effect to run its course depends on the response variable.

CONCLUSION

"Public policy is whatever governments choose to do or not to do" (Dye [1972] 2013, 3), and whatever laws and policies governments enact to regulate civil society can either help or hinder it. In this chapter, I used a time-based approach to investigate how distinct CSO laws affect society and how quickly those effects unfold. Using a specialized time series model to study a sample of 135 low- and middle-income countries, I find that CSO laws have a minimal effect on three high-level response variables, that immediate and long-run effects vary across law types, and that the effect of these laws is not immediate and instead unfolds over several years and sometimes decades. My analysis has only examined the relationship between foreign funding restrictions and high-level measures for civil society, democratization, and foreign funding. A task for future research is to examine whether foreign funding restrictions have a stronger impact on lower-level measures (e.g., the size and number of CSOs present and operating in a country, how much money those CSOs spend, or how many projects they undertake).

My findings are relevant to practitioners and scholars for numerous reasons. First, many analysts treat CSO laws as conceptually equivalent. However, recent work finds different factors predict different law types (DeMattee 2019a, 2020) and has started to trade imprecise binary variables for count variables and cumulative indexes (e.g., Bakke, Mitchell, and Smidt 2020; DeMattee 2020). The findings in this chapter—that distinct CSO laws produce different effects—support this turn toward deeper conceptualizations of the legal institutions that regulate CSOs. Second, many analysts in this research program conduct analyses that model preexisting institutions as nonexistent (for notable exceptions, see Bakke, Mitchell, and Smidt 2020; DeMattee 2019a, 2020). The bias caused by these omitted variables is minimal when laws have only immediate, short-turn effects. However, this chapter's analyses suggest that the long-run effect of CSO laws is much larger than immediate effects. This means that it is necessary to account for preexisting laws and policies when studying how and why governments use laws to regulate CSOs.

This analysis has studied CSO laws as if governments enforce the legal rules they have enacted. This is a tenuous assumption. As many have identified, rules do not enforce themselves, and rules in the book do not always mirror rules in action (Commons 1924; E. Ostrom 2005; McGinnis 2011; V. Ostrom 1976; Pound 1910). Cole (2017, 11–6), working in the Ostroms's tradition of institutional analysis, offers a typology that distinguishes legal rules (de jure) from working rules (de facto). According to Cole's typology, Type 1 working rules include formal legal rules that closely resemble working rules. Type 2 working rules emerge when legal rules interact with social norms to produce working rules that deviate from legal rules. Type 3 working rules are legal rules that share no apparent relation with working rules. A key takeaway of Cole's typology is that we cannot analytically differentiate between Type 1 (no deviation), Type 2 (some deviation), and Type 3 (high deviation) working rules without knowing what the legal rules are *and* how they are enforced. We can locate our analysis in Cole's typology only if we know the rules-in-form and rules-in-use. The implication of this is that we cannot be certain whether a policy effectively incentivizes or constrains behavior without carefully studying them from multiple perspectives.

A limitation of this analysis—like other analyses studying CSO laws—has been the assumption that CSO laws are Type 1 working rules. Acknowledging the difference between rules-in-form and rules-in-use is critical because scholars have identified the inconsistent, subnational enforcement of permissive and restrictive rules in countries such as Algeria, Ethiopia, Kenya, Mozambique, North Korea, and Russia (Snyder 2007; Toepler, Pape, and Benevolenski 2020; Cunningham 2018; DeMattee 2020; Lorch and Bunk 2017). This legal-rules versus working-rules differential is perhaps the least studied yet most important agenda in the research program studying CSO laws.

APPENDIX

Table 6.3   Descriptive Statistics

	Percent	Mean	Std. Dev.	Min	Max.
Response Variables					
Civil Society Vitality		0.7	0.25	0.02	0.98
Level of Democracy		5.7	2.86	0.00	10.00
Foreign Funding Received		54.7	78.34	0.01	928.66
CSO Law Types					
Pooled Law	0.12			0	1
Prohibitive Law	0.03			0	1
Red-Tape Law	0.09			0	1
Notification Law	0.05			0	1
Control Variables					
Constitution Bolsters Commitments	0.26			0	1
Commitment to Guard Human Rights	0.76			0	1
Rule of Law		0.5	0.27	0.02	0.98
Economic Development		4913.9	7239.58	115.79	72670.96
Years		2003.6	5.72	1994	2013

Source: Author created.

Table 6.4 Estimated Contemporaneous Effects of CSO Law Types

	(1) Baseline	(2) Pooled	(3) Prohibitive	(4) Red-Tape	(5) Notification
RV: Civil Society Vitality					
Civil Society Vitality (lag)	0.969***	0.967***	0.967***	0.968***	0.968***
Pooled Law[a]		−0.002			
Pooled Law (lag)		−0.005			
Prohibitive Law[a]			−0.016*		
Prohibitive Law (lag)			<0.000		
Red-Tape Law[a]				<0.000	
Red-Tape Law (lag)				−0.005	
Notification Law[a]					−0.005
Notification Law (lag)					−0.003
Control Variables[b]	YES	YES	YES	YES	YES
R^2	0.975	0.975	0.975	0.975	0.975
AIC	−9509	−9512	−9516	−9508	−9509
RV: Level of Democracy					
Level of Democracy (lag)	0.947***	0.946***	0.946***	0.947***	0.947***
Pooled Law[a]		−0.015			
Pooled Law (lag)		−0.020			
Prohibitive Law[a]			−0.033		
Prohibitive Law (lag)			−0.032		
Red-Tape Law[a]				0.009	
Red-Tape Law (lag)				−0.033	
Notification Law[a]					−0.016
Notification Law (lag)					0.032
Control Variables[b]	YES	YES	YES	YES	YES
R^2	0.962	0.962	0.962	0.962	0.962

(Continued)

Table 6.4 Continued

	(1) Baseline	(2) Pooled	(3) Prohibitive	(4) Red-Tape	(5) Notification
AIC	4467	4470	4470	4471	4471
RV: Foreign Funding Received					
Foreign Funding Received (lag)	0.793***	0.739***	0.793***	0.793***	0.792***
Pooled Law [a]		-2.129			
Pooled Law (lag)		-0.284			
Prohibitive Law [a]			-7.639		
Prohibitive Law (lag)			2.490		
Red-Tape Law [a]				-1.804	
Red-Tape Law (lag)				1.272	
Notification Law [a]					-6.837
Notification Law (lag)					1.846
Control Variables [b]	YES	YES	YES	YES	YES
R^2	0.682	0.682	0.682	0.682	0.682
AIC	27542	27545	27545	27546	27544
Observations / Countries	2643 / 135	2643 / 135	2643 / 135	2643 / 135	2643 / 135
Degrees of Freedom	9	11	11	11	11

Note: Sample and model specifications consistent across all response variables.
[a] Independent variable measuring the contemporaneous effect on the response variable.
[b] Control variables include contemporaneous and lagged effects for Constitution Bolsters Commitments, Commitment to Guard Human Rights, Rule of Law, and Economic Development.
* p<0.05, ** p<0.01, *** p<0.001
Source: Author created.

NOTES

1. This is an extension of the familiar "gardener who tends a plant" metaphor mentioned by Hayek (1944, 18).

2. I thank Professor William Blomquist for this comparison.

3. Highly restrictive laws contain at least one of the following nine provisions: (1) certain organizations are prohibited from receiving foreign funding; (2) certain types of organizations are prohibited from receiving foreign funding; (3) foreign-funded organizations are prohibited from carrying out particular activities; (4) foreign funding can be used only for certain purposes; (5) foreign funding prohibited; (6) foreign funding prohibited for certain activities; (7) foreign-funded NGOs prohibited from working on certain issue areas; (8) foreign-funded organizations prohibited from carrying out particular activities; (9) and use of foreign funding prohibited for particular activities.

4. Moderately restrictive laws contain at least one of the following twelve provisions: (1) government approval for foreign funding; (2) government approval required for particular uses of foreign funding; (3) government may cap the amount; (4) government monitoring of NGO contracts financed with foreign funding; (5) government restrictions on use and source; (6) government restrictions on whether foreign funding can be received; (7) other restrictions on use of foreign funding; (8) requirements for how organizations can receive foreign funding; (9) restrictions on certain types of organizations receiving foreign funding; (10) restrictions on receipt and use of foreign funding; (11) restrictions on sources from which foreign funding can be acquired; (12) and restrictions on use of foreign funding.

5. Minimally restrictive laws contain at least one of the following six provisions: (1) foreign funds are taxed; (2) government notification of foreign funding required; (3) organizations must report source of revenues; (4) reporting and accounting requirements; (5) reporting and accounting requirements for foreign funding; (6) and reporting requirements.

6. I removed Montenegro, South Sudan, and Timor-Leste because they had fewer than ten observations.

7. There are three CSO laws types analyzed: (1) those that prohibit particular activity concerning receiving foreign funding (highly restrictive, prohibitive laws); (2) those that institute ex ante conditions that CSOs must meet before receiving foreign funds (moderately restrictive, red-tape laws); and (3) those that instruct CSOs to take certain action after receiving foreign funding (minimally restrictive, notification laws).

8. A limitation of the analysis is that it does not control for any other aspect of economic freedom aside from rule of law. Whether the types of rules governing formal market interactions also influence the durability of CSOs is grounds for future research.

9. I calculate these temporal dynamics following equations (2) and (21), respectively, in De Boef and Keele (2008, 186–87, 194).

REFERENCES

Aligica, Paul Dragos. 2018. *Public Entrepreneurship, Citizenship, and Self-Governance.* Cambridge, UK: Cambridge University Press.

Appe, Susan and Marcelo Marchesini da Costa. 2017. "Waves of Nonprofit Regulation and Self-Regulation in Latin America: Evidence and Trends from Brazil and Ecuador." In *Regulatory Waves: Comparative Perspectives on State Regulation and Self-Regulation Policies in the Nonprofit Sector*, edited by Oonagh B. Breen, Alison Dunn and Mark Sidel, 154–75. Cambridge, UK: Cambridge University Press.

Bakke, Kristin M., Neil J. Mitchell, and Hannah M. Smidt. 2020. "When States Crack Down on Human Rights Defenders." *International Studies Quarterly* 64 (1): 85–96.

Box-Steffensmeier, Janet M., John R. Freeman, Matthew P. Hitt, and Jon C. W. Pevehouse. 2014. *Time Series Analysis for the Social Sciences, Analytical Methods for Social Research.* Cambridge, UK: Cambridge University Press.

Branch, Daniel. 2011. *Kenya: Between Hope and Despair, 1963-2011.* New Haven, CT: Yale University Press.

Brass, Jennifer N. 2016. *Allies or Adversaries? NGOs and the State in Africa.* Cambridge, UK: Cambridge University Press.

Brass, Jennifer N., Wesley Longhofer, Rachel S. Robinson, and Allison Schnable. 2018. "NGOs and International Development: A Review of Thirty-Five Years of Scholarship." *World Development* 112: 136–49.

Bratton, Michael. 1989. "The Politics of Government-NGO Relations in Africa." *World Development* 17 (4): 569–87.

Bromley, Patricia, Evan Schofer, and Wesley Longhofer. 2020. "Contentions over World Culture: The Rise of Legal Restrictions on Foreign Funding to NGOs, 1994–2015." *Social Forces* 99 (1): 281–304.

Cammett, Melani Claire and Lauren M. MacLean. 2014. "The Political Consequences of Non-State Social Welfare: An Analytical Framework." In *The Politics of Non-State Social Welfare*, edited by Lauren M. MacLean and Melani Claire Cammett, 31–56. Ithaca, NY: Cornell University Press.

Carothers, Thomas. 2006. "The Backlash Against Democracy Promotion." *Foreign Affairs* 85 (2): 55–68.

Christensen, Darin and Jeremy M. Weinstein. 2013. "Defunding Dissent: Restrictions on Aid to NGOs." *Journal of Democracy* 24 (2): 77–91.

Cole, Daniel H. 2017. "Laws, Norms, and the Institutional Analysis and Development Framework." *Journal of Institutional Economics* 13 (4): 829–47.

Commons, John R. 1924. *Legal Foundations of Capitalism.* New York: Macmillan.

Coppedge, Michael, John Gerring, Carl Henrik Knutsen, Staffan I. Lindberg, Svend-Erik Skaaning, Jan Teorell, David Altman, et al. 2018. "V-Dem [Country-Year/Country-Date] Dataset v8." Gothernburg, SE: Varieties of Democracy (V-Dem) Project. https://www.v-dem.net/en/data/archive/previous-data/data-version-8/.

Coyne, Christopher J. and Matt E. Ryan. 2009. "With Friends Like These, Who Needs Enemies? Aiding the World's Worst Dictators." *The Independent Review* 14 (1): 26–44.

Cunningham, Andrew. 2018. "Law as Discourse: The Case of Ethiopia." In *International Humanitarian NGOs and State Relations: Politics, Principles and Identity*. London: Routledge.

De Boef, Suzanna and Luke Keele. 2008. "Taking Time Seriously." *American Journal of Political Science* 52 (1): 184–200.

DeMattee, Anthony J. 2019a. "Covenants, Constitutions, and Distinct Law Types: Investigating Governments' Restrictions on CSOs Using an Institutional Approach." *VOLUNTAS: International Journal of Voluntary and Nonprofit Organizations* 30 (6): 1229–55.

———. 2019b. "Toward a Coherent Framework: A Typology and Conceptualization of CSO Regulatory Regimes." *Nonprofit Policy Forum* 9 (4): 1–17.

———. 2020. "Domesticating Civil Society: How and Why Governments Use Laws to Regulate CSOs." PhD diss., Indiana University Bloomington.

DeMattee, Anthony J. and Chrystie F. Swiney. 2021. "Ostromian Logic Applied to Civil Society Organizations and the Rules that Shape Them." In *The Cambridge Handbook of Commons Research Innovations*, edited by Shelia Foster and Chrystie F. Swiney. Cambridge, UK: Cambridge University Press.

Dewey, John. 1927. *The Public and Its Problems*. New York: H. Holt and Company.

Dimitrovova, Bohdana. 2010. "Re-Shaping Civil Society in Morocco: Boundary Setting, Integration and Consolidation." *Journal of European Integration* 32 (5): 523–39.

Donnelly, Jack. 2013. *Universal Human Rights in Theory and Practice*. 3rd ed. Ithaca, NY: Cornell University Press.

Dupuy, Kendra and Aseem Prakash. 2017. "Do Donors Reduce Bilateral Aid to Countries With Restrictive NGO Laws? A Panel Study, 1993-2012." *Nonprofit and Voluntary Sector Quarterly* 47 (1): 89–106.

———. 2020. "Why Restrictive NGO Foreign Funding Laws Reduce Voter Turnout in Africa's National Elections." *Nonprofit and Voluntary Sector Quarterly* 51(1): 170–189.

Dupuy, Kendra, James Ron, and Aseem Prakash. 2015. "Who Survived? Ethiopia's Regulatory Crackdown on Foreign-Funded NGOs." *Review of International Political Economy* 22 (2): 419–56.

———. 2016. "Hands Off My Regime! Governments' Restrictions on Foreign Aid to Non-Governmental Organizations in Poor and Middle-Income Countries." *World Development* 84: 299–311.

Dye, Thomas R. [1972] 2013. *Understanding Public Policy*. 14th ed. Boston, MA: Pearson.

Easterly, William and Claudia R. Williamson. 2011. "Rhetoric versus Reality: The Best and Worst of Aid Agency Practices." *World Development* 39 (11): 1930–49.

Edwards, Michael. 2004. *Civil Society*. Malden, MA: Polity Press.

Elkins, Zachary, Tom Ginsburg, and James Melton. 2009. *The Endurance of National Constitutions*. Cambridge, UK: Cambridge University Press.

Elkins, Zachary, Tom Ginsburg, and James Melton. 2014. "Comparative Constitutions Project: Characteristics of National Constitutions, Version 2.0." The Comparative Constitutions Project (CCP).

Fukuyama, Francis. 1995. *Trust: The Social Virtues and the Creation of Prosperity*. New York: Free Press.

Gershman, Carl and Michael Allen. 2006. "The Assault on Democracy Assistance." *Journal of Democracy* 17 (2): 36–51.

Gramsci, Antonio. 1971. *Selections from the Prison Notebooks of Antonio Gramsci.* London: Lawrence & Wishart.

Grzymała-Busse, Anna Maria. 2015. *Nations Under God: How Churches Use Moral Authority to Influence Policy.* Princeton, NJ: Princeton University Press.

Gugerty, Mary Kay. 2017. "Shifting Patterns of State Regulation and NGO Self-Regulation in Sub-Saharan Africa." In *Regulatory Waves: Comparative Perspectives on State Regulation and Self-Regulation Policies in the Nonprofit Sector*, edited by Oonagh B. Breen, Alison Dunn, and Mark Sidel, 69–91. Cambridge, UK: Cambridge University Press.

Gyimah-Boadi, Emmanuel. 1998. "African Ambiguities: The Rebirth of African Liberalism." *Journal of Democracy* 9 (2): 18–31.

Habermas, Jürgen. [1962] 1989. *The Structural Transformation of the Public Sphere: An Inquiry into a Category of Bourgeois Society, Studies in Contemporary German Social Thought.* Cambridge, MA: MIT Press.

Hadenius, Axel and Jan Teorell. 2005. "Assessing Alternative Indices of Democracy." Working Paper, Committee on Concepts and Methods: International Political Science Association.

Haugerud, Angelique. 1995. *The Culture of Politics in Modern Kenya, African Studies Series.* Cambridge, UK: Cambridge University Press.

Hayek, F. A. 1944. *The Road to Serfdom.* Chicago, IL: University of Chicago Press.

Hegel, Georg Wilhelm Friedrich. [1821] 1991. *Hegel: Elements of the Philosophy of Right, Cambridge Texts in the History of Political Thought.* Edited by Allen W. Wood. Cambridge, UK: Cambridge University Press.

Henkin, Louis. 2000. "Human Rights: Ideology and Aspiration, Reality and Prospect." In *Realizing Human Rights: Moving from Inspiration to Impact*, edited by Samantha Power and Graham T. Allison, 3–38. New York: St. Martin's Press.

Hill, Michael J. and Peter L. Hupe. 2002. *Implementing Public Policy: Governance in Theory and Practice.* London: Sage.

Hodenfield, Tor and Ciana-Marie Pegus. 2013. *Mounting Restrictions on Civil Society: The Gap between Rhetoric and Reality.* Washington, DC: CIVICUS: World Alliance for Citizen Participation.

Johnson, Noel D. and Mark Koyama. 2019. *Persecution & Toleration: The Long Road to Religious Freedom.* New York: Cambridge University Press.

Kameri-Mbote, Patricia. 2002. *The Operational Environment and Constraints for NGOs in Kenya: Strategies for Good Policy and Practice.* Geneva, CH: International Environmental Law Research Centre.

Kiai, Maina. 2012. "Report of the Special Rapporteur on the Rights to Freedom of Peaceful Assembly and Association." United Nations General Assembly: United Nations. https://www.ohchr.org/en/issues/assemblyassociation/pages/srfreedomassemblyassociationindex.aspx.

Lewis, David. 2013. "Civil Society and the Authoritarian State: Cooperation, Contestation and Discourse." *Journal of Civil Society* 9 (3): 325–40.

Linz, Juan J. and Alfred C. Stepan. 1996. *Problems of Democratic Transition and Consolidation: Southern Europe, South America, and Post-Communist Europe.* Baltimore, MD: Johns Hopkins University Press.

Linzer, Drew A. and Jeffrey K. Staton. 2015. "A Global Measure of Judicial Independence, 1948–2012." *Journal of Law and Courts* 3 (2): 223–56.

Lorch, Jasmin and Bettina Bunk. 2017. "Using Civil Society as an Authoritarian Legitimation Strategy: Algeria and Mozambique in Comparative Perspective." *Democratization* 24 (6): 987–1005.

Maru, Mehari Taddele. 2017. *Legal Frameworks Governing Non-Governmental Organizations in the Horn of Africa.* Kampala, UG: Al Khatim Adlan Center for Enlightenment and Human Development (KACE).

Mayhew, Susannah H. 2005. "Hegemony, Politics and Ideology: The Role of Legislation in NGO–Government Relations in Asia." *The Journal of Development Studies* 41 (5): 727–58.

McGinnis, Michael D. 2011. "Networks of Adjacent Action Situations in Polycentric Governance." *Policy Studies Journal* 39 (1): 45–72.

Mendelson, Sarah E. 2015. *Why Governments Target Civil Society and What Can Be Done in Response: A New Agenda.* Washington, DC: Center for Strategic & International Studies.

Moyo, Dambisa. 2009. *Dead Aid: Why Aid Is Not Working and How There Is a Better Way for Africa.* New York: Farrar, Straus and Giroux.

Mutua, Makau. 2008. *Kenya's Quest for Democracy: Taming Leviathan.* Boulder, CO: Lynne Rienner Publishers.

Mutunga, Willy. 1999. *Constitution-Making from the Middle: Civil Society and Transition Politics in Kenya, 1992-1997, Series on Constitution Making in Kenya.* Nairobi, KE: SAREAT.

Ndegwa, Stephen N. 1996. "NGOs and the State in Kenya." In *The Two Faces of Civil Society: NGOs and Politics in Africa*, 31–54. West Hartford, CT: Kumarian Press.

Oelberger, Carrie R. and Simon Y. Shachter. 2021. "National Sovereignty and Transnational Philanthropy: The Impact of Countries' Foreign Aid Restrictions on US Foundation Funding." *VOLUNTAS: International Journal of Voluntary and Nonprofit Organizations* 32: 204–19.

Ostrom, Elinor. 1990. *Governing the Commons: The Evolution of Institutions for Collective Action.* New York: Cambridge University Press.

———. 2005. *Understanding Institutional Diversity.* Princeton, NJ: Princeton University Press.

Ostrom, Vincent. 1973. *The Intellectual Crisis in American Public Administration.* Revised ed. Tuscaloosa, AL: University of Alabama Press.

———. 1976. "John R. Commons's Foundations for Policy Analysis." *Journal of Economic Issues* 10 (4): 839–57.

———. 1997. *The Meaning of Democracy and the Vulnerabilities of Democracies: A Response to Tocqueville's Challenge.* Ann Arbor: University of Michigan Press.

Poppe, Annika E. and Jonas Wolff. 2016. "Foreign Funding Restrictions: Far More than Just 'An Illegitimate Excuse'." openGlobalRights, April 20. https://www.openglobalrights.org/foreign-funding-restrictions-far-more-than-just-illegiti/.

Pound, Roscoe. 1910. "Law in Books and Law in Action." *American Law Review* 44 (1): 12–36.

Pressman, Jeffrey L. and Aaron B. Wildavsky. 1973. *Implementation: How Great Expectations in Washington Are Dashed in Oakland; Or, Why It's Amazing That Federal Programs Work at All*. Berkeley: University of California Press.

Putnam, Robert D. 1993. *Making Democracy Work: Civic Traditions in Modern Italy*. Princeton, NJ: Princeton University Press.

Rutzen, Douglas. 2015. "Aid Barriers and the Rise of Philanthropic Protectionism." *International Journal of Not-for-Profit Law* 17 (1): 1–42.

Salamon, Lester M. and Stefan Toepler. 2000. "The Influence of the Legal Environment on the Nonprofit Sector." Working Paper, Center for Civil Society Studies.

Schattschneider, E. E. 1935. *Politics, Pressures and the Tariff: A Study of Free Private Enterprise in Pressure Politics, as Shown in the 1929-1930 Revision of the Tariff, Prentice-Hall Political Science Series*. New York: Prentice-Hall, Inc.

Sidel, Mark. 2017. "State Regulation and the Emergence of Self-Regulation in the Chinese and Vietnamese Nonprofit and Philanthropic Sectors." In *Regulatory Waves: Comparative Perspectives on State Regulation and Self-Regulation Policies in the Nonprofit Sector*, edited by Oonagh B. Breen, Alison Dunn, and Mark Sidel, 92–112. Cambridge, UK: Cambridge University Press.

Skocpol, Theda and Morris P. Fiorina, eds. 1999. *Civic Engagement in American Democracy*. Washington, DC: Brookings Institution Press and Russell Sage Foundation.

Snyder, Scott. 2007. "American Religious NGOs in North Korea: A Paradoxical Relationship." *Ethics & International Affairs* 21 (4): 423–30.

Spires, Anthony J. 2011. "Contingent Symbiosis and Civil Society in an Authoritarian State: Understanding the Survival of China's Grassroots NGOs." *American Journal of Sociology* 117 (1): 1–45.

Swiney, Chrystie F. 2019. "The Counter-Associational Revolution: The Rise, Spread & Contagion of Restrictive Civil Society Laws in the World's Strongest Democratic States." *Fordham International Law Journal* 43 (2): 399–456.

Tiwana, Mandeep and Netsanet Belay. 2010. *Civil Society: The Clampdown Is Real - Global Trends 2009-2010*. Washington, DC: CIVICUS: World Alliance for Citizen Participation.

Tocqueville, Alexis de. [1835; 1840] 2010a. *Democracy in America, Volumes I and II*. Edited by Eduardo Nolla. English ed. Indianapolis, IN: Liberty Fund.

———. [1840] 2010b. "Of the Use That Americans Make of Associations in Civil Life." In *Democracy in America*, Volume II, edited by Eduardo Nolla, 895–904. Indianapolis, IN: Liberty Fund.

Toepler, Stefan, Annette Zimmer, Christian Fröhlich, and Katharina Obuch. 2020. "The Changing Space for NGOs: Civil Society in Authoritarian and Hybrid Regimes." *VOLUNTAS: International Journal of Voluntary and Nonprofit Organizations* 31: 649–62.

Toepler, Stefan, Ulla Pape, and Vladimir Benevolenski. 2020. "Subnational Variations in Government-Nonprofit Relations: A Comparative Analysis of

Regional Differences within Russia." *Journal of Comparative Policy Analysis: Research and Practice* 22 (1): 47–65.

Tripp, Aili Mari. 2017. "In Pursuit of Autonomy: Civil Society and the State in Africa." In *Africa in World Politics: Constructing Political and Economic Order*, edited by John W. Harbeson and Donald S. Rothchild, 89–110. Boulder, CO: Westview Press.

Warren, Mark E. 2001. *Democracy and Association*. Princeton, NJ: Princeton University Press.

———. 2011. "Civil Society and Democracy." In *The Oxford Handbook of Civil Society*, edited by Michael Edwards, 377–90. New York: Oxford University Press.

Wiktorowicz, Quintan. 2000. "Civil Society as Social Control: State Power in Jordan." *Comparative Politics* 33 (1): 43–61.

Williamson, Claudia R. 2010. "Exploring the Failure of Foreign Aid: The Role of Incentives and Information." *The Review of Austrian Economics* 23 (1): 17–33.

Wolff, Jonas and Annika E. Poppe. 2015. *From Closing Space to Contested Spaces: Re-assessing Current Conflicts over International Civil Society Support*. Frankfurt, DE: Peace Research Institute Frankfurt (PRIF).

World Bank. 1997. "Handbook on Good Practices for Laws Relating to Non-Governmental Organizations." Washington, DC: The World Bank.

———. 2018. "World Development Indicators (WDI)." Washington, DC: The World Bank.

Young, Dennis R. 2000. "Alternative Models of Government-Nonprofit Sector Relations: Theoretical and International Perspectives." *Nonprofit and Voluntary Sector Quarterly* 29 (1): 49–172.

———. 2006. "Complementary, Supplementary, or Adversarial? Nonprofit-Government Relations." In *Nonprofits & Government: Collaboration & Conflict*, edited by Elizabeth T. Boris and C. Eugene Steuerle, 37–79. Washington, DC: Urban Institute Press.

Part IV

PUBLIC GOVERNANCE

Chapter 7

A Tale of One City

Lavasa as a Coasian Prototype of a Private Urban Development

Vera Kichanova

What does the future look like? A science fiction–inspired megacity with gravity-defying architecture and vehicles might be the first picture that comes to one's mind when asked. With the highest concentration of financial, social, and human capital, large cities are, indeed, the world's incubators of innovation (Glaeser 2013). The structure of urban social and economic life makes it possible, through endless competition, to accelerate the process of discovering new technologies and eventually speeding up human progress.

An organic urban development is a process of trial and error, and imperfections are inherent to living cities (Jacobs 1961). It is due to these very imperfections—or transaction costs, as economists would call them—that an urban environment is so friendly toward innovations. The Coasian paradigm implies that transaction costs should be regarded not as a basis for market failure, but rather as a basis for market opportunity (Candela and Geloso 2019). Public provision of urban commons, however, leaves independent innovators with less opportunities to get involved in this sector—the phenomenon known to economists as *crowding out*. As a result, some urban problems remain unsolved for too long. Instead of trying to change the legal environment, some entrepreneurs might eventually choose to create an alternative jurisdiction. This creates the case for entirely private cities.

I suggest that a private city can be a profitable enterprise and a legitimate alternative to conventional publicly governed cities, should the regulatory environment be friendlier toward such start-ups. To illustrate my point, I chose the case of Lavasa, a private city in India built entirely from scratch over the last two decades. The goal of this chapter is to look at the making of a private city through the lens of Coasian transaction costs theory and derive certain lessons for private cities that will be launched in the future.

While the number of publications dedicated to private urban planning is substantial and growing, a proper assessment of private cities through the Coasian lens has not yet been conducted. Scholars like Chris Webster and Lawrence Lai have published comprehensive studies on private urban governance (Webster and Lai 2003); however, their focus is largely on smaller-scale proprietary communities rather than larger-scale private cities. Foldvary (1994) investigates the potential of a decentralized city where public goods can be provided by private actors, yet he does not analyze the perspectives of purpose-built private cities. Romer (2010) talks about charter cities—a phenomenon overlapping with private cities yet not identical (I outline Romer's idea of charter cities in the literature review section). Finally, existing literature on Coase and urban planning (e.g., Lai and Lorne 2007) overlooks the phenomenon of private cities. The goal of this chapter, therefore, is to fill this gap and apply the Coasian framework specifically to privately built, managed, and governed cities.

One obvious reason why there are very few studies that focus on private cities is that, practically, there are very few private cities in existence. Recurrent attempts by profit-seeking agents to create private cities, as well as the existence of real-life projects that share many crucial aspects with "pure" private cities, indicate that there is a demand for such innovative forms of governance (Bell 2018). There are potential explanations why the market for private cities is currently missing: it could either be the result of an inherent problem in the very business model of a private city or it could be the result of prohibitive external conditions. The best way to discover which of these two explanations is correct would be to assess a real-life attempt to establish a private city.

Private cities can be seen as analogous to the Coasian firm—"islands of conscious power in this ocean of unconscious co-operation" (Coase 1937, 2). This chapter looks closely at the example of Lavasa, a private city in India, through the Coasian lens with the aim to explain its initial relative success and subsequent demise. Step by step, I demonstrate how the strategy chosen by the developer paid off initially but ultimately turned out to be unrobust in the face of unexpected transaction costs arising as a result of a political campaign. My analysis suggests that the same inability of the state government to fulfill its commitments—that is, to maintain the stable rule of law (while keeping monopoly over its territory) that creates a demand for such private oases—is eventually responsible for the demise of such projects. Lack of the rule of law—by no means a specifically Indian problem—creates transaction costs, a starting point for profit-driven innovations in urban planning. Later, the same inefficient governance becomes the main reason why innovators miscalculate transaction costs and find themselves unable to address the problem.

LITERATURE REVIEW

The Problem of Crowding Out in Urban Planning

The enormous concentration of people and knowledge that is immanent in a large city appears to be the primary reason why cities are a fertile ground for innovation. Urban economist Edward Glaeser defines a *city* as "the absence of space between people and firms" (Glaeser 2013, 11). Such close proximity of the means of production lowers transaction costs, making it easier for buyers and sellers to find each other. Yet, an organic urban development is a process of trial and error, and in a living, growing city imperfections are inevitable (Jacobs 1961). It is due to these very imperfections, however, that an urban environment unlike any other enables profit-seeking agents to discover new, innovative ways of solving urban problems. Someone's problem is someone else's opportunity, and it is therefore crucial that cities, which are largely responsible for economic and social progress worldwide, provide a legal regime that welcomes entrepreneurial spirit and rewards innovators.

Speaking in economic terms, those imperfections are called *transaction costs*. Neoclassical economic theory (e.g., Krugman and Wells 2006) regards transaction costs as a classic example of a barrier that prevents market agents from exploiting the gains from trade, giving a rise to potential market failures—a misallocation of resources by an unconstrained, unregulated market that results in a deadweight loss. By this logic, problems familiar to any city dweller—such as unaffordable housing, disputes over land use and construction, and environmental issues, just to name a few—would represent market failures and therefore require some level of top-down urban planning and management on behalf of the municipal government. There is an alternative way to look at transaction costs though: the way advanced by Ronald Coase. The Coasian theory states that transaction costs should be regarded not as a basis for market failure, but rather as a basis for market opportunity (Candela and Geloso 2019). In a world where transaction costs equal zero, there would be no economic activity whatsoever since all the resources would already be allocated efficiently, and the market would be in a peaceful state known as equilibrium (a purely theoretical concept). This, as most would agree, is neither the case for the market in general nor the case for cities.

The Jacobian imperfect city, where transaction costs are non-zero, must be full of opportunities for entrepreneurs to step in and propose a solution that would minimize these costs so as to exhaust potential gains from trade. The fact that some urban imperfections persist must indicate that something prevents profit-seeking agents from using this opportunity. The phenomenon of crowding out—namely, public providers crowding private competitors out of this sector—might be largely responsible for that (Candela and Geloso 2019). Though the era of the urban utopias (or dystopias, depending on one's point of view) of the twentieth century is long gone, the notion of the municipal government as a sole provider of public goods remains barely challenged. Few urbanists today advocate for all-encompassing, top-down urban planning in the spirit of Le Corbusier's modernist proposals (the most notorious being his "Plan Voisin," in which he envisioned downtown Paris rebuilt as an entirely planned car-oriented territory with massive avenues and uniform skyscrapers). At the same time, most urban public goods—from street cleaning to traffic management—are deemed non-excludable by scholars and policymakers alike, and for that reason, they are traditionally placed within the government's domain. Unable to incorporate the "tacit knowledge" that is dispersed in society and not available to anyone in its entirety, the government that attempts to address urban imperfections fails to allocate the resources efficiently (Hayek 1945). Guided by the price mechanism, entrepreneurs are arguably in a better position to deal with these imperfections. However, the government is crowding them out of the market. In that sense, the persistence of urban problems illustrates not a market failure in private governance, but rather a missing market or, more specifically, a failure of the market for private governance to be created in the first place (Candela and Geloso 2018, 484). It is to a large extent due to the crowding out effect—a result of government intervention—that today's cities are not reaching their full potential as incubators of innovations.

The Cost of Changing Rules

Allowing entrepreneurs to eliminate the persisting transaction costs on an urban level, given the role of cities in global economic growth, would have an immense global effect. Over half of the world population lives in cities today—a proportion that is expected to rise to 68 percent by 2050.[1] In recent history, urban population has grown with meteoric speed: from 751 million in 1950 to 4.2 billion in 2018. Effectively, urbanization has become a synonym of progress—chaotic, uneven, at times controversial, but still, by and large, steady, and rewarding progress. For developing countries, addressing urbanization in a smart way is a particularly crucial challenge. High population density paired with inadequate infrastructure results in all sorts of urban plagues from traffic congestion and, consequently, notorious levels of air pollution to the lack of affordable housing, which results in slum creation, poverty, and crime. India alone—a home to 54 percent of the world's urban population—has six out of the ten most polluted cities, according to the

2019 World Air Quality Report.[2] All the urban imperfections mentioned above, which are common for any city, are magnified in places like Delhi or Mumbai. It is no surprise then that urbanization might seem a curse, not a blessing, to some people in a country like India.

Unlocking the entrepreneurial potential of cities would require changing many of the rules according to which cities are governed. But changing the rules is itself a costly political process, with the costs divided unevenly between participants and the gains of each participant rarely reflecting their input (Ostrom 2005). The sophisticated architecture of decision-making on an urban level eventually rewards small but well-organized interest groups, such as the notorious Not in My Backyard groups (NIMBYs), at the expense of the general population.[3] As collective action theory predicts (Olson 1971), those interest groups not only have a stronger incentive to defend the status quo but also face lower transaction costs of self-organizing compared to the rest of the population, which allows them to act more effectively against legal change. This, in turn, discourages a regular urban dweller from participating in the process whatsoever, leaving them satisfied with suboptimal outcomes (Holcombe 2018, 252). Unsurprisingly, even though urban entrepreneurs are well aware that changing the rules would open to them new opportunities to extract profits, the incentives for them to get involved are still very low. Therefore, instead of challenging the existing system, in which the municipal government provides or at least regulates and controls the provision of urban services on a city level, profit-seeking agents can try to fill the gaps in the government's comprehensive master plan and provide an alternative solution. Private urban planning is an example of such a solution.

Private Planning as an Alternative

Private (or market-based) planning plays a visible role in infill urban development—the common practice of developing the vacant patches of land within the city borders and partially relying on existing infrastructure. This is evidenced by the widespread use of proprietary communities, shopping malls, and theme parks. Various scholars (e.g., Pennington 2012; Foldvary 1994; Webster 2007; Andersson and Moroni 2014) highlight the Hayekian potential of private planning to utilize the tacit knowledge dispersed throughout the city (Hayek 1945). Given the non-zero cost of information collection and processing (Webster 2007) and the absence of profit-and-loss incentives, the local authorities are in a weaker position than private planners when addressing the needs of urban dwellers. Unlike the command-and-control approach, private planning, which treats citizens as consumers, allows for continuous piecemeal adaptations to their ever-changing preferences. Unlike participatory planning, private planning discourages NIMBYism, transforming citizens into stakeholders (Pennington 2014, 82) and, ultimately, transform-ing urban planning from a zero-sum to a positive-sum game.

The increased share of private planning could address one type of transac-tion costs, namely that associated with knowledge collection, but eventually it could give rise to another type of transaction costs, namely that related to conflict resolution.[4] Even scholars who generally favor private planning express concerns about the transaction costs arising from a situation where urban land ownership and infrastructure provision is divided between mul-tiple competing profit-making firms instead of an integrated municipal pro-vider (Andersson and Moroni 2014). It is easy to imagine a city where all the land would be divided between gated communities, each governed by some sort of a charter and only taking care of the club goods within its borders. As is the case with borders between countries inhibiting market exchange on a global scale, borders between gated communities would prevent urban dwell-ers from enjoying a primary economic benefit of a city—an opportunity to exchange goods, services, and knowledge with thousands or even millions of other people. Entrepreneurial activity thrives in the presence of clear, simple, and consistent rules. One might say that such fragmentation itself presents multiple market opportunities. Barriers, after all, are simply another example of transaction costs. Yet, because the city, as a whole, remains a public administrative unit, the ultimate monopoly on conflict resolution remains in the government's hands, leaving little incentive for private actors to get involved.

Cities as Firms

To solve this paradox, it helps to look at cities through the lens of the Coasian theory of the firm. Cities of today are, by and large, centrally planned enti-ties with some small islands of infill private planning. An alternative model would be the *city as a firm*, an "island of conscious power in this ocean of unconscious co-operation" (Coase 1937, 3). An entirely private city—owned, managed, and governed by a single entity—could offer the above-mentioned benefits of market-based urban planning while simultaneously addressing the problem of transaction costs arising from the fragmentation of urban canvas. Guided by the price mechanism, private cities might be in a better position to utilize the tacit knowledge of their citizens. Sensitive to profit and loss, private cities would treat their citizens as consumers, while citizens, in turn, would benefit from the financial success of the city as an enterprise and would therefore be motivated to prefer collaboration over conflicts. Similar to how employees in the Coasian model choose to voluntarily give up some of their autonomy and join the firm, citizens may choose to voluntarily outsource some decision-making powers to a landowner to avoid the transaction costs that arise in a conventional city as a result of fragmentation, unclearly defined property rights, and the need for negotiations over common-pool resources. That is somewhat similar to what people do when they join a homeownership association—but here, they would do it on a much larger scale.

What would be the optimal size for such a private city? Like in the case of a Coasian firm, the answer depends on multiple factors and is to be determined by the market in each separate case. A firm expands until the benefits of hiring an additional employee are lower than the cost of buying his or her labor on an open market. From the same perspective, a private city has to be sufficiently large to successfully address the transaction costs. In order to avoid the same issues of hierarchical structures that conventional cities suffer from, it also cannot be too large. Technological and managerial innovations, on the other hand, are capable of expanding the optimal size of a firm. The same could happen in the realm of urban planning as well—yet, for some reason, it does not. Despite the presence of multiple successful examples of smaller-scale private planning—proprietary communities (McCallum 1997), shopping malls (Galantay 1975), hotels (Heath 1957; McCallum 1977), theme parks (Stringham, Miller, and Clark 2010), manufacturing sites (Arne 2002), university campuses, and so on—"pure" private cities barely exist.[5] The legitimate question, therefore, is whether the same benefits of private planning are likely to play a similar role on a larger scale if it were legally possible.

Competition between Cities

Unlocking the potential for innovations in existing cities often requires changing the rules according to which these cities are governed. Changing the rules, in turn, involves transaction costs that may be prohibitively high for entrepreneurs to be offset by the profits they expect to receive once the rules are changed. Citizens, on the other hand, have a second option: instead of changing the rules, they may try changing the place in which they live, thus transferring their skills and assets to jurisdictions that offer a more appealing set of rules. When such voting with one's feet is actually available to citizens, municipalities' financial performance is strongly linked to their attractiveness for current and potential residents. In that case, the benefits of attracting new taxpayers can potentially offset the high cost of changing rules. Eventually, this creates endogenous pressure on local governments toward changing rules according to "consumer" preferences.

Such a model, in which voting with one's feet accelerates competition between municipalities, was famously outlined by Charles Tiebout (1956).[6] He believed that good governance could be commodified, and market-based incentives could then prevail over institutional inertia. Half a century later,

Paul Romer (2010, 7) echoes his arguments by reminding that throughout history "the ability to move between countries in search of better opportunities—to vote with one's feet—was a powerful force for progress." That said, for a common citizen, this very ability is limited by, on the one hand, the prohibitively high cost of relocation and, on the other hand, multiple immigration restrictions. In other words, voting with one's feet has its own transaction costs.[7] Cities may be incentivized to attract the most productive workforce, but in many cases, that would require changing the immigration rules on a higher—national or federal—level, the level over which local municipalities have very little power.

Establishing a new city with its own private jurisdiction can be an alternative solution, an innovative and arguably promising one. In a globalized world when voting with one's feet is possible, the emergence of numerous private cities would eventually create what Fuller and Romer (2012, 5) describe as a market for rules—the world where regular people could choose a set of rules that they find both fair and convenient and where cities as jurisdictions could also compete for residents through offering them more appealing rules.

Importantly, that would eliminate the costs of rule-changing since prospective citizens would explicitly accept the rules by signing some form of a charter (hence the term "charter cities"). Because opting in would be voluntary, that would simultaneously solve the question of legitimacy. Because rules are the main "product" that is being offered in the case of private cities, maintaining the rules would be essential for developers to survive in the competition of jurisdictions. In other words, the goals of the developer (producer) and those of the resident (consumer) would be aligned, which is not necessarily the case for conventional publicly governed cities.

Thanks to technological progress, international travel is cheaper and safer than ever before in human history. The legal aspects of changing jurisdictions, however, remain a major challenge. The government-imposed regulations on international travel—for instance, the need for potential immigrants to obtain not only a job offer but also a legal permission from the host government before relocating—create enormous transaction costs preventing the global market for the labor force from reaching an equilibrium. Here, again, private jurisdictions may offer solutions. Because developers of private cities would be financially interested in attracting the labor force, it would be in their best interest to minimize the costs of relocation. Obviously, good rules alone, however attractive, in the absence of an adequate infrastructure cannot create a city with a steady and growing population. That said, according to Romer (2010, 1), good rules are a scarcer resource today than materials or technologies. The benefits of good rules in a private city, therefore, might be sufficient to cover the costs of physical relocation.

The problem with private cities is that the current system of international law leaves very thin opportunities for them to emerge in the first place. Apart from several instances of *terra nullius* (Latin for land belonging to no one), few of which, if any, are suitable for urban development, all the potentially inhabitable land is legally divided between nation-states. If we put aside exotic and, as of today, largely theoretical solutions like "seasteading" (Quirk and Friedman 2017) or "cryptosecession" (MacDonald 2019), the primary option we are left with would be the so-called special jurisdictions. They come under different names in different countries—new areas in China, economic cities in Saudi Arabia, free trade zones in the UAE, foreign trade zones in the United States, and so on (Bell 2018). All of them can be united under a broader definition of *special economic zones (SEZs)*, which the World Bank defines as:

> demarcated geographic areas contained within a country's national boundaries where the rules of business are different from those that prevail in the national territory. These differential rules principally deal with investment conditions, international trade and customs, taxation, and the regulatory environment; whereby the zone is given a business environment that is intended to be more liberal from a policy perspective and more effective from an administrative perspective than that of the national territory. (Farole and Akinci 2011, 3)

Because SEZs are bound to compete with each other for investments, they are rather sensitive to the market stimuli and open toward innovative governance models. When treating investors as stakeholders, they are likely to give greater freedom and flexibility to private capital. All of these factors could potentially make SEZs a workable framework for establishing private cities.

What Made Lavasa Possible

The national government does not necessarily need to proclaim an SEZ to enable such an experiment. In some instances, there are very specific transaction costs that prohibit the creation of private cities. Therefore, simply repealing a piece of legislation or issuing a new one would be sufficient to permit the creation of the market for private cities. As we shall see later, in the case of Lavasa, it was the so-called "Hill Stations Regulation" passed in 1996 that empowered private developers to build a city from scratch. The reform only slightly relaxed the very specific land use regulations—yet, because there already was a demand for experiments like Lavasa, as soon as the legal obstacle was removed, the market for private cities emerged. That marginal effect appeared to be enough to encourage developers, among them the Lavasa Corporation Limited (LCL), to come up with institutional innovations that would minimize transaction costs even further.

Like any profit-making market agent, prior to starting a project, LCL had to carefully weigh the transaction costs it was facing—for an enterprise to be profitable, they should be substantial enough to create a market opportunity yet not prohibitively high. Given the strong opposition to—and, as a result, a dismal track record of—private-led urbanization projects among Indian civil society, Lavasa from the very first moment was a high-risk enterprise. As we shall see, the developer undertook certain costly steps to avoid accusations that had jeopardized the efforts of its predecessors. Yet, in the situation of Lavasa, over time, the political process became an unexpected and excessive cost that the developer could not properly budget for, resulting in the project being stalled.

Private cities, in a way, find themselves in a catch-22 position: it is the deficit of stable and predictable rules that creates a market for private jurisdictions, but nevertheless, it is the same deficit of good rules that prevents innovators from addressing this problem. Whether this vicious circle can be broken is a question of grave importance for anyone concerned about the future of private cities. The format of this chapter, however, does not allow me to address this question. The goal of this chapter is to illustrate the elements of that vicious circle using the Coasian transaction costs paradigm.

CATCH-22 FOR PRIVATE CITIES: THE EXPERIENCE OF LAVASA

The two pillars of my approach to investigating private cities are *methodological individualism* and the *spontaneous order*. The former means that human goals and actions are the primary object of analysis; the latter means that unintended and unforeseen consequences of such actions constitute the complex social order (Boettke and Coyne 2005). Observing a real-world development of a private city allows me to grasp the formal and, importantly, informal rules and underlying incentives of stakeholders involved rather than simply make conclusions based on the stated goals and official documents (Campbell 2003).

The practical goal of my work is to illustrate what kind of individual motivations market agents were facing at each stage of the development and what kind of transaction costs they had to incur. I pay special attention to the strategic choice that Lavasa Corporation Limited had to make before commencing the development. Essentially, what they had to evaluate were the two different types of transaction costs—those related to piecemeal land buying and those incurred through potential legal disputes. In the end, I demonstrate how the path they chose guaranteed them an initial advantage. Yet, that advantage was not significant enough to sustain the unexpected political opposition.

This section looks closely at the example of Lavasa, a private city in India, through the Coasian lens with the aim to explain its initial relative success and subsequent demise. In many ways, Lavasa is different from similar projects of private cities built from scratch in India or elsewhere. For a number of reasons, which I outline below, it seemed like a rather promising project as it was conceived and during the first phase of development. The whole process, from land acquisition to master-planning and managing the city once it is built, is well-documented, which makes it possible to establish cause-and-effect relationships in the absence of field studies.

Historical Context

India alone—a home to half of the world's urban population—is notorious for the poor quality of urban management. Sadly, Mumbai's slums and Delhi's air pollution are as recognizable symbols of India as the famous Taj Mahal. With the current unprecedented pace of urbanization—every minute about 25–30 Indians move from a rural area to a city—the country's urban population is projected to reach half a billion in the next decade. If the situation with Indian cities remains unchanged, this is going to be a major challenge for the country. Unwilling to wait for reforms, some 45 million Indians have found a refuge behind the gates of proprietary communities (Singh 2019). Amid urban chaos, these enclaves have public security and well-maintained common-pool resources as their main selling point. This option, however, is neither suitable nor affordable for the majority of urban dwellers in India. Driven by a mix of commercial and philanthropic incentives, certain developers are trying to extrapolate the benefits of gated communities to the size of a whole city.

The classic example of a privately developed city in India, and probably one of the most famous examples of private cities worldwide, is Gurgaon (now officially named Gurugram), a satellite city southwest of the Indian capital, New Delhi. With a population of 876,969, Gurgaon serves as a financial and industrial hub for India, being, in fact, a city with the third highest income per capita in the country (after Mumbai and Chennai) and the highest Human Development Index out of all Indian cities.[8] The case of Gurgaon illustrates that a special legal exemption was needed to make such an innovative governance model possible. For Gurgaon, it was the lifting of restrictions on the land acquisition on a state level—along with the absence of the municipal governing body up until 2011—that played a crucial role. Similarly, the creation of Lavasa only became possible after the passing of the so-called "Hill Station Regulation" by the regional government.

Despite its stunning economic success, Gurgaon was not particularly good at providing quality urban infrastructure. Rajagopalan and Tabarrok (2014, 221) believe that while centralized control over land reduced transaction costs, the fragmentation of urban services (e.g., water, electricity, sewage) provision might have accidentally increased them (they name two particular "market failures": the failure to exploit economies of scale and negative externalities). "If the government had allowed, or even required, much larger initial purchases of land then *entire competitive cities* could have been built under the umbrella of a single firm" (ibid., 221, emphasis added). Lavasa can be regarded as one small step in that direction.

A Private Utopia That Didn't Happen

Located approximately 130 miles from Mumbai, Lavasa was conceived as a private city built entirely from scratch covering some 10,000 hectares of land—one-fifth the size of greater Mumbai. The Hindustan Construction Company (HCC), through its subsidiary LCL, acted as both the owner and the manager of the new city with a budget of $30 billion. According to the initial plan, upon completion, the city of Lavasa was supposed to include five self-sustaining towns with a permanent population of 240,000.[9]

HCC, otherwise known to most Indians as a provider of infrastructure megaprojects such as highways and dams, envisioned Lavasa as an embodiment of the principles of New Urbanism, the urban design movement that promotes walkable communities with much of the land set aside for green and open spaces. The corporation promised, for instance, that 80 percent of the population would be able to access the town center within a 15-minute walk. Lavasa's other influences reportedly include the Italian fishing village of Portofino in the Italian Riviera, which lent its name to some of the city's streets and buildings. The master plan of the new city designed by globally renowned HOK architects was given international awards. Everything inside Lavasa—apart from the post office and police stations—was meant to be run by a corporation. Private businesses not only maintained public spaces but also ran schools, hospitals, and other traditionally state-operated municipal services. The mayor's role was played by a city manager, appointed by the board of LCL.

By 2010, the first of these five towns, Dasve, was almost completed. It attracted the initial population of about 10,000 people, and the developer was already considering an IPO. Suddenly, the national Ministry of Environment and Forests (MoEF) temporarily withdrew its planning permission, leading to a one-year-long pause in construction. That, according to some previously conducted case studies (Hadfield-Hill and Zara 2017), became the primary reason for the stagnation of the project. As described by a reporter who observed the situation on-site,

this one-time hilltop paradise is becoming for some a hell on earth. The days of zero crime are over. Garbage collection is sporadic, so litter soils the man-made lake. Storefronts are vacant. Signs of neglect are everywhere: maintenance is late or non-existent. And that's for the construction already done. For the unfinished building works—i.e. most of it—there is little happening. (Anto and Pandya 2018, n.p.)

About a year later, the company got environmental clearance and the construction was resumed. However, by that time, a critical number of investors lost their trust in the future of the project. In 2018, India's central bank was pushing lenders to take defaulters to bankruptcy court. My investigation below is an attempt, by means of transaction costs analysis, to comprehend and decipher the story of Lavasa as a private utopia that didn't happen.

Legal Background

Gurgaon was conceived as a manufacturing site and eventually gained its prominence as a financial center. Lavasa, on the other hand, was initially envisioned as a resort, a contemporary take on a colonial era concept of a "hill station." Similarly, as in the Gurgaon case, it was the passing of specific legislation—in this instance the "Special Regulations for the Development of Tourist Resorts/Holiday Homes/Township in Hill Station Type Areas" passed in 1996 by the Government of Maharashtra state—that eliminated the prohibitive transaction costs and created an opportunity for developers to address the remaining ones.[10]

The passing of the law, apparently, became possible when long-term policy goals coincided with local interests. On the one hand, encouraging private developers to build new cities was part of an overarching urbanization strategy—and a whole range of legal acts on both the national (such as the *2005 Special Economic Zone Act*) and regional (such as the *2006 Maharashtra Special Township Policy*) levels proved effective in that sense. As a result, Parikh (2015, 51) notes, "in just over a decade, the private sector has gone from building apartments to full-scale cities across the country." On the other hand, the 1996 Hill Station Regulation was likely a brainchild of an influential local politician, Sharad Pawar, who was the three times chief minister of Maharashtra (1978–1980, 1988–1991, and 1993–1995) and later minister of agriculture of India (2004–2014). Notably, one of the real estate companies that helped Lavasa to aggregate land, Yashomala Leasings and Finance Private Ltd, had Pawar's son-in-law among its shareholders (Parikh 2015, 115), while Pawar's nephew was Maharashtra's minister of irrigation in 2000–2012 (ibid.). It should not come as a surprise then that in the eyes of the public, the Pawar family was closely linked with the project.

In essence, the 1996 Hill Station reform waived land-ceiling laws for designated areas, allowed the purchase of agricultural land for non-agricultural purposes, and provided substantial tax exemptions for developers. As a result, a new market was created. Multiple market actors saw it as a profit opportunity, among them the 100-year-old HCC.

Land Purchase

Lavasa was not the first attempt to build a private city in India using the window of opportunity opened by a regulatory reform. However, a number of crucial aspects make Lavasa stand out from the rest, most notable of them related to the land purchasing process. First and foremost, the development of Lavasa did not involve any instances of eminent domain—the state's privilege to forcefully acquire private land for projects deemed to be of public importance. For cities developed in public-private partnerships in India, on the other hand, the involuntary purchase—in other words, expropriation—of private land has been a common trait. The developer of Lavasa, in turn, chose a strategy that, as Parikh (2015, 19) asserts, was "not thought to be possible in the Indian context," the one of a piecemeal voluntary acquisition of land from individual villagers.

It is easy to conclude that transaction costs of that chosen strategy must have been enormous. Indeed, because LLC, the purposely created subsidiary of HCC, needed to individually negotiate the purchase of every piece of land with almost a *thousand* individual sellers, the process of assembling the land took over a decade. Two strategies were utilized to limit, at least to some extent, the incurred transaction costs. The first one was engaging with large land aggregators as intermediaries (75 percent of the land was acquired in this manner according to LCL's own data) instead of the original owners. The second was assembling land before the formal announcement of the project. Parikh (2015, 152) sees it as an illustration of LCL abusing the asymmetry of information, since the villages were unaware, when parting with their land, that the rural land would later be used for urban development. Were they to have known the true land value, Parikh goes on, they would have asked for an adequate, higher compensation to reflect the real value of the land as determined by its future use.

The Hayekian approach, however, implies that there is no such thing as an inherent value of a resource, and the real price of any good or service can be only revealed through the process of voluntary exchange on the open market (Hayek 1945). Moreover, there is no "rural" and "urban" land, per se. It is up to the landowner to classify it. In the case of Lavasa, the land only became "urban" and hence many times more expensive once the developer actually provided urban infrastructure there, thus creating an added value. At the time of transferring property rights on land from the original owners to LCL, the agreed upon price reflected the price at which that land was valued on the open market. It was the entrepreneurial activity of LCL—through the provision of houses, physical infrastructure, and, importantly, services like master-planning, management, and marketing—that was responsible for the dramatic increase in the land value. The ultimate market price of the land, therefore, reflects not its "true" value but largely the developer's innovative input. If it was not for Lavasa, nobody would buy that land from its original owners at such a high price.[11] On top of that, LCL offered the land-selling villagers non-monetary compensation in the form of homes and jobs in a newly built city, none of which was required from it by law.

Transaction costs of assembling land were raised even higher by the so-called "holdouts"—villagers who refused to sell their land and move out. Instead of seeking to evict them forcefully, either by using the government's power, formally or informally, or by outright physical compulsion, LCL made a decision to amend a master plan to incorporate holdouts. Those houses were old, mostly poorly maintained, and not well-designed—clearly an eyesore that could have potentially diminished the land value of the brand-new, Portofino-inspired mansions nearby. Nevertheless, the developer had its own pragmatic reasons to choose to make amendments to the original master plan rather than eliminate the holdouts one way or another. This dilemma illustrates what I believe is the most important strategic crossroads LCL encountered in the whole process of town-making. Essentially, LCL was bound to choose between the two types of transaction costs—the one associated with land buying and the other with legal disputes.

Like its many predecessors, LCL could have avoided the painstakingly long process of piecemeal land acquisition by choosing to acquire the land forcefully through state coercion. After all, lobbying and other "gray" methods that are normally labeled as corruption are another way of dealing with transaction costs. Especially given the support from the influential Pawar family, LCL could have potentially lobbied the government into using eminent domain—the legal right to forcibly acquire private land for public use. The Land Acquisition Act of 1984 allowed this option, and, in fact, it had enabled several cases of "land grabs" for projects similar to Lavasa (Sampat 2010, 170)—an option that LCL was most certainly aware of.

For the sake of evaluating transaction costs solely, let us put aside the moral aspects of coercion and assume that LCL chose the second strategy based solely on their economic estimates. While involuntary displacement of rural dwellers for the purposes of development was sadly common in India, the political resistance to the practice eventually became widespread (Parikh 2015). Environmental civil groups have developed a number of legal and media strategies to counter development projects they deem to be violating the rights of indigenous people. The possibility of such opposition against Lavasa and the subsequent costs of conflict resolution apparently served as an incentive for LCL to opt for a voluntary purchase strategy. They decided to rely on the rule of law—that is, to play by the formal rules and rely on the formal rules.

After choosing this option—playing by the rules—LCL then found itself at another crossroads. Again, I am putting aside the ethical aspects and, for the sake of transaction costs analysis, outlining solely economic considerations. The developer had to select the strategy on how to engage with the local residents. Although there is not enough data available in open sources that would allow me to properly interpret the motivation of LCL in their choice and make comparative calculations of expected costs and benefits, I outline below the three potential ways to deal with that issue (keeping in mind that, of course, multiple other strategies were possible as well). These three ways, however, seem to be the most straightforward, and I analyze them to illustrate the role of transaction costs in building a private city.

First, they could have tried to avoid any negotiation and bargaining with the villagers whatsoever, ignoring the dissenting voices and taking advantage of their market power and political support. On the positive side, that would have obviously meant avoiding the transaction costs of negotiation. On the other side, that could have considerably hurt the public image of a project that had been positioned, from its very inception, as community-oriented, committed to the principles of sustainable development, and destined to become a role model for future master-planned cities. Besides, they surely had in mind the possibility of ideologically motivated opposition and probably did not want to grant this argument to their potential critics who would not have missed a chance to accuse Lavasa of being just another "neoliberal" project that put profits over public interest. Unsurprisingly, LCL did not follow this way and decided to engage in a dialogue with the locals.

Second, LCL could have demonstrated their openness to dialogue while, in reality, trying to downplay or outright silence the holdouts (villagers who refused to sell their land and move out) and any other expressions of discontent on behalf of the villagers, occasionally resorting to minor fraudulent practices. Some of the respondents claimed that it was exactly the attitude that the developer demonstrated by, for example, using powerful land aggregators as intermediaries, generating fake documents, and offering smaller compensation than agreed upon ((Parikh 2015, 170). That said, multiple respondents simultaneously admitted that the overall stance of LCL was largely cooperative. As in the first option, the benefits of this strategy would have included saving time needed for negotiation, although it is likely that less time would have been saved since LCL would have still tried to keep the façade of a benevolent agent. The costs, in turn, would have been somewhat similar to those of the first strategy—plus this would have given their critics a chance to accuse them of being hypocritical (cooperative on the surface but "predatory" in reality). This strategy is, arguably, the least optimal, as, in a way, it suffers from the downsides of the other two.

Third, LCL could have tried to strengthen their image of a conscious developer building a city "like no other" by actively engaging with locals and trying to build alliances with local opinion leaders. This would have meant respecting the holdouts and genuinely taking public opinion into account, including occasionally amending their initial master plan whenever asked by the villagers. Evidently, following this strategy would have meant greatly prolonging the timeline of the project, which could have disappointed some of the investors (whose reputation, to a much lesser extent, depends on the public image of Lavasa). That slowdown would have been the downside of pursuing the most "cooperative" strategy. The upside would have included the chance to secure support from villagers and morally disarm the opponents.

As we shall see, the LCL ultimately preferred the third strategy over the other two. On top of what they were required to do by law and by contract, they made several friendly moves to demonstrate their goodwill (e.g., over 300 landowners were offered jobs within LCL). As a result, the majority of villagers who had sold their land to LCL later voiced their support of Lavasa and condemned the ideologically motivated attempts to stall the construction of the city. In a more institutionally stable environment, that could have tipped the scales in LCL's favor to the point where Lavasa would persevere, both commercially and reputationally. In reality, as we shall see, the developer underestimated the political risks.

Until a certain point, the chosen strategy paid off. The individual approach to every transaction over land minimized the possibility of a collective action from the villagers and deprived the environmental activists of what is usually their strongest argument against similar projects. Furthermore, the mere presence of holdouts served as a vivid illustration of LCL's commitment to non-coercion, and in a way, it politically legitimized Lavasa (ibid.). Even more telling, when the political resistance started, it was immediately met by counter-resistance on behalf of the local residents. The latter highlights the pragmatic reasons for LCL to offer villagers homes and jobs in Lavasa—by making them stakeholders, LCL ensured that the locals became interested in Lavasa's success.

Planning Autonomy

The developer envisioned Lavasa as a conglomerate of five small towns with an overall permanent population of 240,000, an employment base of 80,000, and 2 million visitors a year. What was conceived as a hill resort was eventually proclaimed by the CEO of the Hindustan Construction Company, Ajit Gulabchand, a "replicable model for the development of future cities" (Kazmin 2014). As evident from promotional materials and public announcements by Lavasa representatives, what the company intended to sell was beyond real estate alone. The main product was a utopian vision of a city with not only a master plan and "world-class" facilities but also its own unique governance model. The advertising campaign for Lavasa particularly emphasized the two aspects of a prospected city: sustainability and inclusivity. LCL presented Lavasa as the antipode of the existing Indian cities, which one LCL representative interviewed by Parikh (2015, 137) called "handicapped." The fragmentation of both physical infrastructure and political powers in traditional cities resulted in transaction costs that, in turn, created a demand for innovative propositions like Lavasa.

The unique legal status of Lavasa—the one in which a city is owned, managed, and governed by a single private actor—affected its physical layout, too. In a stark contrast with the chaotic character of traditional Indian cities, the new town of Lavasa was built according to an award-winning master plan by renowned architects. A former Mumbai Metropolitan Authority planner was hired by LCL to implement it—after forty years of serving the government, he recalls, he gained more influence and was less constrained than he was when working for a private firm (Parikh 2015, 140).

The legal status of Lavasa vis-à-vis public authorities was further strengthened in 2007 when LCL received the status of a Special Planning Authority (SPA). The latter spared LCL from the obligation to constantly interact with the government and enabled them to levy charges and enter into land lease and sale agreements, thus minimizing transaction costs even further. At that point, LCL effectively became a private government, an example of a special jurisdiction as referred to by Fuller and Romer (2012) and Bell (2018). The new status, however, came with a cost: from that moment on, LCL employees had to be treated as public servants, and all the planning proposals were bound to be publicly discussed. Yet, given that LCL chose to apply for SPA status, the net value of the new status from the transaction costs standpoint was deemed to be positive.

What Went Wrong

The developer of Lavasa chose a long and cumbersome route of voluntary land purchases from hundreds of individual landowners believing that it would save them from even higher transaction costs associated with legal actions. Up until a certain point, the strategy was working well, as barely any legal cases were filed against LCL. As per the district collector's 2007–2008 report, only 5 percent of all transactions resulted in legal cases that ended up in courts. This, along with the absence of collective protests, has a twofold explanation. On the one hand, transaction costs of legal actions, being a negative-sum game, are burdensome for all parties involved. Yet, they are still very unevenly distributed between the sides. If a dispute between LCL and the villagers ends up in court, the developer is significantly more capable of covering their legal costs. On the other hand, villagers were also interested in the success of Lavasa. Certain villagers might have been interested in receiving what they believed was an adequate compensation for land, but very few were interested in stalling or shutting down the development altogether.

Nevertheless, the private city of Lavasa faced strong political opposition, and that became fatal for the project. The fight against Lavasa was spearheaded by the National Alliance of People's movement (NAPM), an umbrella organization that was created in the early 1990s in opposition to market reforms in India. The NAPM incorporates over a hundred organizations, each with their own agenda. Through activism, it addresses topics from feminism to anti-globalism and the "untouchability" problem. Some of the NAPM's most visible and impactful actions are addressing the rights of tribal people. In the case of Lavasa, the NAPM was instrumental in mobilizing local indigenous people against the development.

For the NAMP activists, Lavasa was an obvious target, though not an easy one. By then, the movement had earned a track record for successfully blocking large-scale development projects across India. Some of the most prominent examples include the Sardar Sarovar Dam in Gujarat, which was stalled after a range of environmental activists organized a massive campaign. That campaign included the following: a petition to the World Bank; coverage in foreign newspapers, including *Financial Times* and *The Washington Post*; putting pressure on private investors from other countries; freezing the Hirandani gardens project in Mumbai until the developer incorporated affordable housing in the master plan; and stopping the construction of the Tata Motors car factory in West Bengal, just to name a few.

It is worth noting that the NAMP activists were known to hold particularly strong ideological opposition to the concept of SEZs, which they saw as an embodiment of the "neoliberal," globalist threat to the Indian values and lifestyle. Social activist Medha Patkar, the informal leader of both the NAMP and the anti-Lavasa campaign, famously labeled SEZs as "Special Exploitation Zones," blamed them for "ecological degradation and destruction of livelihood," and pledged to fight against the development of SEZs in India (The Hindu 2010). As a vivid illustration, five SEZs in Goa alone have been blocked following environmental protests (Sampat 2010).

Parikh's interviews with the NAMP activists involved in the anti-Lavasa campaign reveal that it was more the overall ideological rejection of the project rather than particular instances of land rights violation that drew their attention to Lavasa. Initially, the NAPM undertook an attempt to follow their standard procedure and raise concerns about land fraud and displacement—a strategy that had been successful in previous campaigns (such as the Sardar Sarovar Dam).

For Lavasa developers, the decision to engage in piece-by-piece land acquisition was likely motivated by the need to avoid similar accusations—accusations that had buried more than one development project in India by that time (ibid.). Consequently, the NAPM decided to follow a different approach and sue Lavasa for environmental damage. What the NAMP particularly criticized in the case of Lavasa was its declared eco-friendliness—something that opponents unambiguously rejected as greenwashing. For them, accepting Lavasa as a genuine example of sustainable development would create a dangerous precedent of outsourcing to the private sector what they believed was within the realm of government and the broader society.[12] The conflict had, at its core, "irreconcilable views on privatisation and the control and ownership of land" between Lavasa developers and the NAPM activists (Parikh 2015, 45).

In 2010, through a course of public protests, legal complaints, and media campaigning, the activists managed to stall the project on environmental grounds. The prohibitive order by the MoEF to stall the project came just before LCL was planning to file for an IPO on the Mumbai stock exchange. First, the decision stated that LCL had not obtained environmental clearance from the MoEF.[13] Second, it stated that LCL had illegally constructed 47 hectares of real estate at above 1,000 meters above sea level. Parikh (2015) stresses the fact that both conclusions were made by the MoEF based solely on the NAPM's complaint in the absence of an actual environmental assessment. That move, notably, was met with counter-protests by the village communities whose welfare greatly depended on Lavasa's commercial success. The MoEF obligated LCL to "restore the environment" and generally expand its corporate social responsibility program. Ultimately, after LCL fulfilled its part, the development of Lavasa was unfrozen, yet the trust of the investors was apparently lost irreversibly. To them, the fact that LCL had been defeated in the first place meant that LCL was probably not powerful enough to secure the returns on their investments.

In 2017, adding insult to injury, the future of Lavasa was thrown into further doubt as the SPA status of the project was revoked by the Maharashtra government. From that moment on, all project-related proposals required approval from the Pune Metropolitan Regional Development Authority (PMRDA)—an agency that had not existed at the time when Lavasa was conceived—which was another sign of institutional volatility (Kulkarni 2017). A year later, LCL was finally declared bankrupt. Today, Lavasa is described as a "ghost town" and the future of it remains unclear.

NIMBYism on a Global Scale

As the developer, through lengthy disputes with the government, tried to save Lavasa, their defense strategy was based on an argument that Lavasa was a win-win solution for both LCL and the villagers—a Pareto improvement, to put it in economic terms. In court hearings and public announcements,[14] the LCL representatives argued that the development of Lavasa not only benefited the environment—for instance, by planting 600,000 trees—but also significantly improved the quality of life of local people, most importantly through creating over 400 jobs. To stall the project, LCL argued, would be to deprive some 1,000 families of their source of income and damage their chances of getting out of poverty. Importantly, many villagers supported these claims, with some of them testifying that, contrary to the NAPM's narrative, the creation of Lavasa made them better off, not worse (Parikh 2015, 244). Ten years later, the remaining residents of Lavasa are still petitioning the prime minister's office asking for assistance in reviving the project by including the ghost town in its Smart Cities Mission program (Nambiar 2019).

The ideology of the NAPM implies that environmental rights and land rights are closely intertwined when it comes to protecting the rights of the disadvantaged, displaced, and dispossessed. Moreover, it implies that the alleged victims of such dispossession put their traditional lifestyle and untouched livelihood above all other values. In contrast to that, the Hayekian "tacit knowledge" perspective suggests that, for any given individual or community, the hierarchy of values can only be revealed through price-based mechanisms. The costs and benefits of public goods (including environmental goods) remain highly subjective. Therefore, any external judgment—whether by a government planner or by an activist group—is deemed to be subjective and arbitrary as well (Pennington 2012, 44).

The only way to discover whether indigenous landowners valued the abstract "economic progress" above or below the abstract "traditions" would be to observe their voluntary actions and choices—that, practically, was done by LCL at the land accumulation stage. Hypothetical choices (expressed, for instance, via survey, public hearing, or protest rally) do not carry similarly reliable information in the same sense, as nothing is at stake. The NAMP activists who contested Lavasa had no stakes in its development, unlike the local people who willingly agreed to sell their land in exchange for both monetary compensation and job offers. The NAPM's judgment about the "social cost" of the development was based on their own hierarchy of values which they, by means of protests and petitions, managed to impose on people whose well-being depended upon the future of Lavasa.

The role of the NAPM in the case of Lavasa—and I am hereby speaking in strictly economic terms without passing judgments on their ideological position—was the role of a disruptor. By abusing the lack of institutional robustness, which allowed them to freeze the project complying with the formal rules, the NAPM raised the transaction costs to a point where they became too high for LCL to continue the development. This is not unsimilar to the so-called NIMBY movement, which has a significant limiting effect on urban growth in developed cities (Myers 2017). Why then did the MoEF side with the campaigners? Sharad Pawar's brainchild, the Hill Station town project, might have simply become a battlefield between rival members of the Indian ruling coalition. One explanation Parikh suggests (2015, 247) is that the stalling of Lavasa right before its planned IPO was the way Sonja Gandhi, head of the coalition, chose to "discipline" Pawar, then the minister of agriculture and also one of the coalition's leaders. From this angle, the story of Lavasa resembles the same old story of "Baptists and Bootleggers," an odd alliance of two very different interest groups pursuing the same regulatory outcome (Yandle 1983), where "Baptists" from the NAMP, who opposed Lavasa from moral high ground, found an unexpected ally among "bootleggers" from MoEF, who wanted to exert their political control. Lavasa did not fall victim to a particular public campaign, but rather to an overall institutional failure. Indian institutions did not appear to be ready for projects like Lavasa. That said, the mere fact that Lavasa made it further than most of its predecessors in creating a livable private city surely deserves attention.

CONCLUSION

Private cities, as evidenced by Lavasa, could provide a solution to institutional weakness in countries where institutional weakness is a persistent problem. Unfortunately, as evidenced by Lavasa as well, private cities themselves require relatively strong institutions to emerge in the first place. For entrepreneurs to see private cities as a profit opportunity, they must be sure that their investments are secure and that the rules of the game will remain unchanged. Many opportunities like this remain unrealized due to political instability (Romer 2010). From the transaction costs perspective, private cities are in demand when public institutions fail to do their job, but they are also unlikely to emerge when public institutions fail. Changing the status quo—that is, changing the rules for rulemaking itself—is usually more costly than living in the world of imperfect institutions. In light of the collective action problem, the beneficiaries of such a major institutional change are unidentified and dispersed, while the custodians of the status quo are visible and well-organized.

None of the above means, however, that private cities are impossible in the existing legal and political environment. Lavasa, after all, appeared vulnerable to external conditions but otherwise would have been successfully managed internally. It only took a minor piece of legislation to lower transaction costs enough for a private developer to step in and give it a try. The stable interests of both investors and potential residents indicated that the city-as-a-service concept—a city where the governance model is as important a part of the bundle as the physical infrastructure—has potential. In this sense, Lavasa can be regarded as a prototype for future private urban developments. In the Coasian paradigm, "without failure and entrepreneurial losses, there would exist no future profit opportunities for entrepreneurs to discover either" (Candela and Geloso 2019, 12). The next private city would probably learn from Lavasa's experience.

NOTES

1. United Nations. 2018 Revision of World Urbanization Prospects. www.un.org/development/desa/publications/2018-revision-of-world-urbanization-prospects.html.

2. See www.iqair.com/world-most-polluted-cities.

3. NIMBY stands for "Not in My Backyard" and is used as a broad term for anti-development activists.

4. The two, however, can be regarded as two sides of the same coin, which is defined by Kirzner (1973, 227) as the cost "of obtaining the information necessary to enter into and complete bargaining negotiations."

5. Multiple examples of this can be found in *The Voluntary City: Choice, Community, and Civil Society* (Beito, Foldvary, and Tabarrok 1994), a collection of case studies analyzing various aspects of market-based urban development.

6. Another theoretical possibility would be competition for private governance over the city itself, if we regard the city as a special case of a "natural monopoly" in the field of urban governance (Demsetz 1968). The present chapter does not analyze this alternative.

7. That said, the incentives to relocate are at times so strong that for an ever-increasing number of people—both at the national (Arif et al. 2020) and international levels—they outweigh the high cost of foot-voting. Cao (2019, 736) sees the twenty-first-century migration crises as illustrations that, for so many, the need for better living conditions is strong enough to justify leaving everything behind for an uncertain future.

8. See Census 2011: Gurgaon City Population 2011–2021, www.census2011.co.in/census/city/46-gurgaon.html.

9. See Lavasa: Live, Work, Learn, Play, www.lavasa.com/.

10. See www.indiaenvironmentportal.org.in/.

11. Some villagers interviewed by Parikh (2015) later recalled instances of outright aggressive coercion by intermediaries, which, if true, to some extent undermines the claim that the whole process of land gathering was purely voluntary. That said, I

argue that what Parikh calls an asymmetry of information should not be considered a violation of LCL's commitment to voluntary land purchase.

12. As Pennington (2012, 35) notes, the firm and widespread belief that environmental amenities cannot be commodified owes much to the "market failure" discourse, particularly to the idea that private actors have no incentive to take into account negative externalities incurred by urban development.

13. Actually, Lavasa had received clearance from the Government of Maharashtra state, but the MoEF ruled that, given the significant amendments to the original plan, LCL had to ask for clearance from the MoEF instead.

14. For instance, in the *Defamation Pre-Action Protocol Letter of Claim to the English High Court* from September 6, 2009 that is reacting to the article about Lavasa in *The Sunday Times*, it is stated: "Not only is your allegation of deforestation therefore false, but the impression it leaves of environmental vandalism by LCL is contrary to the true position: as a result of LCL's environmental initiatives Lavasa is in fact much greener than before."

REFERENCES

Andersson, David E. and Stefano Moroni. 2014. *Cities and Private Planning: Property Rights, Entrepreneurship and Transaction Costs*. Cheltenham, UK: Edward Elgar Publishing Limited.

Anto, Antony and Dhwani Pandya. 2018. "Lavasa, a Billionaire's Dream Project, Becomes a Nightmare for Bankers." *Livemint*, June 19. https://www.livemint.com /Companies/M4LUKyX5UjzhfhyUthtBCO/Lavasa-a-billionaires-dream-project -becomes-a-nightmare.html.

Arif, Imran, Adam J. Hoffer, Dean Stansel, and Donald Lacombe. 2020. "Economic Freedom and Migration: A Metro Area-Level Analysis." *Southern Economic Journal* 87 (1): 170–90.

Arne, Robert C. 2002. "Entrepreneurial City Planning: Chicago's Central Manufacturing District." In *The Voluntary City: Choice, Community, and Civil Society*, edited by David T. Beito, Peter Gordon, and Alexander T. Tabarrok. Chicago, IL: Independent Publishers Group.

Beito, David T., Peter Gordon, and Alexander T. Tabarrok, eds. 2002. *The Voluntary City: Choice, Community, and Civil Society*. Chicago, IL: Independent Publishers Group.

Bell, Tom W. 2018. *Your Next Government? From the Nation State to Stateless Nations*. Cambridge, UK: Cambridge University Press.

Boettke, Peter J. and Christopher J. Coyne. 2005. "Methodological Individualism, Spontaneous Order and the Research Program of the Workshop in Political Theory and Policy Analysis." *Journal of Economic Behavior & Organization* 57 (2): 145–58.

Campbell, Scott. 2003. *Urban and Regional Planning Program*. Ann Arbor: University of Michigan Press.

Candela, Rosolino A. and Vincent J. Geloso. 2018. "The Lightship in Economics." *Public Choice* 176 (3): 479–506.

———. 2019. "Coase and Transaction Costs Reconsidered: The Case of the English Lighthouse System." *European Journal of Law and Economics* 48 (3): 331–49.

Cao, Lan. 2019. "Charter Cities." *William & Mary Bill of Rights Journal* 27 (3): 717–64.

Chamlee-Wright, Emily, and Virgil Henry Storr. 2011. "Social Capital, Lobbying and Community-Based Interest Groups." *Public Choice* 149 (1–2): 167–85.

Coase, Ronald. 1937. "The Nature of the Firm." *Economica* 4: 386–405.

Colindres, Jorge. 2018. "Democratic Compliance: A Charter City's Obligations under International Law: The Case of the Honduran ZEDE Regime." *Centre for Innovative Governance Research.* https://www.chartercitiesinstitute.org/post/democratic-compliance-a-charter-citys-obligations-under-international-law.

Demsetz, Harold. 1968. "Why Regulate Utilities?" *Journal of Law and Economics* 11 (1): 55–65.

Farole, Thomas and Gokhan Akinci. 2011. "Special Economic Zones: Progress, Emerging Challenges, and Future Directions." *World Bank*, August 1. https://documents.worldbank.org/en/publication/documents-reports/documentdetail/752011468203980987/special-economic-zones-progress-emerging-challenges-and-future-directions.

Foldvary, Fred. 1994. *Public Goods and Private Communities: The Market Provision of Social Services.* Brookfield, VT: Ashgate Publishing.

Fuller, Brandon and Paul Romer. 2012. "How Charter Cities Could Transform the Developing World." *Macdonald-Laurier Institute.* https://www.macdonaldlaurier.ca/files/pdf/How-charter-cities-could-transform-the-developing-world-April-2012.pdf.

Galantay, Erwin Y. 1975. *New Towns: Antiquity to the Present (Planning and Cities).* New York: George Braziller.

Glaeser, Edward L. 2013. "Urban Public Finance." In *Handbook of Public Economics, Volume 5*, edited by Alan J. Auerbach, Raj Chetty, Martin Feldstein, and Emmanuel Saez, 195–257. North Holland, NL: Elsevier Science.

Hadfield-Hill, Sophie and Christiana Zara. 2017. "New Urbanisms in India: Urban Living, Sustainability and Everyday Life." *University of Birmingham.* https://www.birmingham.ac.uk/news/latest/2017/02/Birmingham-develops-blueprint-for-future-Indian-cities.aspx.

Hayek, F. A. 1945. "The Use of Knowledge in Society." *The American Economic Review* 35 (4): 519–30.

Heath, Spencer. 1957. *Citadel, Market and Altar.* Baltimore, MD: Science of Society Foundation.

Holcombe, Randall G. 2018. "The Coase Theorem, Applied to Markets and Government." *The Independent Review* 23 (2): 249–66.

Jacobs, Jane. 1961. *The Death and Life of Great American Cities.* New York: Vintage Books.

Kazmin, Amy. 2014. "India's Modern-Day Hill Station Lavasa Resurrects IPO Plan." *Financial Times*, July 2. https://www.ft.com/content/06e05160-01b7-11e4-bb71-00144feab7de.

Kirzner, Israel M. 1978. *Competition and Entrepreneurship*. Chicago, IL: University of Chicago Press.

Krugman, Paul and Robin Wells. 2006. *Economics*. New York: Worth Publishers.

Kulkarni, Prachee. 2017. "Lavasa in Limbo: How Politics, Environmental Concerns Are Holding Up a Rs 50,000 CR Project." *Firstpost*, May 31. https://www.firstpost .com/business/lavasa-in-limbo-how-politics-environmental-concerns-are-holding -up-a-rs-50000-cr-project-3497529.html.

Lai, Lawrence and Frank T. Lorne. 2007. "Transaction Cost Reduction and Innovations for Spontaneous Cities: Promoting a 'Meeting' between Coase and Schumpeter." *Planning Theory* 13 (2): 170–88.

MacDonald, Trent J. 2019. *The Political Economy of Non-Territorial Exit: Cryptosecession*. Northampton, MA: Edward Elgar.

McCallum, Spencer H. 1997. "The Quickening of Social Evolution: Perspectives on Proprietary (Entrepreneurial) Communities." *Independent Review* 2 (2): 287–302.

Myers, John. 2017. "Yes in My Backyard: How to End the Housing Crisis, Boost the Economy and Win More Votes." *Adam Smith Institute*, August 11. https://www .adamsmith.org/research/yimby.

Nambiar, Nisha. 2019. "Lavasa Residents Seek PMO's Help to Save Project." *The Times of India*, June 29. http://timesofindia.indiatimes.com/articleshow/69998948 .cms.

Olson, Mancur. 1971. *The Logic of Collective Action: Public Goods and the Theory of Group*s. Cambridge, MA: Harvard Economic Studies.

Ostrom, Elinor. 2005. *Understanding Institutional Diversity*. Princeton, NJ: Princeton University Press.

Parikh, Anokhi. 2015. "The Private City: Planning, Property, and Protest in the Making of Lavasa New Town, India." PhD diss., London School of Economics and Political Science.

Pennington, Mark. 2012. "Elinor Ostrom, Common-Pool Resources and the Classical Liberal Tradition." In *The Future of the Commons: Beyond Market Failure and Government Regulation*, edited by Elinor Ostrom, Christina Chang, Mark Pennington, and Vlad Tarko, 21–47. London: Institute of Economic Affairs.

Pennington, Mark. 2014. "Citizen Participation, 'The Knowledge Problem' and Urban Planning: An 'Austrian' Perspective on Institutional Choice." *The Review of Austrian Economics* 17 (2–3): 213–31.

Quirk, Joe and Patri Friedman. 2017. *Seasteading: How Floating Nations Will Restore the Environment, Enrich the Poor, Cure the Sick, and Liberate Humanity from Politicians*. New York: Simon & Schuster.

Rajagopalan, Shruti and Alexander T. Tabarrok. 2014. "Lessons from Gurgaon, India's Private City." In *Cities and Private Planning: Property Rights, Entrepreneurship and Transaction Costs*, edited by David E. Andersson and Stefano Moroni. Cheltenham, UK: Edward Elgar Publishing Limited.

Romer, Paul. 2010. "Technologies, Rules, and Progress: The Case for Charter Cities." *Center for Global Development*. https://www.cgdev.org/sites/default/files/1423916 _file_TechnologyRulesProgress_FINAL.pdf.

Sampat, Preeti. 2010. "Special Economic Zones in India: Reconfiguring Displacement in a Neoliberal Order?" *City & Society* 22 (2): 166–82.

Singh, Manish. 2019. "MyGate Raises $56M to Bring Its Security Management Service to More Gated Communities in India." *TechCrunch*, October 16. https://techcrunch.com/2019/10/16/mygate-security-gated-premises-india/.

Stringham, Edward P., Jennifer K. Miller, and J. R. Clark. 2010. "Internalizing Externalities through Private Zoning: The Case of Walt Disney Company's Celebration, Florida." *The Journal of Regional Analysis & Policy* 40 (2): 96–103.

The Hindu. 2010. "Medha Patkar Terms SEZs as 'Special Exploitation Zone' Projects." *The Hindu*, February 7. https://www.thehindu.com/news/cities/chennai/Medha-Patkar-terms-SEZs-as-lsquoSpecial-Exploitation-Zonersquo-projects/article16813086.

Tiebout, Charles. 1956. "A Pure Theory of Local Expenditures." *Journal of Political Economy* 64 (5): 416–24.

Webster, Chris. 2007. "Property Rights, Public Space and Urban Design." *The Town Planning Review* 78 (1): 81–101.

Webster, Chris and Lawrence Lai. 2003. *Property Rights, Planning and Markets: Managing Spontaneous Cities*. Cheltenham, UK: Edward Elgar Publishing Limited.

Yandle, Bruce. 2011. "Bootleggers and Baptists in the Theory of Regulation." In *Handbook on the Politics of Regulation*, edited by David Levi-Faur, 25–33. Cheltenham, UK: Edward Elgar Publishing.

Chapter 8

The Political Effects of a Polycentric Order in Nigeria

Ifeoluwa M. Olawole

In challenging the centralization of public goods provision, several scholars have focused on the benefits of a polycentric order. Indeed, a major framework of the Bloomington school of political economy posits that individuals can be and are often self-governing (Boettke, Lemke, and Palagashvili 2016). In assessing a polycentric order of governance, Elinor Ostrom and others at the Workshop in Political Theory and Policy Analysis at Indiana University in Bloomington argued that a polycentric, community-based approach to public goods provision creates better incentive structures for the maintenance of public safety (Boettke, Lemke, and Palagashvili 2016). Further, in evaluating polycentric orders, Storr, Grube, and Haeffele-Balch (2017) highlight the importance of privately provided social services in post-disaster recovery in an Orthodox Jewish community on the Rockaway Peninsula in New York. Although in an altogether different context individuals might not always have the choice of whom to receive goods from, a similar theme that persists regardless of context is the diverse marketplace of goods and services provision.

Therefore, apart from challenging the centralization of public goods provision, this approach also asserts that there are alternative forms of governance when it comes to providing essential goods and services. These alternate forms include state and non-state actors in the marketplace of service delivery. What is missing from the extant literature is the political consequence of these polycentric orders or the impact of various producers on political and economic behavior. Specifically, how might these various producers affect the political participation of citizens? Research on such types of consequences of such polycentric orders has been scarce. Indeed, in contexts with such polycentric orders, where the state sometimes delivers public goods and services; where other non-state actors such as faith-based organizations, nongovernmental organizations, international organizations, and multinational corporations provide social services; and where citizens or communities can self-organize to provide club goods, an imperative question to ask is how it shapes political behavior and citizens' proclivity to participate in politics.

Consequently, this chapter examines the impact of such polycentric orders on political participation and within a different political context altogether. It analyzes the political implications and consequences of having many different producers of goods and services, especially within the context of a young democracy, using Nigeria, the most populous nation in sub-Saharan Africa, as a case study. The chapter also examines the impact of different producers of goods and services in Nigeria on the likelihood of citizens contacting elected leaders—a non-electoral form of participation. By understanding how such polycentric orders affect the likelihood of citizens participating in politics in Nigeria, it demonstrates the consequences of such orders in developing nations and younger democracies and, more broadly, the implications for state-society relations. This chapter asks how the existence of multiple providers of public goods and services affects political participation in Nigeria and as such seeks to understand what incentives (or lack thereof) a polycentric system of service delivery creates for citizens in developing nations to contact their elected leaders and participate in governance.

I argue that political attitudes differ depending on *who* provides the basic goods and services. Specifically, that non-state provision of goods reduces political participation and can ultimately lead to the weakening of the state. When the state provides, citizens are more likely to participate; whereas when non-state actors provide, citizens are less likely to participate in politics. I also examine the effects of various non-state actors: self-provision and international and nongovernmental organizations.

To do this, this chapter employs data from extensive field research in Nigeria in 2018 and 2019. During field research, I interviewed civil society actors, political elites, academics and researchers, and ordinary citizens. Altogether, I conducted forty in-depth and semi-structured interviews. I also attended association and community meetings (in Lagos and Ogun states). Further, I had the opportunity to speak with citizens informally about their politics, governance, and the government in Nigeria in informal and ordinary settings. This manner of immersion gave me various opportunities to conduct participant observation that supports the arguments presented in this chapter.

In the following sections, I first examine the theoretical background. I then examine the context within which the argument is framed—Nigeria. Following that, this chapter delves into service delivery and the numerous challenges surrounding it in Nigeria. Thereafter, I present the different producers of goods and services in Nigeria. I then examine the impact of these providers on citizens' political attitude as it relates to engagement with the state. Finally, this chapter concludes with a summary of the chapter and the policy implications of the argument.

THEORETICAL BACKGROUND

Although scholars have presented more complex frameworks that move beyond the dichotomy of "market" and "state" to understand social interactions and governance, when it comes to applying them to developing nations, there are still facets of these frameworks that are underdeveloped. Indeed, the literature has emphasized the advantages of a polycentric system. Polycentric orders contain a variety of autonomous decision-making authorities that sometimes work independently and other times together. In polycentric orders, these decision-making units may involve multiple and overlapping systems of autonomous governments (Storr, Grube, and Haeffele-Bach 2017; Ostrom, Tiebout, and Warren 1961). Organizations within polycentric systems have some degree of autonomy (Boettke, Lemke, and Palagashvili 2016).

To put it in context, earlier works on diverse ways of organizing water provision in metropolitan areas, policing, and public safety revealed that centralized provision of these goods and services undermined their quality (Ostrom 2010). In the case of policing, larger centralized policed departments underperformed compared to smaller departments in similar neighborhoods (Ostrom and Parks 1973). In extending this framework, Boettke, Lemke, and Palagashvili (2016) empirically test a polycentric system using community policing and find that institutions that remove accountability to the community, foster centralization, and prioritize federal initiatives alter the incentives of police in community policing efforts by causing the police to focus on satisfying the demands of the federal government instead of focusing on the needs of the community. Ostrom and her colleagues argued that community-based policing is more successful because individuals have better knowledge of their own circumstances and are more likely to design better rules (Ostrom 2000; Boettke, Lemke, and Palagashvili 2016). This reasoning can be extended to other arguments for polycentric orders that include self- or community governance.

Apart from revealing the overarching benefits of a polycentric order, some scholars have also specifically highlighted the advantages of non-state provision of goods and services. For instance, local actors governing common-pool resources, especially in uncertain situations (Ostrom 1990), or local entrepreneurs providing goods and services for people in post-recovery (Storr, Grube, and Haeffele-Bach 2017). Indeed, these non-state actors can supplement the state in the delivery of goods and services.

There are a few studies that explore the politics of non-state provision in sub-Saharan Africa. Non-state provision is not a new phenomenon in the region, especially with the rising presence of international and other philanthropic organizations. In fact, some have argued that the presence of nongovernment organizations (NGOs) bolsters and supports a more able state (Brass 2016). A large body of literature has examined the impacts of various NGOs, including as a response to state and economic crisis (Bratton 1989; Sandberg 1994), state-NGO relations (Bebbington et al. 1993), impacts on the health sector (Wamai 2004; Palmer 2006), water (Rusca and Schwartz 2012), or on political outcomes like governance (Swidler 2007).

By so doing, these scholars have criticized a monocentric approach to governance that is predicated on a national economic planning, arguing that it involves the concentration of political and economic power in a single agency (Lavoie [1985] 2016). Yet, my own observations and findings from field research in Nigeria show that many citizens respond better to governance when the state is at the helm of service delivery. This bolsters the argument that state provision, as opposed to non-state provision, induces participation among citizens. While I introduce some novel approaches in my broader research agenda, this is not an entirely new approach.

Other scholars have challenged non-state provision in Africa, arguing that the mere presence of other actors in the marketplace of service delivery can erode state capacity—that is, developing their own internal capacity and revenue generation ability (Cammett and MacLean 2014). Indeed, to narrow it down specifically to the consequences of non-state provision for political participation, Bleck (2013) found that parents who enroll their kids in madrassas (Islamic religious schools) are less likely to vote, while MacLean (2011) found that state retrenchment from social services has adverse effects on voting.

However, while several of these studies have examined the effects of NGOs (or one provider) in the political sphere, they have focused squarely on NGOs as a form of non-state provision. They have rarely examined other aspects of non-state provision, especially self-provision of goods and services. Self-provision of goods and services—further expatiated on below—includes goods and services that individuals or households produce themselves. In addition, works on the complexities of the governance systems in developing countries like Nigeria are relatively few. Further, very few have examined the effects of NGO provision of services on state-society relations and citizens' political inclination. This chapter delves into other aspects of non-state provision and examines their consequences for political participation of citizens in Africa. As far as I know, no other study has explored the impact of having a diverse set of actors in the marketplace of service delivery on political participation in Nigeria. I fill these gaps in this study by examining the impact of having a variety of providers on the political engagement of citizens.

When it comes to explaining political engagement of citizens in the region, a lot of studies have focused on voting. Most of the literature on political participation in the developed world uses socioeconomic models (SES) to posit that citizens with higher income and education are more likely to participate in politics (Verba and Nie 1972). However, this model largely fails in developing countries, especially in sub-Saharan Africa. Participation research in Africa reveals the weakness of SES models, with studies showing that the resource-poor participated more than the resource-rich (Isaksson 2010). In addition to voting, participation includes other activities such as contact between citizens and elected officials (Verba and Nie 1972; van Deth 2014). A lot of scholarly work on participation has focused on voting and not this aspect of participation. It is this aspect of participation that this chapter is concerned with: the likelihood of citizens engaging with elected leaders, a form of citizen engagement. What are the consequences of having a mixture of state and non-state providers for the likelihood of citizens engaging with elected leaders?

This aspect of political participation is becoming increasingly important and is a vital aspect of democratization in the region. Apart from increasing accountability, it can also reduce political corruption and increase efficiency of governance.[1] Furthermore, this form of participation allows citizens to contribute to governance in a way that allows stakeholders to create policies based on people's needs (Haque 2003). In more advanced nations, this manner of contact gives citizens the opportunity to voice their preferences and demand accountability (Mueller 2018).

As with the literature on voting, the prevailing explanation for citizen engagement in Africa is based on patron-client relationships, with scholars arguing that personal contact between elected leaders and citizens is clientelistic and bad for governance (van de Walle 2001). But there is contrary evidence to this. In Niger, for instance, evidence suggests that people contact elected representatives for programmatic requests, thereby making personal contact a source of accountability and not only for fostering patronage relations (Mueller 2018). In addition, extant literature emphasizes socioeconomic factors such as education, money, and civic skills that do not fit the African context (Verba, Schlozman, and Brady 1995; Inman and Andrews 2009). A different category of scholars emphasize the institutional environment that motivates participation, such as fiscal decentralization (Moore 1998), source of public revenue (Moss, Pettersson, and van de Walle 2006; Collier and Hoeffler 2005; Paler 2013), and transparency (Krawczyk, Sweet-Cushman, and Muhula 2013). This approach directly links these institutional arrangements to citizens' participation. Yet, empirical reality in Nigeria suggests that despite recent transparency initiatives, citizens themselves are not always able to parse out whether revenue is from oil rents, taxes, or fiscal transfers.

And while the extant literature is concentrated around transparency and institutional explanations, many citizens can be aware of corruption and still be apathetic.

Indeed, several existing models poorly predict participation in developing countries, but they also fail to include the diverse set of actors that interact with citizens. Factors such as income, education, and skills tend to be constant over time, while the inclination to participate shifts over time (Krawczyk and Sweet-Cushman 2017). Consequently, it is necessary to consider other factors in explaining the motivation to engage in political life. Likewise, institutions are relatively constant, but participation among citizens still varies. What explains that variation in this case? There, I explore why participation within the same political system and unit varies and posit that this leads to a stronger understanding of political participation. I do this by considering other actors and examining the effect of polycentricity. Consequently, the delivery of goods and services by different actors affects political participation.

What the existing literature demonstrates is that exposure to various providers of goods and services certainly motivates political behavior. However, these studies leave some gaps. First, they do not establish an adequate mechanism linking polycentric systems or various providers to citizen engagement. Second, these studies examine one good. Yet, Kramon and Posner (2013) argue that using one good to study political outcomes can be misleading. Therefore, this chapter builds upon earlier studies by examining the effects various actors involved in service delivery have on political participation. What is it about state provision then (or lack thereof) that shifts citizens' engagement? In the following sections, I situate this chapter's main argument within the context of the case study and further expand upon the arguments.

THE CONTEXT—POLITICS AND GOVERNANCE IN NIGERIA

Officially created by Britain in 1914, Nigeria makes a good case and ideal setting for this study, and (as I show below) it enables some level of generalization from this case to other developing nations, especially in sub-Saharan Africa. Nigeria is a federal state with a federal capital territory, 36 states, and 774 local governments, and although there is de jure decentralization in place (carrying significant aspects of a polycentric order), the de facto fiscal autonomy of local governments is hindered by various institutional, economic, and political factors, such as the North primarily relying on fiscal transfers. This is why several Nigerian governors in the Southern states have called for more control of fiscal resources, more political resources, and state-led economic development to bolster carrying out the responsibilities with which each tier of government is constitutionally charged. When it comes to delivery of social services and other goods in the absence of such absolute control, however, there are numerous and multiple centers of independent decision-making units that produce goods and services—directly demonstrating poly-centricity. Below, I further delineate these different providers and how their coexistence might affect the likelihood of citizens contacting elected leaders and, more broadly, the relationship of citizens with the state.

Further, in characterizing Nigeria, Kumar (2018) mentions, "as Nigeria goes, so goes as least the developing world." Indeed, the International Monetary Fund (IMF) states that one in six Africans is Nigerian (Campbell 2011). Nigeria is a vital actor in West Africa alongside boasting of half of West Africa's population and being the most populous nation in sub-Saharan Africa. It is very diverse, multiethnic, and has an abundance of natural resources. The aforementioned polycentricity, occurring alongside other structural factors in Nigeria, makes it a vital setting for understanding how polycentric orders affect citizens' political behavior. Given that the nation is also a key regional player, understanding participation in the country broadens our grasp of political participation more generally. The political and economic context in the paragraphs that follow provide the context within which the main arguments of this study arise.

A huge influence on Nigeria's economy is oil. Oil production began in 1958, but it quickly accelerated after the civil war from 1967 to 1970. As the largest oil and gas producer in Africa, oil accounts for about 65 percent of total government revenue (Extractive Industries Transparency Initiative n.d.). Oil revenue accounted for about 80 percent of government revenue in the 1970s and about 90 percent and 76.3 percent of Nigeria's foreign exchange and government revenue at the federal level, respectively, in 1999 (Lewis 2018). After an increase to 79.9 percent of government revenue in 2011, it started to decline. The crash of oil prices began to necessitate the diversification of the economy.

In a paradoxical puzzle, with its abundance of oil and natural resources, Nigeria has an established history of poor governance. A substantial segment of the political science literature focuses on the adverse effects of oil and over-dependence on oil. The "resource curse" is a phenomenon used to conceptualize instances where natural resource wealth is associated with violence, civil and ethnic conflicts, and poor economic growth (Collier and Hoeffler 2002; Ross 1999). Nigeria's oil experience and its intersection with violence, developmental challenges, and strife certainly demonstrate the resource curse thesis. In explaining their frustration with the government as it pertains to the provision of goods and the resulting failed expectations, Nigerians often draw distinctions between abundant revenue and the lack of service delivery, emphasizing the paradox of plentiful revenue generated from oil that does not lead to gains in state provision. At one community meeting, the prevailing narrative from the attendees focused on their failed expectations, especially given the nation's wealth and the resulting absence of the state from provision of goods and services.[2] Many wondered why they had to utilize self-provision and/or other forms of non-state provision of goods and services in a nation with as much wealth as Nigeria, thereby fueling a disinterest and negative perception of the state. It is for this reason that when non-state actors in a polycentric order like Nigeria's provide goods and services instead of the state, the relationship of citizens with the state is impacted. Yet, the burden remains on the state and not on non-state actors to earn legitimacy from citizens.

Indeed, the over-dependence on oil has affected how federalism operates in Nigeria. The system of top-down federalism found in Nigeria can be attributed to oil due to revenue allocation challenges and the imbalance of regional development interests (Ko 2014). Earlier, in the First Republic, subnational governments assumed dominant modes of economic development (Elemo 2018). At the time, the country had four regional subnational governments. Both levels of government held executive, legislative, and judicial authority, while fiscal power was concentrated at the regional level. However, as revenue increased from the oil boom, there was a greater need to concentrate fiscal powers at the top to be distributed to different regions, which created the more centralized fiscal powers that still persist. The "oil-centric political economy" has increased grievances in Nigerian politics and institutions (Suberu 2004), and with the complexities of providers within such a system, citizens become less likely to contact elected leaders.

Despite a volatile history and a democracy marked by coup d'états at various intervals, Nigeria continues to make improvements. Politically, the Freedom House describes it as partly free. This suggests that as a burgeoning democracy, there is a fundamental right of citizens to exercise their citizenship through engaging with elected leaders. Though this hardly directly explains motivations (or lack thereof) of citizens to utilize this citizenship or perhaps the variations across individuals in exercising their citizenship. What, then, explains this variation? Indeed, there are some macro features that might inherently impede participation. For instance, Nigeria certainly still experiences political corruption, and despite periodical elections, experiences with personalistic regimes and long-running presidencies in other African nations demonstrate that elections alone do not necessarily guarantee a liberal society (Zakaria 1997). There have been efforts to reform Nigeria's electoral process and institutions, many of which have contributed to Nigeria's democratic progress and increased expectations of citizens; notwithstanding, Nigerians point to the lack of state-service delivery as significant factors determining whether or not they contact the state.

To be clear, it is not that Nigerians have always been averse to participation of all forms. Nigeria has gone through stages of political development. In pre-colonial Nigeria, when it seemed that power was employed in such a way that did not benefit members of the community, they would come together to rectify that. Women particularly mobilized to oppose unfavorable decisions using religious and social clubs to deploy traditional strategies (Nwankwor 2018). With the presence of colonial leaders, the relationship of citizens and political leaders shifted as motivations of colonial rule changed. The goal of governance for these leaders then transformed from seeking the greater good to maximizing economic profit (ibid.). Segments of the Nigerian population became disenfranchised at various points in the country's political history. In addition, the colonialism rule's efforts to place men at the center of national politics changed the nature of the relationship between ordinary citizens and political leaders. With age and gender restrictions on voting and participating in politics, political marginalization persisted until Nigeria's First Republic (Ekpeyong, Ibiam, and Agha 2015).

However, after the termination of earlier restrictive policies and the subsequent first general election in preparation for political independence in 1960, there was a signal for a better avenue for Nigerians to engage in political life. The military rule interjecting various political stages in Nigeria has also affected Nigerians' disposition toward the government. There is a disconnect between the state and citizens.[3] Notwithstanding, there are still some citizens who engage in political life and participate in governance. Nigerians engage in political life through different forms. Whether it is the costly voting process, attending political rallies, joining political parties, joining sociocultural associations, contacting their elected leaders, and other informal modes of participation. Broadly speaking, however, in recent years, Nigerians have adopted a more apathetic nature toward politics.[4] In addition, there are some institutional barriers that might also affect participation. For example, elected representatives might not even have constituency offices despite receiving the funding to create one, which can restrict access of citizens to them. Electoral participation is not exempt from these barriers: voting remains a highly costly process that often takes the entire day. But despite these issues, many Nigerians still participate in politics. Sixty-five percent of respondents in the Afrobarometer Nigeria nationally represented 2016/2018 surveys voted in the last election. But often voting is a form of participation that is not as broad in scope with implications for state-society relationships. When it comes to the specific form of participation this chapter deals with—citizen engagement—the trend skews differently; only about 17 percent of respondents contact local government councilors. My own participant observation and qualitative interviews suggest that this is not merely a lack of accessibility issue, but rather it is mainly because non-state provision continually erodes state presence and triggers a dissatisfaction that ultimately leads to disengagement and apathy. I conceptualize citizen engagement broadly as citizens contacting elected leaders at all levels. Although the specific conceptualization in this chapter refers to formal processes like contacting leaders, I argue that inferences from this chapter can apply to both formal and informal processes of engagement. People participate in governance and engage through various forms, including social media, attending town hall meetings, or visiting elected representatives. Therefore, what affects citizen engagement? How does a marketplace of service delivery affect this form of political participation?

SERVICE DELIVERY IN NIGERIA

Due to various historical factors, the government plays a significant role in service delivery in several African nations. Service delivery encompasses the provision of goods and services that are diverse and can include health, education, security, infrastructure, as well as law and order. Some of these services are more visible and tangible than others. Service delivery in this study is conceptualized broadly rather than examining a single good because it can be misleading to draw general conclusions about distributive politics by analyzing one good (Kramon and Posner 2013). In addition, this study emphasizes the provider of these goods more than the specific goods and services.

Apart from the salient role service delivery plays in African nations, it is a facet of governance that is often used to measure government performance across the continent. There are certainly various theoretical arguments explaining the extent to which the government should be involved in service delivery. Coordination processes—whether they are traditional, market, or planning—reveal that social orders are formed through various underlying logic (Lavoie [1985] 2016). Market-based arguments posit that the government provides goods in an economy where individuals pursue their private interests (Moghalu and Obikili 2018; Lavoie [1985] 2016); whereas proponents of centrally planned economies view the state as the provider and distributor of goods and services (Moghalu and Obikili 2018). Many systems employ a combination of these opposing systems often due to historical factors and societal attitude. In Nigeria, as with many other African nations, citizens expect goods and social services such as education, good roads, water, and electricity to be provided by the government. This expectation is a significant aspect of the mechanism driving the main arguments in this chapter. On the one hand, as Ostrom argues, citizens co-producing goods and services alongside other actors bolster the efficiency of those goods. On the other hand, however, in some contexts and due to historical factors (like those delineated above), citizens decry such responsibility because they expect the government to fulfill certain roles and obligations in the delivery of goods and services and are frustrated that they instead carry that burden to the extent that they do.

Yet, the delivery of goods and services has been challenging across the continent. These challenges are evident in the high rates of infant and maternal mortality and underdeveloped roads that affect access to health care and hinder agricultural development (Porter 2002; Minten and Kyle 1999). Indeed, service delivery has suffered a continual decline since the 1970s. It is therefore not surprising that there is an abundant wave of scholarship on the provision of goods and services on the African continent. However, although studies abound understanding its determinants (Miguel and Gugerty 2005) or evaluating how it is delivered to citizens (Omotoso 2014), few have studied effects of the presence of diverse providers on political participation.

State responsibility of goods and services is not new in the region. With the arrival of colonialism, the British colonial officers provided social services and created initiatives to relieve the poor (Decker 2010). Social services in traditional societies included building bridges, road construction, market welfare, and public safety (Abegunde and Akinyemi 2014). This revealed a historical precedent of heavy state presence in service delivery. The state assumed a primary role in economic planning and development especially between 1962 and 1980 (Adejumobi 1999). During this period, there was a substantial increase in government provision of goods, including providing education, health, and electricity, among other services.[5] Gradually, however, this responsibility began to decline, coinciding with global capitalist systems (Decker 2010; Abegunde and Akinyemi 2014).

By the 1980s, after the oil price crash, government finances suffered, and Nigeria's economy took a downward turn (Balassa 1981; Moghalu and Obikili 2018). In response to this crisis, the country adopted the Structural Adjustment Programme (SAP) in 1986, an economic reform by the World Bank and IMF with an objective to restructure the economy. This program resulted in cutting expenditures for social services and the elimination of some public goods. In addition to reduction of support for social services and a decline in service delivery, clientelism was expanded during this period. And while patronage systems still exist across the nation, Nigerians still remember and refer back to the era of heavy state presence in service delivery, citing it as instances of better governance.[6] As a result of the state's withdrawal from social services, several other actors have emerged to fill the gap created by the state in what can now be likened to some form of polycentricity—one that allows for private provision of social services as well as state provision. In the next section, I describe these actors. I also highlight some challenges of service delivery in Nigeria.

DIFFERENT PRODUCERS OF GOODS
AND SERVICES IN NIGERIA

While Nigeria has made important strides in more recent years, the country is still saddled with several development challenges, especially as it relates to fulfilling the citizens' expectations. In 2006, between 54 and 70 percent of Nigerians were without access to basic goods such as education, water, health services, and electricity (Amuwo 2008, 25). These challenges still persist in the nation (World Bank n.d.). Nigeria is ranked 152 out of 157 on the World Bank's 2018 Human Capital Index (ibid.). The notion that government failure is directly linked to poor service delivery continues to be widespread.[7] When such government failure coexists with a polycentric order, there are implications for the relationship between the state and citizens.

In developing nations like Nigeria, goods and services are provided through different channels or a combination of different sources. Some aspect of this phenomenon can be viewed through what Ostrom (1996) conceptualizes as "co-production": the idea that goods and services are provided and jointly produced by the state and from the community. This interpretation refers to a single good from different providers. In other instances, and more pertinent to this study is the idea that there are several sources through which citizens receive goods and services (Olawole 2020). To put this into context, a diverse array of actors provides goods and services, operating on both formal and informal levels. Broadly speaking, these providers can be divided into state and non-state actors. State actors are self-explanatory: when goods and services are from the government. The government is not completely absent from service delivery in Nigeria. Nigeria's current design is such that the different tiers of government share the responsibilities of service delivery. Government agencies are charged with delivering social services. Nigeria's institutional design into a three-tier system of federal, state, and local governments means that different levels have different responsibilities. While the responsibility of the federal government includes issues of national security, electricity provision, and monetary policy, the state and local governments share responsibilities in areas of education, health, and agriculture with the state government incurring more share of the burden than the local government. However, given the sentiments of Nigerians that I interviewed regarding the "government" on the whole as one entity, state provision is viewed broadly in this study. Therefore, the state's presence is reflected in primary healthcare centers, government schools, and so on. However, there are discrepancies between government responsibility and the reality of service delivery by the government. The unreliability of these services renders them inefficient to many citizens.

Non-state actors on the other hand represent producers of goods and services, including international organizations, philanthropic organizations, religious institutions, communities, individuals, and local NGOs. The presence of these actors in delivering a wide range of services is not new in the region, although they are becoming increasingly prevalent. For various reasons, such as inadequate performance and lack of state capacity, these actors have had to fill the gap left by the state in service delivery. Consequently, there is private sector delivery of goods that might not necessarily be profit-seeking, but it is driven by a desire to improve lives and communities.

International organizations such as the World Bank, United Nations, and IMF, and private foundations like the Ford Foundation or the Bill and Melinda Gates Foundation all represent non-state actors that are involved in service delivery. Beyond the macroeconomic policies and strategies of large organizations like these, their individual projects are rarely concealed with projects carrying tags delineating donors, such as "funded by USAID." Activities of this aspect of non-state provision range from charitable acts to more organized philanthropy by corporate social responsibility arms of organizations, churches, and other voluntary nonprofit organizations. These actors might use their resources to provide goods and services at low or no cost to citizens. Such goods include tarred roads, education, healthcare, potable water, and other similar projects.

Another aspect of non-state provision involves individuals or households providing goods and services for themselves without input from the government or other non-state actors. I classify this category of non-state provision as "self-provision" and define it as a category of non-state provision whereby individuals or households produce goods and services themselves that could have been provided by the state. A typical example of this in Nigeria is reflected in the number of households that have to build their own borehole water system due to lack of access to pipe-borne water provided by the state. In other instances, many Nigerians have to buy their own generating sets due to the unreliability of electricity provision and the lack of constant power supply. Beyond these, individuals might enroll their kids in private schools, hire their own "gatemen" security for their homes, or visit private health institutions. In Nigeria alone, the number of clients with private security tripled between 1997 and 2001 (Muggah and Frate 2007). In fact, households sometimes call themselves their own "government" because of the extent to which many provide their own goods and services (Abegunde and Akinyemi 2014). Highlighting these salient factors reveals that citizens do not perceive non-state provision systems to address problems in their community as a successful form of governance. On the contrary, it further exposes where the government has failed and evokes strong reactions among respondents.

As an extension of self-provision, another aspect of non-state provision is community-organized provision. This is most evident in the rise of street and neighborhood associations across the country. These associations are the coming together of members of a street or neighborhood for the purpose of advancing their neighborhoods and solving collective problems (Olawole 2020; Egbu, Pat-Mbano, and Obialo 2012). Neighborhoods have street associations that make arrangements for the provision of services such as security, roads, and waste collection.

To many Nigerians, the increase in non-state provision depicts a failure of the government to provide goods and services. These non-state actors fill the void created by the government in the context of service delivery. But how might the presence of these actors impact citizens' political behavior? If citizens provide their own security, water, and roads; community associations create alternatives to government failures; international organizations sometimes partake in service delivery; and yet the state still sometimes provides services, what might the consequences be? What are the implications of these various providers for the relationship between citizens and the state? And how do citizens respond to the various actors? The next section answers these questions with evidence from Nigeria.

POLITICAL IMPLICATIONS OF STATE
AND NON-STATE PROVIDERS

Economic theories posit that competition is vital in the marketplace of service delivery (Boettke, Lemke, and Palagashvili 2016; Storr, Grube, and Haeffele-Balch 2017). But what are the implications of this for political participation? How do state and non-state producers of goods and services affect citizen engagement and relationship with the state? The case examined in this chapter carries some attributes of a polycentric system within which provision of services to address community problems stems from different actors. A precedent of heavy state presence in service delivery heightens citizens' expectations of the government to assume more responsibility. All of which occur in a complicated polity with pervasive corruption and an abundance of natural resources. Simply put, this case presents a unique opportunity to understand the consequences of polycentricity for the behavior of citizens. Providers of goods can shift the orientation of citizens, especially as it has to do with political participation. That is, state delivery of goods and services induces political participation of citizens. On the other hands, non-state provision reduces political participation among citizens as previous scholars noted (Bleck 2013; Aremu 2015; Olawole 2020) and the paragraphs that follow demonstrate. It is paradoxical that non-state provision, though designed to solve problems, evokes negative reactions among citizens toward the state, but there are various reasons why this would be the case. To be clear, I do not argue that the mere presence of non-state provision creates a negative political reaction. Rather, I make the case through ethnographic research, participant observation, and in-depth interviews that non-state provision that solves problems (that citizens believe are the responsibility of the state) weakens the relationship between citizens and the state. There are indeed implications of various providers on forms of political participation. Below I present the model explaining why, despite addressing challenges facing citizens, non-state provision has negative consequences for political participation.

The underlying framework I employ has some similarities with the policy feedback theory in the American politics literature, which posits that when the state cedes responsibility to non-state actors, it can induce apathy and that experiences with social services can induce participation in politics (Mettler 2011; Campbell 2003). Accordingly, a "submerged" state impedes participation and leads to apathy. This type of apathy dissuades citizens from engaging with elected leaders. When non-state actors provide goods and services, Nigerians view this as the state ceding its responsibility. State provision of goods largely affects citizens' perception of the state. Lack of state provision reveals both the failure and inaction of the state, thereby negatively affecting citizens' perception of the state. When citizens perceive the government badly, they are more likely to withdraw from the political process altogether. Critics might argue that when the government shirks what citizens perceive to be its responsibility, the response would be more citizen participation because they will choose to express their grievances. However, citizens only have an incentive to voice their discontent when the state is providing. When it is not, they tend to exit the political system altogether (with no incentive to participate), not by literally leaving their physical spaces (as that would be too costly) but by disengaging from the system. Similarly, citizens tune out the state from quotidian experiences when they assume that they have no reason to benefit from the state. Indeed, providing goods and services for themselves suggests to many Nigerians that that the state has failed. It is this perception that largely translates into a shift in orientation toward the state. Broadly speaking, participation in politics is normally conceptualized as voting and other electoral forms of participation. But participation goes beyond electoral forms and includes participation in governance, specifically citizens' contact with elected leaders. For the latter aspect, the failure of service delivery has been largely to blame for the apathy that dissuades participating in governance.[8]

Further, provision of goods and services by the state fosters an interaction between leaders and citizens that is imperative for democratic governance. State delivery of services renders the state very visible, and this visibility is instrumental in participation. During one of the focus groups I conducted, I found that not only was the government more visible for parents with kids in government schools, but they were also more likely to interact with the state because their kids were in government schools as opposed to private schools.[9] With an interaction established through state provision of goods and services, there will be more incentive on the part of citizens to revisit relationship with the state. As one of the participants in the focus group described, the state's visibility through government schools created an incentive to forge relationships with elected leaders. If states are credited for the provision of a social service, then citizens may feel that their government serves them and will have a greater incentive to demand accountability through contact with elected leaders. In expatiating upon the logic of coproduction, Ostrom (1993) reiterated the perspective that the way production is organized in communities can affect the incentives of users to participate. This view emanates from the idea that citizens are joint partakers and co-collaborators in governance—that is, they are directly involved in making the rules that govern themselves. If citizens view themselves this way, there may be less likelihood of sanctioning the state for its ineffectiveness. However, within the context of Nigeria and similar developing countries, citizens have an expectation of the state as providers of goods and services and would sanction the state. With the state's absence through service delivery, there is hardly any incentive to participate. As one Nigerian I spoke with put it, "Why would I contact them when there is no relationship whatsoever to them?" Such rhetoric was not uncommon among those who received goods and services from non-state actors. Other similar responses were sayings like, "I have no business with them." Perhaps it is possible that these sentiments might have existed even before the non-state entities stepped. However, the presence of non-state provision filling roles meant further damaging of citizens' perception of the government and ultimately dampened state-society relations. Not to mention, non-state provision, by its very nature, generally undermines citizens' capacity to seek accountability, as was the case in Uganda (Katusiimeh 2015).

The interaction of the state and citizens heightens their interests in governance and certainly means they have some "business" with the state. Consequently, goods and services provided by the government yield a "feedback loop" that strengthens accountability and the relationship between state and citizens (Bleck 2013). The more the citizens believe they have to gain from contacting their elected leaders, the more likely they are to do this. As the state provides, accountability and engagement are more likely reinforced. This becomes evident when there is a discrepancy between the budget of a project, for instance, and what is spent on that project in reality.[10] This logic cannot be applied to non-state provision. For instance, even if charity and/or international organizations have budgets, citizens would not feel as entitled to demand accountability when discrepancies between the budget and project occur. Not to mention, citizens are rarely able to get a hold of the budgets of such non-state actors. A community leader and civil society actor gave an example:

> In 2013, I was monitoring the budget of the richest Niger Delta state, Akwa Ibom. And I got to St. Luke government hospital in Annua in Akwa Ibom. There were certain budgetary provisions for the hospital. When I got to the hospital and asked a few questions about a new plant and maternity ward, the nurse first resisted. At first, she asked why I wanted to know. I told her, "Okay, I guess you are not interested in knowing how the 38 million budgeted for the new maternity ward was spent." She said, "38 what?" That immediately got her interested in what I was saying. She called me back, and I opened the budget and showed her right there, written, "38 million naira for the building of a new maternity ward in Annua." She broke down crying and told me the story of how she delivered a baby in a makeshift maternity ward with a Nokia phone torchlight in her mouth the previous day. Since then, she has become active in the open-budget platform. The major tool for getting citizens interested is by showing them what is in it for them. Make "it" as real as possible.[11]

This quote characterizes the argument that state-provided public goods increase citizen participation and demand for accountability. The woman in this example became interested because it was a government-provided service. Apathy is significantly reduced, while the incentive to engage increases when it is government-provided.

Another way through which the provision of goods affects the likelihood of citizens engaging with their elected leaders has to do with trust. Trust remains a fundamental aspect of every society, and it can give rise to reciprocity and cooperation (Ostrom and Walker 2005). In this case, trust can induce reciprocity among citizens, which fuels the desire to cooperate through contacting elected leaders. Indeed, some scholars posit that the lack of trust in government in Nigeria has reduced participation (Omodia 2009; Falade 2015). Where there is no trust in government, citizens are not inclined to engage with their political leaders. What breeds this trust in citizens? It is hard for citizens to trust their government when they perceive them as failing. The majority of individuals, argue Ostrom and Walker (2005), trust conditionally, taking cues from institutional structures of interactions and perceived intentions of their counterparts. I assume that such intentions can be revealed through state provision (or lack thereof) of goods and services. As mentioned, provision on the part of the state fosters interaction with citizens and breeds trust. In the case of Nigeria, there is widespread lack of trust in the government from failure to provide goods and services. Commenting on this, a politician I spoke with said, "citizens have lost confidence in politicians."[12] Another civil society actor said similarly,

> The average Nigerian is not expecting much from the government: what we expect are good roads, water supply, and electricity. We are not even looking at government for credit or micro credit for people in business. I can tell you if you take a survey of all these among Nigerians, we believe the government has failed us and that has affected how we participate see government. So, there is a lot of apathy.[13]

This lack of trust in the government and its institutions can permeate into other aspects. In an interesting contrast, while lack of provision reduces trust in the government, there seemed to be a lot of trust in international organizations and entities. For instance, with the prevalence of the Chinese government and entities, many express favorable dispositions and trust toward them, a stark contrast to their perception of the Nigerian government. As I sat in community engagement meetings and listened in on conversations, the underlying reasoning behind negative perceptions of the state reinforced the idea that as the state cedes its responsibilities to non-state actors and it failed to meet expectations on the part of citizens, trust of citizens in the state diminished.

When non-state actors are prevalent in the provision of goods at services, it reduces interaction of the state and citizens. Perhaps indeed, international and philanthropic organizations or other non-state actors do not have the knowledge problem (identifying and targeting needs) when effectively delivering goods and services, but provision by these entities does not create favorable views of the government. Critics might suggest that even without the presence of non-state provision, citizens would still hold negative views of their government if it failed to provide goods and services. This would overlook the central claims of this study. It is not merely the existence of non-state actors or non-state provision that impedes political participation. Rather, political participation is impeded when non-state provision carries out responsibilities that citizens deem to be the government's. Of course, by providing these goods anyway, non-state actors play a vital role in the society. Yet, by doing this, citizens have an incentive to completely ignore the government, further perpetuating a divide. Provision by the government fosters more engagement and relationship with the state. V. Ostrom (1973) argues that privately provided aid furthers the development of civil associations, something that is necessary for "political capacity." To put this in context, this would be reflected in some non-state actors mobilizing citizens to demand accountability and criticize the state's failure to provide goods and services. On the one hand, this would strengthen participation, and on the other hand, it would undermine state legitimacy (Kushner and MacLean 2015).

Indeed, when I spoke with people who work in the nonprofit sector in Nigeria, it became clear that, in reality, it was not so straightforward. Many of these organizations that provide social services try not to get involved in politics. As a member of the staff of a public health NGO put it: "We do not get involved in politics at all. We are very apolitical."[14] When asked if they ever give any civic education, she said, "No, not at all."[15] A senior member of the staff of a similar organization buttressed this point. Another said, "Most times we try not to be political. No politicians or political things where we are offering our services. When politics come into play, it is more dangerous. There is also no civic education component at all."[16]

In addition, most projects by such international or philanthropic organizations are usually clearly labeled as such. For instance, a World Bank project would carry a tag of "a World Bank Assisted Project." Other organizations not as prominent also try very hard to be visible by printing their names on fliers, printed t-shirts, banners, and vehicles. This way, beneficiaries of projects are able to easily identity who is responsible for providing the service. Although sometimes such international organizations might grant the government legitimacy, it does little to encourage participation. Other non-state actors, mostly civil society organizations, might attempt to motivate citizens to demand accountability. They create several initiatives to get citizens to demand accountability:

> At [an event they organized] we encouraged citizens to speak and many of them spoke about different corrupt practices in the system. We encourage them to demand accountability from these leaders. And we remind them of the tools they can use to do this. The law is a veritable tool that can be used to demand accountability from elected and public officials.[17]

The availability of so many producers in the marketplace of service delivery may also lead to a crowded and complex system that makes it hard for citizens to navigate, which consequently diminishes engagement (Allard 2014). In addition, non-state provision implicitly diminishes capacity from citizens. Whereas state provision empowers citizens and renews a sense of vigor and ownership in citizens, non-state provision—often viewed as charitable—undercuts accountability since citizens are not able to hold non-state actors as accountable as they would state actors (Katusiimeh 2015).

Furthermore, previous studies—drawing from the fiscal exchange thesis—demonstrate how community-provided goods can reduce the likelihood of paying taxes among citizens (Bodea and LeBas 2016). The fiscal exchange theory posits that states get legitimacy from citizens when they provide goods and services. In a similar vein, community-provided goods and services can crowd out the state when they reduce demand for state-provided goods and services and reinforce decisions to tune out the state entirely. By engaging with leaders, citizens are granting legitimacy to the state. Therefore, citizens can withdraw their legitimacy from the leaders when they abstain from participating in governance when the state fails to deliver goods and services.

When it comes to other non-state provision, like self-provision, the consequences are even more far-reaching. Self-provision, especially, crowds out the state and negatively impacts the attitudes and perceptions of citizens toward the state. While one might expect that it would perhaps propel citizens to participate because they seek to sanction the state, I found that it causes them instead to completely tune out the state from quotidian affairs. This manner of provision reduces the belief in the need to engage. A respondent I spoke with in the Opebi area of Lagos exemplified this. In response to suboptimal levels of state provision, her neighborhood association engages in numerous self-help provisions of goods, with access to this network based on the contribution of individuals in the network. Accordingly, this woman and other individuals in this community are less likely to grant the state legitimacy through engagement as their self-help vis-à-vis non-state provision has obscured the state.[18]

From focus group conversations and notes from field research, whether during participant observation or perhaps more structured interviews, I found that it is the perceived failure from an expectation of the government being filled by a non-state actor that impedes participation. Holding other factors constant, if non-state provision is completely removed from the equation (a feat that is impossible), Nigerians would have a much stronger incentive to participate, engage, and demand more accountability from the state. In such a scenario, popular frustrations would escalate as lack multiplies and there would be nowhere else to channel the anger but toward the state. Indeed, in studies of the formation of modern Western European states, societal penetration of the state bolstered tax collection capacity, a cornerstone of legitimacy (ibid.). Provision of goods by non-state actors, even when it does serve a real need of citizens, demonstrates inaction of the government and dissuades citizens from engaging with leaders or participating even more generally.

We need not interpret this to mean that non-state provision must be eradicated. On the contrary, as the above claims have demonstrated, there is a need for non-state provision. Instead, policymakers and other stakeholders must be aware of the complexities of multiple providers where a central actor—the state—is not providing.

CONCLUSION

In a complex political and economic system like the one that exists in Nigeria and some other developing nations, it is almost inevitable that there will be various sources of goods and provisions for citizens. But what are the effects of state and non-state provision on citizens? Specifically, what are their political consequences? This chapter examined aspects of the political and governance context in Nigeria. In addition, this chapter showed the consequences of non-state and state provision for participation among citizens. If political participation is vital for liberalization in this part of the world, and yet the manner of polycentricity hinders participation, what are the implications of this for policy? First, non-state actors must learn to solve the knowledge problem more by seeking to supplement state provision of goods and services. Further, self-provision poses the most danger for participation. Therefore, other non-state actors can still provide for citizens although it is imperative that they work with the governments. Non-state actors have to understand the consequences of development intervention, particularly within the context of democratization. Moreover, there must be a signal from the state that it is not willing to forgo its responsibility to non-state actors. Ultimately, we need not discard non-state provision altogether. Indeed, the onus is on the state—and not non-state actors—to earn legitimacy from citizens and fulfill expectations of citizens.

NOTES

1. Interview with Ken Henshaw, 2018.
2. The community meeting was held in Ago Iwoye (Osun state, Nigeria) on September 14, 2019. It was a town hall meeting of residents of that community, and altogether there were more than seventy people in attendance. Overall, I recorded about seven to ten of those who got up to speak beginning their speech with this narrative.
3. Interview with Ayo Adebusoye, September 13, 2019.
4. Interview with Michael Aregbesola, September 9, 2019.
5. Interview with Michael Aregbesola, September 9, 2019.
6. Two anonymous respondents brought this up during the in-depth interviews. In addition, this was a topic of conversation during the focus group discussion. More on the focus group below.
7. Interview with Michael Aregbesola, September 9, 2019.
8. Interview at BudgIT, August 27, 2019.
9. The focus group comprised of eight participants: five men and three women. The conversation centered around provision of goods and services (including education, health, water, roads, and security). There was variation across the group based on

whether they predominantly attributed provision of their goods to state or non-state actors. Participants were recruited through outreach to personal contacts in Lagos and snowball sampling. This was by no means a random sample of any kind, although it did contribute some nuance as I disentangled the theoretical models. I served as the facilitator of the focus group, asking questions, taking down answers, as well as recording the conversation. The discussion itself took place in a classroom at a government secondary school in the Agege area of Lagos and lasted for about an hour and thirty minutes.

10. Interview with Ken Henshaw, October 29, 2018.
11. Interview with Ken Henshaw, October 29, 2018.
12. Interview with Mr. Avoseh, October 10, 2019.
13. Interview with Peter Egbule, September 2, 2019.
14. Interview at Society for Family Health (SFH), October 21, 2019.
15. Interview at Society for Family Health (SFH), October 21, 2019.
16. Interview at Marie Stopes, Lagos, October 22, 2019.
17. Interview at SERAP, September 17, 2019.
18. Respondent in-depth interview in Opebi, Lagos.

REFERENCES

Abegunde, Ola and Temitope E. Akinyemi. 2014. "Public Policy, Welfarism, and Social Service Delivery in Nigeria: The Case of a Receding State." *Journal of Law, Policy and Globalization* 22: 134–44.

Adejumobi, Said. 1999. "Privatisation Policy and the Delivery of Social Welfare Services in Africa: A Nigerian Example." *Journal of Social Development in Africa* 14 (2): 87–108.

Allard, Scott. 2014. "State Dollars, Non-State Provision: Local Nonprofit Welfare Provision in the United States." In *The Politics of Non-State Social Welfare*, edited by Melani Cammett and Lauren MacLean, 237–56. Ithaca, NY: Cornell University Press.

Amuwo, Kunle. 2008. *Constructing the Democratic Developmental State in Africa: A Case Study of Nigeria, 1960-2007*. Midrand, ZA: Institute for Global Dialogue.

Aremu, Fatai Ayinde. 2015. "Faith-Based Universities in Nigeria and the Consequences for Citizenship." *Africa Today* 62 (1): 3–28.

Balassa, Bela. 1981. "Structural Adjustment Policies in Developing Economies." *World Bank*. http://documents1.worldbank.org/curated/en/318821468739454872/pdf/multi0page.pdf.

Bebbington, Anthony, David Lewis, Kate Wellard, and John Farrington. 1993. *Reluctant Partners? Nongovernmental Organizations, the State and Sustainable Agricultural Development*. New York: Routledge.

Bleck, Jaimie. 2013. "Do Francophone and Islamic Schooling Communities Participate Differently? Disaggregating Parents' Political Behaviour in Mali." *The Journal of Modern African Studies* 5 (3): 377–408.

Bodea, Cristina and Adrienne LeBas. 2014. "The Origins of Voluntary Compliance: Attitudes toward Taxation in Urban Nigeria." *British Journal of Political Science* 46 (1): 215–38.

Boettke, Peter J., Jayme S. Lemke, and Liya Palagashvili. 2016. "Re-Evaluating Community Policing in a Polycentric System." *Journal of Institutional Economics* 12 (2): 305–25.

Brass, Jennifer N. 2016. *Allies or Adversaries: NGOs and the State in Africa.* New York: Cambridge University Press.

Bratton, Michael. 1989. "The Politics of Government-NGO Relations in Africa." *World Development* 17 (4): 569–87.

Cammett, Melani Claire and Lauren M. MacLean. 2014. *The Politics of Non-State Social Welfare.* Ithaca, NY: Cornell University Press.

Campbell, Andrea Louise. 2003. *How Policies Make Citizens: Senior Political Activism and the American Welfare State.* Princeton, NJ: Princeton University Press.

Campbell, John. 2011. "Ngozi Okonjo-Iweala: Nigeria's Next Finance Minister?" *Council for Foreign Relations*, June 27. https://www.cfr.org/blog/ngozi-okonjo-iweala-nigerias-next-finance-minister.

Collier, Paul and Anke Hoeffler. 2002. "On the Incidence of Civil War in Africa." *Journal of Conflict Resolution* 46 (1): 13–28.

———. 2005. "Resource Rents, Governance, And Conflict." *Journal of Conflict Resolution* 49 (4): 625–33.

Decker, Tunde. 2010. "Social Welfare Strategies in Colonial Lagos." http://002784d.netsolhost.com/images/AF_Decker.pdf.

Egbu, Anthony, Edith Pat-Mbano, and Kalu Obialo. 2012. "Public Goods Provision: Informal Response to Government Failure in the Cities of Nigeria." *Theoretical and Empirical Researches in Urban Management; Bucharest* 7 (2): 67–78.

Ekpenyong, Otu Anthony, Okechukwu Egwu Ibiam, and Emmanuel Obiahu Agha. 2015. "Politics in Nigeria: To What Extent Has the Gender Agenda Gained Momentum?" *IOSR Journal of Humanities and Social Science* 20 (5): 1–10.

Elemo, Olufunmbi. 2018. "Fiscal Federalism, Subnational Politics, and State Creation in Contemporary Nigeria." In *The Oxford Handbook of Nigerian Politics*, edited by Carl Levan and Patrick Utaka, 186–206. Oxford, UK: Oxford University Press.

Extractive Industries Transparency Initiative. n.d. "Nigeria." https://eiti.org/es/implementing_country/32.

Falade, D. A. 2014. "Political Participation in Nigerian Democracy: A Study of Some Selected Local Government Areas in Ondo State, Nigeria." *Global Journal of Human-Social Science: F Political Science* 14 (8): 17–23.

Haque, M. Shamsul. 2003. "Citizen Participation in Governance through Representation: Issue of Gender in East Asia." *International Journal of Public Administration* 26 (5): 569–90.

Inman, Kris and Josephine Andrews. 2009. "Corruption and Political Participation in Africa: Evidence from Survey and Experimental Research." https://citeseerx.ist.psu.edu/viewdoc/download?doi=10.1.1.322.4526&rep=rep1&type=pdf.

Isaksson, Ann-Sofie. 2014. "Political Participation in Africa: The Role of Individual Resources." *Electoral Studies* 34: 244–60.

Katusiimeh, Mesharch W. 2015. "The Nonstate Provision of Health Services and Citizen Accountability in Uganda." *Africa Today* 62 (1): 85–105.

Ko, Vanessa. 2014. "Nigeria's 'Resource Curse': Oil as Impediment to True Federalism." *E-International Relations.* https://www.e-ir.info/2014/07/20/nigerias-resource-curse-oil-as-impediment-to-true-federalism/.

Kramon, Eric and Daniel N. Posner. 2013. "Who Benefits from Distributive Politics? How the Outcome One Studies Affects the Answer One Gets." *Perspectives on Politics* 11 (2): 461–74.

Krawczyk, Kelly Ann, and Jennie Sweet-Cushman. 2017. "Understanding Political Participation in West Africa: The Relationship between Good Governance and Local Citizen Engagement." *International Review of Administrative Sciences* 83 (1_suppl): 136–55.

Krawczyk, Kelly Ann, Jennie Sweet-Cushman, and Raymond Muhula. 2013. "The Road to Good Governance: Via the Path Less Accountable? The Effectiveness of Fiscal Accountability in Liberia." *International Journal of Public Administration* 36 (8): 532–43.

Kumar, Raj. 2018. "One Woman's Fight: Ngozi Okonjo-Iweala Memoir Offers Guide to Fighting Corruption." *Devex,* April 19. https://www.devex.com/news/one-woman-s-fight-ngozi-okonjo-iweala-memoir-offers-guide-to-fighting-corruption-92570.

Kushner, Danielle Carter and Lauren MacLean. 2015. "Introduction to the Special Issue: The Politics of the Nonstate Provision of Public Goods in Africa." *Africa Today* 62 (1): vii.

Lavoie, Don. [1985] 2016. *National Economic Planning: What is Left?* Arlington, VA: Mercatus Center at George Mason University.

Lewis, Peter. 2018. "Nigeria's Petroleum Booms: A Changing Political Economy." In *The Oxford Handbook of Nigerian Politics,* edited by Carl Levan and Patrick Utaka, 520–44. Oxford, UK: Oxford University Press.

MacLean, Lauren M. 2010. "State Retrenchment and the Exercise of Citizenship in Africa." *Comparative Political Studies* 44 (9): 1238–66.

Mettler, Suzanne. 2011. *The Submerged State.* Chicago, IL: The University of Chicago Press.

Miguel, Edward and Mary Kay Gugerty. 2005. "Ethnic Diversity, Social Sanctions, and Public Goods in Kenya." *Journal of Public Economics* 89 (11–12): 2325–68.

Minten, Bart and Steven Kyle. 1999. "The Effect of Distance and Road Quality on Food Collection, Marketing Margins, and Traders' Wages: Evidence from the Former Zaire." *Journal of Development Economics* 60 (2): 467–95.

Moghalu, Kingsley and Nonso Obikili. 2018. "Fiscal Policy during Boom and Bust." In *The Oxford Handbook of Nigerian Politics,* edited by Carl Levan and Patrick Utaka, 491–501. Oxford, UK: Oxford University Press.

Moore, Mick. 1998. "Death without Taxes: Democracy, State Capacity, and Aid Dependence in the Fourth World." In *The Democratic Developmental State,* edited by Mark Robinson and Gordon White. Oxford, UK: Oxford University Press.

Moss, Todd J., Gunilla Pettersson, and Nicolas van de Walle. 2006. "An Aid-Institutions Paradox? A Review Essay on Aid Dependency and State Building in Sub-Saharan Africa." Working Paper, Center for Global Development.

Mueller, Lisa. 2018. *Political Protest in Contemporary Africa*. Cambridge, UK: Cambridge University Press.

Muggah, Robert and Anna Alvazzi del Frate. 2007. More Slums Equals More Violence: Armed Violence and Urbanisation in Africa. The United Nations Development Programme.

Olawole, Ifeoluwa. 2020. "The Political Consequences of Public Goods Provision: Evidence from Nigeria." PhD diss., American University.

Omodia, Stephen. 2009. "Elections and Democratic Survival in the Fourth Republic of Nigeria." *The Journal of Pan African Studies* 3 (3): 35–42.

Omotoso, Femi. 2014. "Public-Service Ethics and Accountability for Effective Service Delivery in Nigeria." *Africa Today* 60 (3): 118–39.

Ostrom, Elinor. 1990. *Governing the Commons: The Evolution of Institutions for Collective Action*. New York: Cambridge University Press.

———. 1993. "Covenanting, Co-Producing, and the Good Society." *The Newsletter of PEGS* 3 (2): 7–9.

———. 1996. "Crossing the Great Divide: Coproduction, Synergy, and Development." *World Development* 24 (6): 1073–87.

———. 2000. "Collective Action and the Evolution of Social Norms." *The Journal of Economic Perspectives* 14 (3): 137–58.

———. 2010. "Beyond Markets and States: Polycentric Governance of Complex Economic Systems." *The American Economic Review* 100 (3): 641–72.

Ostrom, Elinor and Roger Parks. 1973. "Suburban Police Departments: Too Many and Too Small?" In *The Urbanization of the Suburbs*, edited by Louis Masotti and Jeffrey K. Hadden, 367–402. Beverly Hills, CA: Sage.

Ostrom, Elinor and James Walker. 2005. *Trust and Reciprocity: Interdisciplinary Lessons for Experimental Research*. New York: Russell Sage.

Ostrom, Vincent. 1973. "Can Federalism Make a Difference?" *Publius* 3 (2): 197–237.

Ostrom, Vincent, Charles M. Tiebout, and Robert Warren. 1961. "The Organization of Government in Metropolitan Areas: A Theoretical Inquiry." *The American Political Science Review* 55 (4): 831–42.

Paler, Laura. 2013. "Keeping the Public Purse: An Experiment in Windfalls, Taxes, and the Incentives to Restrain Government." *American Political Science Review* 107 (4): 706–25.

Palmer, Natasha. 2006. "An Awkward Threesome—Donors, Governments and Non-State Providers of Health in Low Income Countries." *Public Administration and Development* 26 (3): 231–40.

Porter, Gina. 2002. "Living in a Walking World: Rural Mobility and Social Equity Issues in Sub-Saharan Africa." *World Development* 30 (2): 285–300.

Ross, Michael. 1999. "The Political Economy of the Resource Curse." *World Politics* 51 (2): 297–322.

Rusca, Maria and Klaas Schwartz. 2012. "Divergent Sources of Legitimacy: A Case Study of International NGOs in the Water Services Sector in Lilongwe and Maputo." *Journal of Southern African Studies* 38 (3): 681–97.

Sandberg, Eve. 1994. *The Changing Politics of Nongovernmental Organizations and African States*. Westport, CT: Praeger.

Storr, Virgil Henry, Laura E. Grube, and Stefanie Haeffele-Balch. 2017. "Polycentric Orders and Post-Disaster Recovery: A Case Study of One Orthodox Jewish Community Following Hurricane Sandy." *Journal of Institutional Economics* 13 (4): 875–97.

Suberu, Rotimi. 2004. "The Politics of Fiscal Federalism in Nigeria." In *Federalism and Territorial Cleavages*, edited by Ugo Amoretti and Nancy Bermeo. Baltimore, MD: Johns Hopkins University Press.

Swidler, Ann. 2006. "Syncretism and Subversion in AIDS Governance: How Locals Cope with Global Demands." *International Affairs* 82 (2): 269–284.

van Deth, Jan W. 2014. "A Conceptual Map of Political Participation." *Acta Politica* 49 (3): 349–67.

Van de Walle, N. 2001. *African Economies and the Politics of Permanent Crisis, 1979-1999*. Cambridge: Cambridge University Press.

Verba, Sidney and Norman H. Nie. 1972. *Participation in America*. New York: Harper & Row.

Verba, Sidney, Kay Lehman Schlozman, and Henry E Brady. 1995. *Voice and Equality: Civic Voluntarism in American Politics*. Cambridge, MA: Harvard University Press.

Wamai, Richard. 2004. "NGO and Public Health Systems: Comparative Trends in Transforming Health Care Systems in Kenya and Finland." Presentation at the International Society for Third Sector Research Biannual Meeting.

World Bank. n.d. "The World Bank in Nigeria: Overview." https://www.worldbank.org/en/country/nigeria/overview.

Zakaria, Fareed. 1997. "The Rise of Illiberal Democracy." *Foreign Affairs* 76: 22–43.

Part V

ENVIRONMENTAL POLICY

Chapter 9

Environmental Justice, Incentives, and the Unknown

Knowledge Problems, Institutional Incentives, and Responses to Natural Disaster Scenarios

Emil Panzaru

Environmental justice (EJ) is defined as follows: "Most studies in the field equate environmental justice with distributive justice, that is with distributional patterns among social categories" (Bell 2014, 17–18).[1] Therefore, EJ refers to a subfield of social justice that is concerned with whom environmental aid and resources are allocated to (ibid., 18). In particular, EJ argues that they should be allocated to those who are least well-off, where "least well-off" refers not only to those with a lower income but also to people from disadvantaged social backgrounds based on race, gender, health, and occupation. In terms of what might count as a resource or aid to be allocated, these include things like the healthcare provided to the hazards of the environmental space where people live or the quality of the housing that provides people with a sense of security (that they might otherwise lack) (Grube, Fike, and Storr 2018, 578).[2]

If we take EJ as a desirable goal, why do the government individuals that champion it fail to select for incentives consistent with achieving such goals when it comes to natural disasters?[3] Government agents are widely trusted with ensuring that the most vulnerable socioeconomic groups receive resources like medicines (e.g., for asthma, types I and II diabetes, or heart disease—all illnesses that are more likely to affect marginalized people), food, water, electricity, or housing (e.g., trailers, blocks, hotels, or other forms of lodging for people who might not otherwise be able to afford them) after a natural disaster (Bell 2014, 16). But while they may believe that justice is a worthy and noble ideal in the abstract, state agents might fail to act on it in practice. Hence, rather than supply the needy, government actors tend to merely increase their own agency's revenue while pushing the costs of aid onto others (Walker 2010).

There is already a vast theoretical literature in the classical liberal tradition of the Austrian School of Economics that tries to explain this failure to allocate aid and mitigate the effects of natural disasters for the most vulnerable members of society (Chamlee-Wright and Storr 2010; Chamlee-Wright and Storr 2011; Grube and Storr 2014; Storr, Haeffele-Balch, and Grube 2015; Grube, Fike, and Storr 2018; Storr, Haeffele-Balch, and Grube 2018). They try to address the same worry in different ways. The first is to approach the failure as one of knowledge. While government actors might agree on the general aim of EJ, what it means in terms of policies varies among individuals. One reason why this is a problem is that policymakers cannot discover what justice implies for each affected individual in the first place (Hayek 1945; Schmidtz 2011; Lavoie [1985]2015; Gaus 2016; Brennan 2018). Thus, they do not act on people's needs because they *cannot know* what an "environmentally just" standard would mean in terms of how many real houses have to be built, who actually needs food, water, or electricity, which medicines are required, and so on (Johnson, Penning-Rowsell, and Parker 2007, 379). Another more direct answer is that policymakers themselves are not incentivized to act according to each person's subjective desires. Working within a government involves costs and benefits that encourage political actors to focus on maximizing their budgets and ignore the wishes of the very individuals whose lives are affected by those same policies.

Inspired by these traditional answers, my response to the puzzle in this chapter is thus twofold. I focus on the conventional policy measures that attempt to allocate resources following a natural disaster. I then draw on the classical liberal literature to argue that issues of distributing resources during natural disasters are best thought of as knowledge problems. In other words, no one is even capable of assembling all the knowledge regarding who is vulnerable and what they require. That is because such knowledge is, to use F. A. Hayek's phrase, prone to the "circumstances of time and place," meaning that it is contextual, dynamic, and thus oftentimes un-codifiable into words or numbers (Hayek [1982]2013; Pennington 2011; Boettke 2012; Hodgson 2019). The second part of my argument connects this point back to the institutional incentives that state actors face. Because of the knowledge problem, decision-makers can only use the information available to them and mistake this information for knowledge. This then encourages them to expand on their own operations. Simply stated, since they cannot follow the interests of vulnerable people, they follow the familiar logic of budget maximizing instead. As an unforeseen consequence (and contrary to the hopes of advocates), government action thus ends up being inconsistent with the distributional principle of EJ itself.

My main theoretical contribution is in terms of how we should think about the knowledge problem within the EJ literature. The conventional EJ literature assumes the knowledge problem to be a matter of lacking adequate demographic information about those affected by natural disasters. Thus, policymakers fail to act in a manner consistent with EJ because they do not know that the people they are supposed to help are facing structural racism, class barriers, gender differences, ableism, and interactions between these factors (issues of race complicated by stigmas toward gender, for instance). Consequently, the solution to the knowledge problem is a matter of gathering information about the struggles that the least well-off face in their lives (Wegner and Pascual 2009; Walker 2010; Walker and Burningham 2011; Banzhaf, Ma, and Timmins 2019). However, I argue that this misstates the knowledge problem. The knowledge problem refers to fact that any policymaker lacks the context-specific knowledge (referring to the knowledge of each person's life in a specific time and at a particular place) that they need to allocate resources according to each individual's ends.

A secondary upshot of the chapter is to show how the classical liberal view can provide a more effective institutional answer to the environmental justice puzzle than approaches emphasizing government intervention. Given the emphasis on specialist information in the form of demographics and sociology (gender, race, intersectionality), the conventional EJ literature recommends governmental technical solutions applied by policymakers to fulfill the ends of EJ. However, because the knowledge problem is context-specific, this means that technical solutions that depend on prescribed notions (of what EJ should be) do not in fact work. No sociological schema, no matter how well-designed and how well-intentioned the policymaker, will capture the particularities of each person's diverse needs and how these might result in conflicting ends. By contrast, the classical liberal perspective reframes the problem of EJ, not as a technical issue but as fostering the right institutional conditions for an emergent phenomenon. An emergent phenomenon means it is a "bottom-up" process whereby each individual uses the knowledge of their circumstances to socially coordinate with other individuals to possess and discover the institutions that will reconcile their diverse needs and conflicting ends in a manner consistent with EJ (Aligica, Boettke, and Tarko 2019).

The roadmap for the demonstration ahead is as follows. Section I is a critique meant to identify the gaps within existing research that the current text is meant to fill. To start, I give a brief overview of the EJ literature and describe the types of institutions that are said to implement its goals. In so doing, I identify their relative weaknesses in explaining the unintended consequences of government policy. Section II lays out the main argument. It states the knowledge problem associated with the policy measures meant to allocate resources during natural disasters and how states are ill-equipped to deal with it compared to the market process. Then it details the problems of public choice that are derived from this. When trying to determine the content of the policies, political actors will rely on their own connections and try to increase their own influence, opening the door to regulatory capture when it comes to market intervention and a bloated public sector that is slow to recognize and respond to problems. Finally, in Section III, I aim to apply the theoretical discussion to the particular case of New Orleans before and after Hurricane Katrina by drawing on qualitative methods of analysis. The conclusion in Section IV brings these elements together again and suggests that we should be more open to alternatives like liberal institutions (such as markets that are closer to solving knowledge via the price mechanism and decentralized structure) realizing EJ.

EJ: THE CONVENTIONAL VIEW AS SPECIALIST KNOWLEDGE

For the conventional EJ view, knowledge refers primarily to technical information. An emblematic text is Dotson and Whyte's (2013) overview of the epistemic basis for EJ. The text begins by stating a potential problem of knowledge in the following terms: "To say that some ranges of injustices are unknowable is to signal the end of our epistemic capacities to detect and make sense of varying forms of injustice" (ibid., 56). But these limits have to do with an expert understanding of social theory in the form of "the less transparent history of social and political patterns between the tribe [the case study concerned Australian Aboriginal tribes] and the dominant society" (ibid., 59). As such, these obstacles can be overcome if policymakers attune their distributional analysis to reflect on the sociological impact of their own actions, particularly the way their own policies have been unequal and have magnified the differences between social categories. To give a general example, the housing policy of redlining is an instance of a racist pattern of interaction, the unequal effects of which persist in the present in terms of poorer housing for racial minorities, even under the conditions of a natural disaster (an instance of structural racism). And while this text explicitly assumes this epistemic stance, the idea that knowledge is a matter of sociological expertise is widely present in the literature of applied policy EJ (Walker 2010, 2012; Dotson and Whyte 2013; Banzhaf, Ma, and Timmins 2019).

Thus, if actors know what to do to further the goals of EJ, then the conventional account recommends that policies be informed by this sociological data. Drawing on social expertise, government agents could be more self-reflective about their actions by adding to conventional cost-benefit analyses more refined metrics that weigh data on natural disaster impact by age, gender, race in the form of equality impact assessments, gender impact assessments, and health equity audits (Walker 2012, 314). In turn, they could apply this newfound information to their distribution programs in the form of a tiered system of analysis with multiple thresholds of marginalization. They could then assign an order of priority to each level, followed by the allocation to each individual of their resources such as water, food, electricity, and housing, depending on where they land within this hierarchy (Shields 2012, 114). The system could take the form of something akin to means-testing in the case of multiple thresholds to identify who might be hit the worst. And governments could use the same social information to make sure that other institutions like markets also respect EJ. This could be done at first by intervening in markets to ensure that any distribution will not harm the least well-off. The usual way to do this is to have a combination of the following: subsidies for the poorest, regulations that ensure that markets respect health and safety concerns, governments themselves stepping into exchanges to cover insurance on a marginalized person's behalf if there is no house insurer wanting to take the deal, enlarging anti-discrimination legislation to improve the situation of those who are discriminated against (not just in general, but for the environment in particular), zoning laws, and so on. If all of these measures fail, then states can replace the market system with the state-run distribution program.

What are the limitations of this literature? The primarily one is that scientific information is confused with knowledge. This purely technical analysis leaves out an important source of knowledge in people's lives, which the traditional EJ literature refers to as "embodied experience" (Dotson and Whyte 2013, 56). Embodied experiences represent the totality of experiences that have shaped a person's view of EJ. Some of the cited instances of embodied experiences include the cultural differences influencing perceptions of deprivation, the unspoken activities that govern the way people interact with resources, the way past injustices affect the way people react to current injustices, and the way each person processes cultural and past or present events (ibid., 56). This suggests a diversity of beliefs about what ends matter and how EJ interact with said ends, many of which might not be reconcilable because of people's opposing embodied experiences (people with a disposition toward tradition against those who push for progress or the relevance of past racism to today's conditions for some versus the relevance of other factors for others).

Nevertheless, the technical approach does not engage with these experiences as forms of knowledge at all, preferring to refer to them as an "affective" component that often clouds understandings of EJ (Dotson and Whyte 2013,

58). But all this suggests is that there is a separation between what the experts know and articulate as EJ and what the recipients know from their lives and wish to see realized as EJ, given that the former socially separate themselves from the experiences of the latter (Mathers 2012, 66). In terms of what this separation means in practice, by focusing on the outputs that sociology thinks are relevant (sociological data on class, health, infrastructure, poverty lines, and household consumption), health, gender, or social impact assessments do not quantify missed opportunities, such as the type of assistance that people wished was available but was not accounted for. Thus, merely reducing poverty metrics does not automatically result in improving people's lives, especially when this provides them with things such as health options that they do not think are necessary, housing in places where local efforts have already made housing available, other options that individuals will categorically reject as morally dubious, or using a definition of EJ that is controversial.

In turn, the conventional view misses the way policymakers' lacunae influence their behavior when allocating resources. According to the standard literature, government agents act wrongly because they are part of a dominant group in society who see it in their personal interest as a dominant group to ignore sociological information about the marginalized and shrug the financial burden of having to compensate the latter for injustices (Walker 2012; Dotson and Whyte 2013; Bell 2014; Banzhaf, Ma, and Timmins 2019). But to see this as the implication of the knowledge lacunae is to miss the point in the first place. Even the most well-intentioned and demographically representative individuals would struggle to know what to do. That is because the relevant social separation remains between what the experts see and what the people they are acting to help do. What is left for policymakers is to act on their political position rather than on embodied experiences, which, as I make clear in the main argument, results in continuing to promote policies that are unjust.

This is where classical liberalism comes into the mix. This approach is relevant to the argument because it fills the shortcomings in the general EJ literature. First, the classical liberal account integrates contextual knowledge like embodied experiences into its idea of the knowledge problem. In so doing, it explains why experiences like these cannot be captured by technical scientific data—their nature prevents expertise from ever fully grasping them. Second, it looks at the institutional implications of taking the knowledge problem seriously. Namely, institutions such as markets are able to overcome the knowledge problems via the market process itself (with its constituent components in private property, prices, and entrepreneurial profit and loss), whereas deviating from the market process means that states lack the power to adapt to local conditions and recognize people's needs in context (Mathers 2012, 66). Finally, classical liberalism explores the implications of the knowledge problem on politicians by acknowledging that politics (like the market) is a realm where incentives matter, and the incentives that matter to politicians performing resource allocations are squarely the political incentives (like the dynamics of a bureaucracy and rent-seeking) with which they are familiar, not the incentives that the marginalized face that the politicians do not know. Therefore, unlike what authors like Walker (2012) would suggest, classical liberalism does have a perspective on EJ—one that can explain why government agents fail to select the incentives that advance EJ. Even more so, it shows how political actors become a source of injustice themselves (Storr, Haeffele-Balch, and Grube 2018, 5).

THE KNOWLEDGE PROBLEM, NATURAL DISASTERS, AND INCENTIVES

Why is the knowledge problem a matter of context? Recall the phrase "circumstances of time and place" that I mentioned earlier. The phrase suggests the contextual nature of some data. It is local in that it can only be obtained from specific places and people at any one time (Pennington 2011, 3). Moreover, it is therefore also "contextual" in time not just in place, meaning it is fleeting; those same people or resources might be gone tomorrow, and other factors and people might be more relevant today. Even more so, it is often tacit, meaning it is known to most that practice it on a daily basis but cannot necessarily be put into words or numbers.[4] In order to know these circumstances then, an individual would have to make their presence known in a myriad of simultaneously occurring interactions at the right time and with the right people. In practice then, this makes it physically impossible for any governmental actor to access this knowledge—such a person would have to be omnipresent and omnipotent.

And to better understand why a government actor would lack this context-specific knowledge, it is instructive to compare government as an institution (and policymaking as the process) with the entrepreneurial market system. In a market, the context of each person's experience is instantiated by the wide dispersal of private property whereby a person is able to form their own "embodied experience" and exchange what they prefer, either as someone who is buying items that belong to others or selling those that belong to himself or herself. And contrary to neoclassical economics (which assumes perfect competition from perfectly knowledgeable actors), the knowledge problem affects this process too (Kirzner 2018, 93). There are a myriad of exchanges happening at any given time, each with a diversity of people with their own tastes and experiences, and each exchange is prone to sudden unforeseen accidents, many of them involving tacit activities such as manufacturing and business acumen. As a result, potential buyers are often separated from potential sellers. The former people are ignorant of other sellers who could offer them a cheaper deal and the latter are often unaware that there are buyers out there who would be interested in their products (Kirzner 2018, 93).

Nevertheless, the knowledge problem is overcome through the mechanism of prices, entrepreneurship, and profit and loss. Prices serve to communicate the context-specific knowledge that market actors have obtained via private property to other people in the market, even when these events happen on another continent and at another time. This is the moral of Hayek's (1945) example about tin. There is no need for a buyer or seller to witness a problem happening with one good in a different part of the planet or to see the event in real time to know something has happened to make the good scarcer. All they have to do is to look at the item's price and see how it has changed, thus solving the issue of time and place (Hayek 1945). In so doing, prices also serve as a vicarious form of knowledge, meaning that one can acquire other people's knowledge without having to experience it for oneself or articulate it (Horwitz 2004). One does not need to be an economist, a manufacturer, or a business graduate to be a good buyer or seller. One simply has to look at the change in price to learn the impact of other people's tacit actions.

Last but not least, market actors need not be omnipotent or omnipresent to overcome the knowledge problem. Because of the contexts communicated via price signals, they are instead entrepreneurial. The entrepreneur is vigilant to opportunities to bring together potential buyers and sellers. These opportunities are perceived by the entrepreneur via the price system in the form of profit (when the entrepreneur has been successful in identifying new opportunities) or loss (when they have not). The entrepreneur is thus the human element that makes the market process possible—it is her search for profit that spurs her to act on the opportunity to connect buyers to sellers, which in turn causes another change in circumstances that is transmitted to other actors via price signals, who in turn try to adjust to these changes in search of their own profit, and so on (Kirzner 2018, 83).

By contrast, government actors fail to address the knowledge problem because government allocation via policymaking lacks equivalent mechanisms to private property, prices, and profit and loss. First, the allocation of food, water, electricity, medicines, or housing does not presuppose anything like dispersed private property. On the contrary, it involves centralization via a common multitier system of distribution for recipients and, conversely, a transfer via taxes and subsidies from private ownership into the government ownership that is needed to sustain the multitier system. But without the wide dispersal of private property, there is no way to acquire its context-dependent knowledge in the first place. Hence, government agents follow a uniform solution while failing to adapt to local conditions and reacting too late. The results are counter-productive, especially in cases like natural disasters where existing private property cannot compensate for these shortcomings because it has already been severely damaged. For example, housing subsidies encourage building in areas that locals know to be more vulnerable after a natural disaster. Moreover, providing food for the community could hinder the community's own ability to recover by undermining their extant food market. The same scenario can arise when a supply of government medicines crowd out existing pharmacies by making it harder for them to trade, resulting in the government-provided medical aid arriving too late to help survivors.

Furthermore, the dispersal of private property allows buyers and sellers to pursue their own preferences; they buy and sell as they please. By contrast, government goods are put to the use of EJ as EJ is defined by experts. This often contradicts the culture or expectations of locals encapsulated in "embodied experiences" and results in the aforementioned missed opportunities to help. For instance, locals might have trusted local pharmacies with distribution more, as those are the pharmacists with which they are familiar and trust. Or locals might have contradictory and irreconcilable opinions on who is most deserving of food and water in an emergency. (Is it better to aid the disabled first because they cannot supply themselves or the able who might be capable of helping the disabled too?) Government agents are likely to ignore this. Alternatively, locals might have already established neighborhood relationships that government housing is threatening to displace. The separation between experts and locals is thus partly a matter of government actors being oblivious to the knowledge contained within private property.

The problem is further deepened by the fact that government allocation does not involve an equivalent to the price mechanism. The allocation happens instead according to the rationalist criteria of impact assessments. These complement the multitier threshold because they are centralized attempts by experts to reproduce the type of cost-benefit calculations that people themselves would have made. However, these attempts at artificially reproducing the value of social "inputs" (like the value of income or health) will experience the knowledge problem as the calculation problem that Ludwig von Mises ([1920]1990) laid out in "Economic Calculation in the Socialist Commonwealth." Absent a price system, there is no method of communicating the relative value of people's myriad economic choices in the way that the scarcity of tin was communicated in Hayek's example. That is because experts have no means of quantifying different uses for the same resource, and they do not have a way to discover the benefits and costs of using other resources that could have been used instead. Further, they have no way of pricing in future expectations (given that individuals need different amounts of goods at different times). What an impact assessment can do is merely make an educated guess at the relationship between these factors (which falls short of the reality).

Yet, making these calculations is all the more important in the wake of a disaster where there is a sense of urgency to every decision. State actors therefore often do not recognize that health might be important later down the line, whereas shelter is an immediate concern for those who have lost their home. They might not realize that some need goods that are normally not associated with the environment, like access to markets (Herlitz and Horan 2016, 420). And they may act in counter-productive ways when they do try to interrupt the market process by instituting price gouging laws that are supposed to guarantee resources such as food, water, electricity, housing, and medicines but only end up creating shortages instead (as the calculation problem would have predicted).

Moreover, because they do lack the price mechanism, state actors must rely on explicit information alone and cannot use the tacit knowledge embodied in the locals' unspoken activities and culture. Thus, they can only utilize the information they have gathered themselves (as sociological theory or statistical analyses) or, in the best-case scenario, the information that could be communicated to them verbally by the marginalized. Thus, they miss the values of activities, traditions, or habits that cannot be put into words. When trying to rebuild a neighborhood, for example, political actors will often miss out on the importance of getting familiar faces to return because they underestimate the existing capital of people who have grown familiar to each other over the years and thus trust each other to act as a united group (who have certain places near and dear to their heart that government reconstruction might obstruct). Alternatively, they might undermine cultural or religious expressions of generosity that tie people together in the community or prove socially insensitive to their situation without knowing it.

Finally, without an equivalent to a price there is no equivalent for profit and loss either, meaning that political actors are not incentivized to do what entrepreneurs do. This is due to the fact that profit and loss are not just ways for entrepreneurs to discover how to make people better off. They also provide a personal benefit to do so; it pays to enrich others. Further, loss penalizes entrepreneurs who fail to take advantage of the opportunity. Hence, successful individuals are the ones who drive the market process in the direction of progress. Conversely, the policymaker's own incentives are made worse by the absence of prices and profit and loss because they can only focus on the benefits and costs of the actions to themselves (that are a known context) rather than the costs to others (that remain unknown). The decisions about what is an EJ necessity versus what is frivolous become driven by the interests of expanding departments and budgets.

This is where incentive problems present themselves. Because state actors cannot process this flow of information, they act on the information they do know. And what policymakers do know is their own position and their narrow field of expertise. These include not only an employee's salary, prerequisites, reputation, and output but also the organizational structure of the state, the current active and upcoming policies, and so on (Blais and Dion 1990). To this information, we can add the resources they have at their disposal (meaning the total money and equipment spent on making impact assessments, formulating policies, and implementing them). In trying to enact the policies based on what they know, the successful policymaker will expand their position within the state. This is because a higher budget equals more status, and more status leads to a better ability to enact policies. The self-interested bureaucrat is therefore not only an artifact of public choice theory but also the result of the knowledge problem.[5]

Why would this behavior be a problem for realizing EJ? It is because political behavior incentivized by political information favors a type of "redistributing up" that is at odds with the distributive goal of EJ itself. By "redistributing up," I mean that resulting allocations ultimately benefit those who are already well-off at the expense of those who are worse off; the very opposite of what justice is meant to achieve. After all, if status and funding are what are known to matter, then state actors are more likely to cater to those who they know would be able to allocate them more political standing and supply more funding. So instead of distributing to locals, political actors often spend funds for food, water, electricity, housing, or medicines on awarding public contracts to favored private businesses based on the knowledge that said businesses will support them and their policies in the future. The same goes for regulatory capture, whereby companies obtain regulation that hampers their competition (without helping the marginalized in the process).

What is worse is that this behavior is part of a vicious cycle: not only does the lack of context-specific knowledge change incentives, but the incentives in turn promote a systematically different gathering of knowledge that is centered around expert political knowledge. For instance, political actors will seek out the sociological advice that favors increasing their status and securing more funding over advice that is more skeptical of political solutions. In turn, this means that measures that involve more political intervention in housing, food, water, electricity, and medicines after a natural disaster will have the ear of policymakers, even if these do not match the resources that locals would ask for (as is often the case with subsidies, price gouging, or medical regulations).

THE KNOWLEDGE PROBLEM, POLITICAL
BEHAVIOR, AND ENVIRONMENTAL (IN)
JUSTICE: THE CASE OF HURRICANE KATRINA

Policies trying to address the aftermath of Hurricane Katrina serve as an exact illustration of how the knowledge problem generates policymaking incentives that are at odds with EJ. Take the housing policy enacted through Federal Emergency Management Agency (FEMA). When Hurricane Katrina struck the Gulf Coast area in 2005, it caused 1,800 deaths, $100 billion worth of damage, and the displacement of over 40,000 Gulf Coast people in total (Storr, Haeffele-Balch, and Grube 2018, 1). According to the government estimates, there were 200,000 houses destroyed in the New Orleans area. These losses would be covered in a centralized fashion by providing 120,000 trailers in the short term and $16.7 billion of tax money for secure housing solutions intended for the most vulnerable who could not afford to buy or rent a house (Stringham and Snow 2008, 482).

Because the allocation was federal rather than through private property, it immediately ran into the knowledge problem. Thus, FEMA employees had initially estimated there would be twelve trailers per twenty homes for each street, but the true number was higher by eight, such that there were twenty trailers per twenty homes for each street. This resulted in 40,000 trailers instead of the expected 28,000 for which they had budgeted (Stringham and Snow 2008, 485). Additionally, there were difficulties in timing. Some people continued to occupy the trailers long after FEMA agents had assumed they would move out. Some were still present one year after the hurricane had hit and seemingly had no plans to leave even though FEMA workers had assumed that six months would be enough to go back to normal (ibid., 486). Moreover, these same trailers were detracting from the existing housing market, as local landlords who would have been willing to put up their houses for rent now found it cheaper to sell off their properties instead (ibid., 483). On top of that, the allocation was separated from the differing personal and moral priorities of the recipients. For instance, one of the academics writing on the disaster found that he was refused a quick grant of $1,500 that would have helped him in the circumstances immediately surrounding the disaster. Instead, he was offered a free trailer worth $140,000 several months later when he no longer needed any assistance and had settled in with a new landlord. Meanwhile, his acquaintances (who were in a much better position post-Katrina than him) immediately received all the aid that they had requested and were thus prioritized in terms of conflicting needs (ibid., 483).

The problem is not limited to trailers, and it can in fact be traced across other policies, such as health and safety measures. For instance, the government also enforced regulations in the form of commercial permits for medical clinics—pharmacies in New Orleans would have to respect a uniform code of health and safety if they wanted to operate, irrespective of the fact that the situation on the ground had left most of the pharmacies devastated (Storr, Haeffele-Balch, and Grube 2018, 77). This extra rule managed to hinder, rather than help, local private businesses recover from the disaster, as businesswoman Alice Craft-Kerney discovered when she wanted to open a clinic of her own to treat long-standing patients but was refused her permit based on regulations having to do with installing a ramp in the devastated location (ibid., 77). This single gesture delayed treatment for her potential patients by one and a half years on average (ibid., 77). Moreover, the move also pitted authorities against a distrustful public—90 percent of these patients had no existing health coverage but were nonetheless visiting the clinic on a regular basis because they trusted Alice and her business, more so than they did governmental medical interventions (ibid., 77).

The post-disaster situation was further complicated by attempts to eliminate pricing from the allocation of supplies. Instead of having to buy food from others, those in need would have to complete a food application process in order to receive supplies. The process proved to be cumbersome and a Misesian calculation problem. Individuals had to submit a 36-page application on food stamps whereupon they had to guess how much food they thought they would need and whether they thought it was easier for them to acquire said food from other sources like donations, a task that proved impossible for individuals to contemplate on their own (Grube, Fike, and Storr 2018, 578). The worst-off of these individuals were rescued only through the efforts of people like Rabbi Bender of the Achievezer Community Center. Rabbi Bender had prior experience with settling private insurance claims and had the necessary connections in both FEMA circles and the government sector to help applicants navigate the system (ibid., 578). In the meantime, he would often procure water, food, shelter, and medicines for them himself through the Achievezer Community Center, sometimes even buying desk supplies for those who lacked even the basic means of completing an application (a fact that the application process had completely overlooked) (Storr, Haeffele-Balch, and Grube 2018, 83).

The same was true of federal energy supplied to communities. Thus, the Vietnamese community centered around the Mary Queen Catholic Church managed to recover more quickly than other communities in New Orleans (like the Village D'Est area of New Orleans), with 2,000 parishioners already returning to the flooded area despite it suffering significant damage (Storr, Haeffele, and Grube 2018, 108–9). This was due in large part to the strong bonds of shared history (spanning several generations of Vietnamese Americans, including refugees from the days of the Vietnam War) and an existing Catholic religious social network centered around Father Vien and his parishioners; these forms of tacit knowledge made it easier to locate lost relatives and reorganize the church as a center for basic amenities that everyone was familiar with (ibid., 108–9). Nevertheless, the community continued to be deprived of sufficient electricity because the government had misjudged their tacit capacity to mobilize through a lack of pricing. According to official protocol, energy would not be restored on a price basis, but rather only once government agents had judged recovery to have been sufficient and given official regulatory approval—the Vietnamese community would have to wait to be classified as a high recovery area (ibid., 108–9). This oversight in turn created mistrust of government agents in the Vietnamese community, especially in light of past experience of marginalization in the United States (ibid., 108–9). It took Father Vien's personal lobbying with Entergy, the private energy company, to restore power to the neighborhood, which diverted time and money away from recovery (ibid., 108–9).

This brings the discussion full circle back to the lack of entrepreneurial profit and loss in the policies surrounding Hurricane Katrina. Individuals such as Father Vien, Rabbi Bender, Alice Craft-Kerney, and countless others in the aftermath of Katrina were acting like entrepreneurs, connecting potential buyers (in this case, vulnerable people looking for food, water, electricity, shelter, or medicines) and potential sellers (e.g., NGOs, activist groups, community supplies, local businesses). Alice Craft-Kerney managed to do so with her clinic, Father Vien with Entergy, and Rabbi Bender with Achievezer. Unfortunately, the same cannot be said of government employees who, like FEMA disaster assistance employees (DAEs), engaged in activities that were separated from their importance for the aid recipients, but which bolstered the spending and standing of disaster aid. In the case of FEMA's DAEs, this boils down to banal services consisting of activities such as repainting a black gas valve into a red color to conform to regulations on safety labeling in case of gas leaks—even though there was no case of such a leak happening for any of the 40,000 trailers (Stringham and Snow 2008, 484). Though of no importance to the people living in the trailers, such routine actions were a boon for FEMA and its agents, who saw agency spending grow by $5.6 billion to reach the high mark of $16.7 billion. FEMA assumed more and more responsibilities having to do with housing until FEMA agents were eventually responsible for redrawing whole New Orleans neighborhoods (ibid., 482).

This growth in power and status resulted in the "redistributing up" that characterizes injustice. This was the case even when no such outcome was ever intended by honest individuals acting on behalf of FEMA, who oftentimes found themselves working twenty-four hours, traveling for two to six weeks at a day's notice, and attempting to produce high-quality research under pressure (Stringham and Snow 2008, 484). As well-meaning as these individuals were, though, their ignorance as medical authorities who demanded standardized permits hurt those who had no coverage at Alice's clinic the most and helped bigger pharmacies that could afford to spend the money on meeting regulatory demands (Storr, Haeffele-Balch, and Grube 2018, 77). Moreover, relying on food stamp applications also hurt those who (unlike Rabbi Bender) did not benefit from a highly educated background or having extensive connections and familiarity with the policy world. Unsurprisingly, even a 1 percent increase in high school results yielded a higher absorption of funds by 6.5 percent (Grube, Fike, and Storr 2018, 589).

Conversely, some measures were not unintended but were, as Father Vien correctly judged, a deliberate result of public-private lobbying. Not only did public figures fail to supply energy to the Vietnamese community, but officials wanted to open a landfill on that very site. In doing so, they would receive 22 percent of the revenues on the land from a private company that would in turn be in charge of garbage disposal (Storr, Haeffele, and Grube 2018, 110). This public-private collusion was all the more unjust given that the Mary Vietnamese community was among the poorest and most marginalized, with 29 percent of them at the absolute poverty line—2 percentage points above the New Orleans average for poverty (Grube and Storr 2014, 310).[6] It is all the more remarkable that Father Vien and the community successfully mobilized and had their grievances heard through their own lobbying. However, it speaks to the injustices that government agents acting on bad incentives can commit in the wake of disasters that a full $2 billion of the disaster funds are estimated to have been wasted on such instances of corporate collusion, regulatory waste, and (sometimes) even personal kickbacks and financial fraud (Boettke et al. 2007, 366).

Despite these significant flaws though, FEMA agents are incentivized to promote specialist knowledge that emphasizes further centralization and government interventionism. Part of the $16.7 billion that FEMA agents received was spent on research that would make the case for the utility of future FEMA projects dedicated to disaster relief (Stringham and Snow 2008, 484). Unsurprisingly then, the conclusion of these studies was that a high-level government body entrusted with coordinating the actions of federal agents across organizations would have benefited FEMA policies and facilitated the engagement in better government planning through local comprehensive schemes (Grube and Storr 2014, 303). Both these suggested improvements sidestep the knowledge problem altogether—they are simply a new attempt to replace private property with central decision-making and prices with planning. But both these suggestions provide new opportunities for status (in the case of those who will be chairing the government body and/or those liaising with local authorities) and more spending within the department (to create the new positions and maintain them). Future policies implemented by FEMA are thus likely to be just as flawed as they were in New Orleans.

SUMMARY AND FUTURE RESEARCH POSSIBILITIES

As such, the theoretical answer we have given to the dilemma in the thesis is fully represented in practice. To wrap up, the knowledge problem led to the incentive problem, which caused political behavior inconsistent with the goals of EJ. In order to prove this was the case, I examined three different sections while drawing on qualitative methods by introducing the case study of New Orleans before and after Hurricane Katrina. The end response, as seen in Section III, included problems of public choice that were derived from knowledge problems. When trying to determine the content of the policies, political actors will rely on their own connections and try to increase their own influence, opening the door to corruption when it comes to market intervention and a bloated public sector that is slow to recognize and respond to problems. Furthermore, we know that this development was derived from the very nature of disasters, which in Section II was shown to be, in essence, a combination of the same informational and motivational dimensions (and thus states would be ill-equipped to deal with them). And, thanks to Section I, one could see how this situation maps onto the gaps within existing research and how the text filled these in. In line with the outline, I will now bring these elements together again in terms of implications and confess my own shortcomings by suggesting possible avenues for future research.

The consequences of taking the knowledge problem and its incentive corollary seriously should prompt a complete rethinking of the role that public administrators are supposed to play along lines that are usually associated with the classical liberal tradition (Aligica, Boettke, and Tarko 2019, 19). As noted, because of the knowledge problem, public administrators cannot rationally order societies to fit a specific outcome (ibid., 74). Instead, the experiences of ordinary people are what generate the relevant context-specific knowledge in the first place. And it is ordinary people who, finding themselves dependent on the social experiences of others, stumble upon the right solutions. In trying to pursue their own experiences and understandings of EJ and responding to what others know EJ to be, they both arrive at solutions that neither had planned. Yet, these solutions satisfy the needs and ends of both (ibid., 74). It is in this sense that EJ is a bottom-up or emergent phenomenon.

And from the classical liberal point of view, public administrators are not the "fixers" of EJ but rather cultivators of the institutional conditions that allow individuals to engage and sustain this emergent phenomenon (Aligica, Boettke, and Tarko 2019, 74). The ways they can cultivate this capacity are already familiar to every liberal-democratic system—features such as the division of state powers and guarantees for the freedom of individual association, speech, and practice. But all these features have a less familiar, deeper meaning when seen as ways of overcoming the knowledge problem and incentivizing good political behavior (ibid., 19). Thus, allowing individuals to speak their minds, interact with others on their own terms, and pursue their own activities is vital for knowledge of goals like EJ. Free speech and practice are means to acquire knowledge and correct one's shortcomings in experience. Meanwhile, the freedom to associate is a way to try a distributive solution together, even when this might fail, and try again with someone else if it does fail. Moreover, the division of powers is a matter of preserving the emergent phenomenon from potential state abuse by internally constraining the power of state agents—pitting the executive against the judiciary and the legislative (ibid., 66). Yet, it also creates the social conditions for people to organize on their own if state actors do threaten to become abusive—hence the relevance of EJ activism, environmentally conscious neighborhoods, environmental NGOs, and so on (ibid., 66).

On that note, the knowledge and incentive problems have generally been treated as insights that lead to a more classical liberal view of government. Yet, the knowledge problem does not necessarily pertain to one type of conclusion; social democrats such as Hodgson (2019) have used the very same approach to note the coordination and epistemic limits of markets in a general context. It could be that when it comes to hurricanes, floods, and other such events, market processes have blind spots—either because prices really do not communicate everything about a person's context or because people end up failing to find a social solution on their own under extreme duress. Perhaps it is possible to make the opposite case for more government intervention based on epistemic and incentive problems. Finally, the case focused on a specific type of natural disaster scenario (hurricanes). Therefore, its findings might not be generalizable to other situations such as an earthquake, a tsunami, or a volcano eruption. These might or might not feature better government intervention, worse local responses, and so on. Therefore, more empirical analysis is also welcome.

NOTES

1. There is an ongoing discussion about other ways of defining the term and the scope of this definition. For one, original definitions were more inchoate and attuned to the changing needs of activists—sometimes EJ is referred to injustice by various terms, such as rights infringement, discrimination, allocation, or equality of outcome (Capek 1993). With growing academic interest in EJ came the sharper focus on justice as distribution (with a focus on resource and aid allocation). More recently, there has been a move toward diversifying the definition again. Some academics have begun defining EJ as a form of social recognition of oppressed groups, which refers to social status and social power rather than resources (Bell 2014). Alternatively,

environmental justice is seen as a procedural matter, where the focus is not on distribution and allocation but on the right procedures for distribution and allocation (Bell 2014). However, it is arguably the case that the distribution definition remains paramount even in these cases—recognition merely shifts the focus of distribution from the allocation of resources to that of social standing, while the procedural definition focuses on allocation of positions in a process rather than distributing resources (Walker 2012, 10). Moreover, older definitions featured a narrower focus of justice, which was also derived from the needs of environmental activists (Walker 2012). Given these origins, the initial academic focus was on resource management policies and how these policies disproportionately affected some groups over others—hence the early focus on cases like an unequal risk to landfill and pollution exposure (Capek 1993). However, EJ began being applied to an ever-growing list of scenarios. It began to also describe moments of crisis; the latter began with floods, especially in the UK with texts like Walker's. From there, it was subsequently generalized by Walker to natural disasters in general and from thereon to the rest of the literature (Walker 2010, 2012).

2. EJ has little to say about how much is too much when it comes to richer people and only focuses on the needs of the worst-off. This makes it different than a conventional strict egalitarian approach, which suggests that inequality is bad in and of itself and must be reduced when it comes to the advantages that the rich enjoy, even if these advantages do not harm the poor (Walker 2012, 10). It is also different from a prioritarian Rawlsian approach since it can accommodate different levels of need depending on who counts as the "least well-off" in a given situation.

3. A potential criticism of this thesis is that natural disasters are not a good case study for EJ given the uniqueness of their circumstances. Disasters imply devastation on a scale that renders basic necessities such as food and water inaccessible, causes an overwhelming loss of life, and only allows a limited amount of time to rescue affected people from the affected areas. As such, disasters and disaster recovery are a matter of survival where pursuing a just allocation of resources is a luxury one cannot afford in terms of either time or resources. The goal is not inequality in allocation but simply making sure that there is enough water or food to go around for everyone. However, the COVID-19 pandemic (ongoing as of the time of this text) shows how at least some people would prioritize EJ questions above those of survival. One instance of this has been the argument of prioritizing the allocation of vaccines for marginalized individuals as a means of allocating more resources to the worst-off group in society who have already faced higher rates of unemployment, worse health coverage, and more housing evictions than the well-off (Schmidt, Gostin, and Williams 2020, 2023). Insofar as EJ remains a goal then for natural disasters, it makes sense to explore why it might not be realized in practice.

4. And contrary to some suggestions, it would not be possible to simply codify and store this information to then use when crafting a policy by running something like a computer algorithm to store such data. That is because the information is not of a form that could be codified on a computer in the first place due to its tacit, local, and fleeting nature.

5. Criticisms of public choice usually revolve around discussions of self-interest and the link between the budget and self-interest (Blais and Dion 1990). Critics assert that policymakers may not be as selfish as public choice seems to assume, and budget maximizing might not be the best way to maximize one's utility (given that a bureaucrat's interests might vary in turn). However, our discussion proves Niskanen's basic point holds true. Even if policymakers are treated as well-intentioned, what they take to be good is subject to their own knowledge and experience (meaning their own institution), such that it does not coincide with what might be good for the people affected by the disaster. Moreover, decision-makers default to maximizing the budget as the one piece of information they know of (i.e., their own policies and their effectiveness from their point of view). As such, policy actors need not be self-interested to want to maximize their budgets.

6. The same goes for even more run-down neighborhoods like Gentilly (that were populated by predominantly poorer people of color in a close-knit community) where people managed to leverage their social capital to receive informal supplies and support from activists and celebrities (Grube and Storr 2014, 320).

REFERENCES

Aligica, Paul Dragos, Peter J. Boettke, and Vlad Tarko. 2019. *Public Governance and the Classical Liberal Perspective: Political Economy Foundations.* Oxford, UK: Oxford University Press.

Banzhaf, Spencer, Lala Ma, and Christopher Timmins. 2019. "Environmental Justice: The Economics of Race, Place and Pollution." *The Journal of Economic Perspectives* 33 (1): 185–208.

Bell, Karen. 2014. *Achieving Environmental Justice: A Cross-National Analysis.* Bristol, UK: Bristol University Press.

Blais, André and Stéphane Dion. 1990. "Are Bureaucrats Budget Maximizers? The Niskanen Model and Its Critics." *Polity* 22 (4): 655–74.

Boettke, Peter J. 2012. *Living Economics: Yesterday, Today, and Tomorrow.* Oakland, CA: The Independent Institute.

Boettke, Peter J., Emily Chamlee-Wright, Peter Gordon, Sanford Ikeda, Peter T. Leeson, and Russell Sobel. 2007. "The Political, Economic, and Social Aspects of Katrina." *Southern Economic Journal* 74 (2): 363–76.

Brennan, Jason. 2018. "Private Governance and the Three Biases of Political Philosophy." *The Review of Austrian Economics* 31 (2): 235–43.

Capek, Stella M. 1993. "The 'Environmental Justice' Frame: A Conceptual Discussion and Application." *Social Problems* 40 (1): 5–24.

Chamlee-Wright, Emily and Virgil Henry Storr. 2010. "Expectations of Government's Response to Disaster." *Public Choice* 144 (1–2): 253–74.

———. 2011. "Social Capital as Collective Narratives and Post-Disaster Recovery." *The Sociological Review* 59 (2): 266–82.

Dotson, Kristie and Kyle Whyte. 2013. "Environmental Justice, Unknowability and Unqualified Affectability." *Ethics and the Environment* 18 (2): 55–79.

Gaus, Gerald. 2016. *The Tyranny of the Ideal: Justice in a Diverse Society*. Princeton, NJ: Princeton University Press.

Grube, Laura E. and Virgil Henry Storr. 2014. "The Capacity for Self-Governance and Post-Disaster Resiliency." *The Review of Austrian Economics* 27 (3): 301–24.

Grube, Laura E., Rosemarie Fike, and Virgil Henry Storr. 2018. "Navigating Disaster: An Empirical Study of Federal Assistance Following Hurricane Sandy." *Eastern Economic Journal* 44: 576–93.

Hayek, F. A. 1945. "The Use of Knowledge in Society." *The American Economic Review* 35 (4): 519–30.

———. [1982]2013. *Law, Legislation and Liberty: A New Statement of the Liberal Principles of Justice and Political Economy*. 5th ed. London: Routledge.

Herlitz, Anders and David Horan. 2016. "Measuring Needs for Priority Setting in Healthcare Planning and Policy." *Social Science and Medicine* 157 (C): 96–102.

Hodgson, Geoffrey M. 2019. *Is Socialism Feasible? Towards an Alternative Future*. Cheltenham, UK: Edward Elgar.

Horwitz, Steven. 2004. "Monetary Calculation and the Unintended Extended Order: The Misesian Micro-Foundations of the Hayekian Great Society." *The Review of Austrian Economics* 17 (4): 307–21.

Johnson, Clare, Edmund Penning-Rowsell, and Dennis Parker. 2007. "Natural and Imposed Injustices: The Challenges in Implementing 'Fair' Flood Risk Management Policy in England." *The Geographical Journal* 173 (4): 374–90.

Kirzner, Israel M. 2018. *The Collected Works of Israel M. Kirzner: Competition, Economic Planning, and the Knowledge Problem*. Edited by Peter J. Boettke and Frédéric Sautet. Indianapolis, IN: Liberty Fund.

Lavoie, Don. [1985]2015. *Rivalry and Central Planning: The Socialist Calculation Debate Reconsidered*. Arlington, VA: Mercatus Center.

Mathers, Rachel L. 2012. "The Failure of State-Led Economic Development on American Indian Reservations." *The Independent Review* 17 (1): 65–80.

Mises, Ludwig von. [1920]1990. *Economic Calculation in the Socialist Commonwealth*. Auburn, AL: Mises Institute.

Pennington, Mark. 2011. *Robust Political Economy: Classical Liberalism and the Future of Public Policy*. Cheltenham, UK: Edward Elgar.

Schmidt, Harald, Lawrence O. Gostin, and Michelle A. Williams. 2020. "Is It Lawful and Ethical to Prioritize Racial Minorities for COVID-19 Vaccines?." *JAMA: The Journal of the American Medical Association* 324 (20): 2023–24.

Schmidtz, David. 2011. "Nonideal Theory: What It is and What It Needs to Be." *Ethics* 121 (4): 772–96.

Shields, Liam. 2012. "The Prospects for Sufficientarianism." *Utilitas* 24 (1): 101–17.

Storr, Virgil Henry, Stefanie Haeffele-Balch, and Laura E. Grube. 2015. *Community Revival in the Wake of Disaster: Lessons in Local Entrepreneurship*. London: Palgrave Macmillan.

———. 2018. "Entrepreneurs Drive Community Revival in the Wake of Disaster." *The Review of Austrian Economics* 31 (4): 479–84.

Stringham, Edward Peter and Nicholas A. Snow. 2008. "The Broken Trailer Fallacy: Seeing the Unseen Effects of Government Policies in Post-Katrina New Orleans." *International Journal of Social Economics* 35 (7): 480–89.

Walker, Gordon. 2010. "Environmental Justice, Impact Assessment and the Politics of Knowledge: The Implications of Assessing the Social Distribution of Environmental Outcomes." *Environmental Impact Assessment Review* 30 (5): 312–18.

———. 2012. *Environmental Justice: Concepts, Evidence, and Politics.* London: Routledge.

Walker, Gordon and Kate Burningham. 2011. "Flood Risk, Vulnerability and Environmental Justice: Evidence and Evaluation of Inequality in a UK Context." *Critical Social Policy* 31 (2): 216–40.

Wegner, Giulia and Unai Pascual. 2009. "Cost-Benefit Analysis in the Context of Ecosystem Services for Human Well-Being: A Multidisciplinary Critique." *Global Environmental Change* 21 (2): 492–504.

Chapter 10

Unintended Consequences of a U.S. Meat Tax

Alison Grant

WHY A MEAT TAX?

The link between environmental and human health through diet is becoming increasingly important in contemporary research and popular media outlets. As a result, many consumers have become interested in the impacts of food production before it reaches their plates. A U.S. consumer survey conducted by the International Food Information Council (2020) revealed that 70 percent of survey respondents were (at least) somewhat concerned about climate change. Of the respondents who said they were environmentally conscious, over half were particularly concerned about the environmental impact of their food and beverage purchases. Approximately one in five of these individuals mentioned that their concerns always impacted their purchases at the grocery store or other food establishments. The top concerns listed were as follows: "How food is processed" and "how food is grown"? When asked about effective practices to address these concerns, the top-ranked choice was "reduce greenhouse gas emissions originating from food production."

The production, transportation, and storage of all types of food products produce greenhouse gas emissions (GHGEs). If we narrow this down to the major sources of GHGEs within the food sector, livestock production is, by far, the largest source—approximately 71 percent of the entire sector's GHGEs originate from meat production for human consumption, including the process of growing crops for animal feed, land use, and emissions throughout the supply chain (processing, transport, packaging, and retail) (Poore and Nemecek 2018). From a global perspective, livestock production comprises approximately 15 percent of the total anthropogenic GHGEs (Clark et al. 2019; Food and Agriculture Organization of the United Nations [FAO] 2013), although it may be important to note that within the United

States, this number is smaller (less than 10 percent). The smaller proportional impact within the United States is due to the use of advanced land, crop, livestock, and manure management and capture techniques that reduce resulting airborne methane and nitrous oxide emissions into the environment (EPA 2021). Nevertheless, it is clear that the livestock sector is contributing to increasing GHGEs and that, in general, some consumers are revealing concerns about meat's climate impacts and have acted on these concerns by attempting to reduce their personal meat consumption.

Choosing to reduce personal meat consumption is one way in which consumers have taken action, yet some have gone further to say that something should be done at the state or national level to incentivize consumers to reduce total GHGEs via a reduction in meat consumption (IFIC 2020). The former action is a private, individual choice, whereas the latter action proposes a possible restriction on consumer choice (compared to the former action) in the hopes of achieving an improved public good (air quality) through reducing total meat-derived GHGEs. Thus, the goal of this chapter is to assess the latter action—a policy proposal for reducing livestock's impact on human health and the environment. The particular policy proposal at the forefront of this analysis is a U.S. meat tax. This framework can apply to other "sin taxes," such as the sugar-sweetened beverage (SSB) taxes currently implemented in Berkeley, California, and Philadelphia, Pennsylvania.

What could be the unintended consequences of a meat tax? This chapter will begin with an assessment of the negative externality present and if the magnitude of this externality warrants an intervention by utilization of a sin tax. Following this analysis, an overview of the possible unintended consequences, using current meat supply chain data, is explored. This chapter provides some preliminary evidence to suggest that a meat tax policy might produce more harm than good.

MEAT CONSUMPTION AS A NEGATIVE EXTERNALITY

Caro et al. (2017), Säll (2018), and Nordgren (2012) assess the effects of a proposed meat tax in Denmark, Sweden, and the European Union, respectively. Although a meat tax has never been implemented in these nations, the studies conclude that a tax on meat would drive consumers away from meat-derived protein, resulting in a healthier and cleaner environment overall. The common element in each of these analyses is an assumed political theory—that the state can provide the services necessary to lead society closer to a social optimum where externalities are internalized. What seems to be missing prior to the methods in each of these papers is a thorough analysis of (1) a statement of the political theory used and (2) why a meat excise tax is necessary to achieve overall environmental or health goals.

Simon (2013) presents the case for a meat tax by claiming that current economics is "rigged," that is, that supply and demand lead consumers to an outcome that drives individuals to "consume too much meat." Nordgren (2012) states that a meat tax is necessary since there are serious ethical issues that the market does not account for. Both of these papers assume that individuals are not choosing what is best for them and that society would be better off if a centralized decision-making authority guided them to an optimal social outcome.

To assess these claims, I utilize the core theories of mainline economics presented in Mitchell and Boettke (2017). Mainline economics can be summarized into three parts: (1) the market is a process, (2) institutional and cultural contexts shape that process, and (3) political institutions themselves are a product of exchange. The authors note that the natural tendency to exchange will lead to socially beneficial outcomes. A caveat of this is that exchange itself shapes the institutional environment, but there is no guarantee that the right institutional environment will evolve. For a meat tax to be implemented successfully, public policy officials would require knowledge of consumer preferences. Moreover, such consumer preferences would have to be aligned with the idea that their consumption imposes a cost on others by producing GHGEs and eventually contributes to climate change—a result that is experienced by all people. However, such a state of affairs defines away the problem policymakers are assuming to exist, since it presumes the availability of knowledge, ex ante, that only emerges through the act of consumer choice itself and is therefore never given to a policymaker or group of policymakers (Hayek 1945).

Mitchell and Boettke (2017) further mention that, "given the right incentives, individual actions will serve the common good." They are referring to individuals participating in micro-relationships that lead to the appropriate macro-level social outcome, but for the topic of this chapter, I will discuss what this "common good" or desired social outcome means. Does a social outcome include healthy individuals, the welfare of non-human living things, such as animals, or a clean environment? In the section that follows, I will take a step back from the implementation of a meat tax analyzed in the aforementioned studies and ask the simple question that ought to precede this public policy: Why tax meat?

What Is the Negative Externality?

Similar to the SSB tax, there are calls for a policy response on meat consumption due to some evidence of the link between red and processed meat consumption and environmental and health consequences (Miller 2019; Van Zanten, Van Ittersum, and De Boer 2019; Poore and Nemecek 2018). The price change of meat products is calculated, in a sense, by the pass-through GHGEs resulting from meat production and the negative health outcome effects of consuming red and processed meats, which have been quantified as health-related deaths in the current literature (Springmann et al. 2018). The price change in this study for beef and pork products considers a positive environmental cost per unit of meat consumed. This can be seen as a negative externality. A *negative externality* is a cost that is suffered by a third party as a consequence of an economic transaction. To put it in other words, a negative externality must be damaging to other groups not involved in the transaction. The classic response to negative externalities is to internalize them using a Pigouvian tax (Pigou 1920). Put simply, this kind of tax would add a per-unit cost on the product that is producing environmental damage. A Pigouvian tax is an example of how a meat tax, if seriously considered as a policy response in the United States, might be implemented. If we assess the definition for a negative externality mentioned above with each of the literature claims, we can better determine the total externality involved.

First, what is the negative externality in question that may require market interference? Three negative effects of consuming meat have been noted in the literature, all involving the production of meat: (1) health effects of consuming red and processed meat and the studied link between meat consumption and negative health outcomes, (2) welfare of animals used in meat production, and (3) emissions that result from livestock production. In what follows, I will provide the justifications in the literature for defining a negative externality in each of these three categories and subsequently, where necessary, challenge the validity on some of these claims.

Health Effects

Within the U.S. Department of Agriculture (USDA) Scientific Report of the 2015 Dietary Guidelines Advisory Committee (USDA 2015), the U.S. population was encouraged to consume less red and processed meat to have a healthier and more sustainable diet (3). Later in 2015, the World Health Organization (WHO) and International Agency for Research on Cancer (IARC) noted in a report that processed meats are carcinogenic to humans. They concluded this based on sufficient evidence in humans that the consumption of processed meats contributes to the increased risk of colorectal cancers (IARC 2015). Qian et al. (2020) provide results that point to an association of red and processed meat consumption with type 2 diabetes, cardiovascular disease, and cancer. The authors found that replacing meat with plant-protein sources reduces low-density lipoprotein cholesterol and other cardiometabolic risk factors. Since reports like these have been circulating in recent years, some meat consumers have considered reducing meat in or removing it altogether from their diet (NielsenIQ 2018; Reinhart 2018).

Although the literature is clear on the link between meat consumption and negative health outcomes, health effects of consuming red and processed meat are borne by the consumers themselves who are making the decisions to eat meat, reducing the claim that a negative externality is present for health effects specifically. If we assess the claim that this puts stresses on the healthcare system, which could be, in part, paid for by others, then the donors or the taxpayers would need to be affected by this result for this to be an externality. In countries with more socialized healthcare systems, such as Canada, there might be a stronger justification for a negative externality, as the taxpayers pay for primary care. However, even if we assume a socialized healthcare system, it can still be argued that health outcomes do not exhibit signs of an externality *because* of the market process. Rather, one may exist because of government's involvement in that process. Moving back to the current-day United States with minimal shared healthcare costs sponsored by the government, health costs are largely private costs or private insurance-financed. Therefore, the health outcomes of meat consumption do not conform to the definition of a negative externality and do not provide credible justification for a meat tax.

Furthermore, Boudreaux and Meiners (2019) mention that for an externality to truly exist, it must not only have unintended spillover effects on a third party to an exchange, but it must also be *unexpected*. Just as Mitchell and Boettke (2017) stress the importance of the market process, where consumer preferences align with the idea that their consumption does or does not impose a cost on others, Boudreaux and Meiners (2019) note that people adjust their market activities to reflect their expectations. For meat consumption, this could mean consumers shift their meat purchasing behavior to reflect their concerns about meat GHGE, health effects, or animal welfare issues. On the producer side, this could mean meat producers, suppliers, or packers adjust their production behavior to respond to consumers demanding a reduction in the aforementioned concerns. For example, producers that advertise the cage-free nature of their poultry operations or the omega-enriched quality of their eggs are responding to consumer demand for increased animal welfare and human nutrition, respectively. Both the producer and the consumer adjust their market activities to reflect their expectations. Transactions such as the purchase and sale of meat products result in market prices that reflect expected spillover effects (Boudreaux and Meiners 2019). In other words, market prices should already account for any *expected* social cost of meat production and consumption; thus, they would not require any type of price adjustment to include any social costs that are already incorporated into the price.

The claim that meat production and consumption stresses the healthcare system can be seen as a revealed expectation through market transactions. If this expectation is built into the taxpayer's purchase behavior (i.e., taxpayers know they are bearing the cost of meat consumption, whether they are a meat consumer or not), by definition, it is no longer an externality. Indeed, this can still be considered a cost, but it is not a social cost. The health effects of meat consumption must have clear *unintended*, as well as *unexpected*, negative consequences on a third party to the exchange. Neither of these two requirements has been argued in the meat tax debate; thus, they do not provide credible justification for the presence of an externality.

Animal Welfare Effects

The welfare of animals used in meat production can be a cause for concern by others. People for the Ethical Treatment of Animals (PETA) is calling for an excise tax on retail meat products due to the environmental and animal welfare impacts of animal production (PETA n.d.). Individuals within this organization make the claim that conventional meat production practices in the United States are intensive and profit-driven, leaving little concern for the welfare of the animals involved in this process. However, de Jonge and van Trijp (2012) note that stakeholders across the meat supply chain have become increasingly concerned about animal welfare issues, and perhaps compliance and enforcement of animal welfare standards have kept up with general consumer concerns. Further, the authors note that significant market segmentation has occurred to ensure marketing targets that cater to the heterogeneous nature of consumer animal welfare concerns. Meat supply chain businesses have evolved with consumer sentiment on topics of animal welfare. This means that if one individual prioritizes animal welfare in their food choice and another individual, on the other extreme, has no concern for animal well-being, both types of consumers have a segregated avenue in which to purchase their meat products. The cost of those products may not be the same, but the consumer can decide which product is more desirable based on their own willingness-to-pay values for animal welfare characteristics. This undermines the case for an externality since consumers are already paying and internalizing this cost into their decision. Furthermore, the U.S. Animal Welfare Act of 1966 regulates a base-level standard of care for the treatment of animals in production, transportation, exhibition, and research. Handlers are frequently monitored for compliance under this act. However, this does not rule out any harm that could possibly occur.

If we assume some animal harm is occurring, an externality could be present if it is proven that damage occurs to others not involved in consuming meat. This third party could be human beings that value animal well-being, even if they have no relationship to the animals being harmed. Since it is a private decision to eat meat and a third party being harmed has been somewhat identified, this could be considered an externality in some scenarios. But the identification of an externality alone does not justify the requirement of a meat tax policy. Coase ([1960] 2000) posited that in a world without transaction costs, individuals could bargain with one another to efficiently distribute resources. It is useful to think about Coase ([1960] 2000) as an alternative means to counteract an externality. Even in the world we live in—a world with transaction costs—over forty nuisance cases regarding the *Animal Welfare Act of 1966* have gone through the courts, and some have been successful at proving legitimate harm to animals. For example, *Cox v. U.S. Department of Agriculture* 925 F.2d 1102 (8th Cir. 1991) provided a suspension to a kennel owner for violations involving "delivering dogs for transportation in commerce, that were under eight weeks old, failing to hold dogs for at least five days after acquiring them, and refusing APHIS [Animal and Plant Health Inspection Service] inspections." Appropriate animal harm documentation and resources to file claims like these could be barriers for any individual to participate in this process, but this process does provide a means to compensate harm being done without imposing a general form of taxation on all citizens.

Climate Change Effects

GHGEs, from livestock production particularly, have become a topic of discussion in social, political, and economic agendas (Hunter and Röös 2016; Havlík et al. 2013; Stackhouse-Lawson et al. 2012; Garnett 2011; Fiala 2007). Beef production has a larger impact on the environment through emissions than any other type of livestock (Stackhouse-Lawson et al. 2012; Garnett 2011; Fiala 2007). Livestock production comprises 14.5 percent of the total anthropogenic GHGEs (FAO 2019). This is approximately 7 gigatons of carbon dioxide equivalent per year.

On average, 300 kilograms of carbon dioxide equivalent GHGEs are emitted per kilogram of beef protein produced, although there is very high variability in emission intensities due to various operation practices and different inputs that are used in production across the globe (FAO 2019). The breakdown of GHGEs is methane (44 percent), nitrous oxide (29 percent), and carbon dioxide (27 percent) (FAO 2019). If we consider only carbon dioxide, total livestock production accounts for 5 percent of total annual anthropogenic carbon dioxide emissions (Intergovernmental Panel on Climate Change [IPCC] 2006), so beef production emits approximately 3 percent of global carbon dioxide emissions. Methane and nitrous oxide emissions have a larger proportional impact from beef production—44 percent and 53 percent of total annual global methane and nitrous oxide emissions, respectively (IPCC 2006).

There are mixed results behind livestock production and its contribution to climate change. There is disagreement on how much of an environmental impact livestock is having compared to other sectors (Herrero et al. 2010), and the share of livestock emissions to total emissions varies across regions in the world (Pitesky, Stackhouse, and Mitloehner 2009). Regardless, many studies point to the United States, in particular, as a country that overconsumes meat, and a policy response may be necessary for this overconsumption (Miller 2019; Van Zanten, Van Ittersum, and De Boer 2019; Poore and Nemecek 2018; Springmann et al. 2018; Nordgren 2012).

The claim in the literature is that climate change is a cost that will increase throughout time, so there are hidden costs that are not being internalized if individuals are not paying for their utilization of the public good *today*. The time-trend and damage magnitude are difficult to estimate. A classic Pigouvian tax used to internalize this externality depends entirely on being able to quantify the third-party damage. This taxation is a way to translate the information to the consumer, assuming that they do not already have some form of this information. It sends a signal to the consumer that their choice to eat meat is resulting in a negative externality. Yet, Pigou (1920) did recognize how difficult it is to quantify an externality, and any error in quantifying it makes the tax suboptimal. Therefore, there is no guarantee that the consumers are receiving more accurate information with a tax in place than they did without. Once we consider issues in quantification of the added cost, it may then be important to address why a tax could make society better off than a pre-tax scenario.

How Important Is the Externality?

Ostrom (2017) mentions that producer efficiency in the absence of consumer utility is without economic meaning. "When individuals act with the legal independence characteristic of decision-making in market structures in a situation dominated by externalities [. . .] we can conclude that institutional weakness or institutional failure will occur. The magnitude of the weakness or failure will depend on the importance of the externality, or the degree of indivisibility occurring in the public good" (ibid., 51). This begs the question, how important is the externality? The answer can only be decided by individuals making choices and not by centralized decision-makers. Culture plays a large role in this concept. It plays a role in how we feel about harm to health, animals, or the environment. The customs, patterns, and social institutions of a particular social group also relate to market expectations because expectations are influenced by culture. Revisiting the claim by Boudreaux and Meiners (2019), individuals adjust their market activities to reflect their expectations. The externality comprises the *importance* or weight that each individual in society gives to the externality as well as the *unexpected* nature of the spillover effects that could occur by producing and consuming meat. Culture plays a role in each component of the definition of an externality. What may work in Sweden and Denmark may not work in the United States. Particularly, large meat-producing states, such as Texas, may not shift behavior when faced with increased prices for meat. If the policy goal is to curb meat consumption, Texas and other states may not produce results in line with the original policy goals.

EVEN IF AN EXTERNALITY EXISTS, WHY USE A TAX?

Once the externality is defined, we ought to assess the Pigouvian tax versus alternative mechanisms to reduce the externality present. Ostrom (2005) mentions that when analyzing a public good where exclusion is difficult, "designing mechanisms that honestly reflect beneficiaries' preferences and their willingness to pay is challenging." The exclusion of parties is perhaps most difficult when dealing with air quality. Another feature of air quality as a public good is that there is no subtractability, that is, consumption (or contributing emissions) by one does not currently subtract from the flow of services available to others, but the benefits of mitigating climate change are global and, perhaps, far into the future.

When addressed with the issue of taxation, Hayek ([1960]2011) mentions that taxation intervention will always limit the scope of experimentation and thereby obstruct what may be useful developments. Useful developments that could be limited by taxation intervention include the current technological adoption in the meat sector as well as management techniques to mitigate the effects of climate change.

There are many ways in which producers have responded to consumer demands to reduce the livestock sector's impact on GHGEs through current uninhibited market processes. In terms of animal welfare, producers have found ways to market products to reveal the cruelty-free environment that was present in the production of meat products, such as cage-free chickens and range-fed beef. In terms of emissions, producers have adopted methane digesters to reduce methane emissions originating from cattle. Despite U.S. livestock production quantity rising in the last five years, there has been zero growth in U.S. livestock emissions during this period; methane digesters and herd-size management techniques are the main contributors to this trend (EPA 2021).

Unintended Consequences

A meat tax may provide unintended consequences in two ways: (1) limiting productive entrepreneurship and (2) allowing for unproductive entrepreneurship.

Limiting Productive Entrepreneurship

A meat tax may limit the scope of experimentation in meat production. Consumer preferences and choices have driven producers to reduce the externality. As consumers become increasingly interested in the food production systems behind their consumption, producers are incentivized to find new ways to reveal the production practices that are aligned with consumer preferences. The decisions to innovate, in this case, are self-generating, self-modifying, and self-enforcing without the use of the state to guide human action. Uninhibited market forces have driven producers to adopt methane digesters, which dramatically reduce the GHGEs in meat production processes. Methane emissions are reduced through the use of anaerobic digesters (Key and Sneeringer 2011). Anaerobic organisms break down cattle manure and store methane for use as biogas, rather than releasing methane directly into the environment. Currently, 248 methane digesters are operating in the United States and 4.27 million metric tons of carbon dioxide equivalent per year have been reduced through this technology (EPA 2021). What was once considered a possible market failure associated with a negative externality generated a future profit opportunity to innovate a way to reduce the externality.

A meat tax could redirect resources away from the aforementioned private mitigation efforts. The use of taxation may limit the scope of experimentation or prevent these improvements from occurring because taxation would make the production process more expensive. If producers have increased production costs, the incentive to innovate and adopt new technologies is hindered. Methane digesters, herd management techniques, and production practices that satisfy the consumers cost money—any revenue lost is a loss in potential investments toward productive improvements.

Allowing for Unproductive Entrepreneurship

Mainline economics does not assume that humans are perfectly rational or perfectly informed, but rather that humans rely on incentives and information that is provided through a signal, such as prices. Humans weigh trade-offs and opportunity costs when making decisions. When prices rise for certain types of food, humans can respond to increased prices by choosing an alternative food. On the other hand, if prices rise for certain types of food and humans do not switch to an alternative, this may reveal that certain individuals are still willing to pay for the food product subject to the price increase.

Particularly for relatively elastic goods, such as beef and pork products, the law of demand states that when the price of a good, such as meat, increases, the quantity demanded decreases. Put differently, if the price of meat increases due to a tax, the quantity demanded should decrease. Since consumers are subject to a budget constraint, when they buy more of one good, they must give up some quantity of another good. If beef products are subject to a tax, consumers are expected to buy less beef and substitute toward other types of meat or other sources of protein, for which the demand increases relative to beef products. This could be poultry, fish, tofu, or other plant-based products rich in protein.

Alchian and Allen (2018) present some additional implications pertaining to the law of demand, particularly as they relate to the relative margins, such as quality, in which consumption of a particular good is changed. Alchian and Allen (ibid.) further explain a general effect of an added per-unit cost to a consumer good, namely that high-value products now become less expensive relative to low-value products. An addition of a constant, per-unit cost, such as a tax, to a higher-quality grade of particular good, such as beef, will reduce its price relative to a lower-quality grade of beef. This effect, termed the *Alchian–Allen effect*, is relevant to the discussion of a per-unit meat tax because relative consumption will shift from a lower-quality grade of beef toward a higher-quality grade of beef. This would ultimately impact competition *within* the meat industry in terms of those that can produce higher-value (or higher-quality) meats, since a tax would reduce the absolute quantity of meat produced by the industry as a whole. Thus, there are two components within this effect that are relevant to the meat tax discussion. The first component is that higher-quality producers gain a competitive edge relative to the entire meat industry. This is outlined in Section IV using an example. The second component is that a policy result that relatively benefits higher-quality meat producers invites rent-seeking behavior, where higher-quality producers become incentivized to lobby the government to regulate their own industry in this way. The second component is a direct result of the first and therefore will be further developed in Section V following the example in Section IV.

WELFARE EFFECTS

Let's use an example of boneless USDA Choice sirloin steak as high-quality beef and ground beef as low-quality beef. Average prices in the United States in 2018 for sirloin steak and ground beef were $8.40/lb and $3.72/lb, respectively. The quality of the beef is reflected in the differences in price per-unit quantity. Figure 10.1 shows the yearly meat expenditure per capita over time in the United States. As ground beef is cheaper, consumers demand more of the product. Ground beef expenditures have increased over time, mainly due to the decreasing prices relative to average incomes over this period.

Since a meat tax has not yet been implemented, the data does not exist for real price changes due to a meat tax. A simple excise or unit tax can be simulated as a $1/lb tax on all beef products, which would increase average sirloin steak prices to $9.40/lb and ground beef to $4.72/lb. Though absolute prices are increased equally, sirloin steak becomes cheaper *relative* to ground beef.

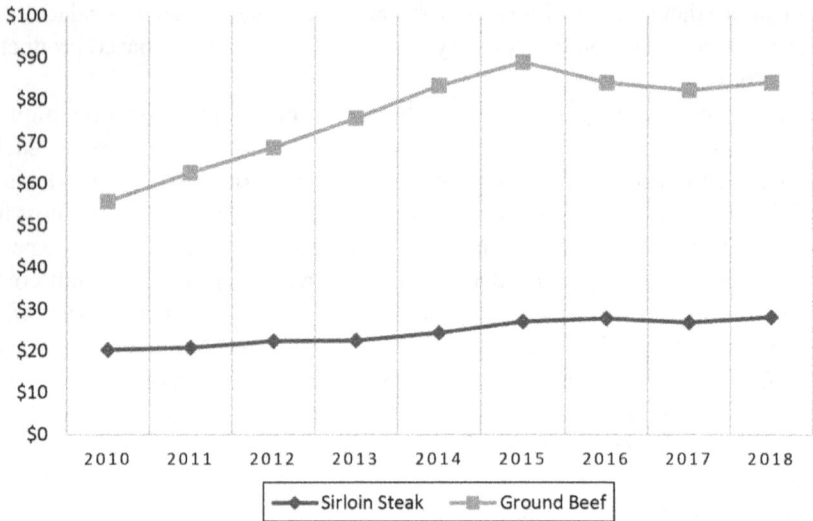

Figure 10.1 Yearly Meat Expenditure Per Capita in the United States, 2010–2018. *Source*: Bureau of Labor Statistics (2020).

Therefore, the low-quality beef now becomes more expensive relative to the high-quality beef. Prior to the tax, a purchase of sirloin steak was equivalent to giving up more than twice (2.26 times) as much ground beef. But with a unit increase in both prices, the new price of sirloin steak is lower relative to ground beef—being only 1.99 times rather than 2.26 times more expensive, even with a tax as small as $1/lb. This gap expands the higher the unit tax is raised.

Figure 10.2 shows the yearly meat expenditure changes due to the $1/lb excise tax if consumers do not change their total consumption subject to new prices. If consumers do not shift their budget shares for beef, the financial burden of buying ground beef would be almost seven times more than sirloin steak. This would have negative implications for low-income groups, as ground beef is bought more often as the main protein item in lower-income households. Since the total food budget stays the same in this example, income-restricted consumers may shift entirely to ground beef as higher costs of ground beef use up the budget faster and could prevent (what would have been pre-tax) purchases of higher-end cuts.

Of course, if consumers face increased prices for selective items, their quantity demanded for the higher-priced items will likely decline, following the laws of demand. The amount of sirloin steak demanded would *increase* relative to the demanded amount of ground beef when the price of each is increased by the same absolute amounts (pound-for-pound). The percentage reduction in demanded amount of ground beef would be greater than that for sirloin steak. Of the total demanded amount of meat, a larger proportion

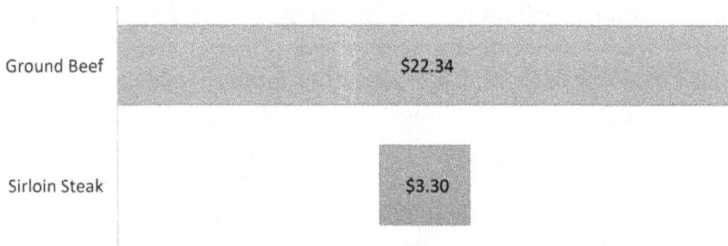

Figure 10.2   Average Yearly Meat Expenditure Changes with a $1/lb Excise Tax. *Source*: Calculated from Bureau of Labor Statistics, 2020 data.

would now be steak sirloin. This then raises the question: Could producers of high-quality meat be aware that meat quantity shares might shift to high-quality meat in the face of a meat tax? Could producers of high-quality meat actually be advocates of a meat tax?

A selective tax on meat products could benefit the individuals and groups who object to meat production on moral grounds (PETA, for instance), but it could also benefit those who might profit from supplying the demands for higher-quality meats or substitute products (the meatpacking or plant-based substitute industry). Hence, the Alchian–Allen effect is relevant for two reasons. The first reason is that higher-quality meat products becoming relatively cheaper when subject to a per-unit tax would relatively benefit the higher-quality meat producers, as mentioned above. The second reason is that, by knowing the first reason, higher-quality meat or substitute product producers would then have the incentive to possibly advocate for this type of taxation policy.

REGULATORY CAPTURE IN THE MEAT INDUSTRY

Regulatory capture is not new in the meatpacking industry. Newman (2018) reveals the lobbying efforts by Chicago meatpacking firms in the early 1900s to halt legislation that harmed them and advocate for government subsidization of the industry. Newman (ibid.) further mentions that these efforts perhaps led to industry consolidation and higher meat prices at the expense of less-endowed competitors. Chung, Park, and Lee (2018) uncover the continued concentration and market power in the U.S. meatpacking industry in the present day, which incentivizes processing firms to draw any small competitors out of the market with government intervention.

The "Bootleggers and Baptists" theory of regulation (Yandle 1983) explains why opposing interest groups might work toward similar goals. Baptists supported alcohol prohibition laws based on their ethical views, while bootleggers supported the same laws based on potential profit gains from legal alcohol prohibition. Thus, two completely different interest groups end up politically supporting the same policy.

Producers of meat are not just the cattle farmers, but they are also the intermediary packers and processors that convert the farm output to consumer goods. The top three meat packers and processors in the United States, by 2019 net sales, are Tyson Foods, JBS USA Holdings, and Cargill Meat Solutions (National Provisioner 2019). Tyson Foods is also the leading donor of political campaigns and lobbying spending for the industry. A meat tax would likely draw the efforts of meat packers and processors to produce high-quality beef cuts, as the price of high-quality beef would become cheaper relative to low-quality beef. High-quality meat producers in this case can also be those that meet the costs of regulatory compliance in terms of product differentiation by the healthy or environmentally friendly traits of their products, not just the physical aspects (such as the different cuts) of the meat. Not only would producer entrepreneurial efforts shift to higher-quality meats, but they would also shift to possible efforts in the participation of the act of regulatory capture.

The entrepreneurial market process is key to understanding any unintended consequences. Institutional changes can redirect entrepreneurship from productive to unproductive purposes. Market externality taxes may give rise to this unproductive entrepreneurship. Hoffer et al. (2014) recognize that Pigouvian excise sin taxes respond to self-serving interests of individuals and groups able to apply effective political pressure on politicians and regulatory agencies, rather than to the public interest itself. There are private motives of interest groups, mainly, the meatpacking industry, that stand to benefit from governmental policy interventions. Figure 10.3 outlines the total dollars spent on lobbying and political campaigns by the meatpacking industry. Peaks in 2008 were mainly a result of lobbying spending for government support through the economic recession. The current spending of the industry is mainly for environmental and food safety regulations as well as immigration policy since labor in this sector relies heavily on immigrants. If the meatpacking industry realizes that it can gain from a meat tax, lobbying efforts might be expanded to satisfy these interests. Since a tax will reduce the absolute quantity of meat produced by the industry as a whole, the Alchian–Allen effect impacts competition *within* the meat industry with regard to those that can produce higher-quality meats, which in turn invites rent-seeking behavior and regulatory capture.

The works of public choice school economists, in particular Buchanan (1987), address another problem—policymaking authorities also face their own incentives, and these incentives are sometimes perverse and create unintended consequences. Hoffer et al. (2014) confirm that sin taxes are subject to the special interests of politicians. If the industry lobby groups are large and powerful enough, politicians have an imperative to get re-elected—they

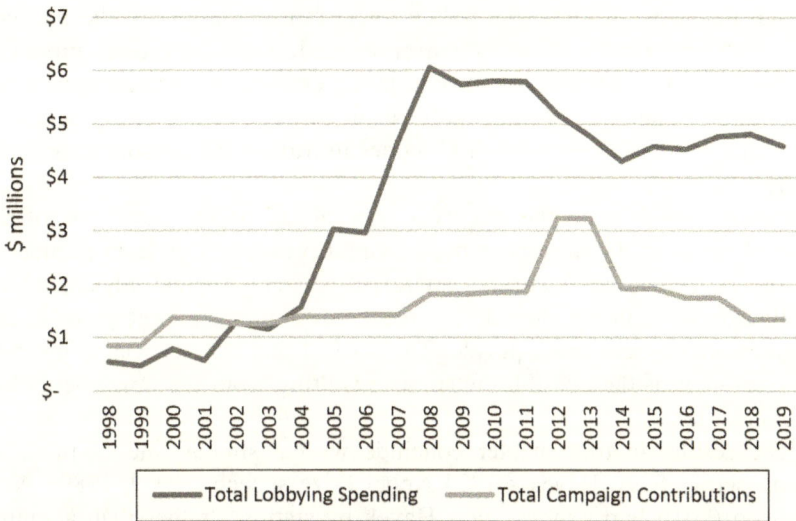

Figure 10.3   Annual Lobbying by Meat Processors and Products in the United States.
Source: Opensecrets.org.

may buy enough votes by supporting well-endowed and loud industries, such as the meatpacking sector lobbyists.

Last, a contribution of Mitchell and Boettke (2017) is the notion that policymakers and researchers should exercise humility. Hayek (1945) alluded to the idea that policymaking authorities are not fully capable—and will never be fully capable due to dispersed subjective knowledge—of possessing all of the information necessary to guide humans to a desired social outcome. If politicians are motivated by the ability to raise revenue or support a special interest group, the original policy goal of internalizing the negative externality to reach this social outcome becomes an oversight. A particular unintended consequence is the creation of another negative externality, namely the social costs associated with rent-seeking.

CONCLUSION

The first two steps in determining whether a policy intervention is required are to (1) determine whether a negative externality is present and (2) determine whether it is important enough to justify government intervention. If a meat tax meets these two requirements, the next step is to analyze possible unintended consequences that might result from this policy intervention. Examples from the supply chain of meat production reveal that it is possible that policy intervention could limit the productive entrepreneurship that is currently underway, including producer technological advancements for mitigating emissions. Further, unproductive entrepreneurship would likely result through rent-seeking behavior in a market that already has high concentration, firm consolidation, and market power.

Further research on the effects of a meat tax on increased consolidation of firms or the disappearance of small processors or farm producers would be beneficial. Increased attention on technological advancements of livestock producers should be considered, as this is a large piece of the unintended consequences puzzle. The goal of this chapter was to provide an overview of the possible outcomes resulting from the implementation of a meat tax.

The results in this chapter conclude with a similar line of thinking addressed in F. A. Hayek's 1974 Nobel Prize speech (Hayek 1989). Neil Chilson (2016, n.p.) summarizes Hayek by stating, "rather than attempting to shape society directly like a sculptor shapes a statue, we must seek instead to understand and to create the right environment for progress, like a gardener in a garden. If the goal in society is not to do more harm than good in our efforts to improve the social order, we should view individuals, including those individuals crafting public policy, as gardeners who cultivate growth. This requires that policies do less engineering or sculpting and more weeding and trimming, allowing for individuals to be free to act and choose in a way that achieves a social outcome resulting from the aggregate of these individual actions." Considering the serious policy proposals currently being brought forward in some states, this information may be useful to policy officials. After careful consideration and questioning of a U.S. meat tax policy, the possible unintended consequences seem like they would outweigh the benefits of targeting emissions and animal welfare concerns through increasing the cost of meat consumption. A meat tax policy might do more engineering and sculpting when society would be better off with more weeding and trimming.

REFERENCES

Alchian, Armen A. and William R. Allen. 2018. *Universal Economics*. Edited by Jerry L. Jordan. Indianapolis, IN: Liberty Fund.

Animal Welfare Act of 1966, 7 U.S.C. "Chapter 54—Transportation, Sale, and Handling of Certain Animals." (2015).

Boudreaux, Donald J. and Roger Meiners. 2019. "Externality: Origins and Classifications." *Natural Resources Journal* 59 (1): 1–34.

Buchanan, James M. 1987. "The Constitution of Economic Policy." *The American Economic Review* 77 (3): 243–50.

Caro, Dario, Pia Frederiksen, Marianne Thomsen, and Anders Branth Pedersen. 2017. "Toward a More Consistent Combined Approach of Reduction Targets and Climate Policy Regulations: The Illustrative Case of a Meat Tax in Denmark." *Environmental Science & Policy* 76 (10): 78–81.

Chilson, Neil. 2016. "A Simplified 'Pretense of Knowledge.'" *Medium.com*, April 4.

Chung, Chanjin, Seongjin Park, and Jungmin Lee. 2018. "Estimating Bilateral Market Power of Processors and Retailers in the U.S. Beef Industry." *Agribusiness* 34 (4): 771–92.

Clark, Michael A., Marco Springmann, Jason Hill, and David Tilman. 2019. "Multiple Health and Environmental Impacts of Foods." *Proceedings of the National Academy of Sciences* 116 (46): 23357–62.

Coase, Ronald H. [1960] 2000. "The Problem of Social Cost." In *Classic Papers in Natural Resource Economics*, edited by Chennat Gopalakrishnan, 87–137. London: Palgrave Macmillan.

de Jonge, Janneke and Hans C. M. van Trijp. 2013. "Meeting Heterogeneity in Consumer Demand for Animal Welfare: A Reflection on Existing Knowledge and Implications for the Meat Sector." *Journal of Agricultural and Environmental Ethics* 26 (3): 629–61.

Cox, E. Lee, and Becky Cox, d/b/a Pixy Pals Kennel, Petitioners, v. United States Department of Agriculture, Respondent. 925 F.2d 1102 (8th Cir. 1991).

Environmental Protection Agency. 2021. "Sources of Greenhouse Gas Emissions." April 14. https://www.epa.gov/ghgemissions/sources-greenhouse-gas-emissions.

Fiala, Nathan. 2008. "Meeting the Demand: An Estimation of Potential Future Greenhouse Gas Emissions from Meat Production." *Ecological Economics* 67 (3): 412–19.

Food and Agriculture Organization of the United Nations. 2013. "By the Numbers: GHG Emissions by Livestock." http://www.fao.org/news/story/en/item/197623/icode/.

Garnett, Tara. 2011. "Where Are the Best Opportunities for Reducing Greenhouse Gas Emissions in the Food System (Including the Food Chain)?" *Food Policy* 36 (1): S23–S32.

Havlík, Petr, Hugo Valin, Aline Mosnier, Michael Obersteiner, J. S. Baker, Mario Herrero, Mariana C. Rufino, and Erwin Schmid. 2013. "Crop Productivity and the Global Livestock Sector: Implications for Land Use Change and Greenhouse Gas Emissions." *American Journal of Agricultural Economics* 95 (2): 442–48.

Hayek, F. A. 1945. "The Use of Knowledge in Society." *The American Economic Review* 35 (4): 519–30.

———. 1989. "The Pretence of Knowledge." *American Economic Review* 79 (6): 3–7.

———. [1960]2011. *The Constitution of Liberty: The Definitive Edition*. Edited by Ronald Hamowy. Chicago: The University of Chicago Press.

Herrero, Mario, Petr Havlík, Hugo Valin, An Notenbaert, Mariana C. Rufino, Philip K. Thornton, Michael Blümmel, Franz Weiss, Delia Grace, and Michael Obersteiner. 2013. "Biomass Use, Production, Feed Efficiencies, and Greenhouse

Gas Emissions from Global Livestock Systems." *Proceedings of the National Academy of Sciences* 110 (52): 20888–93.

Hoffer, Adam J., William F. Shughart II, and Michael D. Thomas. 2014. "Sin Taxes and Sindustry: Revenue, Paternalism, and Political Interest." *Independent Review* 19 (1): 47–64.

Hunter, Erik, and Elin Röös. 2016. "Fear of Climate Change Consequences and Predictors of Intentions to Alter Meat Consumption." *Food Policy* 62: 151–60.

Intergovernmental Panel on Climate Change. 2006. "Emissions from Livestock and Manure Management." In *IPCC Guidelines for National Greenhouse Gas Inventories, Volume 4: Agriculture, Forestry and Other Land Use*, edited by Simon Eggleston, Leandro Buendia, Kyoko Miwa, Todd Ngara, and Kiyoto Tanabe, 10.1–10.87.

International Agency for Research on Cancer. 2015. "IARC Monographs Evaluate Consumption of Red Meat and Processed Meat." Working Paper, World Health Organization.

International Food Information Council. 2020. "Consumer Survey: Climate Change and Food Production." *Food Insight*, April 22. https://foodinsight.org/consumer-survey-climate-change-and-food-production/.

Key, Nigel and Stacy Sneeringer. 2011. *Climate Change Policy and the Adoption of Methane Digesters on Livestock Operations*. US Department of Agriculture, Economic Research Service, ERR-111.

Miller, Margaret Ruth. 2019. "Knowledge, Policy, Action in the Decade of Nutrition 2016-2025." *World Nutrition* 10 (2): 4–7.

Mitchell, Matthew and Peter J. Boettke. 2017. *Applied Mainline Economics: Bridging the Gap between Policy and Theory*. Arlington, VA: Mercatus Center at George Mason University.

National Provisioner. 2019. "The 2019 Top 100 Meat & Poultry Processors." *The National Provisioner RSS*. https://www.provisioneronline.com/2019-top-100-meat-and-poultry-processors.

Newman, Patrick. 2018. "The Big Meat: The Beef Trust, Regulatory Capture, and Government Intervention." Working Paper, SSRN.

NielsenIQ. 2018. "Plant-Based Food Options Are Sprouting Growth for Retailers." *NielsenIQ*, June 13. https://nielseniq.com/global/en/insights/analysis/2018/plant-based-food-options-are-sprouting-growth-for-retailers/.

Nordgren, Anders. 2012. "Ethical Issues in Mitigation of Climate Change: The Option of Reduced Meat Production and Consumption." *Journal of Agricultural Environmental Ethics* 25 (4): 563–84.

Ostrom, Elinor. 2005. *Understanding Institutional Diversity*. Princeton, NJ: Princeton University Press.

Ostrom, Vincent. 2017. *The Intellectual Crisis in Public Administration*. Tuscaloosa: University of Alabama Press.

PETA. n.d. "Tax Meat." *PETA.org*. https://www.peta.org/features/tax-meat/.

Pigou, Arthur Cecil. 1920. *The Economics of Welfare*. London: Palgrave Macmillan.

Pitesky, Maurice, Kimberly R. Stackhouse, and Frank M. Mitloehner. 2009. "Clearing the Air: Livestock's Contribution to Climate Change." *Advances in Agronomy* 103: 1–40.

Poore, Joseph, and Thomas Nemecek. 2018. "Reducing Food's Environmental Impacts through Producers and Consumers." *Science* 360 (6392): 987–92.

Qian, Frank, Matthew C. Riddle, Judith Wylie-Rosett, and Frank B. Hu. "Red and Processed Meats and Health Risks: How Strong Is the Evidence?" *Diabetes Care* 43 (2): 265–71.

Reinhart, R. J. 2018. "Snapshot: Few Americans Vegetarian or Vegan." Working Paper, Gallup, Inc.

Säll, Sarah. 2018. "Environmental Food Taxes and Inequalities: Simulation of a Meat Tax in Sweden." *Food Policy* 74 (1): 147–53.

Simon, David Robinson. 2013. *Meatonomics: How the Rigged Economics of Meat and Dairy Make You Consume Too Much and How to Eat Better, Live Longer, and Spend Smarter*. Newburyport, MA: Conari Press.

Springmann, Marco, Keith Wiebe, Daniel Mason-D'Croz, Timothy B. Sulser, Mike Rayner, and Peter Scarborough. 2018. "Health and Nutritional Aspects of Sustainable Diet Strategies and Their Association with Environmental Impacts: A Global Modelling Analysis with Country-Level Detail." *The Lancet Planetary Health* 2 (10): e451–e461.

Stackhouse-Lawson, Kimberly R., Clarence A. Rotz, James W. Oltjen, and Frank M. Mitloehner. 2012. "Carbon Footprint and Ammonia Emissions of California Beef Production Systems." *Journal of Animal Science* 90 (12): 4641–55.

US Department of Health and Human Services and US Department of Agriculture. 2015. "2015-2020 Dietary Guidelines for Americans." 8th ed. *health.gov*, December. https://health.gov/our-work/nutrition-physical-activity/dietary-guide-lines/previous-dietary-guidelines/2015.

Van Zanten, Hannah H. E., Martin K. Van Ittersum, and Imke J. M. De Boer. 2019. "The Role of Farm Animals in a Circular Food System." *Global Food Security* 21: 18–22.

Yandle, Bruce. 1983. "Bootleggers and Baptists: The Education of a Regulatory Economist." *Regulation* 7 (12): 12–16.

Chapter 11

Institutional Differences in the Stewardship and Research Output of U.S. Herbaria

Alexis Garretson

Biodiversity information is considered a complex good, having aspects of both commo-pool resources and public goods (Gómez-Zapata, Espinal-Monsalve, and Herrero-Prieto 2018; Dedeurwaerdere 2006; Escribano, Galicia, and Arino 2018). While digitized information is essentially a public good that is not destroyed or depleted through use, specimens are degraded through traditional research usage and destructive sampling, including genomic sequencing and chemical characterization, meaning some aspects resemble a common-pool resource. According to the conventional economic thought, both common-pool resources and public goods are subject to overutilization and under-provision, theoretically leading to a market failure that requires government actors to support production and limit free riding (Anderson and Libecap 2014; Suarez and Tsutsui 2004; Escribano, Galicia, and Arino 2018; Hardin 1968; Samuelson 1954). Empirical research has demonstrated that under certain circumstances, private mechanisms such as nonprofits, private universities, and foundations can facilitate the provision of public goods, and they can sometimes outperform government provision of public goods (Candela and Geloso 2018; Skarbek 2011, 2016; Stringham 2015). In addition, the work of Elinor Ostrom demonstrates that the tragedy of the commons can be averted, and common-pool resources can be efficiently managed for long-term use without requiring top-down government intervention (Poteete, Janssen, and Ostrom 2010; Ostrom 1990; Ostrom et al. 1994).

There is also tension within the economic literature between the efficiency of polycentric and centralized systems for the provision of public goods and services. Many scholars argue that polycentric institutions can better solve collective action problems because they are more flexible and can better incorporate local knowledge (Aligica and Tarko 2012; McGinnis

Table 11.1 Summary of the Features, Potential Institutional Priorities, and Examples of the Institutional Types Discussed

	Cultural Sector	Public University	Private University	Public Land
Description	Cultural sector herbaria include herbaria located at botanical gardens, natural history museums, or nonprofit research sites. Herbaria at these organizations may receive government research grants, cultural grants, or other public funding but are not owned or operated by government agencies and are primarily funded by donations and fees.	Public university herbaria are located at public universities. These universities are under state ownership and receive significant public funding through either the national, state, or local government. Herbaria at public universities are often maintained by faculty, graduate students, or curatorial staff and are typically used for academic research and teaching.	Private university herbaria are located at private universities. These universities are not operated by governments, although many receive public funding through tax breaks, publicly funded student loans, and government-administered research grants. Herbaria at these institutions are often maintained by faculty, graduate students, or curatorial staff and are typically used for academic research and teaching.	Public land herbaria may be located at national, state, or local park and recreation, agricultural, land management, or forestry administrations. These organizations are often tasked with collecting and retaining specimens relevant to their scope (e.g., a forestry department may collect specimens relevant to the tree species in their region or associated pests, or a national park may collect specimens of endemic plants in their associated lands).
Priorities and Incentives	Visitor engagement, education, rare plant cultivation, recreation	Education, research, service	Education, research, service	Enforcement of regulations, land administration, visitor engagement, industry relations, recreation
Examples	New York Botanical Garden Field Museum of Natural History Desert Botanical Garden Herbarium Carnegie Museum of Natural History	University of Wisconsin-Madison, Wisconsin State Herbarium University of Kansas Ronald L. McGregor Herbarium University of Wyoming Rocky Mountain Herbarium	Academy of Natural Sciences of Drexel University Vanderbilt University Brigham Young University S. L. Welsh Herbarium Indiana University Deam Herbarium	Mecklenburg County Park and Recreation Florida Department of Agriculture and Consumer Services, Division of Plant Industry Grand Canyon National Park

Source: Author created.

Table 11.2 Distribution of Herbarium Richness Variables and Research Productivity Variables

	Cultural Sector (n=30)	Public University (n=174)	Private University (n=52)	Public Land (n=36)	ANOVA p-value
Specimens	116,791.56±223,471.76ᵃ	54,479.36±100,151.03ᵇ	37,992.08±79,263.06ᵇᶜ	4,040.31±7,125.46ᶜ	0.0005***
Specimens Identified to Species	99,005.20±202,174.01ᵃ	45,742.58±90,030.05ᵇ	32,582.29±72,599.88ᵇ	2,975.19±3,971.88ᵇ	0.001**
Families	217.37±104.98ᵃ	169.72±110.43ᵃ	162.92±85.62ᵃ	97.64±63.39ᵇ	<0.0001***
Genera	1,569.87±1,529.01ᵃ	975.21±912.87ᵇ	830.60±712.88ᵇᶜ	404.39±380.52ᶜ	<0.0001***
Species	7,402.43±10,628.58ᵃ	3,488.98±4,042.96ᵇ	2,787.13±3,515.27ᵇᶜ	908.17±1,099.48ᶜ	<0.0001***
Total Taxa	8,609.27±12,476.82ᵃ	4,015.69±4,768.41ᵇ	3,150.06±4,256.54ᵇᶜ	1,076.24±1,183.02ᶜ	<0.0001***
Types	17,627.90±83,965.76ᵃ	121.96±630.07ᵇ	175.10±809.22ᵇ	0.68±2.61ᵇ	0.011*
Specimens Georeferenced	40,810.50±64,715.56ᵃ	18,034.30±61,907.48ᵃᵇ	7,661.46±23,378.49ᵇ	795.42±1,347.14ᵇ	0.013*
Percent of Specimens Georeferenced	48%±36%ᵃ	26%±33%ᵃᵇ	28%±36%ᵃᵇ	36%±44%ᵇ	0.01**
Specimens Imaged	51,594.00±156,336.23	33,382.05±65,320.47	33,104.92±76,464.21	2,712.44±6,941.53	0.73
Percent of Specimens Imaged	48%±46%	58%±44%	66%±43%	45%±49%	0.13

Notes: A total of 292 institutions are included in the table, distributed across the institution types. If the ANOVA was significant, the superscript letters (a, b, c) designate the grouping results of a Tukey's HSD test. Institutions marked with the same superscript letter do not significantly differ from one another but do differ significantly (P < 0.05) from institutions marked with other superscript letters.
Source: Author created.

2000; Ostrom 2008; Coyne and Lemke 2011). Tarko (2015) suggests that a polycentric framework is part of what contributes to the success of the global scientific community. However, many of these authors recognize that polycentric institutions do not benefit from the economies of scale that can arise from more centralized approaches (Nagendra and Ostrom 2012; Thiel 2017; Ostrom 2010). Larger institutions managing natural history objects benefit from economies of scale by having better access to specialized staff, expensive equipment, and sophisticated storage space. This suggests that the provision of biodiversity data requires understanding the proper scale for the different natural history collection management activities, including specimen collection, long-term stewardship, and research utilization.

Academic, government-run, and cultural sector institutions across the world maintain substantial natural history collections containing biological specimens and physical objects (Suarez and Tsutsui 2004). Because these institutions vary in their size, taxonomic diversity, and research goals, there are significant differences in management priorities. The wide array of institutional frameworks under which natural history collections are managed provide both challenges and opportunities to researchers who rely on these data to produce scientific knowledge. The purpose of this chapter is to assess how the institutional management type impacts the size and richness of a herbarium, the progress toward digitization, and the research output.

INSTITUTIONAL TYPES OF U.S. HERBARIA

Herbaria represent a subset of natural history collections dedicated to the preservation of botanical specimens and dried plant matter (James et al. 2018). According to the Index Herbariorum 2019 report, there are 3,324 active herbaria containing 392,353,698 specimens (Thiers 2019). A herbarium specimen typically consists of exsiccatae—dried plant material mounted on paper with labels indicating key metadata, including date, species identification, and location. In general, herbarium specimens and their associated data are persistent, verifiable, and repeatable (James et al. 2018; L. M. Page et al. 2015; Holmes et al. 2016). Traditionally, these specimens have served as critical sources of data to define a biological community at a point in time or for systematics and taxonomy studies to clarify and define species boundaries (L. M. Page et al. 2015; Besnard et al. 2018). However, expanding digitization efforts enables open access to biodiversity data and allows for big data investigations that would have previously been impossible (Devictor and Bensaude-Vincent 2016).

Presently, the best practices for digitization include not only the databasing of critical specimen metadata but also the georeferencing and imaging of specimens (L. M. Page et al. 2015). Databasing is typically text-based metadata about an item, the date of collection, the date of taxonomic identification, the identities of the collector and the individual identifying the object, the taxonomic identification of the specimen, and locality information that typically includes the county and state of collection and occasionally includes information about soil type, habitat, and biological community (Iwanycki 2009; Heidorn and Wei 2008). Often, the databasing step of digitization includes the assignment of a unique identifier, which may be a collection-specific barcode or a persistent identifier like an IGSN (Hobern, Hahn, and Robertson 2018; Nelson et al. 2015). Georeferencing involves using the text locality information to provide a mapped point location and associated error or uncertainty for the specimen to enable geoanalysis (Murphey et al. 2004). Imaging flat herbarium specimens typically includes the capture, processing, and archiving of a 2D image of the specimen (Nelson et al. 2015; Giraud et al. 2018). Imaging occasionally also includes 3D scans of structures such as fruit or buds of a specimen (Schneider et al. 2018) or microscopic images of pollen or other structures (Allan et al. 2019; Carranza-Rojas et al. 2017). Increasingly, digitization also includes genomics or phylogenetics data related to the specimen, and the digitization best practices may soon include standardized sequencing of specimen DNA (R. D. M. Page 2013; Taylor and Swann 1994; Leavitt et al. 2019).

The availability of digitized specimen data enables biodiversity big data research that was historically impossible. For example, georeferenced specimens can serve as baseline data for defining the impacts of climate change, invasive species, and other anthropogenic changes on plant communities (Lang et al. 2019; Dyderski et al. 2018; Ahern et al. 2010). Imaged specimens allow for studies of plant growth forms and coloration without requiring travel or loan of specimens and also provides a labeled training dataset for deep learning and taxonomic classification (Jimenez-Mejias, Cohen, and Naczi 2017; Collins et al. 2018). These images also contain information about the plant life stage at the time of collection, allowing researchers to assess changes in plant phenology in response to climate change and land use change (Cleland et al. 2007; Everill et al. 2014; MacGillivray, Hudson, and Lowe 2010). Additionally, advances in genomics technology can allow researchers a window into genetic changes and how species are distributed across a landscape through the sequencing and genetic profiling of collection specimens (Cozzolino et al. 2007; Konrade, Shaw, and Beck 2019; Snyman et al. 2018). Digitizing collections and making data publicly available should allow researchers to expand research usage of these collections, but these outputs may be dependent on particular management and institutional approaches to enabling herbarium research.

Different types of natural history institutions have distinct challenges in the process of managing and digitizing their collections (Mayernik et al. 2020). Smaller herbaria often struggle with prohibitively small budgets and few curatorial staff to assist in collection management and digitization tasks (Snow 2005; Harris and Marsico 2017). Herbaria located at larger universities may have a greater number of affiliated researchers, but herbarium management is rarely their primary role, and their particular research area may not meaningfully contribute to specimen collection or curatorial tasks (Feeley and Silman 2011).

Cultural sector herbaria are often co-located with botanical gardens, field research sites, or natural history museums. The shared goals of cultural institutions include serving the public good, attaining financial stability, and supporting staff (Selwood 1999; Giardina and Rizzo 1994; Falk and Dierking 2008). Serving the public good takes a variety of forms, including serving as storehouses of cultural and scientific information, supporting research work on collection holdings, supporting social impact, and providing educational opportunities to the public (Scott 2006; Stanziola 2008). These institutions can vary in size, but their herbarium staff members are more likely to have curatorial tasks and taxonomic assessment as their primary role compared to university staff members. Variations in the curatorial role types and the number of curators may have significant impacts on not only the size and richness of a herbarium but also the progress made on digitization and incorporation into public databases. This ultimately can affect the research output associated with an individual herbarium.

Herbaria located at public land institutions face unique challenges compared to those at academic institutions. Namely, the Sundry Civil Act of March 3, 1879 (20 U.S.C. 59), requires that all physical object collections, including herbarium specimens, must eventually be archived in the Smithsonian Museum of Natural History. This means that, although a significant proportion of the collections are held by other organizations, such as the Bureau of Land Management, the United States Geological Survey (USGS), the National Parks Service, and the Fish and Wildlife Service, federally managed collections are not typically locally managed or archived for long-term stewardship. The lack of accountability for physical objects has led to significant criticism from the scientific and data management community, particularly of the USGS (Office of the Inspector General 2017; Ruch 2018, 2019). A 2018 report highlighted that the agency lacked a policy for biological specimens, and its geological specimen policy had confusing language that could leave specimens at risk of destruction (Ruch 2018). In September 2019, the USGS released their Policy on Scientific Working Collections (United States Geological Survey 2019), and though these policy changes are significant improvements, there are still concerns that these changes will not address risks to natural history collections under their administration (Ruch 2019).

Natural history collections at public lands are rarely collected exclusively for research purposes, and digitization for public research may not be a priority at these institutions. Additionally, the requirement that all physical objects collected by government entities must be eventually deposited into the Smithsonian National Museum of Natural History for long-term archiving may leave publicly managed natural history collections without a strong incentive to manage their specimens for long-term research usage, as the specimens are not yet housed at their long-term home. The bureaucratic burden that this policy places on the limited time and resources of staff members at government agencies can incentivize destruction of valuable specimens. In theory, requiring public land institutions to deposit specimens into the Smithsonian should enable research access and improve stewardship of federally collected physical objects. In practice, however, this policy leads to neglect and insufficient stewardship of the distributed working collections at the USGS and other institutions and often leaves specimens at risk of destruction or degradation due to storage under suboptimal conditions (Ruch 2018).

Much of the digitization progress in the United States has been funded through federal grants, particularly the Advancing Digitization of Biological Collections (ADBC) program, established by the National Science Foundation in 2011. ADBC provides funding to organizations to improve access to digitized specimens in U.S. natural history collections (National Science Foundation 2015). This program established iDigBio, a centralized organization that coordinates the integration of the digital data resulting from digitization projects (Paul et al. 2013; Matsunaga et al. 2013; Nelson 2014). ADBC also supports Thematic Collections Network (TCN), which provides funding to networks of institutions with a shared strategy to digitize specimens from a specific research theme, such as a taxonomic focus or geographic region (Nelson 2014; National Science Foundation 2015). Eligible institutions include two- and four-year public and private colleges and universities; nonprofit, non-academic cultural institutions, including museums, botanical gardens, research labs, and professional societies; and state and local governments. There are presently more than 124,858,708 specimen records, 39,689,496 media records, and 1,623 record sheets aggregated on the iDigBio portal resulting from funding to 925 collections at 317 institutions.

Few herbaria are purely private endeavors, as cultural sector institutions, public universities, private universities, and public land institutions all receive government funding, whether that is in the form of grants, direct support, or through mechanisms like federally funded financial aid programs. However, this does not change the fact that different institutional structures, priorities, and goals can lead to differences in institutional outcomes in the stewardship of natural history objects.

METHODS

Data Collection

Herbaria across North America submit data to the SEINet Regional Networks of North American Herbaria, and I extracted collection-level statistics for a total of 399 submitting institutions on February 21, 2020, using the SouthEast Regional Network of Expertise and Collections portal. This provided aggregated measures of herbarium size: the total number of specimens and the total number of specimens identified to species level. This also included measures of digitization efforts in the collection including the total number and percentage of specimens that are georeferenced or imaged. Additionally, the portal reports measures of herbarium taxonomic diversity, including number of families, genera, species, and total taxonomic groups included in the collection. Finally, the portal also reports the total number of type specimens, or specimens that have permanent taxonomic designations used by other researchers to confirm identifications and define taxonomic boundaries, in the collection. Herbaria outside the United States were excluded from this analysis, and each remaining herbarium was classified as either associated with a public land institution, public university, private university, cultural sector institution, or for-profit organization.

In addition to measures of herbarium richness, five measures of research activity were collected for each herbarium. First, the total number of research staff for each institution was collected through the Index Herbariorum from the New York Botanical Gardens, which provides a list of associated staff members for each indexed herbarium. If an institution did not have an associated staff list, the homepage of the herbarium was used as a source of the number of staff members. For each collection, the total number of Google Scholar search results from a search for the institution name was recorded as a proxy for the number of times the institution name appears in publications, either as an author affiliation, in the acknowledgments, in research methods, or in cited material. This is admittedly a coarse measure of research output, so additionally each staff member affiliated with the herbarium institutions was screened for a Google Scholar page. The total number of research articles and associated citations for each of the staff members with a Google Scholar page was recorded.

Statistical Analysis

To determine the correlations between the variables of interest, the Pearson correlation was calculated for each of the pairwise comparisons. Additionally, a one-way ANOVA was used to determine the association between the institution type and measures of herbarium research output and richness. In outcome variables with an ANOVA significant at $p < 0.05$, a Tukey's HSD test was used to determine the significant differences between the mean values of institutions and statistically significant groupings between the institution types. Finally, the herbarium richness measures were compared to research outcome variables using linear regressions.[1]

RESULTS AND DISCUSSION

Summary of Data Collection

Of the 339 total institutions that submit data to SEINet, 28 were omitted from the present study for having fewer than 10 databased specimens. A further 10 were omitted for being outside the United States, leaving 301 institutions included for further analysis. After categorizing by type, the majority of the herbaria are housed at universities, with 52 at private universities and 174 at public universities. There are a total of thirty institutions that are categorized as cultural sector institutions, primarily housed at botanical gardens and museums. A total of thirty-six institutions are categorized as public land institutions, primarily housed at national parks, other federal institutions such as the Bureau of Land Management and Forest Service, and state or local park departments. Finally, the remaining five herbaria collections are housed at fully private institutions, with two at for-profit companies and three at for-profit nature preserves. Due to the low number of representative collections, the fully private herbaria were excluded from future analysis by type, though the staff associated with the herbaria were included in analyses of research output and herbaria measures.

Across the institutions, a total of 1,102 staff members were found across all herbaria. Because some herbaria shared staff members, this led to 1,024 unique staff members. Of these staff members, 24.31 percent (268) had active Google Scholar profile pages (table 11.3). The distribution of herbaria richness across the remaining types (cultural sector institution, public university, private university, and public land institution) is presented in table 11.2.

Larger Institutions Have Larger and More Diverse Collections

One of the primary findings of this analysis is that herbarium richness in one area is positively correlated with herbarium richness in other measures (figure 11.1, table 11.3). As size increases, the diversity and digitization of the collection also increases. The institution type is also significantly related to measures of herbaria richness, with richer and larger herbaria at cultural sector institutions, followed by private universities, public universities, and finally public land institutions. Consistently, public land institutions lag behind both cultural sector institutions and university institutions across richness measures, suggesting that management features of public land collection institutions may not lend themselves to large and diverse collections.

However, the percent of imaged specimens is negatively correlated with both the percent of georeferenced specimens (r=−0.21, p=0.0001) and the total number of georeferenced specimens (r=−0.11, p=0.04). This negative correlation may suggest that there is a trade-off between digitization task types (figure 11.1). There are very different skill sets and technological requirements to georeference specimens compared to imaging specimens (Nelson et al. 2015; Blagoderov et al. 2012). Standardized imaging of specimens requires, at a minimum, a high-quality digital camera, lighting fixtures, a camera stand, a color scale, and a ruler. This setup can cost upward of $1500, which may be prohibitive for a small herbarium (Harris and Marsico 2017). Therefore, institutions with a limited budget may need to focus on only one digitization task at a time and may focus on georeferencing due to the financial investment required to appropriately image specimens. As digitization tasks expand to include generating genetic data for each specimen, the

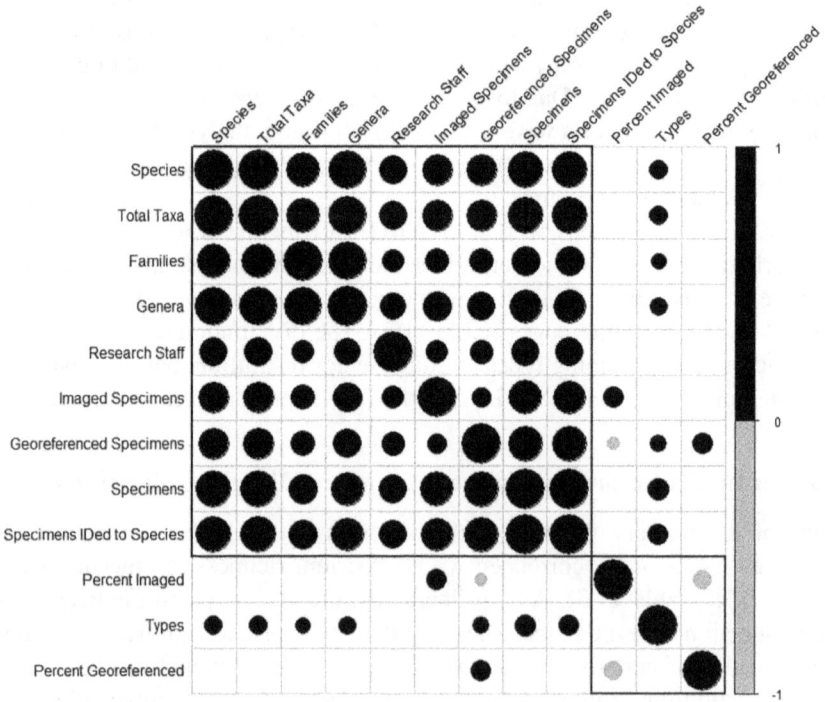

Figure 11.1   Pearson's Correlation between Measures of Herbaria Richness. *Source:* Author created.

financial and technological needs to meet best practices of digitization will grow, increasing the disparity between institutions in digitization completion.

Additionally, the number of research staff at a herbarium is significantly and positively correlated with measures of herbarium richness, except for the number of type specimens in the institution (figure 11.1). In every herbarium, richness, diversity, and digitization analysis of public lands were in the Tukey grouping with the lowest mean, indicating public lands tended to have smaller and less diverse collections (table 11.2). In contrast, cultural sector institutions were in the highest group, indicating larger and more diverse collections. In most assessments, the universities, both public and private, are in an intermediate group. However, in comparing within universities, public universities tended to have higher mean average metrics of diversity than private universities (table 11.2).

Cultural sector institutions outperform other institution types in the size and diversity of their collections. This may be because of the greater amount of overall research activities occurring at these institutions. Because while there were no significant differences in the measures of research outcomes, cultural sector institutions were found to have a higher number of type specimens (an indicator of active systematics research) and a higher percentage of specimens georeferenced (an indicator of active big data diversity research and ongoing digitization) in their collections (tables 11.1 and 11.2). Alternatively, this relationship may be because cultural sector institutions are often co-located with botanical gardens (living collections), leading to easy access to exotic plants that may otherwise be difficult to collect as specimens. While this would increase the number of unique species in the collection, thus increasing the associated biodiversity, this may not adequately support the needs of researchers interested in documenting wild species occurrence and differences across a species's natural range. Increasingly, cultural institutions such as museums and botanical gardens also harness visitor enthusiasm for digitization tasks through citizen science tools, which can support digitization activities (Garretson et al. 2020). Additionally, staff at cultural sector institutions are often not subject to other non-curation tasks, while collectors at public lands may have obligations to collect specific specimens relevant to survey work, and collectors at universities may have additional restrictions on time, including teaching, mentorship, and service (Snow 2005; Ab Rahim et al. 2013; Adams and Griliches 2000).

STAFF AT LARGER AND MORE DIVERSE HERBARIA PUBLISH MORE RESEARCH ARTICLES

No significant differences were found between institution type and measures of collection research output. However, there is a significant and positive

Table 11.3 Results of the Research Assessments for Each Herbaria

	Cultural Sector	Public University	Private University	Public Land	ANOVA p-value
Scholar results for herbarium	41,507.63±123,284.89	261,744.97±802,450.82	215,691.46±679,815.05	67,029.56±228,921.14	0.23
Research staff	8.00±11.80	3.71±5.06	2.51±2.48	1.76±2.29	0.17
Percent of staff with Google Scholar	20.42%[ab]	27.63%[a]	22.90%[ab]	13.16%[b]	0.02*
Average staff articles	127.12±231.50	106.86±134.9	70.13±72.40	84.50±58.7	0.63
Average staff citations	3,663±5,557	4,290±6,218	4,236±7,255	2,640±2,508	0.67

Notes: Reported average number of citations and average number of articles are for researchers with a Google Scholar page.
Source: Author created.

relationship between the number of articles published by staff with Google Scholar pages and measures of herbaria richness (figure 11.2, table 11.3). Particularly, the number of articles by staff members increased with the total number of the research staff at their home institution (b=4.11, $P<0.0001$, figure 11.2A). This relationship also holds between the total Google Scholar results for the researcher name in the absence of a Google Scholar page (b=3.77, $P<0.0001$). There is also a significant positive correlation between a number of herbaria richness measures and the number of research articles of research staff with Google Scholar pages, namely the number of collection specimens ($P=0.0054$), the total taxonomic groups represented by the collection ($P=0.03$), the number of species groups in the collection ($P=0.04$), and the number of type specimens ($P=0.03$) (figure 11.2). Finally, there was a significant difference in the percentage of staff associated with each institution type that had a Google Scholar profile page (table 11.3).

The lack of association between institution type and individual researcher outcomes may be because there are too many confounding factors, like career stage, position type, or age (Beaudry and Allaoui 2012; Gonzalez-Brambila and Veloso 2007; Wang et al. 2017). There may also be differences in the subset of researchers across all institution types that are likely to have active Google Scholar accounts. Particularly, younger researchers may be more likely to have an active online presence, as previous studies have found the age and career stage of a researcher can impact their assessment of the importance of online academic presence (Mierzecka, Kisilowska, and Suminas 2020; Arshad and Ameen 2017; Wang et al. 2017). This may mean that the dataset of researchers used in this study may not be a random sample of researchers at the institutions. However, a positive relationship between herbaria measures and research outcomes means that a larger dataset could reveal significant institutional trends. The association with the number of staff might mean that collaborations and staff community could lead to more research, suggesting that larger institutions may generally have greater research output for any given faculty. This is in line with prior studies of research output of university faculty members that have suggested that larger public universities have greater research output compared to that of smaller private universities (Ab Rahim et al. 2013; Gonzalez-Brambila and Veloso 2007).

CONCLUSIONS

These results demonstrate that there are institutional differences in collection stewardship, and there is a link between institutional type and its effectiveness in contributing to publicly available biodiversity data. The results of this study show that institution type is significantly associated with the size,

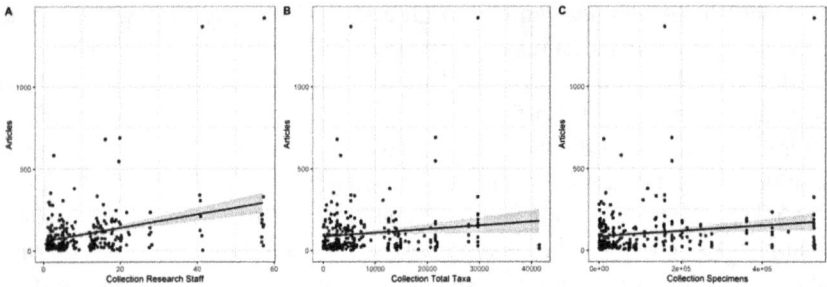

Figure 11.2   Herbaria Staff Published Articles. *Source*: Author created.

diversity, and digitization of a herbarium collection. However, past studies have found that critical occurrence records and rare taxa can be found in small natural history collections (Glon et al. 2017). Small and distributed herbaria may be better able to catalogue and collect unique local flora but may not have the resources to support larger research endeavors. There are also certainly differences in the institutional priorities across all institutions, particularly in the mission, vision, and objectives of the institutions that can drive data collection methods, focuses, and digitization protocols. Additionally, the results demonstrate that as herbaria richness increases, the research output of associated staff increases in kind. This suggests that there may be economies of scale in research output because as the number of researchers grow, research output per researcher grows accordingly. Decentralized, small collections can benefit from local knowledge and unique records, but centralization has significant returns to scale in collection stewardship, digitization, and research output.

Implications of Differences between Cultural Sector and Public Land Institutions

While small herbaria can be important to researchers due to their ability to add unique occurrence information for rare plants (ibid.), these findings suggest that smaller herbaria, particularly those located at public land institutions, may be under-digitized and under-incorporated into the publicly available biodiversity datasets. This may be because smaller herbaria tend to have fewer staff and fewer resources to support data collection, digitization, and access (Harris and Marsico 2017; Snow 2005; Blagoderov et al. 2012). Larger herbaria benefit from scale with respect to personnel, access to technology, and curatorial skill sets that may lead to greater opportunities for collaborative publication, collection research usage, and expansion of the collection. This demonstrates that smaller herbaria can act as polycentric institutions—better able to incorporate local knowledge and particularities of their surrounding region—while other aspects of collection curation, namely digitization and long-term storage, are better suited to more centralized archives. This mismatch between the institutions and researchers best positioned to collect novel specimens and institutions best positioned to digitize and manage the data in the long term represents an ongoing challenge in the management of small collections. This may also represent an important area for increased investment in supporting smaller institutions in building the capacity to support additional digitization and collection activities.

This finding supports the policy requiring federal entities to plan for submission of objects to the Smithsonian Institution. The Smithsonian Museum of Natural History is a public-nonprofit partnership and contains more than 156 natural history specimens. The Smithsonian Museums benefit from economies of scale and often are the first institutions to have access to cutting-edge curatorial technology, including 3D scanners and genomics tools. However, the challenge in implementing this policy, particularly in the USGS, has been that this policy leaves USGS staff without significant investment in the long-term stewardship of the physical objects in question, and often without the training to appropriately store the items to prevent deterioration and destruction. Requiring the development of collection management plans may help address some of these concerns, but it may not be sufficient to ensure proper management of the collection items before they reach the Smithsonian Institution. Like the USGS, many small herbaria need to maintain transition plans for their collections in the event that they lose funding, complete the associated research project, or face other risks to the datasets (Mayernik et al. 2020). Tools like persistent identifiers, such as IGSNs, can help prevent some of these hurdles by ensuring critical metadata are associated with natural history specimens throughout their lifecycle (Hobern, Hahn, and Robertson 2018).

Directions for Future Research

Herbaria are only one type of biodiversity information facility, so assessing whether these trends hold with museums, field stations, and published biodiversity data and literature may be key to further understanding how research institution types and digitization efforts impact biological discovery and knowledge generation. Other studies have suggested that substantial differences exist between universities with and without a medical school, and these institutional differences may be more important than the private/public differentiation (Ahn, Charnes, and Cooper 1988). Finer-grain differences in the institutional type might also be relevant for the understanding of how institutional type might influence the collection richness and research effort, so future studies should consider the age of the institution and its operating budget.

A better understanding of the institutional differences in the digitization of natural history collections can assist in targeting collections that might need additional support through granting agencies, like the ADBC, and can improve our understanding of how policies regulating the deposition of federally collected specimens might impact long-term collection outcomes. Collections of natural history specimens are an invaluable resource in understanding scientific processes, and they contribute to critical research in policy-relevant areas such as public health and pandemic forecasting, monitoring of climate and ecological change, and basic biological research. Ensuring the ongoing protection, digital preservation, and research access to these items is a critical aspect of stewarding our research resources and better understanding our changing environment.

NOTE

1. All data analysis was performed in R (version 3.6.2) with RStudio (version 1.1.453).

REFERENCES

Ab Rahim, Ina Suryani, Aizan Yaacob, Noor Hashima Abd Aziz, Salleh Abd Rashid, and Hazry Desa. 2013. "Research Publication Output by Academicians in Public and Private Universities in Malaysia." *International Journal of Higher Education* 2 (1): 84–90.

Adams, James D. and Zvi Griliches. 2000. "Research Productivity in a System of Universities." In *The Economics and Econometrics of Innovation*, edited by David Encaoua, Bronwyn H. Hall, François Laisney, and Jacques Mairesse, 105–40. Boston, MA: Springer US.

Ahern, Robert G., Douglas A. Landis, Anton A. Reznicek, and Douglas W. Schemske. 2010. "Spread of Exotic Plants in the Landscape: The Role of Time, Growth Habit, and History of Invasiveness." *Biological Invasions* 12 (9): 3157–69.

Ahn, Taesik, Abraham Charnes, and William W. Cooper. 1988. "Some Statistical and DEA Evaluations of Relative Efficiencies of Public and Private Institutions of Higher Learning." *Socio-Economic Planning Sciences* 22 (6): 259–69.

Aligica, Paul D. and Vlad Tarko. 2012. "Polycentricity: From Polanyi to Ostrom, and Beyond." *Governance* 25 (2): 237–62.

Allan, E. Louise, Laurence Livermore, Benjamin W. Price, Olha Shchedrina, and Vincent S. Smith. 2019. "A Novel Automated Mass Digitisation Workflow for Natural History Microscope Slides." *Biodiversity Data Journal* 7: e32342.

Anderson, Terry L. and Gary D. Libecap. 2014. *Environmental Markets: A Property Rights Approach*. New York: Cambridge University Press.

Arshad, Alia and Kanwal Ameen. 2017. "Scholarly Communication in the Age of Google: Exploring Academics' Use Patterns of e-Journals at the University of the Punjab." *The Electronic Library* 35 (1): 167–84.

Beaudry, Catherine and Sedki Allaoui. 2012. "Impact of Public and Private Research Funding on Scientific Production: The Case of Nanotechnology." *Research Policy* 41 (9): 1589–1606.

Besnard, Guillaume, Myriam Gaudeul, Sébastien Lavergne, Serge Muller, Germinal Rouhan, Alexander P. Sukhorukov, Alain Vanderpoorten, and Florian Jabbour. 2018. "Herbarium-Based Science in the Twenty-First Century." *Botany Letters* 165 (3–4): 323–27.

Blagoderov, Vladimir, Ian J. Kitching, Laurence Livermore, Thomas J. Simonsen, and Vincent S. Smith. 2012. "No Specimen Left Behind: Industrial Scale Digitization of Natural History Collections." *ZooKeys* 209: 133–146.

Candela, Rosolino A. and Vincent J. Geloso. 2018. "The Lightship in Economics." *Public Choice* 176 (3): 479–506.

Carranza-Rojas, Jose, Herve Goeau, Pierre Bonnet, Erick Mata-Montero, and Alexis Joly. 2017. "Going Deeper in the Automated Identification of Herbarium Specimens." *BMC Evolutionary Biology* 17: 181.

Cleland, Elsa E., Isabelle Chuine, Annette Menzel, Harold A. Mooney, and Mark D. Schwartz. 2007. "Shifting Plant Phenology in Response to Global Change." *Trends in Ecology & Evolution* 22 (7): 357–65.

Collins, Matthew, Gaurav Yeole, Paul Frandsen, Rebecca Dikow, Sylvia Orli, and Renato Figueiredo. 2018. "A Pipeline for Deep Learning with Specimen Images in IDigBio - Applying and Generalizing an Examination of Mercury Use in Preparing Herbarium Specimens." *Biodiversity Information Science and Standards* 2: e25699.

Coyne, Christopher J. and Jayme S. Lemke. 2011. "Polycentricity in Disaster Relief." *Studies in Emergent Order* 4: 40–57.

Cozzolino, Salvatore, Donata Cafasso, Giuseppe Pellegrino, Aldo Musacchio, and Alex Widmer. 2007. "Genetic Variation in Time and Space: The Use of Herbarium Specimens to Reconstruct Patterns of Genetic Variation in the Endangered Orchid Anacamptis Palustris." *Conservation Genetics* 8 (3): 629–39.

Dedeurwaerdere, Tom. 2006. "The Institutional Economics of Sharing Biological Information." *International Social Science Journal* 58 (188): 351–68.

Devictor, Vincent and Bernadette Bensaude-Vincent. 2016. "From Ecological Records to Big Data: The Invention of Global Biodiversity." *History and Philosophy of the Life Sciences* 38 (13): 1–23.

Dyderski, Marcin K., Sonia Paz, Lee E. Frelich, and Andrzej M. Jagodzinski. 2018. "How Much Does Climate Change Threaten European Forest Tree Species Distributions?" *Global Change Biology* 24 (3): 1150–63.

Escribano, Nora, David Galicia, and Arturo H. Arino. 2018. "The Tragedy of the Biodiversity Data Commons: A Data Impediment Creeping Nigher?" *Database-the Journal of Biological Databases and Curation* bay033.

Everill, Peter H., Richard B. Primack, Elizabeth R. Ellwood, and Eli K. Melaas. 2014. "Determining Past Leaf-out Times of New England's Deciduous Forests from Herbarium Specimens." *American Journal of Botany* 101 (8): 1293–1300.

Falk, John H., and Lynn D. Dierking. 2008. "Re-Envisioning Success in the Cultural Sector." *Cultural Trends* 17 (4): 233–46.

Feeley, Kenneth J. and Miles R. Silman. 2011. "Keep Collecting: Accurate Species Distribution Modelling Requires More Collections than Previously Thought." *Diversity and Distributions* 17 (6): 1132–40.

Garretson, Alexis, Megan Napoli, Natalie Feldsine, Penelope Adler-Colvin, and Elizabeth Long. 2020. "Vernal Pool Amphibian Breeding Ecology Monitoring from 1931 to Present: A Harmonised Historical and Ongoing Observational Ecology Dataset." *Biodiversity Data Journal* 8: e50121.

Giardina, Emilio and Ilde Rizzo. 1994. "Regulation in the Cultural Sector." In *Cultural Economics and Cultural Policies*, edited by Alan Peacock and Ilde Rizzo, 125–42. Dordrecht, NL: Springer Netherlands.

Giraud, Michel, Quentin Groom, Ann Bogaerts, Sofie de Smedt, Hannu Saarenmaa, Noortje Wijkamp, Sarah Philips, and Zhengzhe Wu. 2018. "Best Practice Guidelines for Imaging of Herbarium Specimens." *Innovation and Consolidation for Large Scale Digitization of Natural Heritage* 41: 1–41.

Glon, Heather E., Benjamin W. Heumann, J. Richard Carter, Jessica M. Bartek, and Anna K. Monfils. 2017. "The Contribution of Small Collections to Species Distribution Modelling: A Case Study from Fuireneae (Cyperaceae)." *Ecological Informatics* 42 (2): 67–78.

Gómez-Zapata, Jonathan Daniel, Nora Elena Espinal-Monsalve, and Luis César Herrero-Prieto. 2018. "Economic Valuation of Museums as Public Club Goods: Why Build Loyalty in Cultural Heritage Consumption?" *Journal of Cultural Heritage* 30: 190–98.

Gonzalez-Brambila, Claudia, and Francisco M. Veloso. 2007. "The Determinants of Research Output and Impact: A Study of Mexican Researchers." *Research Policy* 36 (7): 1035–51.

Hardin, Garrett. 1968. "The Tragedy of the Commons." *Science* 162 (3859): 1243–48.

Harris, Kari M. and Travis D. Marsico. 2017. "Digitizing Specimens in a Small Herbarium: A Viable Workflow for Collections Working with Limited Resources." *Applications in Plant Sciences* 5 (4): apps.1600125.

Heidorn, P. Bryan and Qin Wei. 2008. "Automatic Metadata Extraction from Museum Specimen Labels." *Proceedings of the International Conference on Dublin Core and Metadata Applications* 57–68.

Hobern, Donald, Andrea Hahn, and Tim Robertson. 2018. "Options to Apply the IGSN Model to Biodiversity Data." *Biodiversity Information Science and Standards* 2: e27087.

Holmes, Michael W., Talisin T. Hammond, Guinevere O. U. Wogan, Rachel E. Walsh, Katie LaBarbera, Elizabeth A. Wommack, Felipe M. Martins, et al. 2016. "Natural History Collections as Windows on Evolutionary Processes." *Molecular Ecology* 25 (4): 864–81.

Iwanycki, Natalie. 2009. "Guidelines for Collecting Herbarium Specimens." *Royal Botanical Gardens* 5: 1–5.

James, Shelley A., Pamela S. Soltis, Lee Belbin, Arthur D. Chapman, Gil Nelson, Deborah L. Paul, and Matthew Collins. 2018. "Herbarium Data: Global Biodiversity and Societal Botanical Needs for Novel Research." *Applications in Plant Sciences* 6 (2): e1024.

Jimenez-Mejias, Pedro, James I. Cohen, and Robert F. C. Naczi. 2017. "The Study of Online Digitized Specimens Revalidates Andersonglossum Boreale as a Species Different from A-Virginianum (Boraginaceae)." *Phytotaxa* 295 (1): 22–34.

Konrade, Lauren, Joey Shaw, and James Beck. 2019. "A Rangewide Herbarium-Derived Dataset Indicates High Levels of Gene Flow in Black Cherry (Prunus Serotina)." *Ecology and Evolution* 9 (3): 975–85.

Lang, Patricia L. M., Franziska M. Willems, J. F. Scheepens, Hernán A. Burbano, and Oliver Bossdorf. 2019. "Using Herbaria to Study Global Environmental Change." *New Phytologist* 221 (1): 110–22.

Leavitt, Steven D., Rachel Keuler, Clayton C. Newberry, Roger Rosentreter, and Larry L. St. Clair. 2019. "Shotgun Sequencing Decades-Old Lichen Specimens to Resolve Phylogenomic Placement of Type Material." *Plant and Fungal Systematics* 64 (2): 237–47.

MacGillivray, Fran, Irene L. Hudson, and Andrew J. Lowe. 2010. "Herbarium Collections and Photographic Images: Alternative Data Sources for Phenological Research." In *Phenological Research: Methods for Environmental and Climate Change Analysis*, edited by Irene L. Hudson and Marie R. Keatley, 425–61. Dordrecht, NL: Springer Netherlands.

Matsunaga, Andréa, Renato Figueiredo, Alex Thompson, Gregory Traub, Reed Beaman, and José A. B. Fortes. 2013. "Integrated Digitized Biocollections (IDigBio) Cyberinfrastructure Status and Futures." *Proceedings of the Taxonomic Databases Working Group 2013 Annual Conference*: 1.

Mayernik, Matthew S., Kelsey Breseman, Robert R. Downs, Ruth Duerr, Alexis Garretson, Chung-Yi (Sophie) Hou, and Environmental Data Governance Initiative (EDGI) and Earth Science Information Partners (ESIP) Data Stewardship Committee. 2020. "Risk Assessment for Scientific Data." *Data Science Journal* 19 (1): 10.

McGinnis, Michael Dean. 2000. *Polycentric Games and Institutions: Readings from the Workshop in Political Theory and Policy Analysis*. Ann Arbor: University of Michigan Press.

Mierzecka, Anna, Małgorzata Kisilowska, and Andrius Suminas. 2020. "Researchers' Expectations Regarding the Online Presence of Academic Libraries." *College & Research Libraries* 78 (7): 934–51.

Murphey, Paul C., Robert P. Guralnick, David Neufeld, and J. Allen Ryan. 2004. "Georeferencing of Museum Collections: A Review of Problems and Automated Tools, and the Methodology Developed by the Mountain and Plains Spatio-Temporal Database-Informatics Initiative (Mapstedi)." *PhyloInformatics* 3: 1–29.

Nagendra, Harini, and Elinor Ostrom. 2012. "Polycentric Governance of Multifunctional Forested Landscapes." *International Journal of the Commons* 6 (2): 104–33.

National Science Foundation. 2015. *Advancing Digitization of Biodiversity Collections Program Solicitation*. https://www.nsf.gov/pubs/2015/nsf15576/nsf15576.htm.

Alexis Garretson

Nelson, Gil. 2014. "IDigBio: The US National Science Foundation's National Resource for Digitization of Biological and Palobiological Collections." *Proceedings of the Geological Society of America 2014 Annual Meeting*: 1.
Nelson, Gil, Patrick Sweeney, Lisa E. Wallace, Richard K. Rabeler, Dorothy Allard, Herrick Brown, J. Richard Carter, et al. 2015. "Digitization Workflows for Flat Sheets and Packets of Plants, Algae, and Fungi." *Applications in Plant Sciences* 3 (9): 1500065.
Office of the Inspector General. 2017. "Final Evaluation Report – Evaluation of USGS Scientific Collection Management Policy, Report No. 2016-ER-057." *US Department of the Interior*, September 7. https://www.doioig.gov/sites/doioig.gov/files/FinalEvaluation_USGSScientificCollections_Public.pdf.
Ostrom, Elinor. 1990. *Governing the Commons: The Evolution of Institutions for Collective Action*. New York: Cambridge University Press.
———. 2008. "Polycentric Systems as One Approach for Solving Collective-Action Problems." Working Paper, Indiana University Bloomington.
———. 2010. "Beyond Markets and States: Polycentric Governance of Complex Economic Systems." *The American Economic Review* 100 (3): 641–72.
Ostrom, Elinor, Roy Gardner, James Walker, James M. Walker, and Jimmy Walker. 1994. *Rules, Games, and Common-Pool Resources*. Ann Arbor: University of Michigan Press.
Page, Lawrence M., Bruce J. MacFadden, Jose A. Fortes, Pamela S. Soltis, and Greg Riccardi. 2015. "Digitization of Biodiversity Collections Reveals Biggest Data on Biodiversity." *BioScience* 65 (9): 841–42.
Page, Roderic D. M. 2013. "BioNames: Linking Taxonomy, Texts, and Trees." *Peerj* 1: e190.
Paul, Deborah, Austin R. Mast, Greg Riccardi, and Gil Nelson. 2013. "IDigBio as a Resource for the Digitization of a Billion Biodiversity Research Specimens." *Proceedings of the Taxonomic Databases Working Group 2013 Annual Conference*: 1.
Poteete, Amy R., Marco A. Janssen, and Elinor Ostrom. 2010. *Working Together: Collective Action, the Commons, and Multiple Methods in Practice*. Princeton, NJ: Princeton University Press.
Ruch, Jeff. 2018. "Information Correction Request Submitted under USGS Information Quality Guidelines." *Public Employees for Environmental Responsibility*.
———. 2019. "Appeal to the USGS Response to a Request for Correction of Information Submitted under USGS Information Quality Guidelines." *Public Employees for Environmental Responsibility*.
Samuelson, Paul A. 1954. "The Pure Theory of Public Expenditure." *The Review of Economics and Statistics* 36 (4): 387–89.
Schneider, Julio V., Renate Rabenstein, Jens Wesenberg, Karsten Wesche, Georg Zizka, and Jörg Habersetzer. 2018. "Improved Non-Destructive 2D and 3D X-Ray Imaging of Leaf Venation." *Plant Methods* 14 (7): 1–15.
Scott, Carol. 2006. "Museums: Impact and Value." *Cultural Trends* 15 (1): 45–75.

Selwood, Sara. 1999. "Access, Efficiency and Excellence: Measuring Non-Economic Performance in the English Subsidised Cultural Sector." *Cultural Trends* 9 (35): 87–137.

Skarbek, David. 2011. "Governance and Prison Gangs." *American Political Science Review* 105 (4): 702–16.

———. 2016. "Covenants without the Sword? Comparing Prison Self-Governance Globally." *American Political Science Review* 110 (4): 845–62.

Snow, Neil. 2005. "Successfully Curating Smaller Herbaria and Natural History Collections in Academic Settings." *BioScience* 55 (9): 771–779.

Snyman, Sandy J., Dennis M. Komape, Hlobisile Khanyi, Johnnie van den Berg, Dirk Cilliers, Dyfed Lloyd Evans, Sandra Barnard, and Stefan J. Siebert. 2018. "Assessing the Likelihood of Gene Flow from Sugarcane (Saccharum Hybrids) to Wild Relatives in South Africa." *Frontiers in Bioengineering and Biotechnology* 6 (72): 1–23.

Stanziola, Javier. 2008. "Developing a Model to Articulate the Impact of Museums and Galleries: Another Dead Duck in Cultural Policy Research?" *Cultural Trends* 17 (4): 317–21.

Stringham, Edward Peter. 2015. *Private Governance: Creating Order in Economic and Social Life*. 1st ed. New York: Oxford University Press.

Suarez, Andrew V. and Neil D. Tsutsui. 2004. "The Value of Museum Collections for Research and Society." *BioScience* 54 (1): 66–74.

Tarko, Vlad. 2015. "Polycentric Structure and Informal Norms: Competition and Coordination within the Scientific Community." *Innovation: The European Journal of Social Science Research* 28 (1): 63–80.

Taylor, John W. and Eric C. Swann. 1994. "DNA from Herbarium Specimens." In *Ancient DNA*, edited by Bernd Herrmann and Susanne Hummel, 166–181. Berlin: Springer.

Thiel, Andreas. 2017. "The Scope of Polycentric Governance Analysis and Resulting Challenges." *Journal of Self-Governance and Management Economics* 5 (3): 52–82.

Thiers, Barbara M. 2019. "Index Herbariorum: A Global Directory of Public Herbaria and Associated Staff." *New York Botanical Garden's Virtual Herbarium*.

United States Geological Survey. 2019. "USGS Scientific Working Collections Management. IM CSS 2019-01." https://www.usgs.gov/about/organization/science-support/survey-manual/im-css-2019-01.

Wang, Wei, Shuo Yu, Teshome Megersa Bekele, Xiangjie Kong, and Feng Xia. 2017. "Scientific Collaboration Patterns Vary with Scholars' Academic Ages." *Scientometrics* 112 (1): 329–43.

Part VI

TECHNOLOGY POLICY

Chapter 12

Introducing a Theory of Asset Specificity for Hacking Services

Karl Grindal

While not socially productive, a full-time criminal performs work. This requires of the criminal a concentration of mental or physical effort to achieve an intended outcome. This investment of labor time and potential resources will either directly endow the criminal with money or may provide a service or produce a product that can be exchanged for money to acquire their basic needs. Criminologists, such as Cornish and Clark (1997), have explored these parallels through rational choice theories to explain criminal behavior. More specifically, transaction costs analysis has been applied to the domain of organized crime to explain vertical integration (Dick 1995). In institutional economics, transactional costs may be avoided through careful development of complex contracts. However, in illegal markets where contract enforcement cannot be guaranteed through the legal system, it seems reasonable that vertical integration would serve as the logical alternative. Yet, a significant amount of cyber-criminal behavior is distributed and operates through spot markets mediated through the darknet.

Concurrently, significant literature has explored how the information and communication technology (ICT) revolution has lowered the cost of transactions. In addition to near-instantaneous communication reducing the costs associated with moving digital assets, platform economics show how this mediation of the relationship between the consumers and users and the suppliers and producers has also lowered the costs of transactions (Parker, Van Alstyne, and Choudary 2017). Yet, some ICT trends indicate increasing consolidation demonstrated by large corporations benefiting from network effects and urban clusters forming around Silicon Valley.

At the intersection of these two literatures exploring the role of transaction costs is the subject of cyber-criminal enterprises. Sitting within a New Institutional Economics (NIE) perspective, the transaction cost literature assumes that, while rational and self-optimizing, actors lack perfect information and face challenges monitoring and enforcing contracts. While this theory is quite well developed, a more systematic analysis of the underlying transaction costs associated with hacking activity can help explain variability in the organizational structure of hacking criminal enterprise. While a variety of factors can shape transaction costs, asset specificity proves especially important in markets where one-time anonymous transactions without state oversight create significant incentives for opportunism. This theoretical approach helps to explain an empirical finding of Wegberg et al. (2018, 1009) that found dark market "commodification to be spottier than previously assumed."

To this end, this chapter will discuss the applicable literature on asset specificity and explore how five attributes of asset specificity shape hacking behavior. Based on this framework, we can project which kinds of criminal services will trend toward commodification and which are unlikely to. To demonstrate the theory's explanatory power, its effects are explored in vignettes that discuss how darknet-based markets allow individuals to trade credit cards, and states' role in monopolizing advanced persistent threat (APT) capabilities used for trade secret theft. The cyber policy community frequently invokes the language of "imposing friction" or "imposing costs" on adversaries in cyberspace. This language is given greater meaning when viewed through the lens of transaction costs. Consequently, the policy implications of this theory help to identify both opportunities and risks of pursuing a strategy of cost imposition.

LITERATURE REVIEW

Asset Specificity

Oliver Williamson (1975) linked the risk of opportunism to transactions with high asset specificity. This suggests that in buyer and seller relationships where one of the actors faces high exit costs (possibly because of limited competition), the actor with lower exit costs may be able to act opportunistically. Opportunism by the seller might include delivering an inferior product, late delivery, or favorably modifying the terms of exchange. Because of this risk of opportunism, asset specificity, as articulated by Riordan and Williamson (1985), links production and transaction costs with optimal firm and market organization. The risks associated with a sole supplier would encourage a firm to vertically integrate by acquiring the supplier or developing in-house capability. While initially conceptual, this literature quickly acquired "strong empirical support for the importance of transactions cost considerations, especially the importance of asset specificity, in explaining variations in vertical relationships" (Joskow 1988, 115).

Vertical integration may not be necessary if long-term contracts can be designed to comprehensively cover the participants' respective rights and duties (Masten 1988). However, complex contracts can be costly to design and difficult to adjust to changing circumstances. Grossman and Hart (1986) describe vertical integration as the acquisition of the "residual rights of control" by purchasing the suppliers' assets.

Employment, contractual obligations, and state mandates all entail control over others behavior.[1] Joskow (1988, 115) enumerated the factors that shape vertical integration as, "relationship-specific investments, asymmetric information, and the costs of writing, monitoring, and enforcing contractual relationships have emerged as the key factors explaining 'nonstandard' vertical relationships." As for the first of these attributes, Joskow (1987, 169) suggested that "the more important are relationship-specific investments, the longer will be the period of time (or number of discrete transactions) over which the parties will establish the terms of trade ex-ante by contract." As for the last attribute, contract law and tort law of complex market relationships are traditionally enforced through the legal system. In lieu of the legal system and its monopolization of the use of violence, contract enforcement for illegal business operations will often involve an inherent threat of private violence. The consequence of a drug deal gone wrong is thus potentially a shootout rather than a court date.

There are a variety of potential sources for asset specificity. Williamson (1983, 526) identifies four distinct types of transaction-specific investments:

Site Specificity: Moving an asset from one location to another is costly.

Human Asset Specificity: The specific skills or expertise possessed by individuals and related to assets production are costly to transfer.

Physical Asset Specificity: The asset itself may only be used for a narrow purpose that is not easily redeployed.

Dedicated Assets: The production of an asset requires additional or specialized capital investments to the plant or equipment that are unique to a particular customer.

In addition to these factors, Malone, Yates, and Benjamin (1987) added another concept:

Time Specificity: There are time-dependent factors related to acquiring or using an asset, where the required duration can potentially increase transaction costs.

The subsequent framework will explore the implications of each of these types of investments for hacking-based transaction costs. They describe the various ways that costly exit might enable opportunism. Asset specificity should be understood as relating to the challenges of hold-up or a short-term time horizon. These factors are consequently linked to the notion of vertical integration or complex contracts.

The transaction costs literature has been applied to a variety of industries and is specifically relevant to organized criminal behavior. Andrew Dick draws on Shelling to provide a definition of *organized crime* as "a formal governance structure that specializes in providing illegal goods and services to downstream buyers" (Dick 1995, 25). Dick then applies a transaction theory analysis to organized criminal enterprise and asserts that an "organized criminal firm enters only those markets in which its specialized supply of inputs to downstream criminal activities is more cost efficient than having a downstream firm self-supply" (ibid., 26). As evidence of this, his paper highlights the extortion and protection rackets applied to downstream criminal elements such as bookies, prostitutes, and loan sharks.

Wegberg et al. (2018) draw on Oliver E. Williamson for the concept of asset specificity in their empirical assessment of Dream Market, an illicit darknet marketplace accessible with the Tor network that was in operation between 2013 and 2019. The authors used the concept of asset specificity to explain why they identified commoditization as "a spottier phenomenon than was previously assumed" (Wegberg et al. 2018, 1009). The article then went on to hypothesize that "vertical integration probably remains important for more complex and dynamic forms of cybercrime" (ibid., 1023). However, this hypothesis was asserted in their conclusion highlighting the need for additional research. Zhou et al. (2020) build on the Wegberg et al. (2018) paper, also citing Williamson (1985) in their own empirical analysis of illicit sales on Dream Market. Based on their findings, Zhou et al. (2020, 11) make an overly strong claim when they assert that "traditional crime patterns will gradually transfer to anonymous network[s]." This finding seems to equate a shift to online transactions with a shift toward anonymous exchange. Further, this paper misidentifies some of the issues at play, as it fails to incorporate subsequent theoretical development in transaction costs theory. As more empirical analysis is made of these illicit marketplaces, it would be productive for a deeper understanding of the theoretical literature to accompany these empirical findings. This chapter seeks to serve this purpose, providing a more complex theoretical vision of the factors at play.

ASSET SPECIFICITY FACTORS

Site Specificity

Defined by the costs associated with moving assets through space, site specificity is unlikely to be a primary driving factor in cyberspace, particularly with respect to digital assets. The rapid diffusion of broadband Internet speeds has lowered the costs for global communication and transferring information across national borders. Specifically, a culture of anonymous digital communication with persistent handles protects hackers from law enforcement, while sustaining trust-based relationships. This hacking community would consequently avoid the location-specific effects associated with other industries. Yet, future research should confirm that site-specific effects by either urban agglomeration or national preference are not in effect.

As the technology sector seems to thrive within industry clusters, most notably Silicon Valley, the hacking sector could be subject to a similar effect. This would be especially impactful if in-person communication or community ties create a greater capacity for trust, as this would decrease the transaction costs. A secondary subject of interest would be the role of national jurisdictions as hacker sanctuaries. This national responsibility might be characterized along a spectrum of state responsibility ranging from inadequate prohibitions to state executed operations (Healey 2013, 52). If there are strong disincentives to cross-border collaboration by hackers (like increased legal exposure by multiple jurisdictions), this might increase these potential transaction costs and encourage trade within countries.

Human Asset Specificity

Human asset specificity relates to the specialized knowledge, skill, or expertise associated with a particular asset that cannot be easily transferred. While the discovery of new cyber vulnerabilities is likely to be highly specialized, its application would be much less so. The structure of a cyberattack is often described as the combination of an exploit and payload. While the exploit leverages a vulnerability in the target system to acquire access, the payload serves as the functional activity. Open-source hacking tools like the Metasploit Framework allow a hacker to choose from a list of exploits and payloads and configure them before targeting. While cybersecurity professionals can legitimately leverage this tool as part of penetration testing, it also lowers the technical expertise required to hack different devices. Hacking skills may also be transferable when identical technical procedures can be used to achieve distinct criminal ends (i.e., stealing credit card numbers and stealing corporate secrets both involve gaining system access and scanning networks). That said, the more complex the criminal behavior is, the more training and experience would be required to effectively execute the hack and evade detection.

Future quantitative research into the prosecution of the range of online criminal behavior might demonstrate the degree of specialization. Qualitative analysis of hacker activity through interviews or oral histories might reveal the role of specialization in this industry and whether this specialization is a product of skills-based capacity or alternative attributes like marketing or reputation.

Physical Asset Specificity

Physical asset specificity is often linked to the physical or engineering properties of the asset being produced. Where, for example, the manufacturing process requires investment in dedicated castings, this would increase the cost of re-purposing. The aspects of physical asset specificity for a digital product are somewhat distinct. In this respect, stolen account information and trade secrets represent the extreme ends of specificity. Account information is transferable, and multiple buyers might be interested in exploiting the same information acquired through a data breach. Additionally, the structure of stealing account information allows it to be sold individually or bundled, while a variety of users might be interested in purchasing the service. This is consequently a leading factor in determining the value of the service and can broadly be understood as relating to the number and homogeneity of potential buyers that would be interested in purchasing the product.

Dedicated Assets

Dedicated assets are when the production of an asset requires additional or specialized capital investments. The nature of dedicated assets is such that a downstream supplier will avoid making targeted investments that benefit an exclusive customer if it risks them being taken advantage of. The upstream purchaser may realize that the downstream supplier cannot easily transfer the sale to an alternative company, which would allow them to negotiate for more of the economic gains. Models of this form of investment structure were explored empirically by De Vita, Tekaya, and Wang (2010). Applied to cybersecurity, an example of a dedicated asset might be a zero-day exploit tailored to a particular software application used by an intended target.[2] Another example of dedicated assets might be the command and control (C2) infrastructure used to operate a botnet. A botnet is a network of infected computers that a hacker can control from a centralized server. It can take many years to grow a botnet, and law enforcement and technology companies often attempt to "sinkhole" the botnet by redirecting control of the hijacked computers away from the hacker. While botnet instructions can frequently be modified, some botnets like GameOver Zeus are highly sophisticated and are designed to capture banking credentials. The FBI has offered a reward for the capture of Evgeniy Bogachev for his association with GameOver Zeus and has accused him of being the "leader of a gang of cyber criminals" (FBI 2014). The association of complex banking trojans with Russian criminal gangs might be indicative of the kind of vertical integration expected with significant dedicated assets.

Temporal Assets

If digital assets hold their value less than physical assets or show great variance in pricing, the temporal dimension of asset specificity would be particularly dominant for hacking-related activity. Whether looking at ransomware, distribution denial-of-service (DDoS) for hire, stolen accounts, or trade secrets, all are attributes that must either be maintained at cost or lose value over time. With respect to supply, some hacking activities related to availability (like DDoS) might show accelerating costs as the defender begins to respond. However, the accrued costs to the defender might also be non-linear; going down for an hour, a day, or a week will affect various businesses differently.

Alternatively, once information assets are extracted from the network and capable of resale, they are likely to see diminishing value. For example, the value of stolen credit card numbers diminishes once the victim chooses to put a hold on their account, changes the contact information, or when the cards expire. On July 7, 2020, the United States indicted Li Xiaoyu and Dong Jiazhi for a conspiracy to steal biotech trade secrets related to COVID-19 (U.S. Department of Justice 2020). The two hackers were accused of working for both the Chinese Ministry of State Security and their own personal gain. If they had acquired this data (they did not), the value of these trade secrets would have been in their potential to accelerate the production of viable vaccines or therapeutics for the global market. Were the hackers to sit on these designs for one year, Chinese biotech companies interested in the designs may have moved past this level of R&D, and prospective Chinese firms would correspondingly decrease their willingness to pay. The degree to which the value of trade secrets diminishes will depend on whether shifts in innovation and the market retain the utility and exclusivity of the information. The value of trade secrets can consequently diminish if they are not put to use.

Overview

Having walked through each form of asset specificity, we can start to categorize their relevance across different examples of hacking activity, as shown in table 12.1. As discussed previously, different factors would be expected to be in play. Across these asset specificity categories, site specificity is likely

Table 12.1   Categorizing Hacking Activity by Asset Specificity

Hacking Activity	Site Specificity	Human Asset Specificity	Physical Asset Specificity	Dedicated Assets	Temporal Assets
Stolen Accounts	Low	Low	Low	Low	High
Botnet/DDoS	Low	Medium	Medium	Medium	High
Ransomware	Low	Medium	Medium	Medium	High
Stolen Trade Secrets	Low	Medium	High	Medium	High
CI[1] Hacks	Low	High	High	High	High

[1]In this case, "CI" stands for Critical Infrastructure. These hacking attacks are generally seen as being quite rare and requiring significant capability by the actor. In this context, CI Hacks refer to destructive attacks. *Source*: Author created.

the least applicable, while temporal assets seem to be a critical factor across a wide range of hacking activities.

The three levels of variation (low, medium, and high) should be understood as characterizing an average attack. There are individual instances that will be the exception to the rule. For example, stealing account access can require low human asset specificity when an attack entails targeting companies with known unpatched vulnerabilities. However, even capable actors will use known vulnerabilities if that is all that is required. Another notable complexity is that the market relationship for DDoS and Ransomware is structured somewhat uniquely so that the victim is the end-buyer who pays for the hacking services as a ransom.

APPLICATION OF THEORY

Selling Accounts and Personally Identifiable Information (PII)

Research into darknet markets seems to back up the claim that these are structured in such a way that, while the markets themselves are concentrated, the users are non-hierarchical. Norgaard, Walbert, and Hardy (2018) applied an agentistic model to explore the "network structure surrounding the interactions in the Virtual black market" and found it to be "less hierarchical than the network structure of the Ground market" (Norgaard, Walbert, and Hardy 2018, 1). One organizational concern might be that while darknets appear to have numerous sellers, these might represent fronts to a few larger firms. However, research by Tai, Soska, and Christin (2019) mapped vendor handles to sellers using random forest classifiers and hierarchical clustering and found many sellers. Of the 22,163 accounts in the dataset "12,155 operate only one account, and the remainder between 2 and 11 different accounts" (ibid., 1871). Cluster analysis has also been applied to identify buyers on anonymous darknet markets (Zheng et al. 2019).

The company top10vpn.com has developed a Dark Web Market Price Index. Summary results for the 2019 U.S. Version are included in table 12.2. Notably, access to personal financial accounts represents 54 percent of the documented listings. Stolen credit cards account for the largest sum of listings at 25 percent. Credit card theft is associated with the activity of "carding," a form of credit card fraud where the cards are used to purchase gift cards and subsequent products for resale. The third party who purchases credit card numbers from hackers is called a "carder," who through the anonymous sale of goods purchased with the stolen cards dissociates the illicit income with these new earnings. The business practice known as carding is considered by Wegberg et al. (2018) to be the most advanced hacking activity in its commodification. Wegberg et al. (ibid.) likewise identified "cash-out," their term for this personal financial category, as dominating the B2B market on darknets (compared to the sales of botnets, exploits, malware, remote access trojans, and so on).

Looking at the market for goods posted by top10vpn.com confirms that carding is a major service with seventy-three records posted. Other personal financial instruments, including debit cards (fifteen), Paypal (thirty), and bank details (thirty-two), are also well represented. These records are notably more valuable, as demonstrated by the average unit price, than account information for specified services like communication (e.g., phone service), delivery, or travel. While this may be driven in part by the value of the underlying resource as measured in dollars, I suspect it is also because cash is the most liquid asset and thereby the most easily converted. Asset specificity serves as a measure of liquidity. Notably, this listing does not include hacking services, often referred to as "hacking-for-hire." These custom offerings are available on markets; however, these offerings may not include transparent pricing.

Advanced Persistent Threat

Advanced persistent threat, or APT, is defined by National Institute of Standards and Technology (NIST) as "an adversary that possesses sophisticated levels of expertise and significant resources which allow it to create opportunities to achieve its objectives by using multiple attack vectors" (NIST 2020). The term was first coined by Colonel Greg Rattray in 2006 and has since retained a national security connotation not shared by the word cybercrime. Characterized by the persistence achieved through skilled technical experience, APT operations also require significant organizational capacity to maintain access without detection. As these operations are maintained continuously, this means "hackers are getting paid on a permanent basis now

Table 12.2   Dark Web Market Price Index

Category	Records	Percent Avg	Listing Price ($)	Avg Unit Price	Percent Bundled
Communication	17	6	28.19	$9.58	41
Dating	3	1	2.94	$2.94	0
Delivery	3	1	5.20	$5.20	0
Email	8	3	2.56	$1.99	13
Entertainment	10	3	10.52	$9.02	10
Food Delivery	4	1	7.78	$7.78	0
Online Shopping	45	16	9.30	$7.87	4
Personal Finance Bank Details	32	11	162.30	$160.18	3
Personal Finance Credit Card	73	25	54.35	$49.60	7
Personal Finance Credit Reports	4	1	35.00	$35.00	0
Personal Finance Debit Card	15	5	67.20	$67.50	0
Personal Finance Paypal	30	10	301.63	$247.02	7
Personal Finance Western Union	6	2	101.17	$101.17	0
Personal Finance Others	1	0	50.00	$50.00	0
Proof of Identity	19	7	44.47	$38.60	0
Social	4	1	2.42	$2.50	0
Travel	15	5	26.48	$5.81	23

Source: top10vpn.com (2019).

for doing nasty things" (Ask et al. 2013, 37). This long-term compensation can be structured as either complex contracts or as employment.

While traditionally linked with nation-states, the term relates to a capability rather than a management structure. APT groups are linked to many of the most significant attacks that make newspaper headlines, including the significant breaches of governments like those of the Office of Personnel Management, the Democratic National Committee, and Equifax. But many lesser-known incidents have linked APT groups to the targeting of dissident groups and larger corporations. In addition to technical attribution, threat intelligence firms have attempted to link these APT campaigns to national agendas by tracking the targets of these campaigns.

By this logic, one could infer the national origins of the attack when POISON CARP, an APT campaign identified by the Munk School as targeting Tibetan groups, was linked through technical features by Google Project Zero to a campaign targeting the Uyghur community (Marczak et al. 2019). The Chinese government was the likely perpetrator. Beyond these inferences, directly linking an APT group to the responsibility of a nation-state is difficult, as cyber forensic attribution often ends with the responsible machine rather than the guilty person. While indictments of specific responsible individuals remain uncommon, in 2014 the United States indicted five officers in China's People's Liberation Army (PLA) Unit 61398 (otherwise known as APT-1) for the theft of U.S. commercial intellectual property and trade secrets. Along a spectrum of state responsibility, nation-states may directly employ hackers (as in the case of PLA Unit 61398) and non-state groups may operate in countries as criminal elements, where they are vigorously pursued by law enforcement. Between these two extremes, states may create permissive environments or differing levels of support and recognition for domestically operating hacking groups (Healey 2013, 52).

The sale of APT operational services online is rare, but it is not impossible. A group by the name "Babylon APT" was described as offering such services in an article titled "Everything Is Sold as a Service Now, Even an APT Campaign" (Wulkan 2016). This source ultimately states that "whilst non-state sponsored groups exist, well capable of launching APT-like attacks, such as the infamous Anunak, they charge heavily for their service and [do] not publish their capabilities and intents into the world" (Wulkan 2016). This APT group maintained a website that sold their services. However, this sale of services was ultimately renamed C-Market, and threat intelligence firms have since associated the group with the Chinese military. As the evidence for APT groups and their operations is documented in the public reports produced by cybersecurity firms, one potential bias could be that "more advanced groups have a tendency to be better covered than the less technically sophisticated groups" (Lemay et al. 2018, 33). Given that the vast majority of threat intelligence firms are linked to specific regions of the world, the national-jurisdictional site specificity may be particularly applicable here. The sale of trade secrets does not appear to lend itself toward a globalized spot market. Rather, complex knowledge transfer with APT activities is costly and may create complex contractual relationships or vertical integration, be they with private criminal organizations or states.

Vignette Comparison

The two prior hacking examples describe a spot market for stolen accounts and PII and vertical integration for the trade secret theft enabled by APT operations. This corresponding level of vertical integration maps to the description of the asset specificity described in the framework. The behavior of groups involved in intellectual property theft seems particularly designed to avoid the risks of opportunism. Hackers present an ideal case for transaction theory, as dark market transactions can be mediated impersonally like many normal economic transactions. This contrasts with the close community ties of criminal elements in other domains that may present alternative explanations for behavior.

Illegal markets lack the coercive power of the state to enforce contracts. Vertical integration is one potential response. However, risks may also be avoided by adopting complex contracts. Many dark markets have also drawn lessons from legitimate platforms, implementing Amazon-like rating systems that allow customers to operate with greater trust of product or service delivery. Even as the online medium creates the potential for theft of service by buyers and theft of payment by suppliers, reputational incentives can prohibit some of this behavior. Yet, as the transaction costs for targeting a particular victim grow, the incentive for the purchasing party to vertically integrate increases. States are major purchasers of hacking services, and they have done much to acquire this capability either directly into the intelligence service or by employing complex contracts to hire military-industrial contractors that maintain control and secrecy.

CONCLUSION

Given the value of transaction theory for explaining market structure in criminal hacking enterprises, how might policymakers and law enforcement leverage these findings for their own ends? On the one hand, effective work is already being done. Law enforcement has significant experience with taking down dark web marketplaces, including Silk Road in 2014, AlphaBay in 2017, and Wall Street Market in 2019. In some cases, these takedowns enable law enforcement to also target criminal vendors. The hacktivist community Anonymous was significantly disrupted in 2011 when the FBI convinced Hector Monsegur (aka Sabu), an active member of the group, to become an informant. Cyber criminals face a significant risk in trusting the wrong person or infrastructure, as the coercive power of the state could meet them with jail time. These risks of doing business should be understood as relating to the cost of delivering criminal hacking services. So, what more might be done to increase the cost of doing business? Classifying certain online resources by their asset specificity might inform various strategies to increase transaction costs and discourage illegal activity.

If the length of time between a cybersecurity incident and notification of affected parties can be decreased, then the value of many of these assets would be significantly reduced. For example, if real-time notification to consumers of potentially fraudulent charges on their cards could get them to cancel potential charges, this would decrease the value of these assets. A decrease in the money that can be extracted from a random set of x number of credit cards would consequently reduce their value and the number of cyber criminals who find trading in carding markets to be lucrative. While banks in 2020 are fairly effective at identifying fraudulent transactions, they are out of the loop when it comes to how online data breaches could affect their customers. Rather than wait for fraud protection to kick in after an illicit expenditure, proactive information sharing might enable financial service companies to react to their customers' data being breached by changing usernames, passwords, credit card numbers, or pins. Anything that shrinks the value of these temporal assets would decrease the incentive for trading in that commodity.

Dedicated asset costs might also present another area of opportunity where the costs of cyber criminality could be increased. Since Clifford Stoll's (1990) use of a honey pot in 1986 to distract his would-be online assailants, the technique of leaving content of potential interest to an intruder on one's network presents an opportunity to increase search costs for the hacker. But this is just one example. Increasing the difficulty for hackers all along the "cyber kill chain" (Yadav and Rao 2015) would increase dedicated asset specificity, as it increases the targeted effort that must be allocated to monetize access to an organization's network.

It would be a research endeavor unto itself to enumerate the diverse range of potential policy and technical cybersecurity solutions and their impact on transaction costs. The more critical finding from this chapter is the mechanism by which these reforms may produce changes in the structure of criminal enterprise. The addition of asset specificity to the cybersecurity literature helps to explain why policy solutions that increase the costs to cyber criminals may be met with increasingly capable and organized adversaries rather than the elimination of this behavior.

This seemingly perverse incentive should in some ways be viewed constructively. Should evidence suggest that cyber criminality has shifted toward hierarchical structures, be they organized crime or nationalization, this may be understood as progress. It is the goal of policymakers and law enforcement to prevent the formation of spot markets in illicit goods and services. Different strategies will be needed to penetrate organized–and nation-state–sponsored criminality.

This research also highlights the potential risk that may arise if anonymous online markets begin to host complex contracts through smart contracts facilitated by blockchain technology. If these smart contracts are employed on the darknet, it might allow APT operations that are currently used almost exclusively by states and organized crime to be more readily acquired by anonymous non-state actors. As Michael Warner (2014) notes in his book *The Rise and Fall of Intelligence*, larger states have already lost their monopoly on intelligence as small states develop new capabilities. Should smart contracts be efficacious on the darknet, this would risk states losing their monopoly on intelligence to non-states.

NOTES

1. Applied to hacking, this relationship may resemble those between criminal hacking enterprises and sanctioning states. While the state may give the enterprise some degree of free right to target external actors, it may reserve the right to dictate behavior at its whim.

2. A zero-day exploit is a technical vulnerability that has not yet been publicly documented. Once an exploit is published, companies work to patch their systems so that the vulnerability is no longer capable of being exploited.

REFERENCES

Ask, Merete, Petro Bondarenko, and John Erik Rekdal, André Nordbø, Pieter Bloemerus, and Dmytro Piatkivskyi. 2013. "Advanced Persistent Threat (APT) Beyond the Hype." Project Report in IMT4582 Network Security at Gjøvik University College.

Cornish, Derek B. and R. V. G. Clarke, eds. 2014. *The Reasoning Criminal: Rational Choice Perspectives on Offending*. New York: Transaction Publishers.

De Vita, Glauco, Arafet Tekaya, and Catherine L. Wang. 2010. "Asset Specificity's Impact on Outsourcing Relationship Performance: A Disaggregated Analysis by Buyer–Supplier Asset Specificity Dimensions." *Journal of Business Research* 63 (7): 657–66.

Dick, Andrew R. 1995. "When Does Organized Crime Pay? A Transaction Cost Analysis." *International Review of Law and Economics* 15 (1): 25–45.

Federal Bureau of Investigation. 2014. "GameOver Zeus Botnet Disrupted." July 11. https://www.fbi.gov/news/stories/gameover-zeus-botnet-disrupted.

Grossman, Sanford J. and Oliver D. Hart. 1986. "The Costs and Benefits of Ownership: A Theory of Vertical and Lateral Integration." *Journal of Political Economy* 94 (4): 691–719.

Healey, Jason, ed. 2013. *A Fierce Domain: Conflict in Cyberspace, 1986 to 2012*. Vienna, VA: Cyber Conflict Studies Association.

Joskow, Paul L. 1987. "Contract Duration and Relationship-Specific Investments: Empirical Evidence from Coal Markets." *The American Economic Review* 77 (1): 168–85.

———. 1988. "Asset Specificity and the Structure of Vertical Relationships: Empirical Evidence." *The Journal of Law, Economics, & Organization* 4 (1): 95–117.

Lemay, Antoine, Joan Calvet, François Menet, and José M. Fernandez. 2018. "Survey of Publicly Available Reports on Advanced Persistent Threat Actors." *Computers & Security* 72: 26–59.

Malone, Thomas W., Joanne Yates, and Robert I. Benjamin. 1987. "Electronic Markets and Electronic Hierarchies." *Communications of the ACM* 30 (6): 484–97.

Marczak, Bill, Adam Hulcoop, Etienne Maynier, Bahr Abdul Razzak, Masashi Crete-Nishihata, John Scott-Railton, and Ron Deibert. 2019. "Missing Link:

Tibetan Groups Targeted with 1-Click Mobile Exploits." *citizenlab.ca*, September 24. https://citizenlab.ca/2019/09/poison-carp-tibetan-groups-targeted-with-1-click -mobile-exploits/.

Masten, Scott E. 1988. "Equity, Opportunism, and the Design of Contractual Relations." *Journal of Institutional and Theoretical Economics (JITE)/Zeitschrift Für Diegesamte Staatswissenschaf* 144 (1): 180–95.

Migliano, Simon. 2019. "Dark Web Market Price Index – 2019 Update." *Top10VPN .com*, February 20. https://www.top10vpn.com/research/dark-web-market-price -index-2019-us-edition/.

Newman, Lily Hay. 2018. "Fin7: The Billion-Dollar Hacking Group Behind a String of Big Breaches." *Wired*, April 4. https://www.wired.com/story/fin7-carbanak -hacking-group-behind-a-string-of-big-breaches/.

NIST Computer Security Resource Center. "Glossary: Advanced Persistent Threat (APT)." Accessed March 24, 2020. https://csrc.nist.gov/glossary/term/advanced -persistent-threat.

Norgaard, Julia R., Harold J. Walbert, and R. August Hardy. 2018. "Shadow Markets and Hierarchies: Comparing and Modeling Networks in the Dark Net." *Journal of Institutional Economics* 14 (5): 877–99.

Parker, Geoffrey G., Marshall W. Van Alstyne, and Sangeet Paul Choudary. 2017. *Platform Revolution: How Networked Markets Are Transforming the Economy– and How to Make Them Work for You*. Reprint ed. New York and London: W. W. Norton & Company.

Riordan, Michael H. and Oliver E. Williamson. 1985. "Asset Specificity and Economic Organization." *International Journal of Industrial Organization* 3 (4): 365–78.

Stoll, Clifford. 1990. *The Cuckoo's Egg: Tracking a Spy through the Maze of Computer Espionage*. New York: Pocket Books.

Tai, Xiao Hui, Kyle Soska, and Nicolas Christin. 2019. "Adversarial Matching of Dark Net Market Vendor Accounts." Proceedings of the 25th ACM SIGKDD International Conference on Knowledge Discovery & Data Mining - KDD '19. Anchorage, AK, USA: ACM Press.

US Department of Justice. 2020. "Two Chinese Hackers Working with the Ministry of State Security Charged with Global Computer Intrusion Campaign Targeting Intellectual Property and Confidential Business Information, Including COVID-19 Research." July 21. https://www.justice.gov/opa/pr/two-chinese-hackers-working -ministry-state-security-charged-global-computer-intrusion.

Warner, Michael. 2014. *The Rise and Fall of Intelligence: An International Security History*. Washington, DC: Georgetown University Press.

Wegberg, Rolf van, Samaneh Tajalizadehkhoob, Kyle Soska, Ugur Akyazi, Carlos Hernandez Ganan, Bram Klievink, Nicolas Christin, and Michel van Eeten. 2018. "Plug and Prey? Measuring the Commoditization of Cybercrime via Online Anonymous Markets." Proceedings of the 27th USENIX Security Symposium, 1009– 26. https://www.usenix.org/conference/usenixsecurity18/presentation/van-wegberg.

Williamson, Oliver E. 1975. *Markets and Hierarchies, Analysis and Antitrust Implications: A Study in the Economics of Internal Organization*. New York: Free Press.

———. 1983. "Organization Form, Residual Claimants, and Corporate Control." *The Journal of Law and Economics* 26 (2): 351–66.

Wulkan, Ido. 2016. "Everything Is Sold as a Service Now, Even an APT Campaign." *intsights.com*, August 26. https://intsights.com/blog/apt-as-a-service.

Yadav, Tarun and Arvind Mallari Rao. 2015. "Technical Aspects of Cyber Kill Chain." In *Security in Computing and Communications*, edited by Jemal H. Abawajy, Sougata Mukherjea, Sabu M. Thampi, and Antonio Ruiz-Martínez, 438–52. Cham, CH: Springer International Publishing.

Zheng, Panpan, Shuhan Yuan, Xintao Wu, and Yubao Wu. 2019. "Identifying Hidden Buyers in Darknet Markets via Dirichlet Hawkes Process." ArXiv:1911.04620 [Cs, Stat], November 11. http://arxiv.org/abs/1911.04620.

Zhou, Gengqian, Jianwei Zhuge, Yunqian Fan, Kun Du, and Shuqiang Lu. 2020. "A Market in Dream: The Rapid Development of Anonymous Cybercrime." *Mobile Networks and Applications* 25 (1): 259–70.

Index

Italicized *t*'s and *f*'s beside page numbers denote tables and figures, respectively.

About the Contributors

Martha Bradley-Dorsey
Research Affiliate, University of Arkansas

Nathaniel Burke
Assistant Professor of Economics, West Virginia University

Rosolino A. Candela
Senior Fellow, F. A. Hayek Program for Advanced Study in Philosophy, Politics, and Economics, Mercatus Center at George Mason University

Anthony J. DeMattee
National Science Foundation Postdoctoral Research Fellow, Emory University

Dora Duru
Associate at HollingsworthLLP

Rosemarie Fike
Instructor of Economics, Texas Christian University

Alexis Garretson
PhD Candidate in Genetics, Tufts University and The Jackson Laboratory for Mammalian Genetics

Alison Grant
PhD Candidate in Agricultural Economics, Purdue University

Karl Grindal
Postdoctoral Fellow, Georgia Institute of Technology

Roberta Herzberg
Distinguished Senior Fellow, F. A. Hayek Program for Advanced Study in Philosophy, Politics, and Economics, Mercatus Center at George Mason University

Vera Kichanova
PhD Student in Political Economy, King's College London

Neil McCray
PhD, Health Services Research, George Mason University

Ifeoluwa M. Olawole
Quantitative Research Specialist, Mercy Corps

Emil Panzaru
PhD Candidate in Political Economy, King's College London

Thomas B. Storrs
PhD Student in History, University of Virginia

www.ingramcontent.com/pod-product-compliance
Lightning Source LLC
Chambersburg PA
CBHW021809270326
41932CB00007B/117